# THE RECOGNITION OF STATES

# THE RECOGNITION OF STATES

## *Law and Practice in Debate and Evolution*

Thomas D. Grant

PRAEGER

Westport, Connecticut
London

**Library of Congress Cataloging-in-Publication Data**

Grant, Thomas D., 1969–
The recognition of states : law and practice in debate and evolution / Thomas D. Grant.
p. cm.
Includes bibliographical references and index.
ISBN 0–275–96350–0 (alk. paper)
1. Recognition (International law) I. Title.
KZ4041.G73 1999
341.26—dc21 98–35371

British Library Cataloguing in Publication Data is available.



Library of Congress Catalog Card Number: 98–35371
ISBN: 0–275–96350–0

First published in 1999

Praeger Publishers, 88 Post Road West, Westport, CT 06881
An imprint of Greenwood Publishing Group, Inc.
www.praeger.com

Printed in the United States of America

The paper used in this book complies with the Permanent Paper Standard issued by the National Information Standards Organization (Z39.48–1984).

10 9 8 7 6 5 4 3 2

In order to keep this title in print and available to the academic community, this edition was produced using digital reprint technology in a relatively short print run. This would not have been attainable using traditional methods. Although the cover has been changed from its original appearance, the text remains the same and all materials and methods used still conform to the highest book-making standards.

# CONTENTS

# PREFACE

Recognition, the topic of this book, captured my attention as a third-year JD candidate at the Yale Law School. It was autumn 1993, and I was taking W. Michael Reisman's course on public international law. Professor Reisman gave each student the choice of writing either a final examination or a research paper. If electing the latter, the student was to choose a topic of current relevance to public international law and discuss it in the form of an 'incident study.'[1] Interested in the events then still unfolding in Yugoslavia, I thought an incident study a good vehicle by which to examine them. The disintegration of Yugoslavia, gravest European crisis since World War II, had raised a number of problems for international law. Not the least of these was how to address the advent of new states. My writing focused on the decision by Germany to extend diplomatic recognition in December 1991 to Croatia and Slovenia. Recognition had aroused resistance at the time and subsequently drew accusations that a precipitate German diplomacy had exacerbated tensions in southeastern Europe. Some observers even went so far as to place on policymakers in Bonn the blame for the later Bosnian civil war.

This subject eventually led me to undertake research into the law of recognition and, in turn, into a venerable debate over the legal nature of recognition. Though my initial interest had centered around the diplomatic, political, and legal factors influencing an existing state in its decision to recognize, the nature of recognition was an unavoidable question. I soon discovered that the sheer bulk of scholarly matter on the nature of recognition defied rapid assimilation. It in fact demanded a subsidiary research project in its own right. Gaining a command of the literature on the subject—a requirement for any doctoral dissertation—in the case of my research became the core of a related but distinct work. This monograph is the result of an inquiry roughly parallel between my initial research, addressing the determinants of recognition policy, and my doctoral dissertation, addressing the legal consequences of recognition.

A writer tackling a subject as heavily studied as recognition faces special pitfalls. One of these is the risk of not saying anything particularly novel. However, a surfeit of commentary on a field also presents an opportunity. The writer can assist by sorting through the literature and, perhaps, in doing this, will identify patterns and changes in the shape of discourse. Such patterns and changes may in turn reflect something about the subject itself and about intellectual developments more generally. If the aim of this monograph were to present startling insight into its topic, then it falls off the mark. Though readers may well find in the following pages some propositions that are new to them, this by and large is not a book that defends a particular viewpoint, nor is it one that will tend to make readers take a wholly new outlook on the recognition of states. Indeed, readers will discover that much here recapitulates existing work in the field. Furthermore, they will note that the book covers many examples of recognition and, with the exception of the Yugoslav crisis, declines to absorb itself in single cases at the length recommended by the incident methodology that in part inspired my original interest in the subject. In light of the reason I have published this work, these characteristics should come as no surprise.

Recognition has, infamously even, generated a great deal of secondary literature. Because the legal nature of recognition was long a central focus of discussion on the subject, recognition has also generated an appreciable body of tertiary comment. Those who wrote about recognition long characterized each other by their views as to its legal meaning. Some—known as declaratists—viewed recognition as simply noting the attainment of the factual elements of statehood; while others—constitutivists—took the view that the phenomenon itself created the state. A mass of writings emerged, part of which discussed the actual practice of states concerning recognition (the secondary literature) and part of which discussed how scholars were discussing recognition (the tertiary literature). More than a few contemporary writers have declared that the legal nature of recognition has ceased to command attention, but this evaluation is wishful thinking. Public international lawyers who work on the cutting edge of the field indeed have seen themselves clear to passing by what James Crawford called the "Great Debate" over the legal nature of recognition. Nevertheless, a quantity of new literature continues to detain itself with the old question at the core of that debate. And, because many who delve into the recognition thicket continue to work into their explorations some or another statement about the legal nature of recognition, an appreciable amount of writing even continues to ask whether commentators are 'declaratists' or 'constitutivists.' Ink has been spilled, and, though hopefully in diminishing volume, continues to be spilled describing how people describe recognition. It comes as little surprise that Ian Brownlie despaired of the vast corpus on recognition and blamed it for producing "a *tertium quid* which stands, like a bank of fog on a still day, between the observer and the contours of the ground which calls for investigation."[2]

Brownlie's desperation in 1983 was not merely a fit response to scholarly development up to that time; it has also proven prescient. The fog has not lifted but in fact has thickened. The advent of new states since the demise of the Soviet Union and the Socialist Federal Republic of Yugoslavia has produced a great deal of new primary material on recognition, and, spurred by this, the academy and international bar have produced a large addendum to the already substantial literature on the nature of recognition. A comprehensive, critical, and up-to-date analysis of the debate over the nature of recognition is now necessary.

The present book in essence stemmed from a review of existing literature that I undertook in the preliminary stage of research on a doctoral dissertation. As my research continued, the bulk of material in that literature review grew until it began to suggest the contours of several ideas. It began to suggest that the debate over the legal nature of recognition remains sufficiently active to demand an up-to-date and systematic analysis; that some issues often viewed as settled in that debate in truth are still open; and that certain contemporary developments and aspirations in international law may explain the prevailing doctrinal preference for a declaratory view of recognition. Moreover, the literature suggests that the main stream of debate today has shifted away from doctrinal categories and toward questions of legal process.

The kernel from which this book grew also began to prove useful. I found myself frequently consulting the pages of what became the present monograph. In drafting several articles touching on recognition, I discovered here a helpmate to negotiate my way through the voluminous and scattered body of writings on the subject. Whereas without it I would have been forced away from my study for hours to hunt down a sought-after proposition, quotation, or simple fact, with it at my side I often have been able to find the essentials in minutes. The thought began to cross my mind that the work might prove a useful resource to anyone deeply involved in the field.

For these reasons, I was finally urged to bring the manuscript to press. I did not however decide to publish without misgivings. The work may be criticized for a tendency toward the overinclusive. The text is supported by endnotes that in some instances would have proven their points with half the detail. Examples in the text carry on beyond the number necessary simply to develop the thesis at hand. Quotation in places might have conveyed the original authors' ideas if abbreviated—or even paraphrased. But, if I have erred on the side of over-inclusion, this was by design. One aim of this book is to furnish a convenient reference to specialists who demand a grasp of the many-nuanced debate over recognition, especially in its most recent evolution. While not formally structured as a reference work, the book may be used as a guide to what has been written—and to an extent, what has been done—about recognition. At the same time, the ready availability of good bibliographic material in the field[3] would have made the book, were it mainly a literature survey, redundant. I acknowledge that the form in which the work is cast may make it difficult to characterize, but I believe this form in balance best serves its purpose. This is in essence a study of the intellectual history of a facet of public international law which has hardly yet ceased to generate academic discourse.

The work is divided into an introduction, six chapters, and a conclusion. Chapters 1 and 2 describe the two traditional doctrines of recognition, problems associated with either, and grounds for current doctrinal preferences. Chapter 3 further describes bases for the doctrines, and Chapter 4 examines proposed amendments to the definition of statehood. Chapters 5 and 6 propose that the process by which recognition is extended has probably supplanted the legal nature of recognition as the primary subject in the field. Throughout, the reader will find extensive references in the endnotes to the key commentary on cases and questions addressed in the text. Though there are doubtless omissions, an aim here has been to present thorough coverage of an extensive body of scholarship. Pursuant to that aim, the chapters cover such diverse incidents of recognition as post-revolutionary Russia, 'Manchukuo,' Rhodesia and the South African 'Homelands,' East Timor, and the Yugoslav republics. The chief focus is the recognition of states, but where incidents of the recognition of governments, territorial situations, or other statuses have illuminated a point, these too have been addressed.

There are issues concerning recognition in its modern development that fall outside the scope of the present treatment. I do not approach in any detail the legal consequences of recognition and nonrecognition. Nor do I endeavor to address changes in the role recognition plays toward different objects—changes that have brought the decline of recognition of belligerency and of governments, and perhaps raise questions about the coherence of recognition as an institution of international law. This monograph is not intended to exhaust its subject, but, rather, to address the intellectual development of recognition to date and to make some observations about its future. Along the way, it covers some of the widely scattered writings and practice surrounding recognition and brings them together in a single framework.

I hope the material presented here contributes to the evolving debate over recognition. Even more, though, I hope the reader finds it as helpful as I have in forging a path through Brownlie's tertium quid toward solid ground.

## NOTES

1. *See* W. Michael Reisman, "International Incidents: Introduction to a New Genre in the Study of International Law" in *International Incidents: The Law That Counts in World Politics*. W. Michael Reisman & Andrew R. Willard eds. (Princeton: Princeton University Press, 1988), 3; Andrew R. Willard, "Incidents: An Essay in Method," *International Incidents*, 25. The methodology inherent in an 'incident study' proceeds from the assumptions of the New Haven School of public international law. On the New Haven School, see Eisuke Suzuki, "The New Haven School of International Law: An Invitation to a Policy-Oriented Jurisprudence," 1 *Yale Studies in World Public Order* (Yale Stud. W. Pub. Ord.) 1 (1974).

2. Ian Brownlie, "Recognition in Theory and Practice" in *The Structure and Process of International Law: Essays in Legal Philosophy, Doctrine, and Theory*. R.S.J. MacDonald & Douglas M. Johnston eds. (The Hague: Nijhoff, 1983), 627. Writers have made complaints like this for some time and not just about international law. Consider Montaigne, who wrote in his *Essays*, Book iii, Chapter 13, "There's more ado to interpret interpretations, than to interpret things: and more books upon books, than upon any other subject."

3. *See, e.g.*, *Public International Law: A Current Bibliography of Books and Articles* (Max-Planck-Institut für auslandisches öffentliches Recht und Völkerrecht) (Heidelberg: Springer Verlag) (published twice yearly); *Index to Foreign Legal Periodicals*, Thomas H. Reynolds, General Editor (Berkeley: University of California Press) (published quarterly).

# ACKNOWLEDGMENTS

I must acknowledge a number of persons and institutions for their rôles in bringing the present manuscript to press. Professor W. Michael Reisman and Professor James R. Crawford encouraged my interest in public international law generally and gave advice and caveats in the writing of this book. Conversations at Cambridge with John Dugard, Marc Weller, Michael Byers, Sandra Bunn-Altham, Thomas Viles, and Ineta Ziemele stimulated my thinking on various aspects of statehood and recognition. The United States/United Kingdom Fulbright Commission and the Cambridge Overseas Trust provided the funding without which I would not have been able to carry on my work at Cambridge University. Dr. Gordon Johnson, President of Wolfson College, and Dr. Gerald Tanyi, associate at Sullivan & Cromwell (New York), furnished highly-informed guidance to an author new to the business of publishing. Dr. James T. Sabin at Greenwood/Praeger and Philip Trahan and Nicholas Kosar, copyeditors, were most helpful throughout the process of publishing. I must especially thank Robin Fairbairns, of the Cambridge Computer Laboratory, for giving generously of his time and expertise in preparing rather raw word processing files for the publisher. Dr. Charles Schencking pointed me in the right direction for sources on Manchuria and Japanese involvement in the League of Nations; other members of Wolfson College, Cambridge who gave the occasional useful research hint in their own fields are too numerous to list. Suffice it here to mention Robert L. Purves, Ralf Gaensmantel, Talal Debbs, Dr. Thomas P. Harte, and Drs. Ramon and Karina Urbach-Jeffrey.

Finally, my education to date has been encouraged in multiple ways by my parents, to whom I dedicate this book.

Flaws in form and content of this book owe in all likelihood to my ignoring the better advice of some or all of the above.

# ABBREVIATIONS

| | |
|---|---|
| AFDI | Annuaire Français de Droit International |
| AJIL | American Journal of International Law |
| Am. U. J. Int'l L. & Pol'y | American University Journal of International Law & Policy |
| Am. U. L. Rev. | American University Law Review |
| Ariz. St. L.J. | Arizona State Law Journal |
| Austral. YIL | Australian Yearbook of International Law |
| Bos. Col. L. Rev. | Boston College Law Review |
| BYIL | British Yearbook of International Law |
| Cal. L. Rev. | California Law Review |
| Camb. L. J. | Cambridge Law Journal |
| Can. B. Rev. | Canadian Bar Review |
| CanYIL | Canadian Yearbook of International Law |
| Case W'n Res. J. Int'l L. | Case Western Reserve Journal of International Law |
| Colum. J. Transnat'l L | Columbia Journal of Transnational Law |
| Colum. L. Rev. | Columbia Law Review |
| Const. Rev. | Constitutional Review |
| Corn. Int'l L.J. | Cornell International Law Journal |
| Corn. L. Rev. | Cornell Law Review |
| Dalh. L.J. | Dalhousie Law Journal |
| Denv. J. Int'l L. & Pol'y | Denver Journal of International Law and Policy |
| EJIL | European Journal of International Law |
| ELR | European Law Review |
| Emory Int'l L. Rev. | Emory International Law Review |

| | |
|---|---|
| Eur. Arch. | Europa Archiv |
| For. Aff. | Foreign Affairs |
| For. Pol'y | Foreign Policy |
| Ford. Int'l L.J. | Fordham International Law Journal |
| Georgetown L.J. | Georgetown Law Journal |
| Hag. Rec. | Recueil des Cours de l' Academie de Droit International de la Haye |
| HILJ | Harvard International Law Journal |
| Hum. R. Q'ly | Human Rights Quarterly |
| ICLQ | International & Comparative Law Quarterly |
| ILM | International Legal Materials |
| Ind. Y. Int'l Aff. | Indian Yearbook of International Affairs |
| Int. Pol. | Internationale Politik |
| Int'l Org. | International Organization |
| Int'l Stud. Q'ly. | International Studies Quarterly |
| Iowa L. Rev. | Iowa Law Review |
| Irish Jur. | Irish Jurist |
| Israel L.R. | Israel Law Review |
| J. Int'l L. Pol'y | Journal of International Legal Policy |
| Leag. Nat. O.J. | League of Nations Official Journal |
| LNTS | League of Nations Treaties Series |
| Louisiana L. Rev. | Louisiana Law Review |
| Mich. L.R. | Michigan Law Review |
| Mod. L. Rev. | Modern Law Review |
| N.Y.U. J. Int'l L. & Pol. | New York University Journal of International Law & Politics |
| NRGT | Nouveau Recueil Général de Traités |
| Pol. YBIL | Polish Yearbook of International Law |
| RdDI | Revue de Droit International |
| RdDIdSDeP | Revue de Droit International de Sciences Diplomatiques et Politiques |
| Rev. Int'l Stud. | Review of International Studies |
| RGDIP | Revue Générale de Droit International Public |
| Stan. J. Int'l L. | Stanford Journal of International Law |
| Stan. L. Rev. | Stanford Law Review |
| Syracuse J. Int'l L. & Com. | Syracuse Journal of International Law & Commerce |
| Temple Int'l & Comp. L.J. | Temple International and Comparative Law Journal |
| U. Chi. L. Rev. | University of Chicago Law Review |
| UNRIAA | United Nations Reports of International Arbitral Awards |
| U. Penn. L. Rev. | University of Pennsylvania Law Review |
| U. Pitt. L. Rev. | University of Pittsburgh Law Review |

| | |
|---|---|
| UK Cmnd. Papers | United Kingdom Command Papers in International Law and Relations |
| Utah L. Rev. | Utah Law Review |
| Vand. L. Rev. | Vanderbilt Law Review |
| Virg. J. Int'l L. | Virginia Journal of International Law |
| Yale L.J. | Yale Law Journal |
| Yale Stud. W. Pub. Ord. | Yale Studies in World Public Order |

# INTRODUCTION

Recognition is a procedure whereby the governments of existing states respond to certain changes in the world community. It may also be a means by which existing states seek to effect changes in that community. When peoples hitherto contained within existing state structures seek to break free of those structures; when domestic government undergoes radical change; or when territorial status lies in doubt recognition may come into play. Recognition is an authoritative statement issued by competent foreign policy decision-makers in a country. Through it, those decision-makers signal the willingness of their state to treat with a new state or government or to accept that consequences, either factual or legal, flow from a new situation. Recognition at times has implied approval; nonrecognition, censure.[1]

International society in the present decade has confronted radical change. A stable régime dominated by Russo-American rivalry has given way to one of much less certain outline. At least based on a glance at the map, the most remarkable result of the subsidence of the Russian Empire has been a proliferation of new states in Europe and Central Asia. In addition to posing questions about security, economics, and cultural identity, proliferation of states has forced the international community to assess how it greets newcomers. Recognition has long served international society as a device by which to respond to changes in public world order generally and emergence of national communities as new states in particular. There are times when empires and federations stand intact and seemingly immutable, but others when polyglot states prove unable to avert disintegration. When disintegration occurs, recognition takes center stage as an institution both of international relations and international law. As we have witnessed in the last seven years the dissolution of two once-great multi-ethnic states—the USSR and the Socialist Federal Republic of Yugoslavia—recognition today requires renewed study.

My aim here is to summarize a long debate over recognition and to illustrate how recent incidents of recognition have contributed to that debate; to evaluate critically the prevailing theoretical view of recognition; and to trace how recent events have caused the institution to evolve and the terms of debate over it to change.

Two models formed the poles in the classic debate over recognition of new personalities in international law: the *declaratory* model and the *constitutive* model.[2] The cleavage between these reflected differing conceptions of state formation and, indeed, of public order in the world community. Under the declaratory model, the state was viewed as springing forth independent of recognition. Recognition merely acknowledges or *declares* that a community has come to possess all the requisites of statehood. Recognition is *evidence* that a state has come into being, but it is in no way an instrument of that creation. By contrast, under the constitutive model, the state was viewed as having its genesis in recognition. Recognition itself is a requisite of statehood. Recognition forms or *constitutes* the state. The doctrines of recognition therefore differed in how they conceived how states emerge; and in the regulatory role they assigned to existing states in that process.

I begin my examination of recognition with a detailed background of the constitutive and declaratory models. Deficiencies commonly identified in the two models are then discussed, and the traditional debate between declaratists and constitutivists is evaluated. I argue that, though they remain useful as devices for the analysis of recognition, the declaratory and constitutive models no longer mark the most salient dividing line in the law of recognition. Rather, the critical tension in recognition law is concentrated along two axes, in ways related to the traditional debate but distinct from it: first, along an axis between recognition conceived as a legal act and recognition conceived as a political act; and, second, along an axis between a collective and a unilateral *process* of recognition.

To analyze the most recent evolution of recognition, I revisit an alternative model of recognition, first advanced by Hersch Lauterpacht in the late 1940s. The third or 'Lauterpachtian' model contains hybrid features of its predecessors but endeavors to exclude the political distortions which both have admitted to the recognition process. Chapter 5 reviews state practice up to the present decade, asking whether in balance it supports the Lauterpachtian model.

The most telling episodes of recognition in recent years have surrounded the breakup of Yugoslavia. That cataclysm in the Balkans produced a handful of putative new states, and the status of these immediately became a matter of controversy. The breakup of Yugoslavia therefore confronted the world community with difficult issues of state recognition. The response of international society to the new states in the space of the former Yugoslavia is the subject of extended analysis in Chapter 6. This assesses the current direction of the international law of recognition and queries in particular whether a collective régime has evolved to govern the institution.

The six chapters that comprise this work explore a number of aspects of recognition. Though my principal focus is the role of recognition in the advent of new states, it is necessary to examine recognition in its other senses as well. Attention will be given to disputes over territory, to case law concerning recognition of governments, and to other facets of legal acknowledgment of conditions and of changes in condition external to the community extending recognition.

The long-debated issue of defining statehood is taken up in Chapter 1. In particular, the criteria for statehood are examined, with an inquiry into the origins of the most frequently cited enumeration of those criteria, the Montevideo Convention of 1933. Because of its intimate linkage to the definition of the state, the declaratory doctrine of recognition is addressed in conjunction with this analysis of statehood.

Chapter 2 contemplates in comparison and perspective the traditional rival theories of state recognition. Flaws of both are examined, and attention is given in that connection to state practice in foreign affairs, to political activity surrounding recognition in the domestic arena, and to the commentary of publicists. To provide a broad view, Chapter 2 examines scholarship both from the legal academy and from the field of international relations. Toward the end of Chapter 2, the current preference for the declaratory doctrine of state recognition is addressed. I argue that there are links between that preference and contemporary development of international human rights law. Past judicial support for the doctrine is also discussed as a basis for contemporary views.

Chapter 3 evaluates cases oft-cited in the debate over recognition. The meaning of these is scrutinized, and I propose that the purport commonly attributed to much of the case law does not necessarily flow from the decisional texts. Chapter 4 examines another problem of recognition—the conflation of criteria for recognition and criteria for statehood. In four sections, Chapter 4 enumerates and critiques proposals for including new criteria among the elements of statehood. The chapter also scrutinizes a theory (advanced by Akhil Amar, among other Americans)[3] that recognition must take note of domestic constitutional law. Having analyzed the traditional doctrinal struggle over recognition and its current situation, I will then ask whether the law has evolved to change the *process* by which recognition is extended. As will be shown, process now takes center stage in the debate over recognition. Where in light of recent state practice the process of recognition resides along the continuum between politics and law is a final question on which I hope the following chapters may shed some light.

## NOTES

1. For a definition of recognition, see Myres S. McDougal & W. Michael Reisman, *International Law in Contemporary Perspective: The Public Order of the*

*World Community* (Mineola, NY: The Foundation Press, Inc., 1981), 303. *See also* Daniel P. O'Connell, *International Law.* vol. 1, 2nd ed. (London: Stevens & Sons, 1970), 127–28; Ian Brownlie, *Principles of Public International Law.* 4th ed. (Oxford: Clarendon Press, 1990), 87–88.

2. A number of writers have summarized the debate between declaratists and constitutivists. *See, e.g.*, Brownlie, *Principles*, 74–81; James R. Crawford, *The Creation of States in International Law* (Oxford: Clarendon Press, 1979), 16–23; John Dugard, *Recognition and the United Nations* (Cambridge: Grotius Publications Limited, 1987), 7–9; Hersch Lauterpacht, *Recognition in International Law* (Cambridge: The University Press, 1948), 38–66; O'Connell, *International Law*, 128–131; Satyavrata R. Patel, *A Textbook of International Law* (London: Asia Publishing House, 1964), 46–51; Joseph G. Starke, *Introduction to International Law.* 10th ed. (London: Butterworths, 1989), 132–34; Nkambo Mugerwa, "Subjects of International Law," §5.18 ("The doctrinal controversy concerning the nature of recognition in international law") in *Manual of Public International Law.* Max Sørensen ed. (London: Macmillan, 1968), 247, 275–77.

3. Akhil Reed Amar, "Some New World Lessons for the Old World," 58 *University of Chicago Law Review*, (U. Chi. L. R.) 483, 501–502 (*Symposium: Approaching Democracy: A New Legal Order for Eastern Europe*) (1991).

# 1

# THE ONCE-GREAT DEBATE AND ITS RIVALS

Recognition, when debated as a matter of doctrine, was long taken to be better described as either 'constitutive' or 'declaratory' of statehood. The debate had implications for state practice, in that how one described recognition could influence when one believed it proper to extend recognition. A constitutive conception made recognition part of statehood and seemed at times to imply discretion on the part of existing states to bring new states into being. This raised the puzzling scenario of statehood opposable against those states recognizing a new entity but not against others. A declaratory view of recognition, associated by some writers with rule of law, made recognition automatic upon attainment of the criteria for statehood and seemed to reduce the liberty of existing states to choose what entities to regard as states. Declaratory doctrine seemed also to reduce the paradox of entities at once states to some, nonstates to others. However, both doctrines ignored critical factors. Instructions as to how, as a practical matter, recognition is to be extended can only be gleaned from the doctrines by implication. The doctrines do not take adequate account of the composite character of the state, ignoring that statehood is probably best described as a bundle of rights, obligations, and functions. And neither doctrine directly addresses where recognition falls along the spectrum between law and politics.

Nonetheless, because they were the rivals in the debate that once dominated academic discussion about recognition, constitutive and declaratory doctrines are a logical starting point for a study of the evolution of recognition in law and practice. Moreover, though it will be seen later that vital questions about recognition no longer can be answered by simple reference to the two old rivals, writers continue to rely on the terms of the debate and indeed even persist in weighing the merits of the two doctrines.

## THE CONSTITUTIVE MODEL

The constitutive conception of state recognition was summarized famously by Oppenheim: "A state is, and becomes, an International Person through recognition only and exclusively."[1] The central implication of this is that whether or not an entity has become a state depends on the actions of existing states. Recognition by others renders an entity a state; nonrecognition consigns the entity to non-statehood. Though attributes such as possession of territory, stable power over a defined population, and capacity to respect international agreements are elements of statehood, to the constitutivist these are for nought in the absence of recognition. Recognition perfects statehood. Moreover, extending or withholding recognition is a political act. In the words of Lauterpacht, the constitutive conception of statehood "deduces the legal existence of new States from the will of those already established."[2]

It has been said that, from the premise of the constitutive conception, the proposition follows directly that recognition resides at the complete discretion of the existing state. The decision to recognize is subject solely to the 'sovereign' will of the existing state and is made unilaterally, without reference to the actions of other members of the international community or, for that matter, to the objective condition of the entity receiving recognition. Recognition in this view parallels private contract law. Triepel, for example, characterized recognition as a *Vereinbarung* (law-making agreement),[3] and Anzilotti termed the model "constitutive" for the very reason that it describes recognition as generating rights and obligations between two equal actors, free of any overarching law or order, where no such mutual rights and obligations had before existed.[4] Other writers shared the constitutive view.[5] However, a substantial body of opinion rejected the contractual analogy and constitutivism more generally. Some writers objected on logical grounds. Kelsen, Kunz, Diena, and Cavaglieri numbered among those who were troubled by internal inconsistencies in the constitutive theory. To Kelsen, for example, "[t]o maintain that the legal personality of a State is the result of an act in which it is created by that very State is to put forward an assertion reminiscent of the attempt by Baron Munchhausen to extricate himself with the aid of his pigtail from the morass into which he had fallen."[6] While conceiving of recognition as a contractual act has been criticized for logical flaws, Lauterpacht and others identified its chief shortcoming as one of principle: "[T]he cardinal defect of the constitutive doctrine as generally propounded [is] . . . that the constitutive act creative of statehood is an act of unfettered political will divorced from binding considerations of legal principle."[7]

Thus freed from law, recognition, under the constitutive conception, becomes a tool of statecraft.[8] Its status as a legal process is correspondingly cast in doubt. The "high political act of recognition," in the oft-quoted statement of Senator Warren Austin, American ambassador to the United

Nations from 1947 to 1953, was one which "[no] country on earth can question."[9] Recognition, under this model, is not a principled and mandatory response to certain developments within a foreign community. It is, rather, a deliberate measure, taken unilaterally and at the discretion of the individual state.[10] Recognition is not an end unto itself, but a means to further state ends which may themselves bear little or no direct relation to the act of recognition or even to the entity receiving recognition. This view of recognition comported with the theory that international law is *jus gentium voluntarium*—nothing more than voluntary or consensual behavior, manifest in the practice of states. Though not lacking contemporary adherents, such a restrictive view of the contents of international law was more typical of late nineteenth century than of modern thought.[11] It is not surprising that, when state consent was taken as an essential ingredient to all international legal rules, a theory of recognition was preferred which did not posit principles binding on all states. The constitutive model, writers now widely assume, minimized the role of law in the recognition of states. With its emphasis on the power of states to invest legal personality in other communities, constitutivism accented the character of states as free political actors. Following from this, constitutivism implied a world arena absent rights or rules. Georg Schwarzenberger proposed, "New entities which may fulfil the requirements of international persons have no right to recognition."[12] Many constitutivists took the view that recognition is solely a matter between the state recognizing and the community being recognized. If recognition is only bilateral and discretionary, then there exist no structural restraints to censure a state extending recognition when that extension violates legal rules. The disapprobation of third states is irrelevant, as regards conduct over which the individual state enjoys complete discretion. The donor of recognition, assured that only its relation to the recipient matters, does not confront any multilateral mechanism for enforcing legal rules of recognition. Even if the constitutive view admitted somehow of control systems, its emphasis on discretion would still inhibit development of a body of substantive legal rules. The constitutive doctrine, casting recognition as a device of statecraft, a tool of *Realpolitik*, available to forge states out of communities at the will of the recognizing state, provides no apparent means to regulate state conduct and, in any event, no apparent code of conduct. To paraphrase Brierly, the jurisprudence of recognition—as far as a strict constitutivist is concerned—might amount to no more than "an attorney's mantle artfully displayed on the shoulders of arbitrary power"—"a decorous name for a convenience of the chancelleries."[13] Put another way, for the strict constitutivist, "recognition . . . is governed by no rules whatever."[14]

Arguments eventually emerged for a principled approach to state recognition in response and challenge to the morally unsatisfying *Realpolitik* tenor of constitutivism. Evolution of a theory of recognition more tightly bound by substantive legal rules—and perhaps more closely regulated by structures within the community of states—reflected broader trends in thinking about world public order. The initial response to the seemingly unprincipled aspect of constitutivism was a rival view of state formation—the declaratory doctrine. Though declaratory doctrine has enjoyed an ascendancy in contemporary discourse, it was not the lone product of the twentieth century effort to rein in the discretionary aspect of recognition. Hersch Lauterpacht, while maintaining avowedly constitutivist assumptions about how states are formed, substantially revised constitutivism, formulating in the process a distinctive doctrine sometimes characterized all his own. Before evaluating Lauterpacht's project of injecting principle into the constitutive view of recognition, it is necessary to explore the chief rival to constitutivism and, moreover, the bases for its contemporary prevalence.

The Lauterpachtian view of recognition is taken up in Chapter 5. In the remainder of the present chapter, I will summarize declaratory doctrine and examine aspects of its foundation. Chapters 2, 3, and 4 will address contemporary doctrinal preferences and some of the questions these raise; and will compare the two traditional schools of recognition theory.

## THE DECLARATORY MODEL

Unlike the constitutivists, who argued that recognition is necessary to make a state, declaratists characterized recognition as an acknowledgment of statehood already achieved. The two views have led to conflicting interpretations of the legal responsibility of states extending recognition. As a shorthand, I will refer to the state extending recognition as a 'donor' state, the community receiving it, as the 'recipient.' The practical difference between the constitutive and declaratory models of recognition has been described as follows: the former describes recognition as a voluntary act of the donor state; the latter, as an automatic duty.[15] Whether recognition is voluntary or mandatory not only defines the nature of the state, but it also suggests the outline of the society of states. Chen wrote, "In the last analysis, the question of international recognition is but a reflection of the fundamental cleavage between those who regard the State as the ultimate source of international rights and duties and those who regard it as being under a system of law which determines its rights and duties under that law."[16] Recognition, to the declaratist, is a response triggered by certain facts and conditioned by law. When the attributes which international law holds to define a state come to obtain within a community, existing states should declare that fact by according the community recognition. The constitutivist maintains that the state is held to no such duty. A central feature of the declaratory model is that it seems to subject recognition to legal principle, whereas the constitutive model implies recognition to be a mere tool of statecraft. When there arises a set of facts allegedly verifiable in objective fashion, recognition becomes a legal duty. Idealists have applauded the declaratory model for this. Nonetheless, the declaratory model is more complex than a simple dichotomy between *Realpolitik* and idealism would suggest.[17] Declaratory doctrine imposes on existing states the duty to identify when new states have arisen. This in turn demands a clear conception of what constitutes a state. Accordingly, the declaratory approach enmeshes recognition with the definition of statehood. Herein arises the substantial complexity of declaratory doctrine.

## Basic Outline and Criteria of Statehood

The declaratory conception of state recognition denies that the act of recognition alone imparts legal personality. The declaratory conception detaches statehood from the unilateral and discretionary behavior of existing states, making statehood automatic, upon the fulfillment of certain criteria by any entity aspiring to statehood. In the words of one declaratist scholar, "Recognition presupposes a state's existence; it does not create it."[18] Recognition, put differently, simply *declares* "as a fact something which has hitherto been uncertain."[19] It is not surprising that the coexistence of two such divergent theories as the constitutive and declaratory conceptions of state recognition spawned debate.[20] While ending the unfettered discretion which constitutivism seemed to imply, declaratory doctrine presented its own problems. If recognition follows the advent of statehood, donor states must possess a clear definition of 'state.' The challenge of defining 'state' did not obviously arise if states approached recognition under the constitutive view, but, under declaratory doctrine, every act of recognition raises it. This would pose no problem for declaratory doctrine—if the criteria of statehood were clear and the mechanisms for fact-finding well-established. The most daunting task of the declaratory project, however, is concretizing the notion of statehood. Toward this goal, declaratists must enumerate the characteristics defining a state. If these were to become clear (and if authority to determine whether the characteristics obtain in individual cases were identified and agreed upon), then recognition would become much simpler and less politicized. But defining 'state' has proven problematic.

The source most often cited[21] as a textual basis for statehood and thus as a guide for declaratory recognition is the Montevideo Convention of 1933 (*Convention on the Rights and Duties of States*).[22] The Montevideo Convention proposed four criteria for statehood. Under the Convention, the entity aspiring to be regarded as a state must possess a permanent population; it must occupy a clearly defined territory; over its extent must operate an effective government; and it must display a capacity to engage in international relations—such capacity including ability to fulfill international treaty obligations.[23] This list of criteria—to which I will refer as the Montevideo criteria—provides a succinct and perhaps easily employed standard to assess whether a community is a state and, according to the declaratists, whether to extend recognition. It is not however entirely clear that the Montevideo criteria provide a satisfactory definition of statehood. The criteria have held a prominent place in efforts to define statehood, but this may reflect the lack of a better model more than the sufficiency of Montevideo itself. To understand the position of the Montevideo criteria in modern discourse over statehood, it is necessary briefly to explore the background of the Convention.

## Origins of the Montevideo Criteria

The text of the Montevideo Convention standing alone does not explain the origins of the criteria it enunciates. Since its formulation, however, the Montevideo Convention on the Rights and Duties of States has been a primary point of reference in efforts to define statehood. Crawford correctly calls Article 1 of the Convention the "best known formulation of the basic criteria for statehood."[24] The 1930s and 1940s, immediately following the signing of the Convention by the United States and the other Pan-American nations,[25] witnessed ample citation to the Convention. The four-point enumeration of the elements of statehood offered by the Convention has perhaps been even more frequently cited in recent years; citation to the Convention in contemporary discussions of statehood is nearly a reflex.[26] Some important sources, without attributing their definition of statehood to the Convention, repeat the Montevideo criteria nearly verbatim. The United States Department of State, for example, wrote in 1976, "In [judging whether to recognize an entity as a state], the United States has traditionally looked to the establishment of certain facts. These facts include effective control over a clearly defined territory and population; an organized governmental administration of that territory; and a capacity to act effectively to conduct foreign relations and to fulfill international obligations."[27] Though the Montevideo criteria have become the touchstone for defining 'state,' little if any examination is to be found of their origin. References to the Convention in the academic literature of the 1930s and 1940s offer no insight into why the drafters chose the adopted phrasing.[28] Nor, when publicists have mentioned the Montevideo criteria in the last half century, has much light been shed on the matter.

That the framing of the Montevideo Convention has gone largely unexamined may reflect the fact that its content was a restatement of ideas prevalent at the time of the framing. So apparent were the Montevideo criteria to contemporary observers that few thought to inquire as to their basis or origin. At the crux of the Montevideo criteria lay the concepts of effectiveness and territoriality. These concepts may, in the 1930s, have seemed a long-established feature of international law. They indeed were widely assumed to be a mainstay of statehood. Reflecting their prevalence, effectiveness and territoriality were enumerated as a basis for statehood (or of sovereignty) by many leading publicists of the half century leading up to the Montevideo Convention.

Wheaton wrote, "The habitual obedience of the members of any political society to a superior authority must have once existed in order to constitute a sovereign State."[29] Wheaton added this to a definition of statehood which he attributed to classical scholars. Cicero, Wheaton explained, had defined 'state' as "a body political, or society of men, united together for the purpose of promoting their mutual safety and advantage by their combined strength."[30] Power played a central role in Wheaton's definition of statehood. Lorimer also suggested that the effectiveness of a putative state was critical to its claim:

> In order to be entitled to recognition, a State must presumably possess;
>
> (a) The will to reciprocate the recognition which it demands.
>
> (b) The power to reciprocate the recognition which it demands.[31]

Lorimer, who proposed this formula in 1883, would be followed by many others. Hannis Tayler wrote at the turn of the century that both Rome and its successor to organized power in the Mediterranean—the Christian Church—embraced universalist notions of the state. This view contemplated only a single state, encompassing the width and breadth of the known world, and it denied full legal status to entities falling outside the imperium. Roman universalism gave way, however, to a belief that *territorial sovereignty* lay at the root of statehood.[32] The medieval and classical West conceived of the state as a singular instance of human organization, deriving its validity from principle. The early modern thinkers, by contrast, began to admit that there could be a multitude of states, and that it was their effectiveness in controlling a land and a population that lent these legal status. It would be this view which took center stage by the early twentieth century. Scelle, writing in 1932, would describe the state as "une collectivité,—fixée sur un territoire délimité,—juridiquement organisée."[33] Hall, the publicist perhaps most closely approximating the Montevideo criteria before their codification, wrote, "The marks of an independent State are, that the community constituting it is permanently established for a political end, that it possesses a defined territory, and that it is independent of external control."[34] Hall further emphasized the territorial aspect of statehood by emphasizing in particular *permanence* of territorial control. According to Hall, a fugacious people could not qualify as a state: "From the invariable association of land with sovereignty, or in other words with exclusive control over the members of a specific society, to the necessary association of such control with the possession of land, is a step which could readily be made, and which became inevitable when no instances were present of civilised communities without fixed seats."[35] The ideas behind the Montevideo criteria were well-rooted by the time of the Convention—so much so that the arbitrators in *Deutsche Continental Gas-Gesellschaft* (1929) could posit with little explanation that a "State does not exist unless it fulfils the conditions of possessing a territory, a people inhabiting that territory, and a public power which is exercised over the people and the territory."[36]

Consensus on territoriality and effectiveness by the eve of Montevideo probably explains the dearth of examination surrounding the elements of the Convention. However, consensus obscured that these concepts were not absolute. Though the Montevideo criteria were very much a part of the international legal milieu by 1933, territorial power and effectiveness had not monopolized state theory for very long. Well into the nineteenth century, statehood was thought to be bound to a set of political criteria as much or more than to the fact of territorial power. Legitimism was at times the prevailing concept in theory and practice concerning statehood. Though legitimism would eventually fade, its onetime prevalence recommends more careful examination of the assumption that the Montevideo criteria are conclusive as to the nature of statehood.

*Legitimism and Its Decline*

Legitimism was the prevalent theory of sovereignty during the age of monarchy.[37] Eighteenth-century princes were awake to the threat posed to their dynasties by popular unrest, family dissension, and external attack. The system of states at the time rested on the principle of inheritance and equated the state to personal ownership of land by the monarch. Eighteenth-century notions of statehood went so far, famously, to posit an identity between state and ruler—"L'État c'est moi."[38] This system relied on the proposition that a dynasty enjoyed a historic right to rule a state, and, it flowed from this, the prince continued to be the sovereign even if in fact displaced from his throne. Though firmly entrenched for much of the eighteenth century, legitimism would not prove immune to historical contingency. The French Revolution put the doctrine under strain. The collapse of the ancien régime in France was a fact which the monarchies of Europe—essentially all the states of Europe—could scarcely ignore, but to that fact the monarchies resolutely refused to attribute legal effect. With the sheer power of his empire insufficient to unseat legitimist assumptions about statehood, Napoleon resorted to the terms and forms of the European monarchies in a bid for recognition. Bonaparte fashioned himself Emperor and various of his relatives kings of conquered European states.[39] In trying to integrate himself into the ancient system of European dynasties, Napoleon seems to have reaffirmed the notion of dynastic legitimacy. Though existing dynasties took a hostile view of the effort, it may have born fruit as reflected in willingness later in the period of Empire for Napoleon's enemies to treat with him as an equal. At Napoleon's peak, Tsar Alexander I of Russia would hold a 'summit' with the French Emperor on the River Nieman; and Prince Metternich would make several offers of dynastic security to the Bonapartes after French military fortunes had declined. That legitimism survived the French Revolution was evidenced by Napoleonic adoption of its argument and terminology. In the aftermath of Napoleon's bid for European dominion, a Holy Alliance was established by the conservative monarchies. Installing a Bourbon anew on the throne of France, the alliance of Russia, Prussia, and Austria pledged to revive legitimist tests of sovereignty and thus to make dynastic credentials the *sine qua non* of statehood. Under the legitimist theory promoted by the Holy Alliance, an entity could be considered a state "irrespective of the compelling force of facts."[40]

Some contemporary international legal thinkers, however, rejected the strong-form view of legitimism. Justi, Steck, Martens, and Klueber argued that political change in a community could create a new state or government. Such a state or government, according to the more progressive publicists, could enjoy status on the world stage equal to that of other, longer-established ones. The Congress of Aix-la-Chapelle in 1818 nonetheless reiterated the legitimist position. The doctrine was however to face erosion in the face of social and political change during the decades that followed. Though the Congress of Aix-la-Chapelle won the adherence of France and Britain, the latter approached the legitimist thesis with reservation. The Congress, British statesmen made clear, "never was . . . intended as a union for the government of the world, or for the superintendence of the internal affairs of other States."[41] The proposition was gaining force that domestic political reality could trump dynastic legitimacy. Though some powers as late as World War I remained cautious toward revolutionary changes in the structure of states, effective control became, as the nineteenth century progressed, a more important indicator of statehood than historic dynastic prerogative. The disappearance in 1918 of the four great monarchies (Germany, Austria-Hungary, Russia, and Turkey) ended lingering attachment to the idea. For a time, effectivist criteria for statehood held the leading position in international legal theory.

### Montevideo Scrutinized

Despite its prevalence, the enumeration of statehood criteria found in the Montevideo Convention has come under scrutiny. Crawford in particular proposes that effectiveness—the linchpin of Montevideo—is not the sole or even the critical criterion for statehood.[42] States annexed from 1936 to 1940, Crawford notes, continued to enjoy legal personality. Though their governments lost all territorial power, the Polish, Yugoslav, Czechoslovak, and Baltic states retained recognition, at least by the Allied Powers.[43] In the context of the recent civil strife in Somalia, it has also been noted that statehood survives illegal occupation, not to mention disintegration of municipal legal order.[44] To this might be added the observation that entities never before enjoying territorial control have been attributed 'nationhood.' France recognized Poland and Czechoslovakia as 'nations' during World

War I. Though Poland had once been a state, the Polish National Committee which benefited from French recognition was headquartered at Paris; had never had a seat in Poland; and could make no realistic claim of continuity to a state which had disappeared from the map of Europe in 1815. Poland and Czechoslovakia had no territory, yet the act "recognized their right to raise an army, to have a national flag, to have military tribunals authorized to judge their nationals."[45] An extensive set of state-like competences was thus recognized in entities completely lacking territorial foothold.

Crawford proposes that in fact the critical criterion for statehood is independence. While, according to Crawford, diminutiveness, political alliance, belligerent occupation, and illegal intervention do not derogate from independence, a number of factors may. Substantial illegality of origin may put an entity's "title to be a 'State' . . . in issue."[46] Formation of the putative state under belligerent occupation (*e.g.*, Manchukuo) casts doubt on independence.[47] And a putative state experiencing "substantial external control" also may lack the essential attribute of statehood.[48] Crawford notes that there have been no proposals accepted since the Montevideo Convention to codify recognition, and this he attributes in part to a reluctance to announce a clear definition of statehood.[49]

If the community of states today hesitates to announce what constitutes a state, the question arises, why did the Pan-American powers in 1933 decide to do so? For one thing, as I have discussed already, the notions of effectiveness and territoriality prevailed at the time of the framing of the Convention. The ideas were in the air. Several additional factors appear to have militated in favor of such an exercise as well however. First, Latin American states had displayed inclination before to codify international norms. Consider, for example, the Estrada and Tobar Doctrines.[50] Penchant for codification perhaps reflected the Roman law roots of Latin American legal systems. Second, the United States was in the early stages of the Restatements movement. The American Law Institute (ALI) was established in 1923 to promote the "clarification and simplification of the law and its better adaptation to social needs." The Restatements, the ALI's principal work product, are formulated by committees of judges, scholars, and practitioners selected for their eminence in different fields of law.[51] Perhaps the same quasi-legislative, quasi-academic inspiration to organize the common law into code-like compilations which had moved the ALI had also moved United States State Department lawyers. Finally, the internationalism prevalent in much of the interwar world made for a milieu conducive to the Montevideo exercise. Other manifestations of interwar internationalism included the Kellogg-Briand Pact (General Treaty for the Renunciation of War of 1928);[52] the Washington Treaty of 1922 for the Limitation of Naval Armament;[53] the London Treaty for the Limitation and Reduction of Naval Armament;[54] and American participation in the Permanent Court of International Justice.[55] The time was ripe for bringing legal order to international society.

Conditions conducive to a latter-day effort at codifying statehood have proved elusive. Perhaps the most comprehensive discussion of attempts to overhaul the Montevideo criteria is provided by Jorri C. Duursma. According to Duursma, the codification of a definition of statehood was debated during drafting sessions for a *Declaration of the Rights and Duties of States* in 1949; for the *Vienna Convention on the Law of Treaties* in 1956 and 1966; and for proposed *Articles on Succession of States in Respect of Treaties* in 1974.[56] Duursma attributes the difficulty in codifying a definition of statehood to political concerns, the same difficulty that writers and practitioners have noted at least since 1973.[57]

Though international organizations or conferences have not produced a multilateral instrument to replace or supplement the Montevideo Convention as a definition of statehood, publicists like Crawford have proposed revision of the criteria. Many writers calling for revision argue that additional criteria are necessary. While formal efforts to recodify the term 'state' have failed, probably for political reasons, to get off the ground, it would appear that some new criteria have at least tentatively taken places alongside those enunciated in 1933. Putative new criteria have however introduced problems of their own. First, some of what I will refer to as *addenda* to the Montevideo criteria are of doubtful legal status, state practice failing to provide good evidence of their operation. And, second, the accretion of putative new criteria to the definition of statehood blurs the distinction between criteria for *statehood* and criteria for *recognition*. Chapter 4 examines the extent to which four proposed addenda to the Montevideo criteria have rooted themselves in state practice. As for blurring the distinction between statehood and recognition, this difficulty has been noted before by Crawford, among others. Crawford includes "willingness and ability to observe international law" on his list of criteria for recognition. This criterion he distinguishes from "capacity to enter into relations with other states." The former Crawford cautions against characterizing as a requisite of statehood: "[I]t is particularly necessary to distinguish recognition from statehood in this context. Unwillingness or refusal to observe international law may well constitute grounds for refusal of recognition, or for such other sanctions as the law allows, just as unwillingness to observe [UN] Charter obligations is a ground for non-admission to the United Nations. Both are however distinct from statehood."[58] Colin Warbrick also notes difficulty in separating recognition from statehood once supplementary criteria are admitted to the traditional definition. Remarking on a statement by the EC and its member states on January 15, 1992, in which they recognized Croatia and Slovenia, Warbrick draws attention to "a tendency to blur the questions of statehood and recognition." He cites the January 15 statement, "with its reference to republics 'which wish to become independent' but then making reference to factors which do not touch the traditional criteria for statehood," as signal of contemporary confusion on the issue.[59]

A review of the history of the Montevideo criteria suggests that the notion of statehood and sovereignty is, at least in part, historically contingent. What may be counted as a source of sovereignty or a basis to a claim to statehood at a particular time may not be counted as such later on. The historical contingencies surrounding the idea of statehood indeed suggest that any codification such as the Montevideo Convention will eventually require overhaul or replacement. The definition of statehood has been fluid and controversial.[60] This fact, I argue below, is of some importance to the nature of recognition.[61]

## NOTES

1. Lassa F.L. Oppenheim, *International Law: A Treatise.* Sir Hersch Lauterpacht ed., 8th ed. (London: Longmans, Green and Co., 1955), 125.

2. Hersch Lauterpacht, *Recognition in International Law* (Cambridge: The University Press, 1948), 38.

3. Heinrich Triepel, *Völkerrecht und Landesrecht* (Tübingen: Verlag von T.C.B. Mohr, 1899), 102.

4. Dionisio Anzilotti, *Cours de droit international.* Gilbert Gidel trans., 3rd ed. (Paris: Recueil Sirey, 1929) (orig. *Corso di diritto internazionale.* 3rd ed. Rome: Athenaeum, 1928), 160 et seq. Cited at Lauterpacht, *Recognition*, 39 n. 2.

5. Past writers usually cited as constitutivists include Triepel, Le Normand, Liszt, Lawrence, Anzilotti, Kelsen, and Redslob. *See* Heinrich Triepel, *Droit International et Droit Intern.* René Brunet trans. (Paris: Pedrone, 1920) (orig. *Völkerrecht und Landesrecht.* Leipzig: Verlag von L.L. Hirschfeld, 1899), 101; René Le Normand, *La Reconnaissance Internationale et ses Diverses Applications: états, gouvernements, belligerants, principes du droit international* (Paris: Imprime Camis, 1899), 268; Franz von Liszt, *Le Droit International: exposé systematique.* Gilbert Gidel & Leon Alcindor trans. Publications of the Carnegie Endowment for International Peace (Paris: Pedrone, 1927), 52–53; Thomas Joseph Lawrence, *The Principles of International Law* Sir Percy H. Winfield ed., 7th ed. (Boston: Macmillan, 1923), 82; Anzilotti, *Cours de droit international*, 192; Hans Kelsen, "Recognition in International Law, Theoretical Observations," 35 AJIL 605, 608–09 (1941); Robert Redslob, "La Reconnaissance de l'État comme Sujet de Droit International," 13 *Revue de Droit International* (RdDI) 429 (1934).

6. Kelsen, Kunz, and Cavaglieri number among the scholars who have criticized the constitutive conception on logical grounds. To Kelsen, "[t]o maintain that the legal personality of a State is the result of an act in which it is created by that very State is to put forward an assertion reminiscent of the attempt by Baron Munchhausen to extricate himself with the aid of his pigtail from the morass into which he had fallen." Hans Kelsen, "Théorie Générale du Droit International Public: Problèmes Choisis; Chapter III: La Détermination par le droit international du Domaine de Validité des différents Ordres Juridiques Étatiques," XLII(iv) *Recueil des Cours de l'Academie de Droit International de la Haye* (Hag. Rec.) 268–69 (1932).

7. Lauterpacht, *Recognition*, 41.

8. *See, e.g.*, M.J. Peterson, "Political Use of Recognition: The Influence of the International System," 34 *World Politics* 324, 325 (1982).

9. Warren Austin, quoted in Philip Marshall Brown, "The Recognition of Israel," 42 *American Journal of International Law* (AJIL) 620, 621 (1948). *See also* James L. Brierly, *The Law of Nations: An Introduction to the International Law of Peace*. Sir Humphrey Waldock ed., 6th ed. (Oxford: Clarendon Press, 1963), 140 n. 1 (citing *New York Times*, May 19, 1948); D.J. Harris, *Cases and Materials in International Law*. 4th ed. (London: Sweet & Maxwell, 1991), 140 n. 59; Marjorie M. Whiteman, *Digest of International Law* (Washington, DC: Government Printing Office, 1973), 10 (citing UN Security Council Off. Rec. No. 68, 294th meeting, May 18, 1948, p. 16).

10. *The Restatement (Second) of the Foreign Relations Law of the United States* sustains this characterization, at least as regards the distinct but nonetheless related issue of recognizing new governments: "[T]he question of recognizing [a] new regime is one for determination by each state in its own discretion." American Law Institute, *The Restatement (Second) of the Foreign Relations Law of the United States* (St. Paul: American Law Institute Publishers, 1965), §99(1) comment b.

11. Hall has been cited as a leading nineteenth-century exponent of the positivist conception of the "Law of Nations"—the conception that international law consists only of what states in fact do. *See* Hersch Lauterpacht, "The Grotian Tradition in International Law," 23 *British Yearbook of International Law* (BYIL) 1, 21 (1946). *See* William E. Hall, *A Treatise on International Law*. A. Pearce Higgins ed., 8th ed. (Oxford: Clarendon Press, 1924) (orig. 1890).

12. Georg Schwarzenberger, *Power Politics: A Study of International Society*. 2nd ed. (London: Stevens & Sons Limited, 1951), 8.

13. James L. Brierly, *The Outlook for International Law* (Oxford: Oxford University Press, 1944), 13.

14. Brown, "Recognition of Israel," 42 AJIL at 621.

15. Fred L. Morrison, "Recognition in International Law: A Functional Reappraisal," 34 *University of Chicago Law Review* (U. Chi. L. Rev.) 857 n. 7 (1967). This is not to say that the state, under declaratory doctrine, is left powerless in the recognition process. It remains at the discretion of the individual state contemplating recognition to assess whether the attributes of statehood have arisen. Once the individual state has concluded they have, recognition is mandatory. Hall wrote:

> Theoretically a politically organised community enters of right . . . into the family of states and must be treated in accordance with law, so soon as it is able to show that it possesses the marks of a state. . . . For though no state has a right to withhold recognition when it has been earned, states must be allowed to judge for themselves whether a community claiming to be recognised does really possess all the necessary marks, and especially whether it is likely to live. Thus although the right to be treated as a state is independent of recognition, recognition is the necessary evidence that the right has been acquired.

William E. Hall, *A Treatise on International Law*. A. Pearce Higgins ed., 8th ed. (Oxford: Clarendon Press, 1924) (orig. 1890), §26, p 103.

Note too in Hall the emphasis on the evidentiary nature of recognition. Adherents to declaratory doctrine often referred to recognition as "mere evidence of statehood" and the phrase appears prominently in the writings of the declaratory school. Consider for example the *Tinoco* arbitration. 18 *American Journal of International*

*Law* (AJIL) 147 (1924); 1 *United Nations Reports of International Arbitral Awards* (UNRIAA) 369, 376–384 (1923).

16. Ti-Chiang Chen, *The International Law of Recognition, with special reference to Practice in Great Britain and the United States* (London: Stevens & Sons Limited, 1951), 3.

17. In a later editorial comment, Kunz attributed the declaratory doctrine to his 1928 work *Die Anerkennung von Staaten und Regierungen im Völkerrecht (Handbuch des Völkerrechts)* 2. Bd ("Die Lehre von den Volkerrechtssubjekten,"), 3. Abt. (Stuttgart: W. Kohlhammer Verlag, 1928), 218. Josef L. Kunz, "Critical Remarks on Lauterpacht's 'Recognition in International Law,"' 44 AJIL 713 n. 3 (1950).

18. Alan James, *Sovereign Statehood: The Basis of International Society* (London: Allen & Unwin, 1986), 147. *See also* Hermann Mosler, "Subjects of International Law," in 7 *Encyclopedia of Public International Law*. Rudolf Bernhardt ed. (Amsterdam: North-Holland Publishing Company, 1984), 442, 449; Jochen Abraham Frowein, "Recognition," in 10 *Encyclopedia of Public International Law*, 340, 342.

19. James L. Brierly, *The Law of Nations: An Introduction to the International Law of Peace*. Sir Humphrey Waldock ed., 6th ed. (Oxford: Clarendon Press, 1963), 139. John Dugard, *Recognition and the United Nations* (Cambridge: Grotius Publications Limited, 1987), 7.

20. A number of authors summarize the debate between constitutivists and declaratists. *See, e.g.*, James R. Crawford, *The Creation of States in International Law* (Oxford: Clarendon Press, 1979), 16–25; Chen, *Recognition*, Chaps. 1 & 2; Satyavrata Ramdas Patel, *Recognition in the Law of Nations*. 1st ed. (Bombay: N.M. Tripathi, 1959), Chaps. 3–5; Hersch Lauterpacht, *Recognition in International Law* (Cambridge: The University Press, 1948), Chap. IV; Dermott J. Devine, "The Status of Rhodesia in International Law," 1973 *Acta Juridica* (Cape Town) 1, 90–145. Cited in Dugard, *Recognition*, 7. *See also* Johan D. van der Vyver, "Statehood in International Law," 5 *Emory International Law Review* (Emory Int'l L. Rev.) 9, 13–20 (1991).

21. *See, e.g.*, Dugard, *Recognition*, 8 n. 1; James R. Crawford, "The Criteria for Statehood in International Law," 48 *British Yearbook of International Law* (BYIL) 93, 120 (1976–77); M. Kelly Malone, "Comment: The Rights of Newly Emerging Democratic States Prior to International Recognition and the Serbo-Croatian Conflict," 6 *Temple International and Comparative Law Journal* (Temple Int'l & Comp. L.J.) 81, 83 (1992); van der Vyver, "Statehood," 5 Emory Int'l L. Rev. at 14.

22. *Convention on the Rights and Duties of States* (Montevideo Convention) December 26, 1933. 165 League of Nations Treaties Series (LNTS) 19; 28 AJIL (Supp.) 53 (1934) (reprinting text of Montevideo Convention).

23. Montevideo Convention Article I reads, "The state as a person of international law should possess the following qualifications: (a) a permanent population; (b) a defined territory; (c) government; and (d) capacity to enter into relations with the other states." 28 AJIL (Supp.) at 76.

24. Crawford, *Creation of States*, 36.

25. The signatories were Honduras, the United States of America, El Salvador, the Dominican Republic, Haiti, Argentina, Venezuela, Uruguay, Mexico, Panama, Bolivia, Guatemala, Brazil, Ecuador, Nicaragua, Colombia, Chile, Peru, and Cuba. 28 AJIL (Supp.) at 52.

26. *See, e.g.*, David A. Ijalaye, "Was 'Biafra' at any Time a State in International

Law?" 65 AJIL 551 (1971); Michael C. Small, "Enforcing International Human Rights Law in Federal Courts: The Alien Tort Statute and the Separation of Powers," 74 *Georgetown Law Journal* (Georgetown L. J.) 163, 196 n. 240 (1985); P.K. Menon, "Some Aspects of Recognition: Recognition of States," 67(3) *Revue de Droit International de Sciences Diplomatiques et Politiques* (RdDIdSDeP) 161 (1991); Dugard, *Recognition*, 7 & n. 1; Jost Delbrück & Rüdiger Wolfrum, *Völkerrecht* (Berlin: Walter de Gruyter, 1989), 188, 209, 234; Knut Ipsen, *Völkerrecht* (Munich: C.H. Beck'sche Verlagsbuchhandlung, 1990), 56; Rosalyn Higgins, *Problems and Process: International Law and How We Use It* (Oxford: Clarendon Press, 1994), 39; Frederic L. Kirgis, Jr., "Admission of 'Palestine' as a Member of a Specialized Agency and Withholding the Payment of Assessments in Response," 84 AJIL 218, 219 (1990); Ian Brownlie, *Principles of Public International Law*. 3rd ed. (Oxford: Clarendon Press, 1979), 72–73; Anne-Marie Burley, "Law Among Liberal States: Liberal Internationalism and the Act of State Doctrine," 92 *Columbia Law Review* (Colum. L. Rev.) 1907, 1926 n. 45 (1992); Marc Weller, "The International Response to the Dissolution of the Socialist Federal Republic of Yugoslavia," 86 AJIL 569, 588 n. 122 (1992); Holly A. Osterland, "National Self-Determination and Secession: The Slovak Model," 25 *Case Western Reserve Journal of International Law* (Case W'n Res. J. Int'l L.) 655, 676–77 n. 143 (1993); Kevin Sneesby, "National Separation: Canada in Context-A Legal Perspective," 53 *Louisiana Law Review* (Louisiana L. Rev.) 1357, 1377–78 (1993); James A. Casey, "Sovereignty by Sufferance: The Illusion of Indian Tribal Sovereignty," 79 *Cornell Law Review* (Corn. L. Rev.) 404, 431 (1994); Michael E. Field, "Liberia v. Bickford. The Continuing Problem of Recognition of Governments and Civil Litigation in the United States," 18 *Maryland Journal of International Law and Trade* (Mary. J. Int'l L. & Trade) 113, nn. 70 & 72 (1994); Kenneth S. Freeman, "Punishing Attacks on United Nations Peacekeepers: A Case Study of Somalia," 8 Emory Int'l L. Rev. 845, 860 n. 105 (1994); Christian J. Garris, "Bosnia and the Limitations of International Law," 34 *Santa Clara Law Review* (Santa Clara L. Rev.) 1039, 1067 n. 201 (1994); Kathryn M. McKinney, "The Legal Effects of the Israeli-PLO Declaration of Principles: Steps Toward Statehood for Palestine," 18 *Puget Sound Law Review* (Pug. Sd. L. Rev.) 93, 95 n. 10 (1994); William A. Schroeder, "Nationalism, Boundaries, and the Bosnian War: Another Perspective," 19 *Southern Illinois University Law Journal* (S'n Ill. U.L.J.) 153, 155 (1994); Armen Tamzarian, "Nagorno-Karabagh's Right to Political Independence under International Law: An Application of the Principle of Self-Determination," 24 *Southwestern University Law Review* (Sw'n U.L. Rev.) 183, 200 (1994); Cheri Attix, "Between the Devil and the Deep Blue Sea: Are Taiwan's Trading Partners Implying Recognition of Taiwanese Statehood?" 25 *California Western International Law Journal* (Cal. W'n Int'l L.J.) 357, 366 n. 80 (1995); Ruth E. Gordon, "Some Legal Problems with Trusteeship," 28 *Cornell International Law Journal* (Corn. Int'l L.J.) 301, 335 n. 185 (1995); Laurence S. Hanauer, "The Irrelevance of Self-Determination Law to Ethno-national Conflict: A New Look at the Western Sahara Case," 9 Emory Int'l L. Rev. 133, 134 (1995); P. Kenneth Kiplagat, "Legal Status of Integration Treaties and the Enforcement of Treaty Obligations: A Look at the COMESA Process," 23 *Denver Journal of International Law and Policy* (Denv. J. Int'l L. & Pol'y) 259, 261 n. 9 (1995); Daniel Orlow, "Of Nations Small: The Small State in International Law," 9 Temple Int'l & Comp. L.J. 115, 117 (1995); Judith V. Royster, "The Legacy of Allotment," 27 *Arizona State Law Journal*

(Ariz. St. L.J.) 1, n. 4 (1995); Michael P. Scharf, "Musical Chairs: The Dissolution of States and Membership in the United Nations," 28 Corn. Int'l L.J. 29, 32 (1995); Svetozar Stojanovic, "The Destruction of Yugoslavia," 19 *Fordham International Law Journal* (Ford. Int'l L.J.) 337, 359 (1995); Andrew L. Strauss, "Beyond National Law: The Neglected Role of the International Law of Personal Jurisdiction in Domestic Courts," 36 *Harvard International Law Journal* (HILJ) 373, 409 n. 125 (1995); Justus R. Weiner, "Hard Facts Meet Soft Law—The Israel-PLO Declaration of Principles and the Prospects for Peace: A Response to Katherine W. Meighan," 35 *Virginia Journal of International Law* (Virg. J. Int'l L.) 931, 940 (1995); Christine Biancheria, "Restoring the Right to Have Rights: Statelessness and Alienage Jurisdiction in Light of Abu-Zeineh v. Federal Laboratories, Inc.," 11 *American University Journal of International Law & Policy* (Am. U. J. Int'l L. & Pol'y) 195, 235 & n. 223 (1996); Jorri C. Duursma, *Fragmentation and the International Relations of Micro-States: Self-Determination and Statehood* (Cambridge: Cambridge University Press, 1996), 112–13, 116, 118.

27. November 1, 1976 United States Department of State Press Relations Office Notice. Quoted in Eleanor C. McDowell, "Contemporary Practice of the United States Relating to International Law," 71 AJIL 337 (1977).

28. *See, e.g.*, Robert R. Wilson, "International Law in Treaties of the United States," 31 AJIL 271, 283–84 (1937) (inquiring whether the Montevideo Convention is merely declaratory of existing international law or legislative); James W. Garner, "The United States 'Neutrality' Law of 1937," 19 BYIL 44, 62 (1938) (suggesting that the Montevideo Convention invalidates or conflicts with the Neutrality Act of 1937); Felice Morgenstern, " 'Extra-Territorial' Asylum," 25 BYIL 236, 240, 244, 257, 258 (1948) (discussing only the asylum provisions of the Montevideo Convention); C. Wilfred Jenks, "The Conflict of Law-Making Treaties," 30 BYIL 401, 424 (1953) (remarking on the relation between the Montevideo Convention and the Havana Convention of 1928).

29. Henry Wheaton, *Elements of International Law*. Richard Henry Dana, Jr. ed. (as originally published in 1866). James Brown Scott ed., 1936 ed. (Oxford: Clarendon Press, 1936), 29.

30. *Dana's Wheaton*, 25.

31. James Lorimer, *The Institutes of the Law of Nations* (Edinburgh: William Blackwood and Sons, 1883), 109.

32. Hannis Taylor, *International Public Law* (London: Sweet & Maxwell, 1902), 75.

33. Georges Scelle, *Precis de Droit des Gens: Principes et Systematique* (Paris: Recueil Sirey, 1932).

34. Hall, *Treatise*, 18.

35. Ibid., 19.

36. Arbitrators Lachenal, Bruns, and Namitkiewicz, in *Deutsche Continental Gas-Gesellschaft* v. *Polish State*, Ann. Digest, (1929–30) Case No. 5, 11.

37. On eighteenth-century 'enlightened despotism,' see Eugen Weber, *A Modern History of Europe: Man, Cultures, and Societies from the Renaissance to the Present* (New York: W.W. Norton & Company Inc., 1971), 462–66.

38. *See Dana's Wheaton*, p. 27, §19 ("Wherever, indeed, the absolute or unlimited monarchical form of government prevails in any State, the person of the prince is necessarily identified with the State itself: l'État c'est moi.").

39. Weber, *Modern History of Europe*, 540, 542 (noting also that Napoleon re-established hereditary titles such as 'Duke').
40. C.H. Alexandrowicz, "The Theory of Recognition In Fieri," 34 BYIL 176, 190 (1958).
41. *Dana's Wheaton*, 114–17. Quoted in Alexandrowicz, 34 BYIL at 194.
42. Note however that Rosalyn Higgins endorses the Montevideo Convention, declaring that by the Convention the concept of 'state' "continues to be well described." Higgins, *Problems and Process*, 39.
43. *See* Crawford, *Creation of States*, 78–79. The fourth criterion on the Montevideo list Crawford specifically identifies as problematic. Capacity, he writes, "is not a criterion, but rather a consequence, of statehood, and one which is not constant but depends on the status and situation of particular States." Crawford, *Creation of States*, 47. Crawford may have been anticipated in this proposition by Salmond, Gemma, and Kelsen. *See* Oppenheim, *Treatise*, 118 n. 3.
44. Yemi Osinbajo, "Legality in a Collapsed State: The Somali Experience," 45 ICLQ 910, 910–11 n. 4 (1996).
45. *Répertoire de la Pratique Française en Matiére de Droit International Public* (Pratique Française). vol. III (Paris: Centre National de la Recherche Scientifique, 1965), 26–31.
46. Crawford, *Creation of States*, 58.
47. Ibid., 59–60.
48. Citing *Duff Development Co.* v. *Government of Kelantan* [1942] A.C. 797, 800, Crawford lists protectorates in this third category of derogations from independence; (Crawford, *Creation of States*, 61–62); puppet states (Crawford, *Creation of States*, 62–65); and, citing the World War II independence of Syria, purported but largely substanceless grants of colonial independence. Crawford, *Creation of States*, 65–68.
49. Crawford, *Creation of States*, 31 n. 1.
50. *See* 25 AJIL (supp.) 203 (1930); 44 AJIL 617, 621 (1950).
51. *See* American Law Institute, *The Restatement (Third) of the Foreign Relations Law of the United States*. vol. I (St. Paul: American Law Institute Publishers, 1986), Forward.
52. 22 AJIL (supp.) 171 (1928).
53. 16 AJIL (supp.) 41 (1922).
54. 25 AJIL (supp.) 63 (1931).
55. *See* speech by President Warren G. Harding, June 21, 1923, 17 AJIL 533 (1923).
56. 1949 *International Law Commission Yearbook* (ILCY) p. 61, ¶ 69; 1956 ILCY, vol. II, p. 107, ¶ 4 & 1966 ILCY 192; 1974 ILCY p. 19, ¶ 76.
57. Remarks by Mr. Bilge, 1973 ILCY, vol. I, p. 175, ¶39. Quoted in Duursma, *Micro-States*, 113 n. 18.
58. Crawford, *Creation of States*, 72–73.
59. Colin Warbrick, "Recognition of States," 41 ICLQ 480 (1993).
60. Higgins observes that the term 'state' is fluid, changing "depending on the circumstances and the context in which the claim of statehood is made." Compare however with Higgins' advocacy of the Montevideo criteria, which seem to cast statehood in more static terms. Higgins, *Problems and Process*, 39.

61. I discuss the Montevideo Convention and associated problems at greater length in "Defining Statehood: The Montevideo Convention and its Discontents," 37 *Columbia Journal of Transnational Law* 403 (1999).

# 2

# THE DECLARATORY PREFERENCE EXAMINED

Debate over recognition today, where it still dichotomizes between constitutive and declaratory theory, leans generally toward the latter. Writers indeed often say that declaratory doctrine is preferable to constitutivism.[1] Brownlie, while identifying advantages in declaratory doctrine, advises however against viewing the issue as one of mutually exclusive choices: "[T]o reduce, or to seem to reduce, the issues to a choice between the two opposing theories is to greatly oversimplify the legal situation."[2] Brownlie may well be right. Neither doctrine in its strong form holds up under logical scrutiny or is borne out by state practice. Few writers still espouse either doctrine in strong-form. Declaratory doctrine has nonetheless over the last thirty years exercised greater attraction than constitutivism, with writers expressly avowing that recognition reflects but does not create statehood.[3] At a time when the doctrinal debate has come widely to be declared deficient as an explanatory process, persistence of the terms of that debate is curious, and the contemporary preference for declaratory doctrine itself demands explanation.

## CRITIQUES OF CONSTITUTIVISM

For the student of international law hoping that the discipline in fact governs the conduct of states, constitutivism is disillusioning for its tendency to leave recognition to the "unfettered political will" of existing states. Logical defects, however, seem to be the greater impediment to widespread acceptance of constitutive doctrine. Kelsen critiqued the view of recognition as a contractual event. How can a contract creative of legal personality be entered into when one of the parties lacks legal personality at the time of accession? This puzzlement is a subspecies of that which arises generally when considering the positivist conception of international law. Positivism has been said to identify consent among states as the sole source of international obligation.[4] A state, under the principle *pacta sunt servanda*, is bound by those international legal rules to which it consents—and, according to the positivists, to those rules only. But, if the state is absolutely autonomous, how can it bind itself with a promise? Rules governing promises would seem unable to "derive *their* obligatory status from a self-imposed obligation."[5]

Further casting doubt on constitutivism are practical disjunctions. If statehood stems from recognition and is solely a matter between donor and recipient, then a community recognized by one state but not another would simultaneously be a state and a nonstate. This indeed would present, as Brierly put it, "a legal curiosity."[6] The illogic of constitutivism's focus on bilateral action between an existing state and a claimant community has earned ample rebuke. Chen wrote trenchantly:

> [S]ince recognition is accorded by States individually, and simultaneous action cannot be reasonably expected, the international personality thus recognised must, until universality of recognition is achieved, necessarily be partial and relative. The result would be that a State is a member of the international community for one State, but not for another. . . . [S]uch . . . confusion must be extremely embarrassing.[7]

Of greater doctrinal concern is the proposition which seems to flow from constitutivism that an unrecognized community has neither rights nor duties under international law.[8] Denied recognition, does a community enjoy a freedom from the strictures which govern the conduct of states? And do recognized states enjoy a freedom to abuse the unrecognized community in a manner which international law would bar against a state? The declaratist proposition that the state exists independent of recognition avoids these problems.

Moreover, state practice supports the view, allowed by declaratory doctrine in principle, that unrecognized communities are not *terra nullius*. Even in their expansion into Africa, the Americas, and Australasia, Europeans adhered at least in form to the view that aboriginal peoples possessed rights to the territories in question.[9] Excluding the special case of submarine areas beyond the belt of the territorial sea,[10] practice offers little example of *terra nullius*.

By contrast, State practice does show that unrecognized communities enjoy protections which identify them as superior to legal no-man's land. The putative Turkish Cypriot state offers a contemporary example, Israel before recognition an historical one. Brierly notes, in connection with Israel, that Britain treated with the nascent state before recognizing it. Israeli forces had shot down a British aircraft over Egypt in January 1949. Despite nonrecognition, Britain addressed to Israeli authorities Britain's intention to seek compensation. Britain dealt with unrecognized Israel as if the country possessed international legal personality.[11] Though I will suggest later some reasons for doubting the persuasiveness of the Israeli-British aircraft incident as support for declaratory doctrine, the case is often cited to this effect.[12] Another eastern Mediterranean case perhaps offers better support. Cyprus, politically unstable from the time of the Treaty of Guarantee providing for its independence and constitutive structure (1960), was subjected to *de facto* partition in July 1974. Roughly forty per cent of the country came under the control of Turkish Cypriots and the Turkish army, and it was declared an independent Turkish Federated State of Cyprus. Though recognized only by its patron Turkey, Turkish Cyprus, like other unrecognized entities, nonetheless continued to enjoy freedom from external aggression. Indeed, when discussing aggression, albeit in a context broader than Cyprus, the General Assembly declared that "the term 'State' . . . [i]s used without prejudice to questions of recognition."[13] According to the General Assembly, an entity may be termed a state—and thus benefit from the protections against aggression accorded by UN Charter Article 2(4)—whether or not it is recognized.

As a doctrine, the view that all territorial entities enjoy certain protections might be traced to the Enlightenment theory of natural rights.[14] The American Declaration of Independence (1776) posits that the thirteen British colonies in North America possessed a right of petition to express grievance, and, moreover, a right to be free from "usurpations" and other abuses. Henkin writes that Thomas Jefferson, in the Declaration, "took [John Locke's] 'natural rights' and made them secular, rational, universal, individual, democratic and radical."[15] From the text of the Declaration, these rights apparently were viewed by the drafters as prior to statehood—and altogether independent of whether the Colonies were internationally recognized as states. In its second paragraph, the Declaration posits that "it is their Right . . . to throw off [persistently unjust] Government, and to provide new Guards for their future Security." In the thirtieth paragraph, the Declaration assumes a right of petition in the colonies. The declaration that the colonies now form independent states appears only in the final paragraph, and, logically as well as textually, comes after the assertion of rights enjoyed by the non-state colonies. Rights of redress and freedom from oppression the Declaration of Independence places prior to statehood. Insofar as constitutivism implies that the unrecognized community lacks legal personality, both international practice and political theory call that doctrine into question.

Yet another flaw of the constitutive theory is that it is difficult to reconcile to the retroactive juridical effect of recognition. Courts will treat acts of a recognized state as state acts even if they antedate recognition. If it was recognition which bestowed legal personality on the state, a problem arises: "The very idea that legal effect can be given to acts of previously nonexistent entities is fatal to the constitutivist contention. It substantiates the declaratory view that, recognized or not, the *de facto* power exists. Recognition does not 'create' the legal effects, either of the past, or of the future acts of the recognized power. They have legal effects because of the existence of that power. . . . [R]ecognition lift[s] the ban against taking cognizance by the courts of the existence of the new power hitherto ignored."[16] Though some writers doubt that retroactivity is relevant to the nature of recognition,[17] the logical difficulty of reconciling constitutivism and retroactivity has lent further support to declaratory doctrine.

## *CONTRA* DECLARATORY DOCTRINE

Declaratory doctrine notwithstanding, practice suggests that recognition plays more than an evidentiary role and, furthermore, that recognition is more than an acknowledgment of the coming into being of a set of facts tantamount to statehood. First, the express positions of foreign ministries and multilateral organizations contradict the proposition that recognition has both escaped the orbit of bilateral politics and come under the rule of law. Second, past cases and current events have witnessed recognition focus political energies out of all proportion to the role to which declaratists limited it. Third, the unhappy experience of unrecognized communities testifies crudely to the weight of recognition in the society of states. Fourth, a seepage into the criteria for recognition of elements at best tenuously linked to the basic definition of statehood belies the proposition that attainment of the features of the state alone conditions recognition.

### Governments and Multilateral Bodies

Though incorporation of recognition into a legal framework is not strictly part of declaratory doctrine, most advocates of the doctrine anticipated that its ascendency would inject legal principle into recognition. Indeed, the doctrine seems to have started as a reaction against the unprincipled aspects of constitutivism, and its more recent advocates have associated its premises with legality and de-politicization. The stubborn prevalence of politics in recognition therefore casts some doubt on the declaratist view.

Governments and multilateral bodies have expressly drawn attention to the political aspect of recognition which declaratory doctrine is supposed to have reduced. Rather than a fact-finding exercise, recognition, according to the United Nations, has been a political decision on the part of the individual state: "[W]hile states may regard it as desirable to follow certain legal principles in according or withholding recognition, the practice of states shows that the act of recognition is still regarded as essentially a political decision, which each state decides in accordance with its own free appreciation of the situation."[18] The national and political character of recognition was similarly illustrated by American statements, under both the Truman and Eisenhower administrations.[19] French practice has suggested that recognition carries constitutive effect as well: "[Recognition] makes possible the negotiation and conclusion of any executive agreements on matters related to the territory of the new State, likewise the establishment of normal relations between the two States."[20] Capacity to make binding commitments, according to France, stems from recognition. This may have been more explicit earlier in the twentieth century. As noted in the preceding chapter, France extended recognition to Poland and Czechoslovakia "as Nations" during World War I, even though at the time neither possessed even a territory. In September 1917, over a year before the Central Powers capitulated (and at a point when the outcome of the war remained uncertain), France recognized in those nations a right to "raise an army, to have a national flag, [and] to have military tribunals authorized to judge their nationals."[21] An Italian diplomat at the Peace Conferences two years later seemed nonplussed by the proposition that recognition could create legal personality in an entity not endowed with even the most elementary attributes of statehood: "The Allies have recognized the Czechoslovak State; thus, it exists. But this State does not yet have a territory. Can a State placed in such a grave situation join in a treaty to create territory for itself?" the Marquis Salvago Raggi asked. How, he must have wondered, could a "state" lacking the key marks of statehood have the capacity to be a High Contracting Party? Fromageat, legal counsellor of the French Ministry of Foreign Affairs and member of the Editorial Commission for the Versailles Treaty, replied, "[S]uch a State could very well be party to an agreement."[22] Failing the basic requirements of effective control and defined territory—but enjoying recognition—the two new states possessed legal personality.

Recent official views on the nature of recognition further suggest its discretionary and political character.

Iceland, for example, saw fit to employ recognition for a political purpose. Extending recognition to Croatia and Slovenia earlier than most other countries, Iceland viewed the act as one "speak[ing] volumes in itself" and expressing Icelandic sympathy for small states.[23] The Republic of Korea approaches recognition by "considering the specific situations and conditions, especially in terms of political aspects."[24] The Czech Republic, implying that recognition is something other than a mandatory acknowledgment of fact, maintains that "the [recognition] decision . . . is the prerogative of a sovereign state."[25]

Joining states in announcing the discretionary character of recognition, the North Atlantic Treaty Organization describes recognition as "entirely a matter for individual member states."[26] Other multilateral bodies take a similar approach. Though the Charter of the Organization of African Unity (OAU) "does not make provision in the classical sense for recognition of States," the OAU has dealt with state recognition issues "on a case by case basis." The collapse of public order in Somalia led the OAU Council of Ministers to decide to leave vacant the seat of Somalia. Though the Somalian situation did not involve state recognition, it does appear to have witnessed application of the "case by case" approach to recognition of governments.

Also, though the OAU believes that its admittance of a state will "almost certainly impact on the position of its members," recognition ultimately "is left to individual member states in the exercise of their sovereignty."[27] In making recognition decisions for its own purposes, the OAU leaves itself wide latitude to address the politics of each situation; and it maintains that recognition by individual member states is a discretionary act.

Though the Organization of American States (OAS) takes an explicitly declaratory view of recognition, its Charter nonetheless implies that recognition has constitutive effect for certain areas of state competence. Article 3 of the OAS Charter provides that "[i]nternational law is the standard of conduct of States in their reciprocal relations," and, according to OAS counsel, this means that recognition is to be interpreted in accordance with the principles of international law.[28]

Articles 12 and 13 of the Charter address recognition:

> Article 12: The political existence of the State is independent of recognition by other States. Even before being recognized, the State has the right to defend its integrity and independence, to provide for its preservation and prosperity, and consequently to organize itself as it sees fit, to legislate concerning its interests, to administer its services, and to determine the jurisdiction and competence of its courts. The exercise of these rights is limited only by the exercise of the rights of other States in accordance with international law.
>
> Article 13: Recognition implies that the State granting it accepts the personality of the new State, with all the rights and duties that international law prescribes for the two States.[29]

According to the Charter, the OAS views the state as arising before and independently of recognition. However, Article 12 does not explicitly place prior to recognition the capacity to enter into international treaties or to take on other external obligations. The Charter is unambiguous in providing that the *defensive* rights of a polity do not depend upon recognition, but it leaves open to speculation the source of a community's competence to engage actively in international relations. Nonrecognition, under Article 12, does not deny a putative state the authority to run its home affairs and to fend off external aggressors, but Article 13 suggests that it is chiefly *after* recognition that the state may expect to deal actively on an equal footing with others. It may be inferred from the OAS Charter that capacity to engage in international affairs is not complete until recognition. More broadly, it may be that recognition is declaratory of some aspects of statehood but constitutive of others.

From small states to large multilateral organizations, recognition is viewed as a matter of political importance and state discretion beyond that implied in declaratory doctrine. Some organizations, such as the OAS, characterize recognition in a declaratory light, but even under such characterizations, the unrecognized polity is acknowledged to face certain limits which recognition alone seems to remove.

**Political Controversy and Recognition**

A second factor in state practice casting doubt on declaratory doctrine is the political moment of the recognition act. Not only does politics shape the decision whether and when to recognize; decision makers perceive recognition to carry political weight in authoritative processes. The history of American practice illustrates this. The executive branch has for the most part exercised control over recognition policy in the United States, but a string of episodes has witnessed Congress endeavor to influence recognition policy—and on occasion even to seize the President's ordinarily unchallenged initiative over the subject. Congress, in the person of Henry Clay, sparred with successive Presidents over recognizing the former Spanish possessions of the Western Hemisphere. By introducing budgetary measures to set up diplomatic posts in South America, Clay tried to appropriate the recognition power to Congress. Clay's efforts resulted in one House resolution supporting the independence of the Spanish republics, though no incident of explicit Congressional recognition. Nonetheless, Clay demonstrated that the fiscal power of the legislature could be brought to bear on controversial questions of recognition. Moreover, the very fact that Congress saw fit to use its weight on such questions testified to their political import. Indeed further testifying to this, a tug-of-war over recognition persisted between Congress and the Presidency from 1812 through the early 1820s.[30] And that would not be the last time recognition became a focus of legislative-executive rivalry in the United States. Congress pressed the second Cleveland Administration (1893–97) to recognize a Republic of Cuba. (Cuba was in an as yet inconclusive rebellion against Spain). The recognition of Cuba would remain controversial for several years. Under President McKinley, Cuba was the focus of a war between the United States and Spain (1898). A Congressional faction opposed to acquiring colonies incorporated into the war authorization bill a clause effectively recognizing Cuban independence. Recognition precluded annexation, thus accomplishing Congress's anti-imperial objective. Corwin characterized the legislative manoeuvre thus: "Congress contrived to perform an act of recognition of which a foreign government was entitled by international law to take direct notice."[31]

Congress would make several further forays into recognition politics. The Senate passed a resolution in January 1913 recognizing the new Chinese government. The resolution read, "That the present republican Government of China is hereby recognized by the United States of America, with all the powers and privileges of their intercourse and relations with this Government properly appertaining to and in general extending to independent and sovereign governments and nations."[32] The legislature viewed authority to recognize a prize justifying potential violation of separation of powers and open political contest with the executive.

The 1970s and 1980s also brought political sparring over the seat of recognition power. This further demonstrated the political gravity of the matter—a gravity difficult to explain if recognition is conceived as a mere evidentiary statement. Congress challenged the authority of the President to renounce recognition of the Republic of China (Taiwan) in favor of the People's Republic (mainland China). The political branches litigated the matter, and the Supreme Court, in *Goldwater* v. *Carter*, held in favor of the executive.[33] Later interbranch wrestling for the power to recognize centered around Tibet. A House resolution requested Beijing to negotiate with Tibetan exile groups on a footing appropriate to inter-state relations.[34] The exiled Dalai Lama was later described in the Congressional Record as "political leader of the Tibetan people," and Congress received him with some measure of official dignity.[35] The Department of State strenuously dismissed Congressional overtures toward Tibet and made clear that the authority to recognize foreign communities as states was the President's alone.[36] In view of its characterization of recognition as a "mere evidentiary" statement and a simple and nondiscretionary reaction to facts abroad, the declaratory model of recognition would seem to predict little interest in the locus of the authority to recognize. Practice in the United States illustrates, however, that a persistent and at times heated competition revolves around that very matter.[37]

If the record of American practice leaves any doubt as to the political gravity of recognition, the crisis over the recognition of the Yugoslav republics in the early 1990s makes that gravity undeniable. Governments in Europe were occupied in the last months of 1991 with the question of whether and when to recognize Croatia and Slovenia. So too were the chief political parties, the media, and the most important multilateral organs of the Continent. The captivation of polities and their institutions by the Yugoslav crisis counsels caution toward the idea sometimes associated with declaratory doctrine that recognition is a matter of low political order.

### The Disabilities of Unrecognized Communities

As the centrality of recognition to the politics of the donor state casts doubt on some declaratist assumptions, so too does the impact of recognition on the political security of the recipient suggest a creative force in the institution.

Though declaratists have proposed that the position of an entity in the world community is little effected by recognition, recognition in fact formidably advantages its recipients. International law, in similar vein, maintains that the juridical status of an entity is not relevant to its enjoyment of protection against aggression. However, in practice, unrecognized communities are exposed to ravages seldom visited upon the recognized. Brierly acknowledged that the "enforcement of rights and duties [may be] more difficult" absent recognition but maintained that the state enjoys legal existence before recognition. In support, Brierly cited the downing of British aircraft over Egypt in January 1949 by Israeli airmen at a time when Britain had not recognized Israel. Britain nonetheless held that state responsibility ran against Israel.[38] The example seems however to beg a question. If recognition plays but a *de minimus* role in securing a community in international law, why were relations between Britain and Israel of such an unsettled nature to permit the frictions resulting in the 1949 aircraft incident? To be sure, a state may fall to blows with another that it *has* recognized; the litany of European interstate wars demonstrates this. But Anglo-Israeli tensions were partly attributable to the ambiguity in legal status of Israel at the time, and nonrecognition contributed to that ambiguity. The incident which Brierly cited to support a declaratory view of recognition stemmed from a conflict in which may have been a factor the very international weakness caused by nonrecognition. As declaratory doctrine does not contemplate such weakness, Brierly's example is problematic.

It is arguably a fact of international relations that the security of a community suffers impairment through nonrecognition. Empirical evidence has been adduced which suggests unrecognized entities lie in greater jeopardy of extinguishment than full-fledged states. David Strang observes that the years between 1415 and 1987 witnessed 274 non-European entities succumb to conquest. Eleven of these were recognized by most of Europe as states; 263 were unrecognized. Strang advances that virtually every community lacking recognition during the period in question suffered annexation or loss of independence.[39]

Recent international relations scholarship indeed contains support for constitutivism. Terry Nardin wrote in 1992 that existing states perform a constitutive function when assessing whether to admit new entities to international society:

> The rules of International Law . . . are not merely regulatory but constitutive: they not only create a normative order among separate political communities but define the status, rights, and duties of these communities within this normative order. In international society 'states' are constituted as such within the practice of International Law; 'statehood' is a position or role that is defined by International Law, not independent of it. . . . Statehood is itself a status constituted by International Law. And international society is not an aggregate of separate communities but itself a community: a community of communities tied together by its constitutive practices, including those defining the attributes of statehood.[40]

Statehood, Nardin implies, is bestowed upon a community by communities already possessing it.

International relations research also has inquired into how the conduct of existing states affects communities seeking statehood. Alexis Heraclides examines the results of seven attempts at secession (Katanga, 1960–63; Biafra, 1967–70; Southern Sudan, 1961–72; Bangladesh, 1971; Iraqi Kurdistan, 1961–75; Eritrea, 1961–90; and the Moro region of the Philippines, 1972–90) and concludes that diplomatic support, especially in the heightened form of recognition, plays a critical role in securing a community's international legal personality:

> If words are 'cheaper' than deeds . . . , then political-diplomatic or moral support would be more readily available and at a higher level and extent than tangible support.[41] Indeed, in the seven cases examined, the number of states providing the former was somewhat greater than that providing the latter. . . . But upon close scrutiny, it became clear that the level of political-diplomatic involvement was usually low . . . and that its extent was very limited in most cases, whereas the level of tangible involvement was medium or high . . . in well over half the cases. In fact, extensive political-diplomatic support was evident in only one-seventh of the cases, and high-level political-diplomatic involvement . . . was evident in only one-third of the cases. 'Premature' recognition or recognition in defiance of the world community was given [only six times]-five in the case of Biafra . . . and one in the case of Bangladesh. . . . One other . . . secession received recognition: The Turkish Republic of Northern Cyprus was recognized by its patron, Turkey, in 1982. Apparently, . . . states do not generally find the utterance of such words to be 'cheap.'[42]

The weight of recognition has been noted by scholars of inter-state relations.[43] If recognition were merely declaratory of facts and of little impact on membership in international society, then there would be little cost in using it as a symbolic device. Yet, as Heraclides documents, states mete out recognition parsimoniously. International relations scholarship suggests that recognition carries a force which makes states measure their use of it with care.

Stephen A. Kocs concurs with these assessments:

> The law-based model [of international relations], in contrast to neorealism, suggests that the survival rate of political entities should depend above all else on whether they have obtained formal diplomatic recognition in the international society of states. Under international law, the act of recognition symbolizes a fundamental commitment on the part of the international community. It signifies extension of the full panoply of international legal protections to the recognized state. . . . Thus, polities recognized as sovereign states should enjoy a very high rate of survival. Political entities that lack recognition as sovereign states, by contrast, find themselves in a deeply vulnerable position. International law offers them few protections against conquest and elimination by other political actors. It makes sense to expect, therefore, that political entities lacking diplomatic recognition will suffer extinction at a much higher rate than recognized polities.[44]

This may overstate the point. After all, Article 2(4) of the United Nations Charter obliges member states to refrain from the use or threat of force, and the ban protects members of the world body and nonmembers alike.[45]

Communities at the margins of international power processes do not lack all protection. Moreover, recent state practice does not entirely sustain the constitutive proposition at root in Heraclides, Kocs, and Strang's analyses. China has not (as yet) invaded Taiwan; nor is Turkish Cyprus 'up for grabs' to any power able to take it. Nonrecognition rarely if ever has rendered its object *terra nullius*. The UN Charter and its protections against use or threat of force furthered the development of restraint in inter-state relations after World War II, and some of the most recent instances of UN practice have brought legal punishment on states for abuses against domestic communities as well. UN sanctions against Iraq for mistreatment of its Kurdish and Shi'ite communities exemplify how international law may protect the unrecognized. At the same time, there may be some validity to Kocs' point. Nonrecognition has been observed even in the 1990s to diminish the security of a community.

Unrecognized, Slovenia and Croatia faced attack by Serb irregular forces and Yugoslav federal army units. Since recognition, Slovenia has experienced no serious threat (though the threat had diminished some months prior to recognition), and Croatia became comparatively secure, despite the continued alienation of one third its territory. The first two republics to secede from Yugoslavia appear to have gained some security through recognition. Conversely, they had been less secure whilst unrecognized.

A more pronounced demonstration of the risks of nonrecognition is furnished by Chechnya. Mikhail Gorbachev, reformer of the Soviet Union, was briefly unseated by reactionary putschists in August 1991. Though the putschists were ousted, the General Secretary only nominally regained power and his grip on national affairs was permanently weakened. A period of political indirection ensued. Taking advantage of the situation, a former officer of the Soviet strategic forces, Dzokar Dudyaev, declared his north Caucasian homeland an independent republic. Chechnya repulsed an attempt by Russian forces in 1992 to bring the region back in line. There followed two years of more or less independent governance under Dudyaev. According to at least one commentator, the putative Chechen state had a "credible claim" to statehood, as it fulfilled the criteria of the Montevideo Convention.[46] Putting aside whether the Montevideo Convention is a satisfactory definition of the state, Chechnya mounted a stubborn defense when attacked in December 1994, dealing the Russian Army an embarrassing defeat in the first weeks of the assault. Despite its state-like character, Chechnya received little international acknowledgment. Saudi Arabia and Kuwait allegedly expressed interest in diplomatic ties, but the extent to which those states meant to follow up on this is unclear.[47] In any event, recognition would not have been conferred by the opening of foreign missions lower than ambassadorial rank. Unrecognized, Chechnya lay open to attack and when attacked suffered the acquiescence of the world community in the attempted extinguishment of its state-building project. Recent episodes in state formation as well as the history of interstate relations may be argued to corroborate the constitutive theory.

## Conflation of the Criteria for Recognition and Criteria for Statehood

A solution has been advanced to the seepage of politics into recognition but on analysis may raise problems of its own. What at first look like political conditions for recognition, some writers argue are better viewed as new elements of statehood. As I will discuss, putative new elements of statehood tend to reflect contemporary aspirations of the world community—the goal of a strengthened international human rights regime in particular. Under the proposed solution, a community claiming statehood is not a state upon attainment of the four criteria enunciated in the Montevideo convention and traditionally cited as describing the state; further criteria are now called for. The addition of new prerequisites to statehood may explain, within the walls of declaratory doctrine, why recognition is frequently conditioned upon attainment of characteristics initially seemingly political in nature. A link between proposed new criteria for statehood and declaratory doctrine was posited by Devine, but he saw the issue as essentially limited to the non-recognition of Rhodesia after the Unilateral Declaration of Independence.[48] The implications may reach much further. Declaratory doctrine arguably meshes with the evolution of human rights in international law.

The alleged incorporation of new elements into the definition of statehood—what might be called 'addenda' to Montevideo—has occasioned debate. Some writers doubt whether such addenda are deeply entrenched. (Four examples of proposed new statehood criteria are examined in Chapter 4.) The supposed emergence of addenda to Montevideo also has complicated the relationship between state recognition and state creation, thus spurring speculation about changes in these public order processes.

Fawcett and Brownlie were two of the initial exponents of the view that new criteria have changed the definition of the state.[49] According to some critics, however, Fawcett and Brownlie incorporated into the definition of statehood an untenable requirement of "good government."[50] Devine observed that many entities at present universally recognized as states would not satisfy the requirement. As Oppenheim and the Institute of International Law noted, the disappearance of an essential quality of statehood calls for the withdrawal of recognition from the entity thereby no longer a state.[51] If "good government" were an essential quality of statehood,then a number of contemporary states would loose their statehood. Argued Devine, this condition of "international outlawry" would be "impractical . . . and unthinkable."[52] He further pointed out that international practice has never embraced the proposition that statehood lacks where human rights lag.[53]

Fawcett, to whom Devine's critique was replying, characterized the international response to the Rhodesian UDI as evidence of the addition of a new criterion to statehood, but Fawcett argued that Devine exaggerated in terming the new criterion a requirement for "good government." "Good government" was not what the international community insisted be established in Rhodesia. The community, rather, insisted that a very *bad* government be improved. International pressure aimed to secure basic rights for the Rhodesian populace, rights which a white régime had systematically denied. It was the bald defect of Rhodesian governance which drew censure, not fine points of civic order.[54] Fawcett suggested, in a 1966 article, that Rhodesia under Ian Smith exhibited the traditional criteria of statehood more strongly than had Ireland or Burma upon their recognition. The fact of nonrecognition Fawcett attributed to the advent of a new criterion of statehood: "[T]o the traditional criteria for the recognition of a régime as a new State must now be added the requirement that it shall not be based upon a systematic denial in its territory of certain civil and political rights, including in particular the right of every citizen to participate in the government of his country, directly or through representatives elected by regular, equal and secret suffrage [citation omitted]."[55] The proposed new criterion might have more accurately been termed 'internal self-determination' than 'good government.' Fawcett later perhaps moderated his proposition, describing the new criterion, rather than as a new requirement in its own right, as an addition to the traditional requirement of effective government:

> The traditional description of an independent state, as being a community of people, living together in a defined territory under an organized government not subordinate to any other government, may then need the addition of a new criterion: the self-determination of its people. . . . If there is a systematic denial to a substantial minority, and still more to a majority of people, of a place and say in the government, the criterion of organized government is not met.[56]

Existing states do not investigate the minutiae of domestic administration, but gross and purposive human rights violations may disable a putative state. To Fawcett, then, statehood did not require proof of excellence in government, but it had come to encompass criteria above and beyond the traditional ones related to effectiveness.

Crawford too has addressed the criteria for statehood. In opening, he rejects constitutivism, insofar as that doctrine denies concrete statehood criteria and puts the act of recognition in their place.[57] He concludes that statehood remains an important term of art but, as a legal concept, is "one of open texture." Crawford proposes five characteristics of states: (1) plenary competence to perform acts and make treaties with other states; (2) exclusive competence over their domestic governance; (3) freedom from international process, unless they consent either specifically or generally to such process; (4) equality with other states under international law; and (5) benefit of a presumption that derogation from the principles (1) through (4) must be clearly established.[58] Crawford agrees that the 'classical criteria' for statehood are those of the Montevideo Convention. The four Montevideo criteria—defined territory, permanent population, government, and capacity to enter into relations with other states—Crawford says share a basis in the principle of effectiveness. The Montevideo criteria, he explains, focus inquiry on whether a putative state exercises effective power over a population and a defined space.[59] Additional criteria have however been suggested for some time and require that Montevideo be approached guardedly. Most important among criteria not expressly acknowledged in the Montevideo Convention Crawford ranks independence.[60] Others include sovereignty, permanence, a certain degree of civilization, recognition, and legal order.[61] As noted earlier, Crawford includes in his definition of statehood 'willingness and ability to observe international law,' and he characterizes that older addendum to Montevideo under a separate heading from 'capacity to enter into relations with other states'—one of the original four criteria of statehood. The possibilities for confusing conditions for recognition with the putative new elements of statehood have been noted here already.[62]

Expanding upon the definition of statehood can cause confusion, especially in the context of a declaratory view of recognition. Criteria which constitute the state and criteria which trigger recognition must be the same for a theory which views recognition as no more than an announcement of the attainment of statehood. An identity between statehood and recognition has not however been clear in practice.

Dugard finds fault with both Fawcett and Crawford's approach. Dugard argues that international practice (as manifest by the United Nations) fails to support the proposition that a polity unrecognized for reasons of internal political constitution is not a state. Security Council and General Assembly practice refers to such unrecognized entities as being "null and void," "invalid," or "illegal," which suggests to Dugard that they are "without legal effect as States, not because they fail to meet the essential requirements of statehood but because their existence violates a peremptory rule of international law." Dugard emphasizes the distinction between non-existent acts and acts "null and void *ab initio* by reason of their illegality." Guggenheim explained that the absence of certain elements of a putative act is such a grave deficiency that there is no act to be called a nullity; the act is nonexistent.[63] By contrast, other acts are termed legally void because their execution or attainment violated some important legal rule. Dugard proposes that an entity such as Rhodesia satisfied the basic criteria of statehood but violated a peremptory rule of international law then taking form. Rhodesia was a state, *i.e.*, it was not nonexistent—but owing to its racist system Rhodesia was a legal nullity.[64] Dugard's synthesis of the new criteria with the observed practice of international organizations seems a rather convincing extension of the similar effort some years earlier by Crawford. Dugard differs from Crawford chiefly in his reliance on the distinction between "non-existence" and "nullity." The two writers are similar, however, in that they shy from declaring the emergence of an entirely new element of statehood (something Fawcett by contrast did not hesitate to do). Perhaps as importantly, both Dugard and Crawford, though leaning toward declaratory doctrine, acknowledge limits in the traditional classification of recognition theory. Dugard shifts from the constitutivist-declaratist controversy, to an exploration of collective recognition. Crawford focuses on the nature of statehood. The shift of contemporary scholarship away from the old debate, when considered with a view to the flaws in both the declaratory and constitutive schools, suggests two conclusions: first, that the more tenable view of recognition is that it may be in part declaratory and in part constitutive; and, second, that a more important issue today in the law of recognition is the process by which it is granted.

If this latter point is correct—that today's debate is more a search for an acceptable process of recognition than an effort to characterize the phenomenon theoretically—then declaratory doctrine has the further flaw of eroding the legal nature of recognition. As discussed earlier in connection with the origins of the Montevideo criteria, the concept of statehood has indeed evolved over time. How to circumscribe this evolution inside legal principle is a challenge of the contemporary law of recognition. Indeed, it may too be one of the new lines of debate. Declaratory doctrine, with its need to equate every condition for recognition to an element of statehood, does not assist in this challenge. To the contrary, by implying an astonishingly flexible set of criteria for statehood (and thus for recognition), declaratory doctrine tends to untie the fetters of international legal principle. If recognition simply declares the attainment of statehood, then every political condition attached to recognition is impounded in the definition of the state. The changes wrought on the concept of the state by history in its long progression pose adequate challenge to recognition law; to accelerate those changes by enshrining in the concept of statehood every nuance of daily politics and diplomacy may altogether defeat the purpose of a legal description of recognition.[65]

The confusion between the questions "what makes a state?" and "when is recognition to be granted?" focuses attention on yet another flaw of declaratory doctrine, and it also suggests that the terms of the traditional recognition debate may have begun to erode.

## SUPPORT FOR DECLARATORY DOCTRINE

But then what is the attraction of declaratory doctrine? When characterizing their views on recognition, writers still refer to the traditional debate, and there is a present tendency to favor the declaratory interpretation. As already suggested, declaratory doctrine profits in the negative; the constitutivist alternative is riddled with flaws. There may nonetheless be affirmative factors promoting the doctrine. Two in particular deserve attention: first, the attractiveness of the declaratory view in a context of increasing concern over international human rights; and, second, the support for the declaratory view often identified in judicial opinion.

### Human Rights

Preference for declaratory doctrine is perhaps best explained by the way it accommodates contemporary aspirations for international law.

The proposition long went unchallenged that policies of a recognized state, if these and their effects were confined to its own territory, lay beyond the purview of international law. According to one representative writer, it was the "*ensemble* of sovereign States [which formed] the aristocracy of international society,"[66] and the traditional view indeed put the state at least in its domestic dimension above any other legal force. By the close of World War II, however, calls arose to develop international standards for human rights and to make such standards enforceable within the borders of recognized states. Hersch Lauterpacht's *International Law and Human Rights* and *An International Bill of the Rights of Man* (1945)[67] were early and eloquent proposals for a more comprehensive international human rights system. Further academic work followed, with pressure for internationalizing human rights intensifying in the 1970s and 1980s.[68] The United Nations Charter and the Universal Declaration of Human Rights of 1948 lent support to academic writers.[69]

Two UN Covenants pursuant to the 1948 Declaration (*International Covenant on Economic, Social, and Cultural Rights* and *International Covenant on Civil and Political Rights*) were forwarded by the UN General Assembly in 1966 and furthered human rights as an international legal institution as well.

These and other steps[70] notwithstanding, state monopoly over domestic affairs remains robust. The persistence of national jurisdiction has led the advocates of an international law of human rights to recast certain conceptions of international order.

One attempted revision of international organizing principles has been more apparent and widely examined than others: the revision of the relative positions of the state and the individual in international law. As McDougal and Reisman noted, "One of the principal purposes of the human rights program in the United Nations is . . . to increase the protection of the individual against all states, including his or her own."[71] To effectuate the aspiration of protecting individuals, writers have proposed attributing international legal personality to individuals, rather than to states exclusively.[72] A result would be to diminish the status of the state as the primary object of international law. States have resisted this proposal strenuously.[73]

Further eroding the old monopoly of the state as international actor, nonstate regions and population groups have gained status in recent practice. The goal that international law protect people whether or not they form a state of their own arguably has favored declaratory doctrine. Recognition in the declaratory conception does not confer legal status, so the fact that a community is not held by others to be a state cannot deny it legal protection. The distinction between states and nonstate actors would seem to diminish under declaratory doctrine more than it would under the UN Charter force prohibition alone.

The role of the informed public in liberal democracies may explain in part the increase in concern over nonstate regions and their inhabitants. Many of the human rights violations brought to view by the news media involve mistreatment of minority religious, ethnic, or racial groups. Public concern over South Africa, Kurdistan, and Bosnia testifies to this. The desire to curb human rights violations has led commentators to urge a wider reach for international law.[74] Where once it was assumed that the domestic affairs of a state were beyond the scrutiny of the international community, now human rights abuses routinely spur the public to demand sanctions against oppressive governments. Brutality in the municipal sphere has begun to be viewed as a transgression in the international sphere.

Another factor which may be magnifying the position in international law of nonstate communities is the heightened profile of substate regions within new international structures. Most pronounced in this connection is the European Union. The Union, especially through its Assembly of European Regions, may enhance the position of provinces and regions of member states. Substate regions hitherto belonged only to state structures, and these structures were often hostile to regional interests. With recourse only to Madrid, Basques or Catalans were restricted in the pursuit of particularist agendas to a forum in which prevailed political actors who viewed those agendas as an immediate threat. The Union, however, may provide an alternative structure in which to pursue regional rights. Paul Taylor posits that subnational groups have gained strength in the EU quasi-confederation, and that the structure of the EU may promote this trend further.[75] Not broadly contemplated as actors on the international stage while they were simply provinces or regions of a European nation state, some territories may find their profile increased within the alternative political structure provided by multinational organizations. With substate regions gaining in profile, the community of states may become yet more accustomed to treating minority and regional rights as matters of international concern.

Declaratory doctrine accommodates the internationalization of human rights better than constitutivism. If recognition is viewed as constitutive, then the unrecognized community may not yet be an international person in all dimensions. If recognition is viewed as declaratory, then the fact of nonrecognition is of far less legal consequence. Declaratory doctrine, by diminishing the import of the recognition act, has the effect of amplifying the dignity of the unrecognized. This is consistent with a liberalized law of intervention, which in turn aids the international human rights project.[76] The world community did not recognize the Kurds as a state, but it did take measures to protect them (*e.g.*, the Allied enforced 'no fly' zone).[77] Declaratory doctrine, in its diminution of the legal impact of nonrecognition, arguably facilitated humanitarian measures in other cases as well. The Serbian districts which seceded from Croatia in 1991 earned no recognition, yet they were the intended beneficiaries of international demands that Croatia adopt minority rights laws.[78] To analyze the humanitarian crises in the space of the former Yugoslavia or in Iraq through the declaratory lens may facilitate intervention: international society seizes itself of substate questions more readily if legal personality is viewed as prior to recognition. An unrecognized region by contrast lacks legal personality under the constitutive view—or, at any rate, is a less plausible international actor. Under the declaratory alternative, the region takes a place in international law with or without recognition. Relatedly, international intervention in Bosnia and Kurdistan renders the constitutive view less tenable. If recognition alone gives a polity its international status, what explains unrecognized polities benefiting from international action? It is no surprise that confidence in declaratory doctrine gains strength when humanitarian intervention aids unrecognized communities; weakens where humanitarian crisis has remained immune to intervention. The conflict in Chechnya prompted the remark, "One simply cannot ignore the effect of the international community's universal refusal to recognize throughout [Chechnya's] three-year bid for independence."[79] Chechnya was not a target of international intervention, and writers have noted in connection the nonrecognition of that putative state. The same writers, not coincidentally, have taken the view that recognition is constitutive of at least some incidents of statehood.

In diminishing the role recognition plays in elevating a polity to the status of international actor and thus a potential subject for active international protection, declaratory doctrine is in harmony with the human rights project of the last half century.

### Judicial Opinion

The accommodation which declaratory doctrine offers international human rights law has been little noted as a source of the doctrine's current ascendency. However, a number of judicial opinions, both of domestic and international organs, are frequently cited as support for a declaratory view of recognition.

Crawford justifiably terms the famous *Tinoco* arbitration the "*locus classicus* of the declaratory doctrine in judicial holdings."[80] The opinion of the sole arbitrator, Chief Justice William Howard Taft, resolved a dispute between Great Britain and Costa Rica and is excerpted, quoted, or cited in many discussions of recognition.[81] *Tinoco* concerned British business interests in Costa Rica. Two British entities had executed transactions with the Costa Rican government after the overthrow of President Alfredo Gonzalez in January 1917. Gonzalez's Secretary of War, General Tinoco, took power after driving the unpopular Gonzalez from the country. The Tinoco régime adopted a new constitution in June 1917. During its tenure, the régime granted a concession to the Central Costa Rica Petroleum Company, a British corporation, and incurred liabilities to the Royal Bank of Canada in the amount of nearly one million Costa Rican gold *colones*. The Tinoco régime fell in September 1919. Its successor enacted "Law of Nullities No. 41," which declared invalid all contracts concluded between the Tinoco government and private parties. This purported nullification was to extend to currency issues made during the Tinoco administration. Under the law, the Royal Bank of Canada's million *colones* credit was declared irredeemable and the petroleum concession void. Great Britain pleaded for the full sum Tinoco had pledged to the Bank and an injunction to honor the concession.

The British memorial posited that Tinoco's had been the sole and undisputed government *de facto* and *de jure* when the relations in question had been entered into, and that the Act of Nullities was itself a nullity. Central to Costa Rica's defense theory was the fact that Britain had not recognized the Tinoco régime. Costa Rica argued that Tinoco had led neither a *de facto* nor a *de jure* government and that Britain was estopped from asserting the validity of any allegedly governmental acts performed by the Tinoco régime, because Britain itself had declined to recognize that régime.

Chief Justice Taft cited Moore and Borchard for the proposition that acts of usurpers or any *de facto* government bind their successors. He then examined the nature of the Tinoco régime as an issue of fact. Recognition, he wrote, provided evidence of the status of a government: "[I]t is urged that many leading Powers refused to recognize the Tinoco government, and that recognition by other nations is the chief and best evidence of the birth, existence and continuity of succession of a government. Undoubtedly recognition by other Powers is an important evidential factor in establishing proof of the existence of a government in the society of nations." Taft noted that Great Britain, France, and Italy joined their American ally in withholding recognition. However, he went on to scrutinize the rationale behind nonrecognition and the facts obtaining in Costa Rica at the time of non-recognition:

> The non-recognition by other nations of a government claiming to be a national personality is usually appropriate evidence that it has not attained the independence and control entitling it by international law to be classed as such. But when recognition *vel non* of a government is by such nations determined by inquiry, not into its *de facto* sovereignty and complete governmental control, but into its illegitimacy or irregularity of origin, their non-recognition loses something of evidential weight on the issue with which those applying the rules of international law are alone concerned. What is true of the non-recognition of the United States in its bearing upon the existence of a *de facto* government under Tinoco for thirty months is probably in a measure true of the non-recognition by her Allies in the European War. Such non-recognition for any reason, however, cannot outweigh the evidence disclosed by this record before me as to the *de facto* character of Tinoco's government according to the standard set by international law.

Recognition, the sole arbitrator explained, may provide evidence of the status of a régime, but it is not conclusive. Declaratists interpreted this passage to mean that recognition does not constitute the international legal personality of an entity. Chief Justice Taft held that Britain was not estopped by non-recognition. Moreover, he concluded that the undertakings of the Tinoco régime must bind its successor.[82] Though *Tinoco* may be the foundation stone in the case law, a number of other opinions are also frequently cited as signals of the prevalence of declaratory doctrine. These require separate summary, and, together with *Tinoco*, are analyzed in Chapter 3.

## NOTES

1. *See* James L. Brierly, *The Law of Nations: An Introduction to the International Law of Peace*. Sir Humphrey Waldock ed., 6th ed. (Oxford: Clarendon Press, 1963), 139: "The better view is that the granting of recognition to a new state is not a 'constitutive' but a 'declaratory' act; it does not bring into legal existence a state which did not exist before." *See also* Ian Brownlie, *Principles of Public International Law*. 3rd ed. (Oxford: Clarendon Press, 1979), 90–91: "Cogent arguments of principle and the preponderance of state practice . . . dictate a preference for declaratory doctrine." *See also* William E. Hall, *A Treatise on International Law*. A. Pearce Higgins ed., 8th ed. (Oxford: Clarendon Press, 1924) (orig. 1890),19: "States being the persons governed by international law, communities are subjected to law . . . from the moment, and from the moment only, at which they acquire the marks of a State." And see, generally, Ti-Chiang Chen, *The International Law of Recognition, with special reference to Practice in Great Britain and the United States* (London: Stevens & Sons Limited, 1951). Chen's treatise represents perhaps the most thorough-going defense of declaratory doctrine and critique of constitutivism. Recent texts line up firmly in favor of the declaratists as well. *See, e.g.*, D.J. Harris, *Cases and Materials in International Law*. 4th ed. (London: Sweet & Maxwell, 991), 139–40; Burns H. Weston, Richard A. Falk & Anthony D'Amato, *International Law and World Order*. 2nd ed. (St. Paul: West Publishing Co., 1990), 847: "[I]t is clear that recognition does not create the State. It only confirms that an entity has reached statehood." For further citations to declaratists, see Brownlie, *Principles*, 89 n. 7. And for a prominent assertion of declaratory doctrine recently, see Opinion 1 of the Badinter Commission (issued November 29, 1991): "[T]he effects of recognition by other States are purely declaratory." 92 *International Law Reports* (ILR) 165 (1993). The Commission reiterated this view in Opinion 8 (issued July 4, 1992). 92 ILR at 201.
2. Brownlie, *Principles*, 91.
3. Higgins however suggests grounds for a constitutive view of recognition. Rosalyn Higgins, *Problems and Process: International Law and How We Use It* (Oxford: Clarendon Press, 1994), 44–45 (proposing that Germany and the EC recognized Croatia, on December 19, 1991, and January 15, 1992, respectively, before effective power was established by the government claiming to rule a putative Croatian state).
4. W. Friedmann, *Legal Theory*. 5th ed. (London: Stevens & Sons, 1967), 573–76 (listing as exponents of several varieties of positivism Jellinek, Triepel, and Del Vecchio; and identifying as originators of the theory of state sovereignty Bodin, Hobbes, and Ihering).
5. H.L.A. Hart, *The Concept of Law*, (Oxford: Clarendon Press, 1961), 219.
6. Brierly, *Law of Nations*, 138.

7. Chen, *Recognition*, 39–40.

8. Brierly, *Law of Nations*, 138–39.

9. The United States, for example, acknowledged native rights through its treaty practice. *See, e.g.,Treaty of Cession of the Menomonies*, October 18, 1848, 14 *Nouveau Recueil Général de Traités* (NRGT) 1st ser. 244 (1856); *Treaty of Cession of the Chippewa of the Mississippi and Lake Superior*, October 4, 1842, 6 NRGT 1st ser. 610 (1849).

10. One area that may have been treated as a *res nullius* was the sea floor outside territorial waters. *See* Geoffrey Marston, "The Incorporation of Continental Shelf Rights into United Kingdom Law," 45 *International and Comparative Law Quarterly* (ICLQ) 13, 16 (1996).

11. Brierly, *Law of Nations*, 139 n. 1.

12. Crawford also refers to the British-Israeli incident as support for declaratory doctrine. James R. Crawford, *The Creation of States in International Law* (Oxford: Clarendon Press, 1979), 23 n. 89. *See also* Ian Brownlie, *International Law and the Use of Force by States* (Oxford: Clarendon Press, 1963), 380 & note.

13. GA resol. 3314 (XXX). December 14, 1974.

14. On natural rights generally, see John M. Finnis, *Natural Law and Natural Rights* (Oxford: Clarendon Press, 1980); Richard Tuck, *Natural Rights Theories: Their Origin and Development* (Cambridge: Cambridge University Press, 1979).

15. Louis Henkin, *The Age of Rights* (New York: Columbia University Press, 1990), 85. *See also* Steven Cherensky, "A Penny for Their Thoughts: Employee-Inventors, Preinvention Assignment Agreements, Property, and Personhood," 81 *California Law Review* (Cal. L.Rev.) 597, 629 (1993) (noting natural rights basis of Declaration of Independence).

16. Chen, *Recognition*, 184–86.

17. De Visscher proposed that retroactive acknowledgment of legal acts after recognition "does not follow either from the legal nature of the act of recognition or from any principle of international law." Instead, De Visscher characterized retroactivity as a legal fiction necessary to streamline international decision processes. Charles De Visscher, *Theory and Reality in Public International Law*. P.E. Corbett trans. (Princeton: Princeton University Press, 1957), 235. In support of Chen's view, however, see J. Mervyn Jones, "The Retroactive Effect of the Recognition of States and Governments," 16 *British Yearbook of International Law* (BYIL) 42, 54–55 (1935); Joseph Nisot, "Is the Recognition of a Government Retroactive?" 21 *Canadian Bar Review* (Can. B. Rev.) 627, 630, 640 (1943). But arguing against the very principle of retroactivity, see Quincy Wright, "Recognition, Intervention and Ideologies," 7 *Indian Yearbook of International Affairs* (Ind. Y. Int'l Aff.) 89, 93–94 (1958–59).

18. UN Secretariat, UN Docs. S/1466; SCOR, 5th Year, Supp. Jan./May 1950 at 19.

19. *See* "United States Position on Recognition of de facto Governments" (presented at First Meeting of the Inter-American Council of Jurists, Rio de Janeiro), 1950, MS. Department of State. Quoted in Marjorie M. Whiteman, *Digest of International Law*. vol. 2 (Washington, DC: Government Printing Office, 1973), 8–9. Secretary of State John Foster Dulles, "Our Policies Toward Communism in China" (address delivered June 28, 1957 to convention of Lions International, San Francisco, California), XXXVII Bull., Department of State no. 942 (July 15, 1957) 91,

93–94. Quoted in Whiteman, Digest, vol. 2, p. 13.

20. *Répertoire de la Pratique Française en Matiére de Droit International Public* (Pratique Française). vol. III (Paris: Centre National de la Recherche Scientifique, 1965), 15.

21. *Pratique Française*, vol. III, 26–31.

22. *Pratique Française*, vol. I, 532. Quoting from *Recueil des actes de la Conférence*, Partie IV, C, no. 1, p. 62.

23. Interview by telephone with Erik Sigmundsson, Deputy Permanent Representative of Iceland to the United Nations, October 12, 1992 from New Haven, Connecticut by author.

24. Letter to author from Cho Won-Myung, Assistant Representative, Korean Mission in Taipei, March 22, 1996. On file with author.

25. Letter to author from Rudolf Hykl, Press Secretary, Embassy of the Czech Republic, Washington, DC, March 2, 1992. On file with author.

26. Letter to author from N.W.G. Sherwen, Office of Information and Press, North Atlantic Treaty Organization (NATO), Brussels, March 19, 1996. On file with author.

27. Letter to author from Ben M. Kioko, Head of Legal Division of the Organization of African Unity (OAU), March 27, 1996. On file with author. Mr. Kioko also noted that the OAU has not dealt with recognition of non-member states or governments, and that the June 1994 Tunis meeting of the OAU saw aired a proposal to exclude the delegation of Rwanda, on bases similar to the earlier barring of the Somali delegation. The proposal was voted down. The Legal Division of the OAU, according to Mr. Kioko, is presently preparing a set of guidelines on nonrecognition of governments and the circumstances under which the OAU will withhold recognition.

28. *Charter of the Organization of American States*, signed at Bogotá, April 30, 1948, USTIAS 2361; 2 UST 2394. Letter to author from William Berenson, Acting Assistant Secretary for Legal Affairs of the OAS, April 1, 1996. Letter on file with author. Mr. Berenson also notes that the OAS has a collective procedure for granting permanent observer status. Croatia applied for that status in 1995, and the OAS granted it. Slovenia had not yet made a request for observer status. Countries now with Permanent Observers to the OAS are Algeria, Angola, Austria, Belgium, Bosnia and Herzegovina, Croatia, Cyprus, the Czech Republic, Egypt, Equatorial Guinea, Finland, France, Germany, Greece, the Holy See, Hungary, India, Israel, Italy, Japan, Kazakhstan, South Korea, Latvia, Lebanon, Morocco, the Netherlands, Pakistan, Poland, Portugal, Romania, Russia, Saudi Arabia, Spain, Sweden, Sri Lanka, Switzerland, Tunisia, Ukraine, and the United Kingdom. The European Union also has an observer. Former Permanent Observers now members of the OAS are Canada, Guyana, and Belize.

29. OAS Charter, Articles 12 & 13.

30. Edward S. Corwin, *The President: Office and Powers 1787–1957. History and Analysis of Practice and Opinion.* 4th rev. ed. (New York: New York University Press, 1957), 186–88.

31. Corwin, *President*, 189.

32. Senate Joint Resol., January 2, 1913. Quoted in Green Haywood Hackworth, *Digest of International Law*. vol. I (Washington, DC: United States Government Printing Office, 1940), 162.

33. 444 U.S. 996 (1979).

34. 133 *Congressional Record* (Cong. Rec.) H5217–30 (June 8, 1987).

35. "Proposal for Peace and Accommodation in Tibet—Statement of the Dalai Lama," 133 Cong. Rec. H3641 (Sept. 22, 1987).

36. State Department concern over Congressional reception of the Dalai Lama reflects an historic hesitancy to accord official dignities to representatives of unrecognized states or regimes. In this connection, note Secretary of State Seward's instructions to the American minister in Paris to avoid even an "informal interview" with a representative of the unrecognized Emperor of Mexico. John Bassett Moore, *Digest of International Law*. vol. I (Washington, DC: Government Printing Office, 1906), 147, 147 n. c, 210. On the 1980s tension between a Presidential pro-China policy and Congressional sympathy toward Tibet, see W. Gary Vause, "Tibet to Tienanmen: Chinese Human Rights and United States Foreign Policy," 42 *Vanderbilt Law Review* (Vand. L. Rev.) 1575. On Tibet generally and its international position, see Michael C. Van Walt van Praag, *The Status of Tibet: History, Rights, and Prospects in International Law* (London: Wisdon, 1987).

37. Harold Koh, curiously enough in a book critical of legislative deference to executive foreign policy decisions, accepts the received view that Congress has little constitutional role in recognizing new states. Harold Hongju Koh, *The National Security Constitution: Sharing Power after the Iran-Contra Affair* (New Haven: Yale University Press, 1990). Koh refers to recognition as a long-established executive monopoly (Koh, National Security Constitution, 194) and attributes the monopoly to "executive practice endorsed by judicial decision and congressional approval" (Koh, *National Security Constitution*, 159). The constitutional provision (in Article II, Section 3) that the President "shall receive Ambassadors and other public Ministers" gives the President, in Koh's words, "virtually unfettered power to recognize or not recognize foreign states and governments" (Koh, *National Security Constitution*, 259 n. 3). He also describes recognition as "an issue over which the Constitution has been read to grant the president plenary power" (Koh, *National Security Constitution*, 44). Koh refers to the recognition power of the President numerously in passing and essentially without critical comment. See, Koh, *National Security Constitution*, 69, 75–78, 80–81, 109.

38. Brierly, *Law of Nations*, 139 n. 1. Crawford makes a similar point: "Non-recognition of North Korea and Israel was not regarded as precluding the application of international law rules to the Korean and Middle East wars." Crawford, *Creation of States*, 23 n. 89. Citing Brownlie, *Use of Force*, 380 & note.

39. David Strang, "Anomaly and Commonplace in European Political Expansion: Realist and Institutional Accounts," 45 *International Organization* (Int'l Org.) 143 (1991).

40. Terry Nardin, "International Ethics and International Law," 18 *Review of International Studies* (Rev. Int'l Stud.) 29, 23, 26 (1992). Nardin goes on to write that if an entity rejects international law it renders itself a nonstate.

41. Heraclides proposes that the support states tender secessionist communities may be ranked from least to greatest as follows:

(1) Expression of concern over the conflict;

(2) Call for peace talks in a framework of territorial integrity and unity;

(3) Call for open-ended peace talks, admitting of a right to self-determination in the secessionists; and

(4) Recognition.
Alexis Heraclides, "Secessionist Minorities and External Involvement," 44 Int'l Org. 341, 369 (1990).

42. Ibid., 369–70.

43. For another international relations study alluding to the constitutive character of state recognition, see Alan James, "System or Society?" 19 Rev. Int'l Stud. 269 (1993).

44. Stephen A. Kocs, "Explaining the Strategic Behavior of States: International Law as System Structure," 38 *International Studies Quarterly* (Int'l Stud. Q'ly) 535, 545 (1994).

45. Malcolm N. Shaw, *International Law*. 3rd ed. (Cambridge: Grotius Publications Ltd., 1991), 686.

46. *See* Duncan B. Hollis, "Accountability in Chechnya—Addressing Internal Matters with Legal and Political International Norms," 36 *Boston College Law Review* (Bos. Col. L. Rev.) 793, 815 (1995). According to Hollis, the Chechen experience does not support declaratory doctrine. He proposes that constitutivism is substantiated by the failure of the international community to extend protection to the unrecognized Chechen state. Other writers, without stating so directly, have implied that recognition has constitutive effect in international law. For example, Koh, discussing the status of states and individuals in international law, writes, "When one country recognizes another, it does not merely bestow rights horizontally on the other state, it also grants rights vertically to individuals holding property pursuant to arrangements with the newly recognized state." Harold Hongju Koh, "Transnational Public Law Litigation," 100 *Yale Law Journal* (Yale L. J.) 2347, 2378 (1991). Professor Koh appears not to doubt that recognition has at least some constitutive effect. And Colin Warbrick proposes that, during the crisis of the disintegration of Yugoslavia, Great Britain and other European states took a view that recognition was constitutive: "Although the [EC guidelines of December 16, 1991, on recognizing new states] can be reconciled with orthodox views of statehood and recognition at a formal level, reliance on recognition as some kind of constitutive device has not seemed far away in practice." Colin Warbrick, "Recognition of States," 41 ICLQ 473, 480 (1992). Warbrick is arguably echoed in Judge Skubiszewski's Dissenting Opinion in *East Timor*: "Recognition leads to the validation of factual control over territory and to the establishment of corresponding rights." *Case Concerning East Timor* (*Portugal* v. *Australia*). *ICJ Reports*, 1995, p. 265, ¶ 131. *See also* Cheri Attix, "Between the Devil and the Deep Blue Sea: Are Taiwan's Trading Partners Implying Recognition of Taiwanese Statehood?" 25 *California Western International Law Journal* (Cal. W'n Int'l L.J.) 357 n. 3 (1995). Though constitutivism has some adherents, few of them ratify the doctrine overtly.

47. Vladimir Yemelyanenko, "Russia–Chechnya: A Forced Love Affair," *Moscow News*, November 18, 1992. Cited in Hollis, "Chechnya," 36 Bos. Col. L. Rev. at 803 n. 65. Given Yemelyanenko's apparent sympathy for the Chechens, his report of Saudi and Kuwait overtures deserves a touch of skepticism. Inquiries by the author to the Saudi and Kuwaiti foreign ministries about recognition of Chechnya have not been answered.

48. *See* Dermott J. Devine, "Requirements of Statehood Re-examined," 34 *Modern Law Review* (Mod. L. Rev.) 410, 415–16 (1971).

49. *See* J.E.S. Fawcett, *The Law of Nations* (London: The Penguin Press, 1968),

38; Brownlie, Principles, 67. Cited in Devine, "Statehood Re-examined," 34 Mod. L. Rev. at nn. 3 & 4.

50. Devine,"Statehood Re-examined," 34 Mod. L. Rev. at 410.

51. Lassa F.L. Oppenheim, *International Law: A Treatise*. Sir Hersch Lauterpacht ed., 8th ed. (London: Longmans, Green and Co., 1955), 150–51; 30 *American Journal of International Law* (AJIL) (supp.) 186 AJIL (1936).

52. Devine, "Statehood Re-examined," 34 Mod. L. Rev. at 411.

53. Ibid., 411–12.

54. Rhodesia's five million blacks had essentially no political representation, while the whites, fewer than two hundred thousand in total, ran the country. On international response to the UDI, see Myres S. McDougal & W. Michael Reisman, "Rhodesia and the United Nations: The Lawfulness of International Concern," 62 AJIL 1, 3 (1968).

55. J.E.S. Fawcett, "Security Council Resolutions on Rhodesia," 41 BYIL 103, 112 (1965–66).

56. Fawcett, *Law of Nations*, 38.

57. Crawford is probably best described as a declaratist holding strong reservations. See Crawford, *Creation of States*, vii–viii, 16–25.

58. Crawford, *Creation of States*, 32–33.

59. Ibid., 36–48.

60. Ibid., 48–71.

61. Ibid., 71–76.

62. Ibid., 72–73.

63. Paul Guggenheim, "La Validité et la Nullité des Actes Juridiques Internationaux," 74 *Recueil des Cours de l'Academie de Droit International de la Haye* (Hag. Rec.) 191, 204 (1949). Cited at John Dugard, *Recognition and the United Nations* (Cambridge: Grotius Publications Limited, 1987), 131 n. 29.

64. Dugard, *Recognition*, 130–31.

65. Crawford makes a related point when he asks "whether, given the existence of international law rules determining what are 'States,' those rules are sufficiently certain to be applied in specific cases, or else have been kept so uncertain or open to interpretation as not to constitute rules at all." Crawford, *Creation of States*, 35.

66. Georg Schwarzenberger, *Power Politics: A Study of International Society*. 2nd ed. (London: Stevens & Sons Limited, 1951), 102.

67. Sir Hersch Lauterpacht, *An International Bill of the Rights of Man* (New York: Columbia University Press, 1945).

68. *See, e.g.*, Rosalyn Higgins, "Derogations Under Human Rights Treaties," 48 BYIL 281 (1976–77); Richard B. Lillich and Frank C. Newman eds., *International Human Rights: Problems of Law and Policy* (Boston: Little, Brown and Co., 1979); Myres S. McDougal, Harold D. Lasswell, & Lung-chu Chen, *Human Rights and World Public Order: The Basic Policies of an International Order of Human Dignity* (New Haven: Yale University Press, 1980); Tom J. Farer, "The United Nations and Human Rights: More Than a Whimper Less than a Roar," 9 *Human Rights Quarterly* (Hum. R. Q'ly) 550 (1987). Cited at Brownlie, *Principles*, 564 n. 49.

69. *Universal Declaration of Human Rights*, General Assembly resolution 217(III), UN Doc. A/810, December 10, 1948.

70. For comprehensive overviews of the rise of human rights as an element of international law, see Brownlie, *Principles*, 564–80; Brierly, *Law of Nations*, 291–99;

Myres S. McDougal & W. Michael Reisman, *International Law in Contemporary Perspective: The Public Order of the World Community* (Mineola, NY: The Foundation Press, Inc., 1981), 148–53; 941–62. The two 1966 Covenants (ICESCR and ICCPR) are extensively discussed in Jorri C. Duursma, *Fragmentation and the International Relations of Micro-States: Self-Determination and Statehood* (Cambridge: Cambridge University Press, 1996).

71. McDougal & Reisman, *Public Order*, 941.

72. Individual legal personality in the international sphere has been posited by the following: Philip C. Jessup, *A Modern Law of Nations: An Introduction* (New York: MacMillan, 1948), 68–93; Carl Aage Nørgaard, *The Position of the Individual in International Law* (Copenhagen: Munksgaard, 1962); Giuseppe Sperduti, "L'Individu et le Droit International," 90 Hag. Rec., II, 733–838 (1956) (examining at length the position of the individual in international law); Max Sørensen, "Souveraineté Territoriale de l'État," 101 Hag. Rec., III, 141–44 (1960) (noting though "[t]he cases in which the individual is authorized to plead directly before an international organ are . . . very restricted," the individual is increasingly a beneficiary of rights at international law); Oppenheim, *Treatise*, 638. Cited at Brownlie, *Principles*, 553 n. 1, 581 n. 21. *See also* Myres S. McDougal & Gertrude C.K. Leighton, "The Rights of Man in the World Community: Constitutional Illusions versus Rational Action," 59 Yale L.J. 60 (1949).

73. Great Britain, for example, refused to recognize jurisdiction in the European Court on Human Rights until 1965, on grounds that the statute of the Court contemplated natural persons as international persons. Foreign Secretary, UK *House of Commons Debates* (H.C. Debs.), vol. 574 at col. 867 (July 29, 1957); Brownlie, *Principles*, 594. Proposals to give international legal personality to corporations have also run aground quickly. *See* Ignaz Seidl-Hohenveldern, *Corporations in and under International Law* (Cambridge: Grotius Publications Limited, 1987), 4, 23–26.

74. *See* Natan Lerner, *Group Rights and Discrimination in International Law* (London: Martinus Nijhoff Press, 1991), 9; Christopher J. Greenwood, "Gibt es ein Recht auf humanitäre Intervention?" *Europa Archiv* (Eur. Arch.) 93 (1993) (addressing UNPROFOR in Yugoslavia); Roman Wieruszewski, "International Response to the Human Rights Violations in the Territory of the Former Yugoslavia," 19 *Polish Yearbook of International Law* (Pol. YBIL) 203 (1991–92) (more general examination of the Yugoslav human rights situation by a former CSCE monitor and later UN Center for Human Rights staff member); Wolfgang Wagner, "Zwischen Neuer Weltordnung und Wachsender Anarchie," 1991/92 *Internationale Politik* (Int. Pol.) 1, 20 (proposing that defense of the Kurds in Northern Iraq marked a revision in the principle of non-intervention).

75. Paul Taylor, "The European Community and the State: assumptions, theories and propositions," 17 Rev. Int'l Stud. 109, 115 (1991).

76. *See* Greenwood, "Humanitäre Intervention," 4 Eur. Arch. at 93. *See also* Hans-Peter Gasser, "Internationalized Non-international Armed Conflicts: Case Studies of Afghanistan, Kampuchea, and Lebanon," 33 *American University Law Review* (Am. U. L. Rev) 145 (1983); Louise Doswald-Beck, "The Legal Validity of Military Intervention by Invitation of the Government," 56 BYIL 189 (1985); Paul C. Szasz, "The Protection of Human Rights through the Dayton/Paris Peace Agreement on Bosnia," 90 AJIL 301 (1996); Olivier Corten, "La résolution 940 du Conseil de sécurité autorisant une intervention militaire en Haïti: l'émergence d'un principe de

légitimité démocratique en droit international?" 6 *European Journal of International Law* (EJIL) 116 (1995).

77. 47 *Yearbook of the United Nations* 428–29 (1993).

78. *See* "First Report from the Foreign Affairs Committee Session 1991–92. Central and Eastern Europe: Problems of the Post Communist Era," *United Kingdom Command Papers in International Law and Relations* (UK Cmnd. Papers) (1992), Cmnd. 1969 (Stating, "Following our . . . recognition of the Republic of Croatia, we have continued to insist that the Croatian Government should improve Croatia's minorities legislation, as suggested by the Arbitration Commission of Lord Carrington's Conference").

79. Hollis, "Chechnya," 36 Bos. Col. L. Rev. at 816. Hollis argues that the internal character of the Chechen crisis precludes its regulation through such instruments as the Geneva Convention on international armed conflict. Human rights organs took the lead in addressing Chechnya, and human rights instruments were cited as the main point of contact between the crisis and international law. The Chairman of the UN Commission on Human Rights gave a statement on February 27, 1995 expressing "deep concern" over disproportionate use of force and "deploring" violations of humanitarian law. E/1995/23. *See* 49 *Yearbook of the United Nations* 819–20 (1995). In its statements on Chechnya, the European Union similarly referred to humanitarian law (Code of Conduct of the Organization for Security and Cooperation in Europe; Additional Protocol no. 2 of the 1949 Geneva Convention). *Press Communication* 15/95, February 6, 1995. Quoted in Antonio Tanca, "La Politique Etrangère et de Sécurité Commune de l'Union européene en 1995," 7 EJIL 447, 450, 454 (1996).

80. Crawford, *Creation of States*, 20–21.

81. *See, e.g.*, Michael Akehurst, *A Modern Introduction to International Law*. 6th ed. (London: Routledge, 1987), 57, 60–61; Brownlie, *Principles*, 89; Harris, *Cases and Materials*, 148–50; McDougal & Reisman, *Public Order*, 308–15; Shaw, *International Law*, 250; Weston, Falk & D'Amato, *International Law*, 851–853; Hans Kelsen, *Principles of International Law*. 1st ed. (New York: Holt, Rinehart and Winston, Inc., 1952), 402–03 n. 98; Alfred Verdross & Bruno Simma, *Universelles Völkerrecht* (Berlin: Duncker & Humboldt, 1984), 391, 879; Gerhard von Glahn, *Law Among Nations: An Introduction to Public International Law*. 4th ed. (New York: MacMillan Publishing Co., Inc., 1981), 115.

82. 18 AJIL 147 (1924); 1 *United Nations Reports of International Arbitral Awards* (UNRIAA) 369, 376–384 (1923).

# 3

# DOCTRINES OF RECOGNITION: TEXTUAL EVIDENCE

Writers arguing for the declaratory doctrine relied widely on Chief Justice Taft's decision in *Tinoco*. A handful of other decisions also were put in service to the proposition that recognition evidences rather than constitutes international legal personality. This chapter reviews and analyzes the cases routinely cited in the doctrinal debate over recognition. A question raised here is whether the cases marshalled as evidence for one side of the debate in fact supported the position for which they are familiar. Any textual support for a doctrinaire view of recognition is scarce. It may even be that some of the texts recruited to demonstrate the nature of recognition were over-interpreted. In closing, I argue that, in light of a fair reading of the cases and recent legislation, it is misleading to dichotomize between declaratory and constitutive theory.

## THE DECLARATORY CASES

A number of decisions widely viewed to have communicated support for declaratory doctrine involved the Bolshevik Revolution in Russia or disturbances in Mexico and Central America. This section analyzes the decisions most often identified as the judicial loci of declaratory doctrine. After summarizing the portions of their holdings tending to substantiate a declaratory view of recognition, I will return to them, and to *Tinoco* as well, and examine more carefully their implications for international law.

### Mexico and Central America

*American Banana Co.* v. *United Fruit Co.*[1] arose out of an action to apply the Sherman Antitrust Act to recover treble damages for alleged misconduct by the defendant in Central America. United Fruit Company had been purchasing banana plantations throughout Central America with the apparent aim of monopolizing the banana trade.[2] An American named McConnell set up a rival plantation in Panama, at the time a province of Colombia. The United Fruit Company allegedly instigated the Panamanian governor to advise his government at Bogotá to concede the area of McConnell's plantation to Costa Rica, despite confirmation in a recent arbitral award of Colombian sovereignty there. Independent Panama (Panama was severed from Colombia in 1903) tried to reassert its rights under the award, but Costa Rica sent soldiers to seize the plantation, now owned by the American Banana Company, which had bought it from McConnell. One Asua initiated *ex parte* proceedings before a Costa Rican court, won the plantation in a court award, then sold it to the United Fruit Company. American Banana initiated suit in the United States. Justice Holmes, writing for the Supreme Court, stated that the fact of control was more important than the juridical status of the territory; thus the Costa Rican award was entitled to legal effect, and, as a state act, would not be scrutinized by an American court: "[A] seizure by a state is not a thing that can be complained of elsewhere in the courts. The fact, if it be one, that *de jure* the estate is in Panama, does not matter in the least; sovereignty is pure fact."[3] That Costa Rican seizure of Panamanian territory had earned no *de jure* recognition did not, according to Justice Holmes, deprive of legal effect subsequent Costa Rican acts arising out of the seizure.

Two later cases involved commodities purchased from the authorities of an unrecognized régime in Mexico. In *Ricaud* v. *American Metal Co.*,[4] Ricaud and Barlow bought a quantity of lead bullion in 1913 in El Paso, Texas. The bullion was sold them by authorities pledging allegiance to the revolutionary general, Carranza, and the proceeds allegedly went to fund the revolutionary army. American Metal Company brought suit, however, alleging the bullion belonged to it and had been illegally seized by Carranzist forces. American Metal argued that seizure by a *de facto* but unrecognized authority amounted to banditry and could not effectuate a passing of title. The Supreme Court reversed a lower court holding in favor of American Metal. Though it lacked recognition at the time it seized the metal, the Carranza government was treated as a normal sovereign and its expropriation given legal effect.[5] Justice Clarke, who authored the opinion in *Ricaud*, wrote for a similarly disposed Court in *Oetjen* v. *Central Leather Co.*[6] General Villa, Carranza's "Commander of the North," levied a 'revolutionary tax' on the city of Torreon. This amounted to a punitive tariff against persons sympathetic to Huerta, Carranza's rival in the civil war. One such person was in the business of hides, in Justice Clarke's words, "in a big way." Villa took the hides without compensating their owner and sold them to Oetjen, an American. The Central Leather Company had, however, previously paid the *Huertista* hide merchant for a large delivery of the things, only to witness the transaction frustrated by Villa's levy. Arguing that it alone had good title to the hides, Central Leather sued Oetjen to attach them. The Court concluded that Central Leather had no recourse, but before Mexican courts or through diplomatic channels.[7] The 'revolutionary levy' by an unrecognized but *de facto* authority won legal effect. Both *Ricaud* and *Oetjen* would be cited in the next group of cases.

### Soviet Cases

From the overthrow of the Tsar until the early 1920s, the situation in Russia was unsettled. In the hope of shoring up the Eastern Front and preserving order in Russia, the United States and the Allies were quick to extend recognition to the Provisional Government established after the February Revolution of 1917 under Alexander Kerensky. However, when Vladimir Lenin ousted Kerensky the following autumn, the same countries withheld recognition from the resultant Russian Socialist Federated Soviet Republic. The United States only accorded recognition in November 1933, and Great Britain, though recognizing earlier, declined to reestablish diplomatic ties to Russia until December 1929. The United States went so far as to continue acknowledging members of Kerensky's diplomatic mission in Washington as the legal representatives of Russia.[8] One product of the radical changes in and international isolation of Soviet Russia was an avalanche of commercial litigation. Many of the cases involving Soviet Russia demanded that courts determine the status of Soviet decrees. On a number of occasions in this context, the New York Court of Appeals addressed the nature of recognition.

*Wulfsohn* v. *Russian Socialist Federated Soviet Republic*[9] involved furs allegedly owned by an American citizen and confiscated by the Soviet government. Wulfsohn, alleged owner, sued on the theory that Russia, having as yet not been recognized, lacked the protection of sovereign immunity. Justice Andrews wrote for the New York high court and disagreed: "The result we reach depends upon more basic considerations than recognition or nonrecognition by the United States. Whether or not a government exists, clothed with the power to enforce its authority within its own territory, obeyed by the people over whom it rules, capable of performing the duties and fulfilling the obligations of an independent power, able to enforce its claims by military force is a fact, not a theory. For its recognition does not create the state, although it may be desirable."[10] The Court decided that Russia, though its government remained unrecognized, was, like a fully recognized national authority, not amenable to suit outside its borders.

*Sokoloff* v. *National City Bank of New York* (1924) differed from *Wulfsohn*, in that in *Sokoloff* the revolutionary government was not impleaded and, moreover, the Court of Appeals declined to give legal effect to those of its acts at issue in the litigation.[11] Sokoloff had an agreement with National City Bank to place $30,225 (US) in a bank account in Petrograd. The money reached the Petrograd account without incident but after the October Revolution was seized by the Soviet government. Sokoloff, to recover the money, sued National City Bank on the theory that seizure by an unrecognized régime could have no legal effect and the money thus remained in the eyes of the law in possession of the bank. Judge Cardozo agreed. However, in a thorough discussion at least partly consisting in dicta, the judge explored the nature of recognition and gave some credence to the view that existence of a government or state is independent of recognition:

> Courts of high repute have held that confiscation by a government to which recognition has been refused has no other effect in law than seizure by bandits or by other lawless bodies. *Russian Commercial & Industrial Bank* v. *Comptoir D'Escompte de Mulhouse*, [1923] 2 K.B. 630, 638; S.C., H. of L., 40 T.L.R. 837; *Banque Internationale* v. *Goukassow*, [1923] 2 K.B. 682; *A.M. Luther* v. *James Sagor & Co.*, [1921] 1 K.B. 456, S.C., [1921] 3 K.B. 532. It would be hazardous, none the less, to say that a rule so comprehensive and so drastic is not subject to exceptions under pressure of some insistent claim of policy or justice. . . . Juridically, a government that is unrecognized may be viewed as no government at all, if the power withholding recognition chooses thus to view it. In practice, however, since juridical conceptions are seldom, if ever, carried to the limit of their logic, the equivalence is not absolute, but is subject to self-imposed limitations of common sense and fairness.[12]

In the case at hand, Judge Cardozo found no "insistent claim of policy or justice" to recommend giving legal effect to the acts of the unrecognized Soviet régime, and National City Bank, despite the expropriation of its Petrograd assets, remained liable to Sokoloff. At the same time, the decision suggested that, under certain circumstances, acts of an effective administering power could be held lawful even in absence of recognition. This commentary, though not essential to the case at bar, added *Sokoloff* to the cases often cited as supporting the declaratory view.

The Court of Appeals did give effect to Soviet acts in *Russian Reinsurance Co.* v. *Stoddard.*[13] An insurance company had been nationalized by the RSFSR. Judge Lehman, writing for the Court, stated that the key factor, rather than recognition of the Soviet government, was whether a "government there exists, clothed with power to enforce its authority within its own territory." Determining that the Soviet government was indeed paramount in Russia, the Court held that the nationalization deserved legal acknowledgment, and Russian Reinsurance Company thus was held not liable for assets lost to the nationalization.[14]

Last among the Soviet cases meriting attention here is *Salimoff* v. *Standard Oil Co.*[15] Various oil lands fell to Soviet nationalization decrees. Standard Oil thereafter purchased quantities of the chief product of these lands. Russian private citizens in America who claimed still to hold title sued Standard Oil, seeking payment for the petroleum. Chief Judge Pound, writing for the Court, concluded that the nationalization decree caused title to pass. He wrote in an oft-quoted passage, "As a juristic conception, what is Soviet

Russia? A band of robbers or a government? We all know that it is a government. The State Department knows it, the courts, the nations, and the man on the street know it. If it is a government in fact, its decrees have force within its borders and over its nationals. . . . To refuse to recognize that Soviet Russia is a government regulating the internal affairs of the country is to give to fictions an air of reality which they do not deserve."[16] In *Salimoff*, nonrecognition did not diminish the legality of domestic Soviet acts.

### Other Cases

A German-Polish Mixed Arbitral Tribunal was seised of a controversy between a German corporation and Poland.[17] Deutsche Continental Gas-Gesellschaft had owned property in Warsaw when that city had been part of the Russian Empire. Warsaw became the capital of a reconstituted Polish state in 1918, so the company's Warsaw assets came to lie under Polish jurisdiction. A Polish Committee of Liquidation expropriated Deutsche Continental's Warsaw property in December 1923, under authority of Article 297 of the Treaty of Versailles (allowing redress for damages inflicted on the Allied and associated powers during the Great War). The company argued that, upon the date the Treaty of Versailles went into effect (January 10, 1920), Russia had not ceded, and thus had not recognized Polish title over, the former Congress Poland. (Congress Poland was the portion of the country given to Russia at the Congress of Vienna in 1815). Polish control, the company argued, had been recognized only over those Polish lands formerly part of Germany. Accordingly, as the Versailles provisions for restitutory liquidation reached only assets on the territory of the state conducting the liquidation, Poland had no authority to seize Deutsche Continental's Warsaw assets.[18] The tribunal, comprised of the jurists Lachenal, Bruns, and Namitkiewicz, rejected recognition as immaterial: "[T]he recognition of a State is not constitutive but merely declaratory. The State exists by itself and the recognition is nothing else than a declaration of this existence, recognized by the States from which it emanates."[19] Thus, whether Russia recognized the Polish State in the borders Poland itself claimed was not dispositive. Control, not recognition, is what mattered. The expropriation was upheld.

The *Reparations for Injuries* case,[20] arising from a United Nations General Assembly request for an advisory opinion, confronted the International Court of Justice with the question whether the United Nations has capacity to bring against a *de facto* government an action for injury to a UN agent. Noting that "the progressive increase in the collective activities of States has already given rise to instances of action upon the international plane by certain entities which are not States,"[21] the Court held that the UN possessed legal personality toward member states of the world body and nonmember states alike.[22] Recognition, the opinion implied, did not decide the issue.

Judge Alvarez, in an Individual Opinion, proposed the further rationale that the UN must avoid classing members as inferior to nonmembers by subjecting only the former to liability.[23]

The *Socony Vacuum Oil Company Claim* addressed the status of the Independent State of Croatia (the NDH) during World War II.[24] Socony Vacuum Oil Company was an American enterprise with facilities in Yugoslavia. The portion of these falling within the NDH was seized by the NDH government sometime in the period 1941–45. Socony alleged consequential losses of $11,325,000 and sought redress before the International Claims Commission. The Commission had been set up to adjudicate claims between United States nationals and Yugoslavia arising out of losses from wartime expropriation.[25] Socony argued that Yugoslavia was the successor state to the NDH and that Yugoslavia had exercised *de facto* control over much of Yugoslavia (including Croatia) during part of the relevant time and, moreover, was the sovereign *de jure* over the whole of the country, at least in the eyes of the United States. In support, Socony adduced that the United States had continued to recognize King Peter II and the Royal Government-in-Exile for the duration of Axis occupation and partition. The Commission rejected the Socony claim. "Croatia," it wrote, "had all of the characteristics of a 'local *de facto* government' or 'a government of paramount force.' "[26] Yugoslavia's legal continuity did not change the fact that during the relevant time its government lacked control over, and thus responsibility for acts undertaken in, Croatia. Continuing recognition of Peter II and his government was not dispositive.

## THE CASES SCRUTINIZED: A MIXED MESSAGE FROM THE JURISTS

The cases summarized above are widely cited to prove a restricted role for recognition. But do they unambiguously testify that recognition is declaratory? The international incidents at root in the cases indeed gave the jurists occasion to propose a narrow and evidentiary role for recognition. At the same time, the very decisions so often cited as support for declaratory doctrine contain signals as to a constitutive role for recognition. These signals have come in at least three forms. First, a number of cases dealing with unrecognized entities refer prominently to executive statements addressing the entities in question. Indeed, in some cases, judges have asserted the fact of nonrecognition to be immaterial, yet decision has turned upon government memoranda or briefs tantamount (or nearly so) to recognition. Judicial reliance upon so-called executive "green lights" implies a role for formal acknowledgment which declaratory doctrine would seem little to admit. Second, when addressing entities not universally recognized, jurists sometimes have belied their assertions of the legal immateriality of recognition by cataloguing meticulously those countries which have in fact recognized. The judges note that, though important states may have withheld recognition from an entity, others granted it. Judges in several cases indeed seem to have gone out of their way to document instances—often numerous—of international acknowledgment of the entity in question. This suggests a difference between partial nonrecognition and universal nonrecognition. While they disclaim the importance of recognition, the jurists find it relevant to emphasize that the international community did not deny recognition altogether. Finally, the case law illustrates a split view of recognition. The decisions often cited in connection with recognition dealt with contests in private law, and the jurists implied that recognition matters less for private transactions than it does for public—or what are sometimes termed 'high political'—acts. Several jurists, while disclaiming any importance for recognition as regarded the private disputes before their courts, took pains to emphasize the constitutive effect of recognition, as regarded *public* purposes. This implies that the nature of the transaction in question affects the role of recognition.

### Quasi-Recognition or 'Green Lights'

Judges in the United States have often looked to the executive for a signal how to treat foreign governments implicated in a legal action before American courts.

This has been the practice of the courts for some time.[27] At least as early as the 1890s, executive authorities received judicial notice when recognition questions arose. A New York state court in *Hassard* v. *United States of Mexico* vacated an attachment won by a plaintiff against Mexico and the Mexican states of Tamaulipas and San Luis Potosi.[28] The decision seemed to turn on an instruction by the United States Attorney General to the United States Attorney for the Southern District of New York. The United States Attorney, on Washington's orders, moved to vacate the attachment, and, on little analysis, the court granted the motion, holding that sovereign immunity applied to the defendants, regardless of nonrecognition. As to the peculiar position of the intervenor, the court declared that whether the United States Attorney had standing was not a question which had to be reached: the case was an *ex parte* proceeding, "a nullity *ab initio*," for the court never had jurisdiction over the defendants.[29]

A Comment in the *Yale Law Journal*, cited by Judge Cardozo in *Sokoloff*, acknowledged a role for executive 'green lights,' at least in cases touching on political matters: "[I]t is undoubtedly true that recognition by the political department of the Government is in many cases vital to establish the capacity of a plaintiff government to sue in the courts. The important question to determine is the character of the suit and the issue involved. When either of these is political in its nature, the court properly turns to the executive for guidance as to the political status of the plaintiff government."[30] While the Comment took the view that recognition was essentially evidentiary and not constitutive,[31] it allowed that acknowledgments by the executive branch at times influenced the courts.[32]

Just such an acknowledgment was critical to Chief Judge Pound's decision in *Salimoff.*[33] The case required the court to assess the legality of acts of the unrecognized Soviet government. Chief Judge Pound quoted a United States Department of State memorandum pertaining to the Russian government. The Department began by noting that the United States continued to withhold recognition from the Bolshevik régime, recognizing instead the Provisional Government as the sole successor to Imperial Russia. The memorandum then openly, if reservedly, acknowledged the reality of the situation:

> (2) The Department of State is cognizant of the fact that the Soviet régime is exercising control and power in territory of the former Russian Empire and the Department of State has no disposition to ignore that fact.
>
> (3) The refusal of the Government of the United States to accord recognition to the Soviet régime is not based on the ground that that régime does not exercise control and authority in territory of the former Russian Empire, but on other facts.[34]

The State Department was at pains to emphasize that the United States did not recognize the Soviet government. At the same time, the Department was not silent on the issue of Soviet capacity. The court quoted the Department to prove that a form of executive acknowledgment had been tendered to the suspect entity. The extent to which the court quoted the Department suggests how important the court thought the issue. Though acknowledgment fell short of recognition, acknowledgment implied that Soviet Russia had a status higher than that of an entity subject to express nonrecognition. Moreover, the court relied on that acknowledgment. How an existing state regarded the Soviet state was, then, not without juridical consequence. The declaratists' interpretation was right, insofar as the Soviet state would have existed in *some* sense with or without external authorities taking note of it, but it is debatable whether the court would have given effect in New York to the Soviets' disposal of legal title absent the go-ahead from the American executive. At least in one dimension, "quasi" or *de facto* recognition was creative of legal consequences.

This is not to say that even under a strong-form version of declaratory doctrine recognition would have no place in court proceedings. It is the declaratory thesis that recognition is evidence of statehood. The decisions often taken to stand for the declaratory thesis suggest however that executive pronouncements as to the status of foreign entities may be doing something more than *showing* what the situation is. Executive acknowledgment is, in many of the decisions, the *only* evidence of which the courts took notice. Pound wrote that even "the man on the street" knew that a communist government ruled Russia, but surely the Chief Judge did not rely on that observation as a ground of decision. The Department of State's acknowledgment of Soviet Russia was the deciding factor. Reliance on this factor implies an importance in it greater than declaratory doctrine would admit.

Judicial reliance on executive acknowledgment drew adverse remark from writers. Borchard, for example, wrote, "The courts were . . . confused by their own practice of referring to the executive for information as to the status of the Soviet Government (when the real issue was the *existence* of that government, a fact requiring no executive declaration and susceptible of ordinary proof)."[35] Borchard's position decoupled the capacity of a new régime to produce legal results from acknowledgment or recognition by existing states. Borchard may have assigned howevertoo much foreign affairs competence to the courts. He offered no clue as to the mechanics of a court ascertaining the status of a putative government overseas. Nor did he delve into the constitutional difficulty of court involving itself in foreign policy, one of the soundest preserves of executive discretion. "[R]ecognition," Borchard concluded, "should have been eliminated from consideration as irrelevant and immaterial." Nonetheless, courts looked to the executive for guidance as to the legal personality of foreign entities. That Borchard should so have protested the practice further suggests the prominent role executive signal played in judicial assessment of the status of states and governments. It may be that the courts simply did not believe themselves competent to make such assessment alone. It may too however be that the courts were not entirely sure that those entities were legally fully formed without some sort of recognition.

A number of comparatively recent cases illustrate that the judiciary continued to place stock in government pronouncements regarding the standing of régimes or states of doubtful legal status. Far from viewing recognition or nonrecognition as "mere evidence," the courts tended to view executive statements relating to the legal status of statal or parastatal entities as conclusive. In *Klinghoffer* v. *SNC Achille Lauro*,[36] an elderly passenger on a pleasure cruise was killed by terrorists affiliated with the Palestine Liberation Organization (PLO). The victim's estate sought to attach assets belonging to the PLO in New York. The PLO pleaded immunity under the Foreign Sovereign Immunities Act of 1976. Chief Judge Oakes, writing for the United States Court of Appeals for the Second Circuit, emphasized American nonrecognition of the PLO and denied the organization protection under the 1976 Act.[37] Absent contrary indication from the executive, the PLO was not a state. In another case, attorneys for the national airline of Panama tried to appear on their client's behalf, but the federal district judge barred them. The airline was an instrumentality of the unrecognized government of General Manuel Noriega. According to the court, it was because the executive office of the United States had denied the Noriega régime recognition that intervention by attorneys of that government was not permissible.[38]

In *Republic of Liberia* v. *Bickford*,[39] an entity alleging to be the government of Liberia sought to attach monies placed with defendants by an earlier Liberian government. The entity, the Interim Government for National Unity of the Republic of Liberia, did not enjoy formal recognition from the United States, but, in contrast to its position in *Klinghoffer* and *Air Panama*, the Department of State did inform the district court that the executive branch viewed as acceptable a grant of standing to the alleged government. This quasi-acknowledgment of the government in question was critical in the court's assessment of the case.[40] Go-ahead from the State Department was again determinative of an American court's approach in *Millen Industries*.[41] An American company sued an instrumentality of the Republic of China (Taiwan) for allegedly injurious actions of its government. The Court of Appeals had to decide whether to apply the Foreign Sovereign Immunities Act to Taiwan, an unrecognized state. As *amicus curiae*, the United States filed a brief instructing that "there are no foreign policy interests of the United States in our present relations in the Far East that should bar adjudication of the present suit." The Court of Appeals held that the controversy was justiciable. That formal recognition was lacking did not bar proceedings; declaratists would have cited this as evidence that recognition does not bestow international personality or competence. Such cases, however, may equally illustrate not that formal recognition is immaterial, but that executive statements, at once short of recognition yet indicative of some acknowledgment of the community in question, are determinative. Absent such statements the courts in *Klinghoffer* and *Air Panama* declined to treat the unrecognized entities as states or governments. If recognition were 'merely' evidence of legal personality, it was also, at the end of the day, the only evidence that mattered. When inquiring whether an entity possesses legal personality, courts have been uncomfortable looking anywhere but to official statements of recognition. Though this phenomenon may simply be one of courts seeking reliable evidence, the result once they find such evidence is the attribution of legal effect to undertakings by a foreign state. Without the "evidence," the courts would not treat the undertakings as statal acts with juridical consequence. Surely, part of statehood is the expectation that a state's acts have legal effect. Put another way, an element of statehood is that certain things a state does are opposable against other states and against private parties before the courts of other states. In the cases discussed so far, an element of statehood appears to derive from external acknowledgment, even if short of formal recognition.[42]

But what of cases where entities are neither recognized in formal diplomatic declarations nor acknowledged by lesser executive signals? If such entities as these can be treated as legal persons, then surely, the declaratory view must prevail.

### Nonuniversal Nonrecognition

Entities recognized in no way whatsoever by the foreign policy makers of the country in which the court was seated or by the sovereign of the parties at bar nonetheless have been treated as possessing legal personality. This supported the declaratory view. However, certain of such cases frequently cited to show judicial adoption of declaratory doctrine in fact equally implied a constitutive force in recognition. Judges confronted by an entity not recognized by their own sovereign noted meticulously that other sovereigns *had* recognized. It did not escape notice, in short, that nonrecognition was not universal. Some courts wrote as if compelled to illustrate the nonuniversal scope of nonrecognition. If courts believed it necessary to show that at least some states had extended recognition, then the courts must have viewed recognition as material to legal personality—perhaps even formative of it. Cataloguing instances of recognition would indeed be curious if recognition were unimportant to the legal status of the entities in question. Like executive 'green lights' or 'go-aheads' from the local sovereign, instances of recognition from abroad were duly noted in the decisional law.

The tribunal in *Deutsche Continental Gas-Gesellschaft*, celebrated for downplaying recognition, emphasized that Poland had indeed been recognized by numerous states. "In the course of the first months of 1919," the tribunal wrote, "the new Polish State was recognised by a number of Powers. From 15 December, 1918, Poland was admitted to the negotiations of the Peace Conference."[43] Moreover, by attending the Peace Conference, Germany itself had implied recognition: "The full powers of [Poland's] delegation were admitted without reservation by the delegation which negotiated on behalf of Germany. Finally, the Treaty of Peace was signed on 28 June, 1919 by Germany and Poland. . . . It seemed indisputable that the signing of a treaty of this kind, without any reservations whatsoever, implied full recognition of the State with whom the treaty was signed. . . . Accordingly, the existence of the Polish State was officially recognised before 10 January, 1920, *inter alia*, by Germany."[44] Without expressing its argument in terms of estoppel, the Tribunal may well have relied on that doctrine when it rejected Germany's denial that Poland was a state. Germany had at least implicitly recognized the Polish state, so Germany ought not have been allowed to argue that Poland was a non-state. *Deutsche Continental Gas-Gesellschaft* aside, Chief Justice Taft rejected an estoppel argument in the *Tinoco* arbitration. Rejecting estoppel was consistent with the declaratory approach usually attributed to Taft's *Tinoco* opinion, for arguing that recognition estopped a state from denying the legal personality of another would place a legal force in recognition which declaratory theory does not readily accommodate.[45] If recognition binds one state to treat with a polity as a state, then recognition bestows upon that polity a crucial attribute of statehood—formal equality in international relations. Taft was consistent with declaratory doctrine, insofar as he denied application of estoppel but, as will be shown shortly, he did indeed note the nonuniversal scope of nonrecognition, much as had done the arbitrators in *Deutsche Continental Gas-Gesellschaft*. Drawing attention to recognition by other states is superfluous if it is correct that statehood is made by internal processes alone.

If membership in the United Nations can be equated to recognition of the Organization by the member State, then *Reparation for Injuries* furnishes another example of judicial notice of nonuniversal nonrecognition. *Reparation for Injuries* held that the United Nations possessed legal personality toward all states, whether or not members of the organization. It was the overwhelming inclusiveness of the United Nations that led the International Court of Justice to hold that instances of nonmembership did not free any state from denying the body's international legal personality. Recognition, in the form of membership, did not have to be universal for the personhood of the UN to be opposable against all (opposable *erga omnes*). Because "fifty States, representing the vast majority of the members of the international community," did recognize the UN, the UN had the power to sue nonmembers. *Reparation for Injuries* has been taken to mean that recognition does not create legal personality. If however recognition does not create legal personality in at least some aspect, then the ICJ placed inordinate weight upon recognition. The better view is that the ICJ, while attempting to downplay the constitutive role of recognition, nonetheless felt compelled at least tacitly to admit some formative power in international acknowledgment.

A case arising out of the Axis occupation of Yugoslavia also occasioned judicial reference to the nonuniversal character of a nonrecognition. In the *Socony Vacuum Oil Company* Claim, the International Claims Commission aimed to do two contradictory things. On the one hand, the Commission aimed to discharge liability from Yugoslavia for acts undertaken on Croatian territory during the period Croatia was a satellite state of Germany. This required emphasizing that Croatia had been independent of Yugoslav authority. On the other hand, the Commission did not wish to clothe the fascist NDH with so much dignity that its acts took on legal validity; treating the NDH as an international person would have made it difficult to avoid declaring Yugoslavia the legal successor to the NDH, and thus difficult to avoid imputing to Yugoslavia liability for the NDH's misdeeds. To reach the desired result, the Commission had to indulge in somewhat tortured reasoning, simultaneously showing that the NDH was an entity sufficiently statelike to incur upon itself state responsibility; and that Yugoslavia had itself remained the only real state in the space of Yugoslavia—and thus the only authority in that space competent to incur liability. In the course of its reasoning, the Commission made two interesting references to recognition. First, the Commission took the view that acts of the Croatian state had no legal validity, the United States and its Allies having for the duration of the war recognized as sovereign over Croatia only King Peter II of Yugoslavia and his Government-in-Exile. The United States and the Allies never recognized the NDH. Presumably, the Commission reasoned that an entity denied recognition, whatever the entity's factual situation, was denied legal capacity. In arguing that Croatia—not Yugoslavia—bore responsibility for the seizure and liquidation of the assets of the Socony Vacuum Oil Company, the Commission took a different approach. It related that the fascist régime was paramount over much of Croatia during World War II; and that the Axis powers and their associates had recognized the NDH.[46] The Croatian state enjoyed some capacity, and this stemmed from the situation on the ground—and recognition. For both propositions, as much as they might have contradicted one another, the Commission cited acts of recognition. The result, on scrutiny, looks like having the cake and eating it too. Recognition by the Allies established that Yugoslavia's legal personality and its *de jure* possession of Croatia were never interupted, thus protecting Yugoslavia from successorship to fascist liabilities. Recognition by the Axis secured Croatia's legal personality, at least to an extent sufficient that the NDH would alone bear the burden of wartime torts. Here was presented one of the logical flaws of constitutivism—an entity at once a state and a nonstate. Contradiction aside, the *Socony* argument reflected constitutivist assumptions about formation of state capacity. This facet of *Socony* raises doubts whether the holding is as good support for declaratory doctrine as it is often made out to be.

The *Tinoco* arbitration furnishes perhaps the most prominent example of judicial citation to recognition by states other than those directly implicated in the case. Chief Justice Taft emphasized that nonrecognition of General Tinoco's régime was far from universal. This, he implied, substantially diminished the meaning of nonrecognition by Great Britain. According to the Chief Justice, Tinoco had been recognized as president of Costa Rica by many nations; to wit, Bolivia, Argentina, Chile, Haiti, Guatemala, Switzerland, Germany, Denmark, Spain, Mexico, Holland, the Vatican, Colombia, Austria, Portugal, El Salvador, Romania, Brazil, Peru, and Ecuador. At a time when there were far fewer states than today (some fifty independent countries at the outbreak of World War I), this list embraced an appreciable fraction of the world community. Perhaps lending even more weight than its length was the diversity of the list. Acts of recognition take on more collective force when they emanate from representatives of different segments of the community; less when they come from a limited bloc of nations.[47] The Tinoco régime was recognized by states representing a broad spectrum of geography and politics. The chief partners among the Central Powers, Germany and Austria, recognized. Several respected European neutrals also recognized—Switzerland, Denmark, and Holland. The Vatican, with its special moral constituency, joined in extending recognition. This may have encouraged the numerous Catholic nations which also recognized—Spain, Colombia, Peru, and Ecuador, among others. The largest and most important powers of South America, Brazil and Argentina, recognized. Of particular note, two of the five signatories of the Treaty of Washington of 1907 recognized. The Treaty read in pertinent part, "The governments of the contracting parties will not recognize any one who rises to power in any of the five republics in consequence of a coup d'état or by a revolution against a recognized government until the representatives of the people by free elections have reorganized the country in constitutional form."[48] Guatemala and El Salvador—half of the signatories for which the question of recognition was pertinent—recognized Tinoco as ruler of Costa Rica. Finally, even two Entente countries recognized. Portugal and Romania, albeit relatively minor participants in the Allied cause, nonetheless further broadened the representation.[49]

Despite implying that recognition did not decide the contest, Chief Justice Taft exhaustively catalogued what recognition the government did receive. And that recognition, as the arbitral decision displayed, was substantial. Recognition appears to have had a more important role in *Tinoco* than is commonly acknowledged. In the very least, for the Tinoco régime to have enjoyed the status necessary to give its acts legal force, Taft believed that its nonrecognition had to be nonuniversal. "The merits of the policy of the United States in this non-recognition," Taft wrote, "is not for the arbitrator to discuss, for the reason that in his consideration of the case, he is necessarily controlled by principles of international law, and however justified as a national policy non-recognition on such a ground may be, it certainly has not been acquiesced in by all the nations of the world, which is a condition precedent to considering it as a postulate of international law." What Taft meant was that universal nonrecognition would have produced a different result. Universal nonrecognition would have legally erased Tinoco's government from the international sphere. Universally denied the acknowledgment of states, a régime would not possess the status necessary for its acts to have legal force. International legal personality, it followed from Taft, required at least some recognition. *Tinoco* was in line at least as much with constitutive as with declaratory theory.

When the validity at international law of acts performed by the new Soviet régime came into question, courts again catalogued the states that had extended recognition. The New York Court of Appeals held in *Russian Reinsurance Co.* v. *Stoddard*[50] that an insurance company was not liable to policy holders for company assets seized by the Bolsheviks. The seizure was adjudged legal despite nonrecognition of Soviet Russia by the United States, and *Stoddard* has thus been taken to represent the view that recognition does not create legal capacity. Judge Lehman, writing for the New York high court, enumerated however the nations that had recognized the revolutionary government. Austria, Estonia, Lithuania, Latvia, Persia, Great Britain, Turkey, Afghanistan, Finland, Poland, Germany, Italy, Greece, Norway, and Sweden had recognized, and Denmark and Czechoslovakia had concluded trade agreements with Russia since November 1917.[51] This list had effect like Taft's in *Tinoco*. It reinforced the proposition that Soviet Russia was a legal person able to make its domestic acts opposable in tribunals abroad. Again, a judge concluded that it was necessary to show the nonuniversal character of an instance of nonrecognition. Nonuniversal nonrecognition differs from refusal to recognize by the entire membership of the international community. It does not appear that a state altogether lacking recognition can be argued an international person in all dimensions of the concept. Recognition—even if by only a portion of the community—may well be involved in giving a state some aspect of its international legal vitality.

### International versus Domestic Effect, Public versus Private Acts

The classic declaratory case law dealt by and large with private interests, albeit interests implicating interstate relations. The capacity of a community to enter treaties, join international bodies, and engage in the full panoply of what are sometimes called "high political acts" must be distinguished from matters such as internal territorial administration, continuity of enterprise contracts, and recordation of deeds, licenses, marriages, or debts. This is a venerable distinction.

Warren discussed the judicial response to acts of the rebel states during the American Civil War. In *The Supreme Court in United States History*, he observed that the High Court distinguished between two types of government act when deciding what recognition to give various measures taken in the South during the Rebellion:

> The legal status of the Confederate States and of their legislation during the war was settled by the Court as early as 1870, in *Hickman* v. *Jones*, 9 Wall. 197, in which it held the Confederate Government to be 'simply an armed resistance to the rightful authority of the sovereign'; and all its acts were held invalid so far as they were in aid of the rebellion. While the more radical Republican leaders were insistent that all legislation of every kind enacted by the various States of the Confederacy were illegal and void, the Court took a more conservative and rational view; and in *Horn* v. *Lockhart*, 17 Wall. 570, in 1873, it decided that the acts of the several Confederate States 'so far as they did not impair or tend to impair the supremacy of the National authority or the just rights of the citizens under the Constitution, are, in general, to be treated as valid and binding.' The existence of a state of insurrection and war did not loosen the bonds of society or do away with civil government.[52]

The results of the quotidian functions of government, then, were upheld by the United States courts after the war, but enactments pursuant to the rebel cause were not.[53] Perhaps the following distinction elucidates a principled difference between the two: the former are acts implicating only internal administration and have little impact on the external personality of the polity; the latter, by contrast, define the relationship between the polity and the outside world. Acts in furtherance of the Rebellion were acts aimed at shaping the relationship among nations; marriages, trusts, probate proceedings, and contracts had no direct link to the posture of the Confederacy toward the Union or the other powers of the day. Rejecting the Confederacy meant denying enforcement of any acts linked to the Confederacy's claim to be an international person. It did not mean throwing into disarray ordinary legal expectations at the level of the common citizen.

In another case following the Civil War, the Supreme Court had to determine whether certain acts of fiscal policy by the rebel government of Texas were owed recognition by American courts. Chief Justice Salmon P. Chase, writing for the Court, held that a transfer of federal bonds by the rebel treasury was invalid. However, the Chief Justice noted a difference between mundane governmental functions and extraordinary ones. The liquidation of a bond issuance fell under the category of high political acts and would not be viewed as valid when done by an unrecognized authority. By contrast, acts done in the day-by-day administration of a territory and people were to be given juridical recognition, even though the authority that had executed the acts itself had not been recognized by the country in which the deciding tribunal sat.[54] For some purposes, then, whether or not a government or state has received recognition is legally immaterial. Courts view recognition as "mere evidence" when inquiring whether a putative state has the basic capacity to do 'lower-level' things. Whether recognition is "mere evidence" of capacity to engage in *high political acts* is another question. It may well be more.

This however raises its own question—what acts are high political acts? An answer is crucial to parties seeking to predict judicial outcomes in cases where status of an authority is in doubt. Yet comparing *Texas* v. *White* (where official acts were denied legal effect) and *Wulfsohn* or *Salimoff* (where official acts were accorded legal effect) does not initially reveal a principled standard. It may be plausibly argued that the government acts involved in the Soviet cases were no less "high political" than the bond conversion in *White*. Expropriation (whether of furs or oil) is probably a less common occurrence in the 'life' of a state than government borrowing and transactions in the secondary market related to government borrowing. The key here may well be historical context. Calm reflection about the Civil War was unlikely in Reconstruction America. In a highly charged atmosphere, courts can be expected to take an expansive view as to what acts are "high political." Nonrecognition may in such an atmosphere therefore nullify a much wider range of purported state activity than after the air has cleared. In *Texas* v. *White*, the Court indeed seems to have stretched the definition of high politics downward. The result was to deny profit to the putative beneficiaries of fairly mundane government conduct. In a relaxed atmosphere, conversion of bonds might not have fallen into the category of high politics. The more politically heated the context, the more acts likely to be categorized as political. Politics following the Civil War was arguably as heated as at any time in American history. Thus the Court strained to include as many Confederate acts as possible within the category of the high political.

The relationship between historical/political context and the definition of high politics was demonstrated in other places as well. After World War II, part of eastern Germany was incorporated into the Soviet Union. This, formerly the northern half of East Prussia, became a province of the Russian republic of the USSR and was renamed Kaliningrad. Even mundane legal acts such as recordation of deeds were nullified and records burned as a matter of policy. In the bitter atmosphere following Nazi invasion of Russia, it is not surprising that an expansive view was taken as to what acts of the predecessor régime to deny legal effect. The definition of "high political" fluctuates. Variables of historical context notwithstanding, the distinction proposed in *White* may help predict judicial outcomes in cases concerning recognition.

Knowing how a court will decide particular cases, though it would be invaluable to the practitioner, does not alone however say much about the systemic impact of a line of decision. Judicial attribution of legal effect to acts emanating from a particular authority or situation does not always give rise to legal consequences in all dimensions. The difference between the international and the domestic dimension of an authority or situation is acute where recognition is in doubt. A number of cases involving challenges to United States sovereignty further illustrate the difference.

In *MacLeod* v. *United States* (1913),[55] plaintiff shipped a cargo of rice to the island of Cebu in the Philippines. Cebu in fact was under the control of rebels. The rebels had resisted Spanish rule, and now were refusing to acknowledge the new sovereign, the United States. The rebels collected a tariff to finance their 'republic.' The plaintiff shipped its cargo to Cebu and paid the rebel authorities the required duty. On reaching Manila, however, the cargo vessel was levied another tariff, this time by the United States Customs Service. The Supreme Court held that the plaintiff need not pay the tariff to the United States, as it had already paid the *de facto* authority in that part of the Philippines where the cargo first touched shore. The Supreme Court had addressed an arguably more serious challenge to American sovereignty in *United States* v. *Rice* (1819).[56] Great Britain invaded the fledgling American Republic in 1812. During this invasion, the port of Castine, Maine was occupied and temporarily administered by British forces. Ships calling there paid tariffs to British authorities. Justice Story, writing for the Court, instructed that those ships did not owe tariffs to the United States customs office. In both the Cebu and Castine cases, it is doubtful that the United States or the United States' courts meant to add juridical weight to the *de facto* situation. America was not about to attribute legal validity to seizure of pieces of the national territory by a rebel force or foreign power. However, acts of administration, such as tax and tariff levies, lacked an international aspect, and, therefore, giving them legal effect did not seem to the Court to risk altering the international legal status of the territories concerned. In the cases discussed earlier involving disturbances in Mexico and Central America, courts might have deliberated over executive intentions toward the countries and governments in question. It was even possible to be agnostic about who ruled such foreign territory. In the Cebu and Castine cases, by contrast, there could have been no doubt: putative rebel states and foreign occupation of American soil were to be resisted—not recognized. Nonetheless, just as in some of the cases discussed earlier, certain acts of an unrecognized government or acts taking place within an unrecognized situation were treated as legally valid. In the case of rebel governments in foreign countries, this might have been interpreted as lending approval—or recognition—to those governments. In the Castine and Cebu cases, however, such an interpretation is out of the question. The courts could not have been aiming to validate a seizure by force of American territory. Acknowledging legal force in the acts of the rebels on Cebu and of the British occupiers at Castine was not tantamount to recognizing the international claims implicit in rebel and British action. The Cebu and Castine cases illustrate the distinction between measures of daily governance which neither reflect nor influence the position of the state in external affairs and high political acts which are the manifestations of a state's international personality.

Several of the cases among those often cited as evidence of the declaratory nature of recognition overtly acknowledge this distinction. Judge Andrews, for the New York Court of Appeals in *Wulfsohn* (1923), wrote that it was important to consider the public-private distinction when assessing the status of government acts. "[R]ecognition," he wrote, "may become important where the actual existence of a government created by rebellion or otherwise becomes a political question affecting our neutrality laws, the recognition of the decrees of prize courts, and similar questions."[57] But, Andrews continued, "[within its own territories] its jurisdiction is exclusive and absolute. It is susceptible of no limitation not imposed by itself."[58] Andrews assigned a possible role for recognition, where high political acts—or those touching on external affairs of the putative state—are implicated. Where only private matters are concerned, the reality of administrative power is more important than outside acknowledgment of that power.

The internal-external distinction may also have entered into analysis. Judge Andrews made a statement shortly after *Wulfsohn*, in which he posited a difference between domestic and foreign policy acts, and, moreover, proposed different roles for recognition, depending on the type of act at issue. In *Russian Socialist Federated Soviet Republic* v. *Cibrario* (1923),[59] the Soviet government had hired an agent to purchase movies in the United States. The agent allegedly embezzled Soviet government funds. The RSFSR sued to recover. The Court of Appeals upheld dismissal of the suit, on the grounds that the unrecognized Soviet government lacked standing before the New York courts. On recognition and the position of the Soviet state in international affairs, Judge Andrews wrote for the Court, "So long, indeed, as the new state confines its action to its own citizens and to the limits of its own territory, it may well dispense with such recognition. But if it desires to enter into the great society of nations, all the members of which recognize rights to which they are mutually entitled, and duties which they may be called upon reciprocally to fulfil, such recognition becomes essentially necessary to the complete participation of the new state in all the advantages of this society."[60] The reality of the Soviet régime Judge Andrews would not deny, insofar as that reality concerned space and people within the borders of Russia. However, lacking recognition by the United States, the Soviet régime did not have legal capacity outside Russia. Recognition did not matter for the acts of the Russian government at home. It was vital if Russia was to conduct her affairs abroad.

The year after *Wulfsohn* and *Cibrario*, another New York case brought a similar announcement of the public-private, external-domestic distinction. Judge Cardozo in *Sokoloff* (1924)[61] visited the case law of Reconstruction America, noting that acts of the unrecognized régimes of the Confederacy "were held to be nullities when they worked injustice to citizens of the Union, or were in conflict with its public policy." Acts reaching outside the Confederate borders or touching on the principles of the Union were void. "On the other hand," Cardozo wrote, "acts or decrees that were just in operation and consistent with public policy were sustained not infrequently to the same extent as if the governments were lawful."[62] Nonrecognition of the Confederate governments did not deny legal force to certain of their acts—namely, those acts addressing private rights and restricted in their effect to the Confederacy. Nonrecognition was immaterial to lower-level enactments and fatal to higher-level ones. The case at bar involved claims against National City Bank for assets deposited in the Petrograd branch of the bank but confiscated by the Soviet régime. Judge Cardozo looked upon the Soviet confiscations as sufficiently international in their effect that they could not be validated by American courts, absent American recognition of the Soviet government. Applying his teaching about the post-bellum cases, Cardozo denied the confiscations legal effect, and National City Bank remained liable to Sokoloff.

In *Salimoff* (1933),[63] the distinction between domestic and external power was again acknowledged. The New York high court noted, "Writers have been inclined to view that, where a *de facto* government reigns supreme within its own territory, the courts should give full effect to its decrees, in so far as they affect private rights."[64] The role of recognition depended on the nature of the acts under review. "The government may be objectionable in a political sense," the Court wrote, but "[i]t is not unrecognizable as a real governmental power which can give title to property within its limits."[65] Again were emphasized the two factors which I posit may diminish the role of recognition: the private character of the act and the limitation of its effects—or at least of its execution—to the domestic arena. Many acts either have few external repercussions or require no exercise of power beyond a government's domestic competence. Such acts may be given legal effect abroad even where the government that promulgated them is not recognized. Nonrecognition does not deter judicial enforcement of the acts. The high political act, by contrast, has little vitality absent recognition of the sovereign initiating it. Recognition, as regards the high political act, appears to create an aspect of international personality in the actor.

Where acts with no high political connection have been denied recognition by courts abroad, writers have disapproved. In *Pelzer* v. *United Dredging Co.*,[66] a Mexican court appointed an American widow administratrix of the estate of her husband, who had died intestate. The United States did not recognize the contemporary Mexican government, and the New York Court of Appeals held the Mexican appointment a nullity. Edwin Dickinson called the holding a "miscarriage of justice."[67] Courts may treat as legal acts done by a foreign entity, provided the acts are unrelated to its claim to international status. Whether the country in which the courts sit recognizes the foreign entity does not matter. Nonrecognition alone does not provide grounds for declining to treat the results of quotidian governmental functions as legal. Dickinson's response to the *Pelzer* case illustrates again the distinction between the public and private, the external and domestic. It has long been expected that these be treated differently. Most of the cases that writers identified as supporting the declaratory view addressed private rather than high political acts. Insofar as they did address the latter, the cases seem to have admitted a constitutive effect in recognition.

That recognition may have different effects in different situations is not a new idea, but it has retained currency. Karen Engle, aiming to "mediate the tension between the constitutive and declaratory theories of recognition," argues that recognition is declaratory with regard to private acts, constitutive with regard to public.[68] According to C.H. Alexandrowicz, this may be an ancient distinction. Justi published an essay in 1760 in Frankfurt, and this Alexandrowicz identified as "one of the first . . . efforts to sort out problems of recognition in a fairly systematic way." Justi's essay, *Discussion of the question whether the protests of third monarchs against the election of a person to the throne of an elective monarchy are justifiable in the law of nature and the law of nations*, argued that *de facto* control acquired by a monarch by external agencies (*i.e.*, a foreign army) takes on legal force only through recognition. Recognition of a claim arising in that way is therefore constitutive of rights. By contrast, control acquired by domestic election or through heredity requires no recognition to enjoy legal force. Title is perfected whether or not control is recognized. Recognition of this type of control is thus merely declaratory.[69] A dual character may also have been identified in recognition by Wheaton, who, according to Alexandrowicz, "abandons the conception of homogeneous sovereignty, divides it into internal and external and makes the latter dependent on the consent of States."[70] Other writers too have noted that the effect of recognition seems to differ with different objects. James Crawford writes of the *Tinoco* arbitration: "But this was a case of recognition of governments, and it is arguable that, whilst recognition of governments might be declaratory in effect, recognition of new States is not."[71]

The impact of recognition, also suggests Crawford, may vary with the uncertainty of a situation. Recognizing a polity very near statehood but perhaps falling short by one or two criteria may have more than evidentiary effect: "Such recognition may well be constitutive of legal obligation for the recognizing or acquiescing State; but it may also tend to consolidate a general legal status at that time precarious or *in statu nascendi*. Recognition, while in principle declaratory, may thus be of great importance in particular cases."[72] The effect of recognition is constant neither across the different targets toward which recognition may be directed nor across the different purposes for which a particular target may be recognized.

## THE PUBLIC/PRIVATE DISTINCTION IN MUNICIPAL LEGISLATION

Municipal legislation of the last twenty years further illustrates that the nature of recognition varies depending upon the context in which it operates. National legislatures have adopted the public/private distinction. To avoid confusion like that which surrounded nonrecognition of Soviet Russia, several states have enacted statutes that grant standing to corporations organized under the laws of unrecognized states. The Foreign Corporations Act 1991[73] lets a corporation, though from an unrecognized state, appear before UK courts as if it were from a recognized state:

> (1) If at any time—
>
> (a) any question arises whether a body which purports to have or, as the case may be, which appears to have lost corporate status under the laws of a territory which is not at that time a recognised State should or should not be regarded as having legal personality as a body corporate under the law of any part of the United Kingdom, and
>
> (b) it appears that the laws of that territory are at that time applied by a settled court system in that territory,
>
> that question and any other material question relating to the body shall be determined (and account shall be taken of those laws) as if that territory were a recognised State.

Australia earlier enacted a law to similar effect. The Foreign Corporations (Application of Laws) Act 1989[74] makes provision for choice of law in situations involving foreign-organized companies appearing before Australian courts. The Act also provides:

9. (1) It is the intention of the Parliament that the application of this Act is not to be affected by the recognition or non-recognition, at any time, by Australia:

(a) of a foreign state or place; or

(b) of the government of a foreign state or place; or

(c) that a place forms part of a foreign state; or

(d) of the entities created, organised or operating under the law applied by the people in a foreign state or place.

(2) Without limiting subsection (1), it is also the intention of the Parliament that the application of this Act is not to be affected by the presence or absence, at any time, of diplomatic relations between Australia and any foreign state or place.

The Australian Act goes somewhat further than its British counterpart, in that it provides for entities organized under the laws of unrecognized *governments* as well as states, and it similarly treats entities from states with which Australia does not have diplomatic relations. This may reflect differing government policies on the recognition of governments. Britain had abandoned recognition of governments by 1980, while Australia, around the time of the drafting of its Foreign Corporations Act, was just in the process of discontinuing the practice.[75] The clause reaching companies from states lacking diplomatic relations with Australia may reflect the instability of the practice of government recognition at the time. Where government recognition has been abandoned, disapprobation toward a régime is now expressed by breaking off diplomatic ties.[76] With Australian policy in flux, the Act provided for both the older method—government nonrecognition—and the newer—the breaking of diplomatic ties. The Act covered not only state recognition but a number of practices that might be considered cognates to state recognition as well.

Acts such as the British and Australian acts demonstrate that governments and lawmakers have taken note of a distinction between recognition as an artifact of international relations and recognition as an influence upon private law. During the House of Commons debate over the UK Foreign Corporations Act, the Solicitor-General, Sir Nicholas Lyell, said, "I should make clear that the Bill does not change our policy or practice on the recognition of states in any way."[77] Foreign policy remained untouched, then, by the extension of standing to corporations organized under the legal systems of unrecognized states. The Lord Advocate, Lord Fraser of Carmyllie, stated the separation of public and private law explicitly: "The matters at issue are ones of private international law, which deals with ordinary legal relationships involving different legal systems. The problem is that these matters have, quite unnecessarily, been linked with public international law, which deals with relationships between states."[78] Lord Fraser, like the Solicitor-General, went on to underline that the Act would not "affect one iota the Government's policy on the recognition of states."[79]

The High Court interpreted the 1991 Act, correctly it would seem, and permitted standing to an entity from the unrecognized state of the Turkish

Republic of Northern Cyprus (TRNC). In *Anastasiou (Pissouri) Ltd.*,[80] a UK ministry had accepted import certificates issued by the TRNC to a fruit-and-vegetable export company, Cypruvex. A Greek competitor of Cypruvex, Anastasiou (Pissouri) Ltd., challenged UK approval of the TRNC-issued certificates, on the grounds that these violated a 1972 Association Agreement between the EC and the Republic of Cyprus. (The Agreement had required that certificates issue from the competent authorities of the Republic of Cyprus. The Greek party argued that, as the TRNC is not the Republic of Cyprus, neither the TRNC nor any of its agencies could be competent to issue the certificates). The High Court, in December 1992, referred the matter to the European Court of Justice under Article 177 of the EC Treaty. At a point late in the proceedings, the Turkish exporter and its UK subsidiary moved to intervene. Popplewell, J., writing for the High Court, noted Greek "anxiety that by allowing the Turkish Applicants to intervene, legitimacy in one form or another will be conferred on the TRNC and that they will use the Court as a forum to establish their legitimacy."[81] Justice Popplewell relied on the Foreign Corporations Act 1991 however and concluded, "I do not accept that by giving them leave to intervene that it is likely to lead to any sort of recognition of the TRNC or to suggest its legitimacy or sovereignty."[82] Nonrecognition could leave untouched rights involving private conduct yet affirm the intent of the nonrecognizing state to deny the unrecognized community international legal personality.[83]

*Anastasiou* went to the Court of Justice of the European Communities and was decided by that tribunal on July 5, 1994.[84] Unlike the British High Court, the Court of Justice did not rule favorably for the Turkish Cypriot party. The Opinion of Advocate-General Gulmann began by noting Security Council resolution 541 (1983) which calls upon states not to recognize the TRNC.[85] The Advocate-General went on to relate in detail the history of communal strife and international mediation efforts in Cyprus.[86] He noted in particular a follow-up Security Council resolution, resolution 550/1984: "[The Security Council repeats] the call upon all States not to recognize the purported state of the 'Turkish Republic of Northern Cyprus' set up by secessionist acts and calls upon them not to facilitate or in any way assist the aforesaid secessionist entity."[87] The ECJ held that certificates issued by the TRNC could not be accepted.[88] In support of this holding, the Advocate-General focused on the EC-Cyprus Association Agreement[89] rather than the status of the TRNC under international law. Indeed, the Advocate-General expressly declined to consider whether acceptance of the certificates issued by the TRNC violated the UN resolutions calling for nonrecognition.[90] Nonetheless, the Advocate-General's Opinion emphasized the fact of nonrecognition; rejected arguments analogizing the case to the Namibia situation addressed by the ICJ in 1971;[91] and pointed out that close intergovernmental cooperation, necessary for the certificates system to work, was in tension with UN calls for avoiding actions which might tend to validate the secession of the TRNC from the Republic of Cyprus. The possibility that transactions with TRNC officials might effect the position of the TRNC in public international law seems to have influenced the ECJ holding. Though the Court of Justice in *Anastasiou* did not reach a conclusion supportive of the Foreign Corporations Act 1991, the impact of the case on public law and EU external policy arguably placed the contest outside the class of private disputes which the Act was intended to address.[92] The difference in outcome between the UK and EU courts may have had less to do with divergent conceptions of recognition than with a difference of opinion as to whether the case at bar was one of private or public law.

The United States has also enacted legislation insulating commerce from the effects of nonrecognition. Though the Taiwan Relations Act of 1979[93] is limited in its scope to one American trading partner, the principles which it embodies resemble those of the British and Australian acts.

The United States and its allies had advocated the continued membership of the Republic of China in the United Nations but changed policy in 1971. General Assembly resolution 2758 (XXVI) expelled the Taiwan delegation, and the Chinese seat on the Security Council was subsequently taken by the People's Republic.[94] On December 15, 1978, the United States and the People's Republic of China fully normalized relations; the United States abrogated a Mutual Defense Treaty of 1954 between itself and the Republic of China; and the consular status of the Taiwanese embassy in Washington was revoked. In an unusual exercise, the United States 'de-recognized' the Republic of China.[95] The post-1978 situation was problematic however. The United States and the Republic of China (Taiwan) derived mutual benefit from their highly-developed commercial relations.[96] A situation which might produce a rupture in trade between the two was unacceptable. The response to the new situation was the Taiwan Relations Act of 1979. The Act provided for an exchange of non-government offices between the United States and the Republic of China;[97] and it provided for the continued normal intercourse between the United States and Taiwan in virtually all fields except diplomatic relations:

(1) Application of United States laws generally

The absence of diplomatic relations or recognition shall not affect the application of the laws of the United States with respect to Taiwan, and the laws of the United States shall apply with respect to Taiwan in the manner that the laws of the United States applied with respect to Taiwan prior to January 1, 1979 [the date of de-recognition]. . . .

(b) Application of United States laws in specific and enumerated areas

(1) Whenever the laws of the United States refer or relate to foreign countries, nations, states, governments, or similar entities, such terms shall include and such laws shall apply with respect to Taiwan. . . .

(3)(A) The absence of diplomatic relations and recognition with respect to Taiwan shall not abrogate, infringe, modify, deny, or otherwise affect in any way any rights or obligations (including but not limited to those involving contracts, debts, or property interests of any kind) under the laws of the United States heretofore or hereafter acquired by or with respect to Taiwan.

(B) For all purposes under the laws of the United States, including actions in any court in the United States, recognition of the People's Republic of China shall not affect in any way the ownership of or other rights or interests in properties, tangible and intangible, and other things of value, owned by or held on or prior to December 31, 1978 or thereafter acquired or earned by the governing authorities on Taiwan.

(4) Whenever the application of the laws of the United States depends upon the law that is or was applicable on Taiwan or compliance therewith, the law applied by the people on Taiwan shall be considered the applicable law for that purpose. . . .

(7) The capacity of Taiwan to sue and be sued in courts in the United States, in accordance with the laws of the United States, shall not be abrogated, infringed, modified, denied, or otherwise affected in any way by the absence of diplomatic relations or recognition.

(8) No requirement, whether expressed or implied, under the laws of the United States with respect to maintenance of diplomatic relations or recognition shall be applicable with respect to Taiwan.[98]

The Act, though restricted in ambit to a single bilateral situation, had, as regarded that situation, effect similar to the British and Australian Acts: though creatures of an unrecognized state,[99] corporations would not be prejudiced in matters not touching upon the high political act of recognition. Indeed, the American law appears to have gone somewhat further, or at least to have accomplished similar aims in greater detail. The Act preserves virtually every aspect of Taiwan-US relations. Yet at the same time, it leaves intact the decision to withhold (or, as the case may have been, to withdraw) recognition from a foreign community.[100]

Municipal law in several important states today observes a distinction between the effects of recognition in the public and private spheres.[101]

## TRANSFORMING THE DEBATE?

Recognition, "a subject full of paradoxes and curiosities,"[102] presents a new source of puzzlement in its scholars' continuing reference to the categories of a debate which many of them simultaneously characterize as exhausted. Contemporary analysis (though not in all instances)[103] tends to pay tribute to the debate without detaining itself over doctrinal preferences.[104] The prevalence of opinion in favor of declaratory doctrine is amply noted. But, though the two doctrines today occasion less debate than they once did and it is generally assumed that one of the two old rivals is the "better view," scholars and jurists continue to use both the terms 'declaratory' and 'constitutive' when discussing recognition. Why do the terms persist?

For one thing, as I have discussed so far, there do remain serious issues surrounding the nature of recognition. An uncritical survey of recent literature might obscure this; the assumption that a declaratory view is "the better view" is for the most part in contemporary discourse left unexamined. Scrutiny of the foundations of the declaratory view, as I hope to have shown, suggests however grounds for doubt.

The other reason that the terminology of the old debate remains alive is that recognition poses questions which declaratory doctrine answers better than constitutivism, but others for which constitutivism provides the more satisfactory reply. Hersch Lauterpacht, perhaps foreshadowing the eclipse of the old debate, proposed in 1947 that recognition constitutes some rights but merely declares the existence of others:

> Although recognition is . . . declaratory of an existing fact [the presence of the conditions of statehood], such declaration . . . is constitutive, as between the recognizing State and the community so recognized, of international rights and duties associated with full statehood. Prior to recognition such rights and obligations exist only to the extent to which they have been expressly conceded or legitimately asserted, by reference to compelling rules of humanity and justice, either by the existing members of international society or by the people claiming recognition.[105]

Presumably, the right against external aggression, if asserted by an unrecognized community, would fall under Lauterpacht's category of rights independent of recognition. On the other hand, rights of a more active nature are perhaps more dependent on recognition. This formulation and variants of it have recurred in discussions of recognition. The effects of recognition have also been noted to be pronounced, where the community recognized did not enjoy firm footing in international society. Crawford acknowledges that recognition of states not yet fully formed may well carry constitutive effect, a proposition which other authors accept, including Shaw.[106] Furnishing another example of the persistence of the terms of the traditional debate, it has been argued that recognition might be constitutive of the State's capacity to perform public acts, declaratory of the State's capacity to provide the framework for private law.[107] In a further variant, it was argued that recognition might be declaratory as regards domestic capacity of the State, constitutive as regards external capacity.[108]

If ever declaratory doctrine or constitutivism seems ascendant as a characterization of the nature of recognition, events seem to suggest reasons for moving back toward the other view. The general preference for declaratory doctrine, for example, may have been offset by the recognition of Bosnia[109]—and possibly by the nonrecognition of Chechnya.[110] As the ideas summarized above suggest, recognition will continue to be described at times in constitutive terms, at times in declaratory terms.

On examination, however, it also appears that the dual use of the terms of the old debate has brought about a change in their application. While acknowledging the declaratory nature of recognition generally, Duursma notes that recognition "can have constitutive effect in certain cases," such as those in which entities recognized as States lack the basic criteria for statehood.[111] The Vatican City, though recognized as a State in international law, lacks a permanent population. Recognition of the Vatican City, then, Duursma posits has had a constitutive effect.[112] Its lack of actual independence from France renders Monaco, under Crawford's criteria, a non-State, yet it, too, is recognized. Duursma calls the recognition of Monaco constitutive. Simultaneously, she proposes that at some future time, once Monégasque independence has been secured in practice, the "constitutive effect [of the recognition of Monaco] will turn fully declaratory."[113] Duursma uses the terms of the old debate not so much to describe recognition generally as to describe specific instances of recognition.

The two classic doctrines of recognition today are no longer self-contained theories. Nor are they mutually exclusive. Instead, the declaratory and constitutive doctrines are lenses which assist observers in focusing their analysis of particular incidents of recognition. They are used in tandem to describe different aspects of recognition and to describe the distinguishing features, not so much of the institution of State recognition generally, as of particular incidents of recognition. Two conceptions which once separated opposing schools in a 'great debate' over the nature of recognition have retained their vitality—as means to characterize individual events. Thus, Warbrick[114] and the Judge *ad hoc* in the recent *Genocide* opinion[115] refer to the recognition of Bosnia-Herzegovina as 'constitutive.' The publicists do not cite the recognition of Bosnia-Herzegovina as evidence of the 'constitutive nature' of recognition; they use the expression 'constitutive recognition' to describe that discrete event. Another illustration of the terms of the old debate in their contemporary usage is found in one publicist's analysis of the peace process in Cambodia: "[W]hereas the recognition of states and governments is best regarded as declaratory only, the recognition of the SNC was clearly constitutive."[116] The term 'constitutive' here describes recognition of a new governmental structure in Cambodia—not the nature of a general form of international legal action. Krec´a's usage, and possibly Warbrick's as well, invests in the term 'constitutive' a connotation of censure. This, too, was not seen in the traditional usage: publicists may have criticized the constitutive conception of recognition (*see*, *e.g.*, Chen), but in the main they did not use the term to censure particular instances of State conduct. Writers and jurists seem to have fashioned out of the terms of the old debate a new vocabulary.

In Chapters 5 and 6, I will argue that the most important issues surrounding recognition today are not chiefly doctrinal. Before turning to the new debate over recognition, it is helpful however to examine what is arguably an artifact of the declaratory doctrine—accretion of new criteria to the definition of statehood.

## NOTES

1. 213 U.S. 347 (1909) (Holmes, J.).
2. On the founding of the United Fruit Company and the Central American milieu

around the time of *American Banana*, see Lester D. Langley & Thomas Schoonover, *The Banana Men: American Mercenaries and Entrepreneurs in Central America, 1880–1930* (Lexington: The University Press of Kentucky, 1995), 33–44.

3. 213 U.S. at 356.

4. 246 U.S. 304 (1918) (Clarke, J.).

5. *Ricaud*, 246 U.S. at 307. Act of state doctrine renders nonjusticiable in the courts of one country certain actions done by the government of another country. Though not a bar to jurisdiction *in limine* like sovereign immunity (*see* Foreign Sovereign Immunities Act of 1976, 28 U.S.C. §§1330 *et seq.*; State Immunity Act 1978 (UK); State Immunity Act 1982 (Canada); *Litrell* v. *United States of America* (no. 2) [1994] 2 All ER 203 (Court of Appeal, Hoffman LJ)), act of state doctrine restricts the subject matter that a court may adjudicate. For example, transfer of property pursuant to a public purpose, when done by a recognized government, is an action to which a court under the doctrine will attribute legal effect without further inquiry. The doctrine was central to many of the cases addressing recognition. On act of state doctrine, *see* Margaret A. Niles, "Judicial Balancing of Foreign Policy Considerations: Comity and Errors Under the Act of State Doctrine," 35 *Stanford Law Review* (Stan. L. Rev.) 327, 330–31 (1983); *Buttes Gas & Oil Co.* v. *Hammer* (nos. 2 & 3) [1981] 3 All ER 616 (Wilberforce LJ) (accord among UK, Iran, Sharjah, and Umm al Qaiwan accepting assertion by Sharjah of twelve-mile territorial sea held nonjusticiable).

6. *Oetjen* v. *Central Leather Co.*, 246 U.S. 297 (1918) (Clarke, J.). Cited, among other places, at Rosalyn Higgins, *Problems and Process: International Law and How We Use It* (Oxford: Clarendon Press, 1994), 217.

7. *Oetjen*, 246 U.S. at 304 (1918).

8. This recognition continued until the early 1920s. Lassa F.L. Oppenheim, *International Law: A Treatise.* Sir Hersch Lauterpacht ed., 8th ed. (London: Longmans, Green and Co., 1955), 294 note.

9. *See, e.g.*, Ian Brownlie, *Principles of Public International Law*. 3rd ed. (Oxford: Clarendon Press, 1979), 89 n. 9; Karen Engle, "Views from the Margins: A Response to David Kennedy," 1994 *Utah Law Review* (Utah L. Rev.) 105, 114.

10. *Wulfsohn* v. *Russian Soviet Federated Socialist Republic*, 234 N.Y. 372, 138 N.E. 24, 25 (1923).

11. *Sokoloff* v. *National City Bank of New York*, 145 N.E. 917 (NY Ct. Apps. 1924) (Cardozo, J.). *Sokoloff* has been cited by numerous writers as representative of the declaratory view. *See, e.g.*, Brownlie, *Principles*, 89 n. 9; Engle, 1994 Utah L. Rev. at 112 & n. 42 (describing effort to "mediate the tension between the constitutive and declaratory theories of recognition"); Jost Delbrück & Rüdiger Wolfrum, *Völkerrecht* (Berlin: Walter de Gruyter, 1989), 193; Hans Kelsen, *Principles of International Law*. Robert W. Tucker ed., 2nd ed. (New York: Holt, Rinehart and Winston, Inc., 1966), 401, 403, 408. *See also* American Law Institute, *The Restatement (Third) of the Foreign Relations Law of the United States*. vol. I (St. Paul: American Law Institute Publishers, 1986), § 414, p. 280, reporter's note 6.

12. *Sokoloff* v. *National City Bank of New York*, 145 N.E. 917, 918 (1924) (Cardozo, J.).

13. 240 N.Y. 149, 147 N.E. 703 (1925) (Lehman, J.).

14. 240 N.Y. at 157, 147 N.E. at 705. The Court reached this result by finding it lacked jurisdiction. As a sovereign entity, the Soviet Government was immune from

suit in a foreign court.

15. 262 N.Y. 220, 186 N.E. 679 (1933) (Pound, C.J.). Citations to *Salimoff* include the following: Brownlie, *Principles*, 89 n. 9; Engle, 1994 Utah L. Rev. at 112–13; Delbrück & Wolfrum, *Völkerrecht*, 193, 202, 488; Kelsen, Principles, 408; Laurence S. Hanauer, "The Irrelevance of Self-Determination Law to Ethno-national Conflict: A New Look at the Western Sahara Case," 9 *Emory International Law Review* (Emory Int'l L. Rev.) 133, 167 n. 119 (1995).

16. 186 N.E. at 682.

17. *Deutsche Continental Gas-Gesellschaft* v. *Polish State*, Ann. Digest, (1929–30) Case no. 5, 11. For references to *Deutsche Continental*, see, e.g., Oppenheim, *Treatise*, 126 n. 1 (calling the arbitral decision in *Deutsche Continental* "a pronouncement in favour of the declaratory view"); Brownlie, *Principles*, 89 n. 9; Delbrück & Wolfrum, *Völkerrecht*, 128, 189; Alfred Verdross & Bruno Simma, *Universelles Völkerrecht* (Berlin: Duncker & Humboldt, 1984), 380, 961.

18. *Deutsche Continental Gas-Gesellschaft*, 12.

19. *Deutsche Continental Gas-Gesellschaft*, 13.

20. *Reparations for Injuries Suffered in the Service of the United Nations*. ICJ Reports, 1949, p. 174. Cited at Brownlie, Principles, 89 n. 9; Delbrück & Wolfrum, *Völkerrecht*, 211, 216; Kelsen, *Principles*, 283, 285; Luan Low & David Hodgkinson, "Compensation for Wartime Environmental Damage: Challenges to International Law after the Gulf War," 35 *Virginia Journal of International Law* (Virg. J. Int'l L.) 405, 469 (1995) (proposing that its own constitutive documents and purposes give the Security Council of the United Nations its international competence); Verdross & Simma, *Völkerrecht*, 31; Joakim E. Parker, "Cultural Autonomy: A Prime Directive for the Blue Helmets," 55 *University of Pittsburgh Law Review* (U. Pitt. L. Rev.) 207, 227 & n. 155 (1993) (noting that the United Nations was held to have international legal personality, though it is not a State); Julianne Peck, "The United Nations and the Laws of War: How Can the World's Peacekeepers Be Held Accountable?" 21 *Syracuse Journal of International Law & Commerce* (Syracuse J. Int'l L. & Com.) 283, 301 & n. 106 (1995) (same point as Parker, "Cultural Autonomy," 55 U. Pitt. L. Rev. 207); *Restatement (Third) Foreign Relations Law US*. vol. I, §223, p. 142, reporter's note 1; vol. II, §902, p. 350, reporter's note 3.

21. *Reparations*. ICJ Reports, 1949 at p. 178.

22. ICJ Reports, 1949 at p. 185.

23. ICJ Reports, 1949 at p. 191.

24. *Socony* is frequently cited. *See, e.g.*, Brownlie, *Principles*, 89 n. 9; Delbrück & Wolfrum, *Völkerrecht*, 129; Verdross & Simma, *Völkerrecht*, 397.

25. *See* International Claims Settlement Act (1949) Public Law 455, 81st Cong., 2nd sess. (64 Stat.12).

26. *Socony Vacuum Oil Company Claim*, 21 ILR 55, 60 (1954).

27. Relying on the executive for recognition decisions is consonant with a generally-observed judicial deference to the political branches in foreign policy. Though the courts do interpret international law (*see The Paquete Habana*, 175 U.S. 677, 700, 20 S.Ct. 290, 299, 44 L.Ed. 320 (1900)), they have seldom denied presidential primacy over foreign affairs. This apportionment of powers is often attributed to *United States* v. *Curtiss-Wright Export Co.*, 299 U.S. 304, 57 S.Ct. 216, 81 L.Ed. 255 (1936) (Sutherland, J.). For a critique of *Curtiss-Wright* deference, see Harold Hongju Koh, *The National Security Constitution: Sharing Power after the*

*Iran-Contra Affair* (New Haven: Yale University Press, 1990), 135–42.

28. 29 Misc. Rep. 511, 61 N.Y. Supp. 99, 66 N.E. 1110 (S.Ct., App.Div., First Dep't 1899).

29. 66 N.E. at 1110.

30. "Comment: Can an Unrecognized Government Sue?" 31 *Yale Law Journal* (Yale L.J.) 534, 536 (1922).

31. 31 Yale L.J. at 534.

32. For discussion of another example of an executive green light in the recognition context, see Louis Connick, "The Effect of Soviet Decrees in American Courts," 34 Yale L.J. 499 (1925). Connick noted that in connection with *Russian Government* v. *Lehigh Valley RR*, 293 Fed. 133 (SDNY 1923), Secretary of State Charles Evans Hughes sent a letter on February 19, 1923 to Lindley M. Garrison, counsel to Lehigh Valley RR. The letter acknowledged that the Provisional Government had fallen and that the Soviet régime had replaced it. Borchard noted use of a green light in *Gov't of Mexico* v. *Fernandez* (1923), a case before the Superior Court for Essex County, Massachusetts. Edwin M. Borchard, "The Unrecognized Government in American Courts," 26 *American Journal of International Law* (AJIL) 261, 264–65 (1932).

33. *Salimoff*, 262 N.Y. 220, 186 N.E. 679.

34. United States Department of State, quoted in *Salimoff*, 186 N.E. at 681.

35. Borchard, "Unrecognized Government," 26 AJIL at 263.

36. *Klinghoffer* v. *SNC Achille Lauro*, 937 F.2d 44 (2nd Cir. 1991) (Oakes, C.J.).

37. 937 F.2d at 48.

38. *Republic of Panama* v. *Air Panama International SW*, 745 F.Supp. 669, 671–73 (S.D. Fla. 1988) (Hoeveler, D.J.).

39. 787 F.Supp. 397 (SDNY 1992) (Conboy, D.J.).

40. 787 F.Supp. at 401.

41. *Millen Industries* v. *Co-ordination Council for North American Affairs*, 855 F.2d 879 (D.C. Cir. 1988) (Sentelle, J.).

42. *Transportes Aereos de Angola* v. *Ronair*, 544 F.Supp. 858 (Del. 1982) (Latchum, C.J.) offers another example where an executive statement guided the court in assessing standing of an unrecognized entity. And in *United States* v. *Noriega*, 808 F.Supp. 791 (1992) (Hoeveler, D.J.), a *de facto* head of state, who was trying to obtain dismissal of indictments issued against him *in absentia*, was denied head of state immunity. The court noted that a rival head of state enjoyed recognition by the US government.

43. *Deutsche Continental Gas-Gesellschaft*, 13 [Digest text].

44. *Deutsche Continental Gas-Gesellschaft*, 13 [part Digest text, part Tribunal text].

45. Recent analysis of equity in international law sheds doubt on Taft's view of estoppel in *Tinoco*. Thomas M. Franck & Dennis M. Sughrue, "Symposium: The International Role of Equity-as-Fairness," 81 *Georgetown Law Journal* (Georgetown L.J.) 563 (1993). "Even in the absence of detrimental reliance, a nation may be estopped, under an implied principle of 'good faith,' from contesting the legally binding effect of its promises." 81 Georgetown L.J. at 567. By contrast, Taft took the conventional view of the doctrine and implied that an act (recognition in the instant case) could create obligation only if the act induced detrimental reliance. Taft did not rule out that recognition could generate obligation. Extrapolating from estoppel, Taft indicated that recognition absent detrimental reliance generates no obligation. It

follows that recognition that *does* induce detrimental reliance generates obligation. It is an important incident of statehood that certain obligations toward the state are opposable against other states. States are obliged, for example, to accept that "acts of state" generate legal consequences. Insofar as Taft allowed that obligation toward a state can stem from recognition, he implied a constitutive effect in recognition.

46. *Socony*, 21 ILR at 55.

47. International jurists have noted that the number of parties to a treaty is relevant to determining the force of the treaty as a general law-making instrument. The more parties, the stronger the evidence that the treaty represents a generally applicable international norm. *See Reparations. ICJ Reports*,1949 at pp. 171, 185. If something like this were to work in connection with recognition, then recognition of an entity as a state would become opposable against all states when the number of states recognizing it as such reached a sufficient number. What number would be sufficient is unclear. It may also be that the normative effect of recognition increases not only with the sheer number of states extending recognition to an entity, but also with the *diversity* of those states. Recognition of the Japanese satellite state in Manchuria had little general normative effect, partly because only a small handful of states recognized it, but possibly also because almost all the recognizing régimes were of one type (right-wing dictatorships). Perhaps it is the case that lack of number and lack of diversity raises a presumption that an entity has received recognition for reasons of ideology rather than law.

48. *Treaty of Washington*. December 20, 1907 (signed by Costa Rica, Guatemala, Honduras, Nicaragua, and El Salvador). Reprinted in 2 AJIL (supp.) 229–30 (1908).

49. Portugal the arbitral decision lists as having recognized Tinoco on August 14, 1917; Romania on November 15, 1917. Romania had by that date been occupied by the Central Powers. It is not clear from the text of the arbitral decision whether the Romanian government extending recognition was a satellite régime under the influence of Vienna and Berlin; a government-in-exile; or a government relocated to the small portion of Romanian soil not occupied by the Central Powers in their 1916 invasion. Portugal had joined the Allies on March 9, 1916. *See* James Brown Scott, "The Entry of Portugal into the European War," 10 AJIL 351 (1916) (reprinting texts of the German and Portuguese declarations of war). *See also* A. Pearce Higgins, "Enemy Ships in Port at the Outbreak of War," 3 *British Yearbook of International Law* (BYIL) 55, 61 (1922–23). Romania had declared war against Austria-Hungary on August 27, 1916, and Germany declared war against Romania the following day. 23 *Revue Générale de Droit International Public* (RGDIP), Docs. Sec., 197–99 (1916) (reprinting full texts of the declarations of war). At least one, and possibly two, Allied Powers recognized the controversial Costa Rican régime.

50. 147 N.E. 703 (NY Ct. Apps. 1925) (Lehman, J.).

51. 147 N.E. at 705.

52. Charles Warren, *The Supreme Court in United States History*. vol. ii (Boston: Little, Brown & Company, 1922), 139.

53. Greenwood and Lowe observe that later case law upholds this distinction, allowing that "perfunctory acts of administration undertaken by unrecognised authorities in territory under their control may be recognised as valid." Christopher Greenwood & Vaughan Lowe, "Unrecognised States and the European Court," 54 *Cambridge Law Journal* (Camb. L. J.) 4, 6 (1995) (discussing *United States* v. *Insurance Companies*, 89 U.S. 99 (1874) and, following the rule therein, *Upright* v.

*Mercury Business Machines*, 213 N.T.S. 2d 417 (1961)).

54. *Texas* v. *White*, 74 U.S. (7 Wall.) 227, 240 (1868) (Chase, C.J.).

55. 229 U.S. 416, 33 S.Ct. 955 (1913) (Day, J.).

56. 4 Wheat. 246, 254 (1819) (Story, J.).

57. 138 N.E. at 25.

58. 138 N.E. at 26.

59. 139 N.E. 259, 235 N.Y. 255 (1923):

60. 139 N.E. at 261, quoting Henry Wheaton, *Elements of International Law*. 2nd ed., 39. *See* Henry Wheaton, *Elements of International Law*. Richard Henry Dana, Jr. ed. (as originally published in 1866). James Brown Scott ed., 1936 ed. (Oxford: Clarendon Press, 1936).

61. *Sokoloff* v. *National City Bank of New York*, 145 N.E. 917 (NY Ct. Apps. 1924) (Cardozo, J.).

62. 145 N.E. at 918–19.

63. *Salimoff*, 186 N.E. 679.

64. 186 N.E. at 681.

65. 186 N.E. at 682.

66. 193 N.Y. Supp. 676 (1922).

67. Edwin D. Dickinson, "The Unrecognized Government or State in English and American Law," 22 *Michigan Law Review* (Mich. L.R.) 29, 31 (1923–24).

68. *See* Engle, 1994 Utah L. Rev. at 112 n. 42.

69. C.H. Alexandrowicz, "The Theory of Recognition *In Fieri*," 34 BYIL 176, 179–80 (1958).

70. Ibid., 195.

71. James R. Crawford, *The Creation of States in International Law* (Oxford: Clarendon Press, 1979), 21.

72. Crawford, *Creation of States*, 74. Shaw echoes this proposition. See Malcolm N. Shaw, *International Law*. 3rd ed. (Cambridge: Grotius Publications Ltd., 1991), 246.

73. Foreign Corporations Act 1991: An Act to make provision about the status in the United Kingdom of bodies incorporated or formerly incorporated under the laws of certain territories outside the United Kingdom. 1991 c.44; July 25, 1991.

74. Act No. 183 of 1989: An Act relating to the law to be applied in determining certain questions relating to foreign corporations, and for related purposes [Assented to December 29, 1989].

75. Stefan Talmon, "Recognition of Governments: An Analysis of the New British Policy and Practice," 63 BYIL 231, 241–43 (1992) (proposing reasons for the change in British recognition policy and noting other countries abandoning government recognition). Britain announced on April 25, 1980 that it would henceforward recognize only states and not governments. Talmon, "Recognition of Governments," 63 BYIL at 231. Australia discontinued the practice of recognizing governments only in 1988, so the new policy was barely settled when the Act was passed. On Australian practice in the 1980s, see "Recognition," 10 *Australian Yearbook of International Law* (Austral. YIL) 280 (1987) (discussing Australian recognition policy toward the Turkish Republic of Northern Cyprus (TRNC); non-recognition of a Bolivian government; and recognition policy toward Kampuchea, the People's Republic of China, the two Koreas, South African Homelands, the PLO, and an Australian natural person claiming independence for his real estate holdings). The most extensive recent

treatment of recognition of governments is M.J. Peterson, *Recognition of Governments: Legal Doctrine and State Practice, 1815–1995* (New York: St. Martin's Press, Inc., 1997). Peterson examines the shift away from recognition of governments and argues that states ceased to employ recognition in connection with governments because there began to be accepted a duty to recognize governments on the basis of their effectiveness alone. In consequence, withholding recognition (which must be an option if recognition is to retain substance as an institution) was no longer possible. Peterson, *Recognition*, 35.

76. Besides the United Kingdom and Australia, states which have abandoned the institution of government recognition include Austria, Belgium, France, Germany, Switzerland, Canada, New Zealand, and the Netherlands. Talmon, "Recognition of Governments," 63 BYIL at 247–48. Such states, if their policymakers decide to express approval or disapproval of a new government, now do so by drawing attention to the level at which they intend to conduct diplomatic relations with the government. Disapproval is communicated by downgrading relations, breaking off relations, or leaving unchanged an already-low level of relations; approval by upgrading relations, initiating or reinitiating relations, or continuing an already-high level of relations. Other states have not so clearly abandoned recognition of governments. Ireland is evidently one example. *See* Clive R. Symmons, "Irish Policy and Practice on Recognition," 28 *Irish Jurist* (Irish Jur.) 175, 177 (1995). Though generally not recognizing or expressly declining to recognize governments, the United States in some situations of heightened political sensitivity does resort to the mechanism. Talmon cites situations in which the United States has expressly recognized a government: the Peoples' Republic of China after 'de-recognition' of Taiwan; Panama after the overthrow of the Delvalle Government by General Noriega; Paraguay after the overthrow of General Stroessner by General Rodriguez; Iran after the replacement of Mohammed Reza Shah Pahlavi by Prime Minister Mehdi Bazargan. Talmon, "Recognition of Governments," 63 BYIL at 245. I would include two further cases on the list of recent American practice in recognizing governments: the continued recognition of the government of Father Jean-Bertrand Aristide and Prime Minister Robert Malval in Haiti following the September 1991 coup by Army Lt. General Raoul Cedras and installation of puppet leader Emil Jonassaint (see Howard W. French, "4 Aristide Backers Slain in Haiti as Tensions Rise," *New York Times* (N.Y. Times), May 24, 1994, sec. A, p. 4, col. 4); and the recognition of the Kabila régime and its decision to change the name of Zaire to 'Democratic Republic of the Congo' following the overthrow of Marshal Mobutu in May 1997 (*see Keesing's Record of World Events*, vol. 43:5, May 1997, p. 41621).

77. *House of Commons Hansard* (Coms. Hans.), 17/07/91, col. 413.

78. Foreign Corporations Act 1991 (UK): House of Lords Debate, April 22, 1991, col. 67.

79. House of Lords Debate, April 22, 1991, col. 68. One academic writer also noted that the Act promotes a decoupling of commerce from public international law. Ilona Cheyne, "The Foreign Corporations Act," 40 *International & Comparative Law Quarterly* (ICLQ) 983, 984 (1991).

80. R. v. *Minister of Agriculture, Fisheries and Food,* ex parte *S.P. Anastasiou (Pissouri) Ltd and Others*, High Court, Queen's Bench Division, February 23, 1994 (unpublished report). Reprinted at 100 ILR 244 (1995).

81. *Anastasiou (Pissouri)* (QB), 100 ILR at 252.

82. 100 ILR at 254.

83. For commentary on *Anastasiou (Pissouri)*, see Christoph Vedder & Hans-Peter Folz, "The International Practice of the European Communities: Current Survey," 7 *European Journal of International Law* (IEJIL) 112 (1996); Nicholas Emiliou, "Cypriot import certificates: some hot potatoes," 20 *European Law Review* (Eur'n L. Rev.) 202 (1995) (Emiliou is an officer of the Republic of Cyprus Ministry of Foreign Affairs).

84. *R.* v. *Minister of Agriculture, Fisheries and Food, ex parte S.P. Anastasiou (Pissouri) Ltd and Others* (Case C-432/92) Court of Justice of the European Communities (ECJ), July 5, 1994. Reprinted at 100 ILR 257 (1995).

85. *Anastasiou (Pissouri)* (ECJ), 100 ILR at 263.

86. *Anastasiou (Pissouri) (ECJ)*, 100 ILR at 267–69.

87. Advocate-General's Opinion, *Anastasiou (Pissouri)* (ECJ), 100 ILR at 268, quoting Security Council resol. 550/1984.

88. *Anastasiou (Pissouri)* (ECJ), 100 ILR at 302; ¶ 67 original text.

89. *Anastasiou (Pissouri)* (ECJ), 100 ILR at 284; ¶ 69 original text.

90. *Anastasiou (Pissouri)* (ECJ), 100 ILR at 284; ¶ 70 original text.

91. *Anastasiou (Pissouri)* (ECJ), 100 ILR at 280; ¶ 58 original text. The ECJ distinguishes the *Namibia* case on factual grounds and further expresses the view that the European Commission in the case at bar overstated the degree to which international conduct toward a territory, the status of which is not recognized, should be conditioned by the interests of the inhabitants of the territory. The International Court of Justice held in the *Namibia* case (*Legal Consequences for States of the Continued Presence of South Africa in Namibia (South West Africa) notwithstanding Security Council Resolution 276 (1970)*. Advisory Opinion, ICJ Reports, 1971, p. 16) that UN member states were obliged to deny recognition to South Africa's continued administration of Namibia; but also called on the member states to implement nonrecognition in a manner which visited the least possible economic hardship upon the inhabitants of Namibia.

92. Not all observers would agree. Greenwood and Lowe criticized the ECJ holding in *Anastasiou*, for the very reason that it ran against "the trend in state practice and case law regarding recognition in recent years . . . away from treating unrecognised states as though they did not exist and towards acceptance of day-to-day acts which were not in themselves contrary to the public policy of the forum." Greenwood & Lowe, "Unrecognised States," 54 Camb. L. J. at 5. Greenwood and Lowe cite the Foreign Corporations Act 1991 as indicative of the trend they identify. They also reject the ECJ's distinguishing of the *Namibia* holding. Greenwood & Lowe, "Unrecognised States," 54 Camb. L. J. at 6.

93. 22 U.S.C. §§ 3301 *et seq.* (Chapter 48—Taiwan Relations).

94. Huang-Chih Chiang, *The International Legal Status of Taiwan* (Thesis Presented for the Degree of Doctor of Philosophy to the Faculty of Laws in the University of London (Queen Mary and Westfield College) (1996)), 75–79.

95. President Jimmy Carter's decision to de-recognize was challenged by Senator Barry Goldwater, but the source of controversy was whether the Executive could de-recognize without consulting Congress. *Goldwater* v. *Carter* did not address whether 'de-recognition' is a valid act under international law. *Goldwater* v. *Carter*, 444 U.S. 996 (1979). *See* David J. Scheffer, "The Law of Treaty Termination as Applied to the United States De-Recognition of the Republic of China," 19 *Harvard International*

*Law Journal* (HILJ) 931 (1978).

96. *See* Virginia K. DeMarchi, "United States-Taiwan Relations: *New York Chinese TV Programs, Inc.* v. *U.E. Enterprises, Inc.*, No. 91–7694, slip op. (2d Cir. January 24, 1992)," 33 HILJ 631, 637 n. 31 (1992) (presenting statistics on growth of Taiwan-United States bilateral trade between 1979 and 1990).

97. An "American Institute in Taiwan," designated by the President of the United States, carries on relations with Taiwan. 22 USC §3305. The Act provides for a reciprocally-scaled "Taiwan instrumentality" in the United States to represent the government of the ROC in America. 22 USC §3309.

98. 22 USC §3303 (a).

99. The term 'state' must be used advisedly in reference to Taiwan. Taiwan does not claim independent statehood; it claims to be China. *See* Chiang, *Status of Taiwan*, 291–304. Chiang calls the "one China policy," espoused both by Taipei and Beijing, "one of the most perplexing questions for international scholars." Chiang, *Status of Taiwan*, 291.

100. Commenting on the Act, see Mark J. Harty, "United States-Taiwan Relations. Taiwan Relations Act," 20 HILJ 731 (1979); DeMarchi, "*New York Chinese TV*," 33 HILJ 631.

101. It may be that other states have enacted legislation like the UK, Australian, and American acts, but, in an on going survey, the author has yet to find any close analogues.

102. J.G. Starke, "Recognition in International Law" in Starke, *Studies in International Law* (London: Butterworths, 1965) (originally appeared as article in *Australian Quarterly* 1950, I), 91.

103. *See, e.g.*, Myres S. McDougal & W. Michael Reisman, *International Law in Contemporary Perspective: The Public Order of the World Community* (Mineola, NY: The Foundation Press, Inc., 1981), 301–431 (emphasizing issues such as putative duties of recognition and nonrecognition and the collective or unilateral nature of recognition; but not addressing directly the classic declaratory-constitutive debate).

104. Characteristic contemporary discussions of the doctrine are found in Crawford, *Creation of States*, 19; John Dugard, *Recognition and the United Nations* (Cambridge: Grotius Publications Limited, 1987), 7–8; and Jorri C. Duursma, *Fragmentation and the International Relations of Micro-States: Self-Determination and Statehood* (Cambridge: Cambridge University Press, 1996), 110–11 & 111 n. 10.

105. Hersch Lauterpacht, *Recognition in International Law* (Cambridge: The University Press, 1948), 6.

106. Crawford, *Creation of States*, 74; Shaw, *International Law*, 246.

107. Engle, 1994 Utah L. Rev. at 112 n. 42.

108. Alexandrowicz, "Recognition *In Fieri*," 34 BYIL at 179–80 (1958) (discussing eighteenth and nineteenth century views on recognition).

109. Danilo Türk welcomes a constitutive approach. He argues that, if a State or international organization recognizes a State with "deficient effectiveness," the entity extending recognition must "be ready to assist these newly recognized states effectively." Danilo Türk, "The Dangers of Failed States and a Failed Peace in the Post Cold War Era," 27 *New York University Journal of International Law & Politics* (N.Y.U. J. Int'l L. & Pol.) 625, 626 (1995). The judge *ad hoc* in the jurisdictional phase of the *Genocide* case, Milenko Kreća, criticizes what he argues marks a con-

stitutive leaning in current State practice. The qualification "self-proclaimed," used by the press and the United Nations in reference to the Serb and Croat republics in Bosnia, he writes, "can have legal meaning only within the reasoning of constitutive theory on the recognition of States." *Application of the Convention on the Prevention and Punishment of the Crime of Genocide (Bosnia and Herzegovina* v. *Yugoslavia)*. Dissenting Opinion, ICJ Reports, July 11, 1996, p. 18, ¶ 20.

110. *See* Duncan B. Hollis, "Accountability in Chechnya–Addressing Internal Matters with Legal and Political International Norms," 36 *Boston College Law Review* (Bos. Col. L. Rev.) 793 (1995). *See also* Trent N. Tappe, "Chechnya and the State of Self-Determination in a Breakaway Region of the Former Soviet Union: Evaluating the Legitimacy of Secessionist Claims," 34 *Columbia Journal of Transnational Law* (Colum. J. Transnat'l L.) 255 (1995).

111. Duursma, *Micro-States*, 115.

112. Ibid., 419.

113. Ibid., 315.

114. Warbrick identifies in EU practice surrounding Bosnia-Herzegovina "reliance on recognition as some kind of constitutive device." Colin Warbrick & A.V. Lowe, "Recognition of States," 41 ICLQ 473, 478 (1992).

115. Milenko Kreća, Judge *ad hoc* in the *Genocide* case, characterizes Western Europe's recognition of Bosnia-Herzegovina as an "instrument" to establish conditions suitable for a peace agreement. *Genocide*. Dissenting Opinion, ICJ Reports, 1996, at p. 25, ¶ 26.

116. Steven R. Ratner, "The Cambodia Settlement Agreements," 87 AJIL 1, 11 (1993).

# 4

# CRITERIA FOR RECOGNITION OR CRITERIA FOR STATEHOOD?

Whichever model is viewed better to describe the international law of recognition, publicists and practitioners have proposed numerous additions to the traditional list of prerequisites of statehood. It is unclear however whether states in their recognition practice have accepted such criteria as binding. In this chapter I will describe four of the more persistently promoted putative additions to the characteristics of statehood, and I will inquire which if any are necessary before an entity is properly declared a state.

A distinctive aspect of declaratory doctrine—perhaps a flaw—is that it tends to conflate criteria for recognition and criteria for statehood. If recognition occurs automatically on attainment of the traits of statehood, then any factor which conditions recognition must belong to the definition of 'state.' Acceptance of declaratory doctrine would make what states say is necessary for recognition necessary for statehood as well. Such a formula could upset expectations about which actors in international society are full legal persons. The addition of criteria beyond those enumerated at Montevideo also poses difficulty under the constitutive model. As I will explore later in this chapter, the constitutive view of recognition too easily admits politics into what would be ideally a legal process. Multiplying criteria, and, moreover, leaving unclear whether they are criteria for recognition or criteria for statehood, makes recognition readily deferrable and thus all the more prone to political manipulation. Lorimer expressed concern over ill-defined requirements of statehood and recognition: "Each State is to say, not only whether or not a given community fulfils the requirements of international existence, but is, moreover, left to determine what these requirements are. It can thus twist both facts and law to the gratification of its passions or its prejudices."[1] Open-ended and ill-defined standards erode the legal character of a system. It is not altogether clear whether either of the traditional doctrines fosters standards conducive to legality.

It has indeed been in the face of Lorimer's warning that writers have proposed what might be called addenda to the Montevideo criteria—additional elements in what makes a state. Even before the Montevideo Convention, additions were being proposed to the four criteria that later became known by their enumeration there. Self-determination, discussed immediately below, is one such early addition. In time, the collection of addenda to the 1933 list grew. These addenda, it may seem, take on different characteristics, depending on which of the traditional doctrines of recognition is imposed on them. Through the constitutive lens, recognition itself becomes the *sine qua non* of statehood. All other factors, though possibly interesting, ultimately cannot restrain the donor of recognition, nor compensate for lack of recognition. Through the declaratory lens, in seeming contrast, the addenda put new legal requirements on what may be called a state, and, by extension, may seem better to control recognition. Under declaratory doctrine, recognition and statehood are mutually assimilated, for the former is conditioned upon attainment of any and all features of the latter; whatever is called a criterion of statehood must too be called a criterion of recognition. But because of this very correspondence, if an expansive view is taken of new criteria for statehood, it is not at all clear whether declaratory doctrine offers much more restraint on recognition than constitutivism. Constitutivists may call the addenda to the definition of statehood criteria for recognition—to call them criteria for statehood would imply legal restraint on what an existing state may call (or decline to call) a state, and such restraint runs against the discretionary grain that is the fiber of constitutivism. Declaratists may well call the addenda attributes of statehood, but the correspondence between statehood and recognition that is the heart of declaratory doctrine there too makes the addenda criteria for recognition. Declaratory doctrine arguably does no more than rearrange the geography of discretion, moving discretion from the timing of recognition to the definition of statehood. In the end, if left to modify the definition of 'state,' the declaratist little more admits to control over recognition than the constitutivist.

Though there are arguably more,[2] at least four proposed new criteria for statehood here merit address: self-determination, democracy, minority rights, and constitutional 'legitimacy.'

## SELF-DETERMINATION

President Woodrow Wilson endeavored to make self-determination a precept of international law. " 'Self-determination' is not a mere phrase," the President told Congress. "It is an imperative principle of action, which statesmen will henceforth ignore at their peril."[3] While the rhetoric of self-determination came into its own toward the end of World War I, recognition of governments during the nineteenth century may have foreshadowed the principle.[4]

The United States withheld recognition from two régimes established in the 1850s, on the grounds that they relied so heavily on the support of outside parties that indigenous autonomy was compromised. The Rivas government in Nicaragua, between 1854 and 1856, owed its existence to an American adventurist. And Maximilian occupied his throne in Mexico City (1854–67) essentially as a French proxy. Neither régime received recognition from the United States.[5] Nineteenth century American practice provided antecedents for self-determination, so, when in 1917 the United States sought principled grounds for entering the war in Europe, reliance on self-determination was not unnatural.

As an effective element in international relations, however, self-determination fell rapidly by the wayside. Indeed, even Wilson's own secretary of state would later indicate that at the Versailles peace conference he had had misgivings about it. Robert Lansing wrote, "The phrase is simply loaded with dynamite. It will raise hopes which can never be realised. It will, I fear, cost thousands of lives. In the end it is bound to be discredited, to be called the dream of an idealist who failed to realise the danger until too late to check those who attempt to put the principle in force. What a calamity that the phrase was ever uttered! What misery it will cause!"[6] Lansing would not be the last to suggest that adverse consequences might flow from the doctrine attributed to Wilson. Philip Marshall Brown, noting its inquiry into the domestic affairs of states, unflatteringly compared self-determination to the doctrine of legitimism espoused by the Holy Alliance after the Congresses of Vienna and Aix-la-Chapelle.[7] And in 1955, a British delegate to the UN committee drafting the *International Covenant on Economic, Social and Cultural Rights* and the *International Covenant on Civil and Political Rights* warned that self-determination was "political dynamite."[8] Perhaps the delegate had read Lansing.

Self-determination did exhibit some, if only momentary, vitality at the close of World War I. International acceptance of new states in the space of Habsburg Austria-Hungary, Ottoman Turkey, and Romanov Russia was related to self-determination. But other events immediately after the Great War diminished the weight of self-determination in practice. The Allies had made pledges that certain ethnic communities would become states. When Kurdistan and Armenia failed to receive material or political support, however, doubt was shed on the depth of commitment of the major powers to the principle. Once the civil war in Russia had concluded successfully for the Bolsheviks, there began a partial revival of the Russian Empire, quickly extinguishing fledgling states in Georgia, Azerbaijan, Ukraine, and Belorussia, as well as suppressing rumblings of independence across Turkestan and Siberia. The absence of effective Western protest against Russia further eroded self-determination as an operative norm. The first great test of self-determination as a guide to international practice was not a success.

A search of the post-World War I record turns up few if any cases where self-determination was applied without reservation. One writer maintains that the transfer by plebiscite of the Burgenland from Hungary to Austria in 1919 was "one of the few territorial changes in which the popular ideal was allowed full play, unencumbered by major considerations of strategy or recompense."[9] The plebiscitary transfers of the Memelland and portions of Silesia (respectively, to Lithuania and Poland) arguably deserve mention as well.[10] In any event, the record was spotty at best.

Lansing had indeed suggested a potent objection. Taken to its logical extreme, self-determination would result in international entropy. The Committee of Rapporteurs appointed by the League of Nations to address the Åland Islands question came to a similar conclusion and stated the problem explicitly:

> This principle [of self-determination] is not, properly speaking a rule of international law and the League of Nations has not entered it in its Covenant. This is also the opinion of the International Commission of Jurists [studying the Ålands question] . . . It is a principle of justice and of liberty, expressed by a vague and general formula which has given rise to most varied interpretations and differences of opinion . . . To concede to minorities . . . or to any fraction of a population the right of withdrawing from the community to which they belong because it is their wish or their good pleasure, would be to destroy order and stability within States and to inaugurate anarchy in international life.[11]

Anxiety was widespread that to admit of a right to self-determination would make unviable state structures on which world order in no small part relied. Few inter-war jurists or writers attributed the principle legal status. Though discredited between the wars, self-determination would attract renewed interest after World War II. European retreat from colonial empire in the 1950s and 1960s led writers and politicians to address the legal status of popular secession.[12] As the West European colonial powers withdrew from Africa and Asia, dozens of new states began to assert independence. Especially when such assertions were unilateral, problems of recognition arose. Writers in the 1960s and 1970s reconsidered the language of self-determination as a means to evaluate the new claims to statehood.[13] A number of international declarations would complement this trend in academic thought.

Offering textual support for self-determination early in the post-war era, the twenty-first article of the *Universal Declaration of Human Rights* (1948) announced that government stems from the will of the people governed.[14] The *Declaration on the Granting of Independence to Colonial Countries and Peoples* (1961), building on the theme of the earlier United Nations text, addressed decolonization.[15] Toward the end of decolonization, another United Nations document—*Declaration on Principles of International Law*

*Concerning Friendly Relations and Cooperation Among States in Accordance with the Charter of the United Nations*—stated, "[E]very state has the duty to promote, through joint and separate action, realization of the principle of equal rights and self-determination of peoples."[16] Recognition would seem to offer one mechanism by which to fulfill the duty posited in this formulation: existing states, identifying a discrete national community seeking statehood, would be obliged to protect (and advance) that community in its quest for statehood; the act of recognition would demonstrate that existing states expected the community to be accorded the full dignity due a state. A corollary to a directive that states employ recognition to foster self-determination might be that recognition is appropriate only for a community enjoying self-determination. This admittedly does not directly follow, but the UN texts do seem to posit some relationship between statehood and recognition on the one hand and self-determination on the other. Several ICJ cases also support self-determination: the *Namibia Opinion*,[17] the *Western Sahara Case*,[18] and the *East Timor Case*.[19] Sources both political and judicial have pressed to include self-determination among the criteria for statehood and among the criteria for recognition as well.

Publicists toward the end of the era of decolonization and after intensified their support for self-determination. Crawford proposes that self-determination is a criterion for statehood. The ambit of self-determination, he notes, has not been decided, and the concept remains as much a matter of politics as law.[20] From this, he further notes that it is not at all clear that self-determination has risen to a peremptory norm of international law.[21] Nonetheless, Crawford writes, "A significant body of practice attests to the reality of the link [between statehood and self-determination]."[22] As elsewhere in his work, Crawford focuses here on how territory is organized, arguing that four categories may be eligible for self-determination: (1) entities whose right to self-determination is established by international agreement, particularly mandated, trust, and non-self-governing territories; (2) existing states, minus parts of existing states which fall into one of the other categories; (3) entities belonging to a state but denied self-government; and (4) any other entities where states agree to apply self-determination "as an appropriate solution or criterion."[23] Crawford supports the integration of a rule of self-determination into the definition of statehood.[24]

Duursma also argues that self-determination is involved in defining what entities may be recognized as states and, moreover, has become a rule of international law:[25] "It is not just a pragmatic principle," Duursma writes, "but a right which has to be respected.[26] An *opinio juris sive necessitatis* has been formed and proved not only in the colonial context but also more recently in a non-colonial European context."[27] The scope of self-determination according to Duursma is broad. The right belongs to all peoples, not just those under alien subjugation. To be beneficiaries of the right, a group must (1) have the character of a 'people'; and (2) bear a close relationship to a territory. The benefits of the right thus do not run to minorities or to newly settled peoples, though over time, populations such as those of European origin in North America, South Africa, and Australasia may acquire the traits of a people entitled to the right.[28] This limit notwithstanding, Duursma's view of self-determination is considerably more expansive than Crawford's.

Duursma must however concede that self-determination faces a counterbalance in the principle of territorial integrity. This is not a new proposition.[29] Peoples with a connection to a territory possess a right to self-determination, but their exercise of the right is constrained by the right of existing states to territorial integrity. The key question is "when does the right of self-determination take precedence over the obligation to respect the territorial integrity of a State."[30] From this, Duursma suggests an interesting, and I think novel, formulation about state recognition. The recognition of states is no stranger to controversy in international law. State practice has witnessed crises over the recognition of putative new states,[31] and the legal meaning of recognition itself is uncertain. New views on the subject are welcome. Duursma proposes that recognition amounts to a signal that the burden in favor of territorial integrity has shifted: "In each case the right of self-determination has to be weighed against respect for the territorial integrity of a State. It is in this weighing process that international recognition becomes relevant. Recognition does therefore not imply that a right of self-determination exists, but that the right of self-determination offsets the inviolability of the territorial integrity in the given case."[32] The idea of offsetting an *inviolable* value might raise questions—if inviolable how can the value be offset? Duursma's formulation is useful nonetheless. It provides a framework for investigating state practice and *opinio juris* surrounding the difficult matter of balancing self-determination and territorial integrity. Furthermore, it suggests one possible legal consequence of recognition—burden shifting.

The principle of territorial integrity poses little problem in the most common cases of self-determination. An independent people forming the permanent population of an independent state has, like all peoples with a tie to a territory, the right to self-determination. Exercise of the right by such a people does not clash with the territorial integrity of any state. The right of the people to merge their state with another illustrates the scope of the right of self-determination when it does not confront issues of territorial integrity.[33] Neither do colonial peoples in Non-Self-Governing and Trust Territories pose a problem. The United Nations declared integration of colonies to the metropole a fiction which it would not recognize.[34] Therefore, independence of European colonies did not disrupt the territorial integrity of the metropolitan states.[35]

Trouble arises however where colonies have historical or legal ties to a neighboring territory. Can colonial independence disrupt the territorial integrity of proximate states? This question led Duursma to discuss colonial enclaves, such as East Timor, West Irian, Belize, Ifni, Gibraltar, Walvis Bay, Hong Kong, Macao, and Goa, Daman and Diu. Three conclusions might be reached about these territories: (1) if a colonial enclave once belonged to a state other than the colonizing state, then the inhabitants of the enclave are probably not a distinct people (and thus not proper beneficiaries of the right to self-determination); (2) there is no legal obligation to consult the inhabitants if the territory is small and connected geographically to a neighboring state claiming the territory; and (3) nothing in state practice excludes that small enclaves lack a right to self-determination, except in the case of "micro-entities which have formed a clear distinct territory over the centuries, the political history of which cannot be assimilated to that of other States."[36]

The most difficult case is that of secession from the metropole itself. What institution has the competence to decide when self-determination trumps territorial integrity? Duursma posits that this decision cannot rest with the metropolitan state; if it did, "it would result in the denial of the international character of the competing rules in question."[37] A likely outcome of such an assignment of competence would be that states would never attribute the right of self-determination to secessionist minorities on their own territory. Defining of competence in international law, however, tends to rest in large part with individual states. I am unsure whether Duursma, in locating at international level the competence to decide the balance between self-determination and territorial integrity, has sufficiently taken into account the discretion enjoyed by states in setting their responsibilities under international law. The recognition of the secessionist republics in Yugoslavia raised questions about the collective nature of recognition: did international law require recognizing states to coordinate their policy with others? It appears that an expectation had arisen by 1991 that states carry out recognition in a collective framework, but each recognizing state appears to have retained the discretion to choose in how broad a collective framework to place itself. The states recognizing Croatia and Slovenia in December 1991 (chiefly Germany and Austria) did so earlier than the majority of Europe seemed to believe prudent (or legal), but the recognizing states nonetheless repeatedly acknowledged a requirement to recognize collectively. The requirement was announced expressly—and also by implication (the recognizing states characterized their acts of recognition as collective). However, the early-recognizing states liberally construed the term "collective"; it was up to them to define the framework of collective reference. Duursma is insightful to posit that a rule is necessary to mediate the tension between self-determination and territorial integrity. She may however underestimate the competence of the individual state to decide where to place the competence to conduct the proposed mediation.

Even if Duursma's assumption is flawed that the competence to decide the relative weight of the two competing principles rests with the international community, Duursma makes a number of interesting observations about the way the community evaluates secessionist claims. Critical to Duursma's proposed mechanism of international evaluation is the institution of state recognition. Central government authorities in a federal state may oppose secession, but "[t]hrough the act of recognition, a preference is expressed for the full right of self-determination of the secessionists." As pointed out above, Duursma sees recognition as a burden-shifting device. If before recognition, the burden rested with the secessionists to prove that their independence would not threaten the territorial integrity of the parent state, after recognition, the burden shifts to the parent state to prove that continued integration does not derogate the secessionists' right to self-determination. In the case of recognition from many states, recognition is even more than a burden-shifting mechanism: such recognition puts "the 'old' State . . . under the obligation to respect the territorial integrity of the 'new' State."[38] Widespread recognition, for Duursma, is determinative.

This formula raises a question: when is recognition sufficiently widespread to overcome the presumption favoring territorial integrity? I would propose that recognition takes on added weight when it originates from (1) powerful states; and (2) a representative cross-section of the international community. Thus recognition from twenty Latin American states is not as likely to produce the burden shifting Duursma proposes as recognition from half as many states, representing Latin America, Western Europe, Eastern Europe, the space of the former Soviet Union, the Arab world, Africa, and East Asia. Nor might recognition from thirty or forty states comparatively weak in terms of the effective power processes of the world community have as much impact as, for example, recognition from the United States, Japan, and France. It is worth noting again in this connection that the number of parties to a convention is relevant to determining the impact of the convention on general international law. The more parties, the greater the possibility that the convention represents a generally applicable international norm.[39]

Linking recognition to self-determination and territorial integrity attributes a certain constitutive force in recognition. Indeed, Duursma argues that recognition can "remedy the possible non-fulfilment of a criterion for statehood."[40] Thus recognition can create elements of statehood lacking in the objective situation of the putative state. At one time writers on the subject primarily debated whether recognition constituted the object community as a state or merely declared that that community had attained the criteria of statehood. Before the 1990s, the view came generally to be held that recognition was declaratory rather than constitutive.[41] State practice since the dissolution of the USSR and the Socialist Federal Republic of Yugoslavia (SFRY) has, however, led to a reevaluation of this view.[42] Duursma, in identifying a constitutive force in recent recognition practice (her example of the federal state resisting secession but being overruled by generalized recognition clearly refers to the SFRY case), has contributed to the post-Cold War reevaluation of recognition.

Duursma also takes up, in connection with secession, the much debated issue of human rights and statehood. Human rights violations, since the nearly universal nonrecognition of Rhodesian independence,[43] have reduced the prospects for recognition of states perpetrating them. States created through or resting upon violations of *jus cogens* have been denied recognition, with nonrecognition of Manchukuo a forerunner.[44] It may even be that delicts, as they reduce some actors, enhance others. Instead of focusing on how human rights violations can diminish the legal status of their perpetrators, Duursma asks whether being a victim of such delicts entitles a people to recognition. If a people suffers an oppression denying it *jus cogens* rights, does the people thus acquire under self-determination a right to secede? Duursma concludes, after analyzing Nagorno Karabakh and Bangladesh, that violations of fundamental rights do not independently place self-determination ahead of the competing value of territorial integrity. The violations may provide evidence in support of secession, but they do not alone shift the burden against the parent state.[45]

Other factors also provide evidence favoring self-determination. The total disruption of an existing state may expedite recognition of new states.[46] And federal units may generally have an easier time securing self-determination in face of the territorial integrity principle than other pieces of a parent state. This leads to an interesting observation. It may be that the law of secession gives no preference to federal units over lesser entities. However, the prior existence of a putative independent state as a federal unit may make proof of statehood easier. The putative state is accustomed to self-administration, and the political desirability of independence has been tested during its federal existence. Other states can approach the putative state with some confidence in its ability to exert effective control over its territory. Duursma notes that the fifteen union republics of the USSR received recognition quickly, whereas Abkahzia, Chechnya, and South Ossetia (lower-level entities within the Russian and Georgian republics) proved unable to establish independence, at least as a matter of international law.[47] If a federal unit was illegally annexed, it may achieve recognition yet more readily than other federal units. Consider the Soviet Baltic republics. But, again, Duursma emphasizes that it is not a rule of law which produces this phenomenon. Concluding that practice concerning secession is inconsistent, Duursma characterizes disputes over secession as essentially political. Reciprocal use of force by a state and secessionists continues, though outside international law: "The balance between the right of self-determination and the inviolability of the State's territorial integrity has thus been struck not by a rule of law, but by the law of the strongest, one of the first principles to be rejected by international law."[48] International law enters contests over secession only in connection with minority rights, humanitarianism (as in the law governing the conduct of warfare), and *uti possidetis juris*.[49] A secession struggle ends only when the secessionists quit or win international protection for the territorial integrity of their putative State.[50]

Duursma doubts whether self-determination has become *jus cogens*. The principle is, she writes, nonderogable, with regard to Non-Self-Governing and Trust Territories and peoples which form existing states. But self-determination is not *jus cogens* in situations where self-determination will disrupt the territorial integrity of a state. In such situations, self-determination, Duursma posits, declines to an ordinary norm of international law. The burden in proving the relative weight of the two competing principles is shifted in favor of self-determination however after a secessionist community has received recognition.[51]

Other writers have examined whether state practice evidences a rule of self-determination. Dugard, for example, proposes that certain norms of international law have recently become peremptory, namely self-determination and respect for human rights. These, he argues, have not so much become part of the definition of statehood, as rules which must not be violated in the formation of the state.[52] It would appear that Dugard aims to explain the nonrecognition of Rhodesia, Northern Cyprus, and the former South African homelands, yet maintain declaratory doctrine. Rhodesia, Northern Cyprus and at least one of the former homelands (the Transkei) possessed the attributes traditionally viewed as sufficient for statehood.[53] In them operated coherent governments controlling defined territories and populations, but these putative states went or remain unrecognized. Dugard finds untenable the assertion that such entities were not in some very real sense states. To explain their nonrecognition, he proposes instead that their formation was at odds with the new norms of self-determination and human rights. Their creative moment thus poisoned, the entities were disabled as international legal persons. Dugard's proposal stems in part from similar ideas forwarded by Fawcett and Crawford.

Fawcett[54] and, later, Crawford[55] both grappled with expanding precedent in the areas of self-determination and human rights, and, like Duursma, both tried to accommodate the precedent within the law of recognition. Fawcett wrote, "[T]o the traditional criteria for the recognition of . . . a new State must now be added the requirement that it shall not be based upon a systematic denial in its territory of certain civil and political rights, including in particular the right of every citizen to participate in the government of his country."[56] Crawford makes a somewhat bolder proposition. "[A] new rule," he writes, "has come into existence, prohibiting entities from claiming statehood if their creation is in violation of an applicable right to self-determination."[57]

The degree to which the criterion of self-determination has joined the definition of statehood can be gauged by examining state practice. Several cases from the last quarter century may help evaluate the proposal, put forward to differing degrees by Fawcett, Dugard, and Crawford, that self-determination now forms part of the essential attributes of the state. Rhodesia and the South African 'homelands' provide the standard starting point.

Rejecting British demands for a one-man-one-vote system, whites in South Rhodesia in 1965 unilaterally declared independence from the United Kingdom. The resultant régime of Ian Smith effectively denied both democracy and self-determination to over ninety-five percent of the inhabitants of the country. Few international actors assumed regular relations with the Smith régime. None formally recognized Rhodesia's putative independence. In addition, against the rogue government the community of states enforced a number of economic and political sanctions.[58] The response of the world community at least implied that self-determination by then constituted a part of the definition of statehood at international law. Self-determination had almost certainly become a *political* imperative, at least in a case of notorious infringement. Nonetheless, the legal parameters of the principle would remain a matter for debate.

The Republic of South Africa, in a racist policy considerably more complicated than that pursued by Rhodesia, established a series of Bantustans or "homelands."[59] These black-only territories, ensconced within South Africa, controlled land of marginal value; in some cases consisted of mutually non-contiguous enclaves;[60] and subsisted under local régimes notionally black-led but dependent upon South Africa. The international community denied recognition to the homelands from their inception in 1976,[61] and the United Nations, amplifying an earlier condemnation of South African apartheid,[62] criticized the establishment of the Bantustans as well.[63] When the Ciskei was created, the United States issued a particularly pointed reply. The American Deputy Permanent Representative to the United Nations, Kenneth Adelman, stated, "Just as the United States did not recognize Transkei, Venda and Bophuthatswana, so we will not recognize Ciskei. Why this homelands process continues when its ideology has been discredited, when its perpetuation has become ludicrous and when its practice is grounds for greater scorn remains a mystery."[64] The United States unambiguously rejected South Africa's alleged acts of state formation. The reaction of the United Nations and individual members of the community of states suggested that self-determination had begun to constitute a requisite of statehood.

Other examples point the same way. The National Liberation Army of Vietnam invaded Cambodia in 1979 and deposed Khmer Rouge dictator Pol Pot. Observers may well have celebrated the end of Khmer Rouge reign-by-terror, but the replacement régime, installed by the Vietnamese army and dependent upon Vietnam, failed to win recognition outside the Communist bloc. A deficit in self-determination was apparently the fatal flaw. If not the definition of statehood (at issue was recognition of a government) then the conditions for *recognition* appear to have acquired a new element.[65] In a more recent visitation of the matter, Judge Oda filed a Separate Opinion in the *East Timor* case. He wrote, "The principle of self-determination of peoples has been recognized by the United Nations Charter and in the jurisprudence of the Court; it is one of the essential principles of contemporary international law."[66]

## DEMOCRACY

While the era of decolonization has established some right in national groups to self-rule, whether citizens within such groups have a right to control their governments democratically is much less certain. The principle of self-determination may invalidate rule from without, but it says much less about the processes through which is conducted rule from within.

Like the proposed requisite of self-determination, democracy began tentatively to emerge as a criterion in the recognition of governments at least as early as it appeared in analyses of the recognition of states. Where a government used extreme violence or simply ignored electoral process in order to achieve power, established states hesitated to extend recognition. The ascent of the Karageorgevitch Dynasty in Serbia was perfected in a coup, the bloodiness of which shocked the opinion-forming public in the West.[67] The 1903 change of Balkan dynasty was denied recognition for some time.[68] Louis Napoleon established the Second French Empire in 1852 peacefully—but undemocratically. Switzerland and the United States, among others, withheld recognition.[69]

State practice concerning democracy only began to grow in earnest however in the late twentieth century. Writers assessing more recent instances of recognition and nonrecognition[70] have argued that state practice has accreted a criterion of democracy to the prerequisites of statehood. Supporting incorporation of democracy into the law of recognition, Crawford notes that states hesitated to recognize Guinea-Bissau after its unilateral declaration of independence from Portugal. This may have been motivated by concern over the undemocratic character of the revolutionary régime.[71] Response to the break-up of the Soviet Union further demonstrated that states now seem to attach weight to democracy. In deciding whether to recognize the secessionist republics, the European Community and the United States required that the aspirants to statehood undertake democratic reform.[72] Nonrecognition of the Noriega régime in Panama and the Cedras junta in Haiti also support a democracy requirement for recognition.

In considering whether and when to recognize Croatia, Slovenia, Bosnia-Herzegovina, and Macedonia, states indicated that the governments of those republics had to demonstrate adherence to democratic norms before recognition be extended.[73] Before January 1992, the European Community particularly wrestled over recognizing Croatia and Slovenia. The debate later shifted to Bosnia-Herzegovina and Macedonia. The European states formally incorporated democracy into the prerequisites for the receipt of recognition. On December 16, 1991, the EC held an Extraordinary Ministerial Meeting at Brussels, and the Member States adopted a set of guidelines for recognition. The *Declaration of 'Guidelines on the Recognition of New States in Eastern Europe and in the Soviet Union'* touched on democracy, reading in pertinent part, "[The Community and its Member States] affirm their readiness to recognize . . . those new States which, following the historic changes in the region, have constituted themselves *on a democratic basis.*"[74] The EC guidelines reached a broad audience of operative decision-makers-diplomats, politicians, and writers. The frequency of reference to them during the Yugoslav recognition crisis suggests that they may well have informed international practice. Professed commitment to the December 16 *Guidelines* did not however translate into practice uniformly. Recognition proceeded apace for Croatia despite some unanswered questions over General Franjo Tudjman's methods of governance, and Bosnia received recognition several months later with doubts lingering over whether the polyglot state's nascent institutions would function democratically. Democracy was overtly declared a principle relevant to recognition but did not play a deciding role in all cases.

Evidence of the emergence of democracy as an international legal prerequisite for statehood is not as solid as like evidence of self-determination. Though there may well have been a legal element in the pertinent state practice, it is difficult to disentangle from politics. The dissolution of the Soviet Union introduced instabilities into an international system that had long presupposed the permanence of the Communist bloc. It may be that the demand for proof of democratic institutions offered a means, acceptable to the policy-shaping public in the West, to delay recognition of the successor states as long as possible. The decision to delay was not however clearly based on law. Precipitous recognition of the Soviet secessionists, it was apprehended, risked a worldwide crisis. While nonrecognition was not long-lasting, the demand for proof of democratic institutions did serve as an effective, albeit temporary, break on events—a mechanism to slow a process which, for many state actors, had begun to appear far too fast. The three former constituent republics of the USSR slowest to win recognition not coincidentally lay in regions most likely to have raised international concern: the Caucasus and Central Asia. In Azerbaijan former communists would win election by a suspicious 90 per cent margin. In Georgia a celebrated poet and popular nationalist, Zviad Gamshakordia, drifted toward fascism. And in Uzbekistan a Brezhnevesque government hardly revised the Soviet mode of governance. Adoption of democracy as a prerequisite for recognition would certainly have delayed acceptance of the new states led from Baku, Tblisi, and Tashkent; and indeed democracy the western powers cited as the stumbling block there. However, in the face of evidence that democracy was still not taking root, recognition was in due course extended to these new states. The West seems to have awaited stability in Moscow, rather than democracy in the republics, and this would imply that geopolitical strategy was more at work than international law. The requirement of democracy as a condition for recognition may have been at the time no more than a practical means to "put the breaks" on a recognition process which the chancelleries feared could, if let spin out of control, foment disorder in the space of a superpower in the grips of an already perilous transition. Nonetheless, once cited as a justification in statecraft, a principle may acquire a normative force independent of its political utility in the course of a single incident. Saying that democracy matters may eventually make it matter.

In May 1997, a rebellion in Zaire unseated the régime of President Mobutu Sese Seko. The rebel leader, Laurent Kabila, declared himself president, constituted a government absent the leader of parliament, and renamed the country 'the Democratic Republic of Congo.' Kabila's ascent, though undemocratic, received rapid recognition, even, puzzlingly, from states which had for some time refrained from employing recognition upon changes of government. Response to events in Zaire/Congo may have been conditioned on the widespread opprobrium in which Kabila's predecessor had come to be held. Whoever replaced Mobutu was likely to enjoy a moment of tolerance. Its reasons aside, recognition of Kabila did not strengthen the emergent norm of democracy in international law. For the time being, it remains doubtful whether democracy is an entrenched element of the law of recognition.

## MINORITY RIGHTS

The Europe which emerged after the collapse of communism and retreat of Russia contains many minority communities which identify more with a foreign state than with the one in which they live. Such communities have remained a potential source of tension.[75] Perhaps the greatest danger posed by minorities is their tendency to render assistance to one another across state borders, thus potentially destabilizing a region. Though without commenting directly on the danger of such cross-border activity, the Permanent Court of International Justice in the *Greco-Bulgarian Communities Case* (1930)[76] was aware of the international dimension presented by the minorities question: " '[C]ommunity' is a group of persons living in a given country or locality, having a race, religion, language and traditions of their own and united by identity of race, religion, language and traditions in a sentiment of solidarity, with a view to preserving their traditions, maintaining their form of worship, ensuring the instruction and upbringing of their children in accordance with the spirit and traditions of their race and *rendering mutual assistance to each other*."[77] The secession of constituent republics of Yugoslavia and the Soviet Union focused on minority communities the attention of a western leadership and media which, for nearly half a century, had had little reason to concern themselves with the 'nationality question.'

Prior to the Second World War, however, the minorities of central and eastern Europe—especially southeastern Europe—had attracted a great deal of attention. Before World War I, European powers sometimes expressed concern over the rights of religious minorities.[78] Treaties addressed the rights of Catholics in Protestant-ruled countries,[79] the rights of Protestant minorities and Protestant states amid Catholic powers,[80] the rights of Muslims in Christian countries,[81] and the rights of Christians in the Ottoman Empire.[82] From religion, the focus during and after the World War I settlement shifted to ethnic groups. The treaties between the Allied Powers and new[83] or reconstituted[84] states contained clauses designed to protect ethnic minorities. The peace treaties with the defeated powers Austria,[85] Hungary,[86] Bulgaria,[87] and Turkey[88] contained such clauses, and declarations were required of other newly created states to demonstrate respect for minority ethnic groups.[89] Minority protection became a central concern among diplomats and international lawyers as well.[90]

With the one-time hotbed of European ethnic discontent chilled under Soviet hegemony, the post-World War II era witnessed concern over minority rights turn elsewhere. It would be states emerging out of the overseas colonial empires which raised new cases of the old question. The *Universal Declaration of Human Rights* of 1948 guaranteed the recognition of minorities.[91] A related *Convention on Prevention and Punishment of the Crime of Genocide* was also adopted by the United Nations in 1948.[92] And Article 27 of the *International Covenant on Civil and Political Rights* (1966) read, "In those States in which ethnic, religious or linguistic minorities exist, persons belonging to such minorities should not be denied the right, in the community with the other members of their group, to enjoy their own culture, to profess and practise their own religion, or to use their own language."[93] A Committee of Human Rights would hear minority rights complaints, under the framework of the 1966 Covenant. Many complaints brought before that body concerned indigenous peoples.[94]

Thus the focus of minority rights shifted over time: from denominational communities, to ethnic groups in central and eastern Europe, to former colonies, to indigenous tribes. The end of the Cold War would draw international attention back to Europe. Along the Baltic littoral at the close of World War II, the Soviet Union expelled a series of long-seated German-speaking communities. In place of the German minority (members of which had enjoyed disproportionate representation in the merchant and aristocratic classes in Lithuania and Latvia), Stalin settled ethnic Russians. At the same time, substantial fractions of the majority ethnic groups were deported to distant parts of the USSR. By the end of the 1940s, the Russian populations of Estonia, Latvia, and Lithuania not only far exceeded the old indigenous German populations; Russians constituted majorities in some towns (*e.g.*, Narva in Estonia) and dominated all aspects of government and the economy.[95] At the same time, however, the coming decades of 'Sovietization' would hardly erode the distinct identity of the Baltic nationalities, and, in fact, the Russian presence intensified animosity, providing, as it would, a conspicuous reminder of the forced expatriations of the 1940s. When the Baltic republics declared independence from the USSR,[96] it was speculated that the long-aggrieved native majorities would take vengeance against the Russians in their midst.[97]

The independence declarations of Croatia and Slovenia in June 1991 engendered similar concern. Croatia in particular was a source of worry: some twelve percent of its inhabitants were ethnic Serbs, and a history of violence marred relations between the majority and minority races. Signaling that guarantee of minority rights might have been emerging as an element of recognition law or practice, the member states of the European Community (European Union after February 1992), announced jointly their concern that the new states might disregard the rights of minorities within their boundaries. In a Report to the European Parliament (issued May 26, 1992), the Committee on Foreign Affairs and Security stated the view of the Community toward protection of minority rights: "None of the governments [in the space of the former Yugoslavia] must be permitted to subordinate the interests of others totally to its own. There are joint responsibilities that cannot be simply evaded, *e.g.* respect for human rights and the cultural and ethnic rights of minorities."[98] A number of conditions for recognition were made explicit. Crucial among these was that the new states make constitutional provision for the protection of minorities.[99] The constitutional requirements were consistent with the December 16, 1991, *Guidelines on the Recognition of New States*. The *Guidelines* required, among other things, "guarantees for the rights of ethnic and national groups and minorities in accordance with the commitments subscribed to in the framework of the CSCE."[100] The Community sufficiently conveyed the seriousness of this condition that the leaders of neither Croatia nor Slovenia believed it could be ignored: both states incorporated into their new constitutions provisions guaranteeing the rights of minorities.[101]

Minority rights in international law had a long genealogy. State recognition however had not previously been enmeshed in the minorities question. Insistence by the EC that minority rights receive formal guarantee, preferably through enshrinement in constitutional text, represented a new pressure on the norm governing recognition.

## CONSTITUTIONAL 'LEGITIMACY'

At least among American writers, if not among the wider community of decision-makers, another addition to the law of recognition has been proposed. Since the demise of Europe's two polyglot communist states (Yugoslavia and the Soviet Union), academic lawyers have suggested that any secession must possess a certain *constitutional* legitimacy if the state it generates is to receive recognition. To American legal writers, studied in federalism and its relation to constitutional law, the addition of a prerequisite of 'constitutional legitimacy' has exercised a particular attraction.

It may seem at first blush improbable that a deciding factor for recognition would be whether the entity aspiring to statehood seceded from its parent in a manner constitutionally proper within the laws of the parent. The political will to secede implies dissatisfaction with the prevailing laws and institutions of the parent state, if not their outright rejection. And the act of secession, if successful, itself nullifies those laws and institutions, at least insofar as they were instrumentalities of the union that the secessionists have dissolved. Secession seems by its very purpose and purport to exclude whole respect for the laws of the parent state. The logic of secession notwithstanding, Americans commenting on post-Cold War Europe have proposed that secessionist states satisfy domestic constitutional requirements before they receive recognition.

*Texas* v. *White*,[102] which I have already mentioned in connection with recognition and private law, can also be taken as a starting point in the American discussion of the constitutionality of secession. Texas sued to enjoin redemption of a quantity of United States bonds, held by two individuals, White and Chiles, and to compel surrender of the bonds to the Texas state treasury. (The Supreme Court possessed original jurisdiction.) A Military Board, during the Civil War, had received payment from White and Chiles as consideration for the bonds, and the Board conveyed the bonds to them. However, the alleged authority of the Board to execute such a transaction derived from the government of Texas whilst the state of Texas belonged to the Confederacy. Chief Justice Salmon P. Chase, writing for the Court, declared the contract by which the bonds changed hands "null, void, and of no effect."[103]

The *White* decision was rendered in the wake of the Civil War, which, it must be borne in mind, was an immensely costly war and, moreover, a war fought to reverse secession. It should, then, come as little surprise that the United States Supreme Court displayed little patience in *Texas* v. *White* for the proposition that the Constitution makes allowance for the unilateral departure of a constituent state from the federal Union:

> By . . . [the Articles of Confederation] the Union was solemnly declared to 'be perpetual.' And when these Articles were found to be inadequate to the exigencies of the country, the Constitution was ordained 'to form a more perfect Union.' It is difficult to convey the idea of indissoluble unity more clearly than by these words. What can be indissoluble if a perpetual Union, made more perfect, is not?[104]

The Supreme Court therefore declined to recognize the conveyance between the Military Board and defendants White and Chiles. American writers have agreed with Chief Justice Chase's view of secession as announced in *Texas* v. *White*,[105] and when considering international law, some have imported this hostility toward secession into their analysis of recognition. The proposal has followed from this that a secessionist community, to be recognized, must have abided by the constitutional rules of the parent state.

The American experience of fiercely defending federalism is consistent with a constitutional criterion. American national identity is as well. The United States does not define its nationhood by ethnic or linguistic links.[106] Whereas the European states which developed from the late eighteenth through the nineteenth centuries relied on a close identity between ethnic-linguistic nationalism and their state-building projects, the cornerstone of American statehood and nationality alike is the Constitution of 1787. Though some citizens argued that the United States possessed an Anglo-Saxon ethnic identity, from the Foundation the American republic claimed immigrants and descendants of immigrants from diverse parts of Europe. The abolition of slavery and extension of citizenship to African-Americans diversified the ethnographic base of America even more. And the last century and a quarter witnessed further additions to an already rich ethnic mosaic. "Americanness" does indeed exist, but it is a more fluid and elusive concept than the ethnic identities which are the foundation of many older nation states. Constitutional law in the United States provides more than a framework for governance; the Constitution symbolizes the Nation. The paramountcy of the Constitution both as a legal document and as an embodiment of the national identity may explain why American legal scholars have exported constitutional law into the law of secession. Erosion of the Constitution challenges American nationhood.[107]

Municipal constitutional status has interested Latin American policy makers as well. It was a former foreign minister of Ecuador, Dr. Tobar, after whom was named a doctrine of nonrecognition of illegal changes in government. The Tobar Doctrine provided, "The American Republics for the sake of their good name and credit, apart from other humanitarian or altruistic considerations, should intervene in the internal dissensions of the Republics of the Continent. Such intervention might consist at least in the non-recognition of *de facto*, revolutionary governments created contrary to the constitution."[108] The states of the Western Hemisphere would apply the Tobar Doctrine to changes of government in Nicaragua,[109] El Salvador,[110] and elsewhere.[111]

While a constitutional criterion is understandable in the American context, applying it universally exposes its flaws.

Even in the Western Hemisphere itself, the notion of a constitutional grounds for nonrecognition came under fire. The Tobar Doctrine of nonrecognition was deemed invalid by the Mexican foreign ministry. In repudiating the doctrine, Mexican Secretary of Foreign Relations, Don Genaro Estrada, established what would come to be known as the Estrada Doctrine:

recognition and nonrecognition of *governments* is not proper policy, and the state contemplating a change in the internal organization of another should simply respond to the *de facto* situation.[112]

Not all American constitutionalists' take an absolute view on secession. Cass R. Sunstein, for example, concedes that "[i]n some cases, a right to secede will be fully justified as a matter of political morality," but finds it nonetheless important to emphasize that secession lacks any constitutional justification. Joining the federal unions which many constitutions have created, Sunstein explains, waives legal right to secession.[113] Akhil Amar notes that the secession of the South from the American Union was under U.S. law illegal and argues, by extension, that secessions in post-Cold War Europe were also illegal.[114] It is in this, what might be termed strong-form manifestation of the American constitutionalist view, that the proposition is open to question.

Taken in narrow terms—that is, in terms of municipal law—the propositions of the American commentators are sustainable: uncontrolled self-dissolution a federal order can hardly endorse in its constitutive texts or allow in practice. However, in the broader compass of international law, an insistence on domestic constitutionality is not entirely logical.[115] Constitutionalism as a criterion for statehood lacks force in theory as well as practice.

The proposition is dubious that recognition of new states, a process traditionally entrusted to the foreign affairs authority of a state and possibly even within the province of international decision-making, should be subject to such an essentially parochial rule as that governing internal federal relations. Whether one subscribes to the view of international law as superior to municipal law (after Lauterpacht)[116] or to the view of international law as a basic norm of national law (after Kelsen),[117] the role of constitutionality in adjudging secession remains minimal. If international law supersedes domestic, then artifacts of international law (*e.g.*, self-determination and territorial integrity) override the domestic constitutional mandate. If international law is an integral part of municipal law, then domestic institutions must reconcile the transnational with the parochial in their nation's codified or constitutionalized norms; however they do this, the result does not rebound to change international law. Kelsen proposed that international law permeates domestic law; not that the rules in force in a single state define public international law for all states. Notwithstanding the role assigned international law in the parent state, the question posed to other states (*i.e.*, whether to recognize the secessionist) is answered by reference to international law, as understood by the world—not the parent state. Recognition, though perhaps unilateral and discretionary, remains a subject of international law.

This may at first blush appear self-contradictory. Recognition would seem to have little to do with law, if it is unilateral and discretionary. However, the issue here is one of legislative competence. If any rules govern the effects and the propriety of recognition, they are rules legislated by the world community. The world community may legislate international law in numerous ways. It may codify rules through multilateral conventions, either general or particular. It may form a body of juristic opinion through organs of dispute resolution, both permanent and ad hoc, as well as through the teachings of the most qualified publicists. It may shape rules through state practice.[118] The world community may also decline to legislate. Lack of a clear-cut rule at a given time on a given matter does not have the effect of stripping the world community of its law-making competence. Even if recognition is at present purely political—that is to say, a unilateral and discretionary process—recognition remains a subject susceptible to international legislation. In the traditional view of recognition—recognition as a unilateral act left to individual state discretion—it is the absence of an international norm on recognition, not the operation of a municipal rule, which sets the parameters of state conduct. A self-help regime of recognition does not come from national legislation, but from a supposed vacuum of relevant international law. Whatever the content of the norm governing recognition—whether it is discretionary or rule-bound, unilateral or collective, some intermediate form among these, or *contentless*—international society retains legislative competence. The nature of recognition—a statement by one state toward another (or toward a community aspiring to statehood)—makes recognition a subject of international rather than municipal law. A proposal to introduce municipal ordering principles into the law of recognition is therefore dubious.

As a subject of international law, recognition is not governed by rules lacking crossborder effect. The norm governing recognition historically has, indeed, contained only elements with substantial bearing on relations among states. Self-determination, democracy, and guaranties to minorities—the first three of what I have discussed as addenda to the Montevideo list—all possess fairly evident contacts to international affairs. Self-determination means that distinct national groups have the right either to organize themselves under a state particular to the group or to manage some aspects of their own affairs within another state. To deny such right would call into question the nation state, still arguably a key organizing force in public international law and international relations. Democracy is a less firmly-rooted criterion, but it is nonetheless arguable that democracy constitutes such an important principle to the leading state actors today that it deserves some degree of acknowledgment in the law of recognition. Further, proponents of democracy would argue, undemocratic régimes are a destabilizing element in the international system. (Consider North Korea and Iraq, as well as the classic proposition that democracies do not go to war against one another.) The third proposed addendum, minority rights guarantee, serves a certain systemic international interest as well. Such guarantee assuages the fears of proximate states whose ethnic brethren might face persecution under alien rule, and they quiet domestic opposition, the activities of which could otherwise spill into the inter-state arena. It should also be recalled that minority rights and democracy have received international support, most recently in the cases of Haiti and Iraqi Kurdistan. The first three addenda—self-determination, democracy, and minority rights—bear close links to international order. Domestic constitutional text does not.

Finally, the proposed criterion of constitutionality possesses little momentum in state practice—at least in terms of constitutionality *qua* constitutionality.[119] A comparison of two cases demonstrates this. Writers in the 1920s and 1930s assumed that the constitutive norms of the British Commonwealth provided no right to secession.[120] However, Eamon de Valera did sever all remaining ties between Ireland and the United Kingdom, and the last steps of this secession (in the 1930s) were peaceful.[121] By contrast, the Soviet Constitution explicitly permitted secession, and any attempt to assert independence from Moscow was suppressed.[122] Taken together, Ireland and the Soviet republics reveal no correspondence between constitutional provision for secession and actual conduct of the parent state. Whether constitutional text influences the decision by foreign states whether to recognize a secessionist is also dubious.

The constitution in force at the time of the disintegration of Yugoslavia had been created in 1974 by amendments to a preexisting constitution. Article 1 provided the textual basis for a federal Yugoslavia, declaring the country a "state community of voluntarily united nations and their Socialist Republics."[123] Article 5 provided that any republic could secede, but only with unanimous consent of the others. Under this rule, secession of Croatia and Slovenia was illegal. However, such municipal illegality played little role in staying states from recognizing the independence of the former constituent republics.

While state practice is not much moved by the intrinsic legal value of constitutions, it is concerned with systemic implications of unconstitutional conduct. Disregard for the strictures of the constitutional legal order within its parent state frees an independence-seeking entity to behave in a manner disruptive of the order within, at the very narrowest, its immediate federal community. As a precedential matter, such disregard poses a danger. Unilateral, willful conduct within the near community may spill over or be generalized to conduct within the international community. Unilateral action, oblivious to constitutive rules both in the parent federation and in the broader community of states, is a threat that may be described in terms of constitutionality and from which valid international concern may arise. The legal source here is not however the parent state's constitutional text. Unfettered discretionary conduct by new states may exact an unacceptable toll on an order increasingly rooted in collective action and collective decision-making. Neither idealist concern over the innate value of constitutions nor incorporation of domestic constitutional law into public international law is a good reason to involve constitutions in the process of recognition. Rather, insofar as constitutionality can join the roster of recognition criteria, it would do so in anticipation of the international systemic costs incurred when unconstitutional behavior is generalized from within federation boundaries to the external world. What the American writers identify as a constitutional criterion for recognition may in truth be the principle of territorial integrity. The principle is well-established, but it has its source in state practice and *opinio juris*, as well as in treaty and convention texts—not in municipal law. In any case, constitutionality *per se* has not yet generated a body of state practice and *opinio juris* like that surrounding the emergent norms of democracy and minority rights.

The plausible objection under international law to 'unconstitutional' secession—that a régime unmindful of internal constitutional law may well, on that precedent, equally disregard the law of states—differs from the objections of American writers. Amar attaches importance to constitutionality for its own sake. Cobban, by contrast, was antagonistic toward secession for reasons of systemic risk—but not quite the same systemic risk as identified here. Cobban wrote, "Since [secession] is generally a work of destruction, and a breaking down of established connections, it can hardly be a good thing in itself."[124] Though an absolute rule of sovereignty would be tantamount to totalitarianism, Cobban wrote, an absolute right of secession would lead to anarchy. Possessed of that right, minority communities everywhere, from the French of North America to the smallest ethnic group Africa, would splinter off their parent states, rendering international order as we know it unviable (based as international order is on states).[125] According to Cobban, the threat of runaway secession comes from self-determination taken too far, not constitutionality ignored.[126] My proposition, then, follows Cobban at least in the broad sense: the potentially adverse systemic effect of secession is what convinces statesmen to restrain communities from seeking statehood. It is in accord with Amar, in the narrow sense that constitutionality matters: if an independence movement treats municipal constitutional norms cavalierly, what are the prospects that as a state it will respect international law?

Rejecting 'constitutional legitimacy' as a gauge for recognition should not however exclude municipal law from the analysis of a claim to statehood. Alan James has proposed that possession of an independent constitution distinguishes states from non-states:

> It is frequently said that the criterion [sic] for statehood consist of territory, people, and government. However, this is insufficient for the formally unhindered playing of the international game. There are many entities which display these characteristics—the constituent states of federations, for example—which make no international appearances. The reason is simple. Such appearances can be made by territorial entities in their own right only if they have an additional qualification—what states, in this connection, call sovereignty. . . . The content given, by states, and just in this specific

connection, to the concept of sovereignty, is constitutional independence. A territorial entity must have a constitution which is independent of other constitutions to be termed, in the specified sense, sovereign, and hence able to look forward to membership in the collectivity of states.[127]

James proposes the constitution as a measure of statehood, but not in Amar's sense. Amar argues that adherence to constitutional rules is prerequisite to formation of a new state; James argues that constitutional independence signals that a putative state is really independent. The two are related in that both conceive of an international legal process inquiring into domestic constitutional law. They differ in that Amar would exclude from recognition a fully independent polity which violated municipal law of the parent state. James would focus inquiry not on the mode of independence but on its fact.

It was once assumed that statehood consisted simply in the ability of a government to exercise control over a definite territory and people. How it governed or how it came to govern did not matter as much as the fact of power. Changes in how we approach recognition or define statehood have however pushed to amend the traditional view. It may even be that changes in conceptions of recognition and statehood have pushed the law away from mere reflection of fact toward principles with normative content. Perhaps with law no longer wedded to the idea of territorial power, the way will be open to idealist reform. However, not all writers who rejected legal positivism assumed that adding a criterion such as democracy in fact would make recognition more principled. Lauterpacht wrote, "Once considerations of that nature are introduced as a condition of recognition, the clear path of law is abandoned and the door wide open to arbitrariness, to attempts at extortion, and to intervention at the very threshold of statehood."[128] Changes in a norm, though inspired by human rights concerns or the goal of a legally regulated international society, may create new avenues for political opportunism.

A further caveat is necessary. Criteria for recognition which spring from political calculus have entered international usage from time to time. The criteria of self-determination, democracy, minority rights, and constitutionality may well number among the politically-inspired amendments to traditional views in the field. As such, their positions in international law are less secure than the more basic criteria. Politics is not new to international law, nor is international law closed to reform initiated in the political dimension. However, state practice is sometimes characterized as conditioned by legal obligation when, on scrutiny, politics, not law, is the real force motivating practice. Several criteria arising over the past century and a half did not last long and thus did not turn into law. Resolution Number XXII of the Emergency Advisory Committee for Political Defense of the Inter-American Treaty (December 23, 1943) declared that no government in the Americas at war with the Axis powers or aiding in the Allied war effort would recognize a new American government coming to power through force, unless recognition was agreed upon by the parties. The criterion for recognition was that the new government "complies with the inter-American guarantees for the defense of the Continent."[129] This anti-Axis criterion, in retrospect, was destined for obsolescence. Not so clearly time-bound but nonetheless ultimately insecure in international law was Secretary of State Stimson's policy, in response to Japan's creation of Manchukuo, that the United States would not recognize states originating from violence.[130] Nineteenth-century practice furnished another example of an essentially political criterion failing to persist and become legally binding. The Holy Alliance (Prussia, Austria, and Russia) vowed to suppress democracy and nationalism in order to preserve against these new political forces the existing monarchical order. *Legitimacy* became the by-word for imperial statesmen when evaluating new governments and states. If a claimant community did not have at its head a 'legitimate' royal household, then recognition would be collectively denied.[131] By the late nineteenth century, when nationalism and popular governance had gained strength, legitimacy, in the sense promoted by the Holy Alliance, was no longer a criterion for recognition. Political conditions for recognition which the world community or regional groups have tried to incorporate into international or regional law in few instances have had a stable existence.

## NOTES

1. James Lorimer, *The Institutes of the Law of Nations* (Edinburgh: William Blackwood and Sons, 1883), 107.

2. *See* Thomas D. Grant, "Defining Statehood: The Montevideo Convention and its Discontents," 37 *Columbia Journal of Transnational Law* 403 (1998).

3. President Woodrow Wilson, to the United States Congress, 56 *Congressional Record* (Cong. Rec.) 1,952 (1918).

4. It has been suggested that the ideas associated with the term 'Wilsonianism' did not originate with the twenty-eighth President and were not actually given much effect by that President. David notes that Wilsonianism was espoused by prominent members of the early Franklin Roosevelt administration (including William Phillips, the under secretary of state; Cordell Hull, the secretary of state; James F. Byrnes, the leading Democrat in the Senate; and Edward M. House, Wilson's chief advisor on Europe and FDR's foreign policy expert in 1933) but was followed between 1913 and 1921 by Wilson himself only sporadically. Moreover, Fromkin proposes that Wilsonianism was not original but an amalgam of ideas coming into the fore in the decades prior to Wilson's presidency. David Fromkin, "What is Wilsonianism?" XI *World Policy Journal* (World Pol'y J.) 100, 106 (1994) For an exhaustive examination of the use and legal development of the term 'self-determination,' see Jorri C. Duursma, *Fragmentation and the International Relations of Micro-States: Self-Determination and Statehood* (Cambridge: Cambridge University Press, 1996), 8–109. Duursma focuses particularly on UN practice.

5. M. J. Peterson, "Recognition of Governments Should Not Be Abolished," 77

*American Journal of International Law* (AJIL) 31, 37 (1983). Self-determination was not the only consideration which shaped the American stance toward these two régimes. Certain perceived national interests were also in play. The United States during the nineteenth century professed to follow the Monroe Doctrine, *i.e.*, that European influence in the Western Hemisphere be limited to that already entrenched. In its original formulation, the Doctrine held:

> [W]e should consider any attempt on their part to extend their system to any portion of this hemisphere as dangerous to our peace and safety. With the existing colonies or dependencies of any European power we have not interfered and shall not interfere. But with the governments who have declared their independence and maintained it, and whose independence we have . . . acknowledged, we could not view any interposition for the purpose of oppressing them, or controlling in any other manner their destiny, by any European power, in any other light than as a manifestation of an unfriendly disposition toward the United States.

Message of President Monroe, December 2, 1823. John Bassett Moore, *Digest of International Law*. vol. vi (Washington, DC: Government Printing Office, 1906), 402, §936. The adverse response to Maximilian was informed as much by the Monroe Doctrine as by international law.

6. Robert Lansing, *The Peace Negotiations, A Personal Narrative* (Port Washington, NY: Kennikat Press, 1921), 97–98. Quoted, in part, in Alfred Cobban, *The Nation State and National Self-Determination* (London: Collins, 1969) (1st ed., Oxford: Oxford University Press, 1945), 62.

7. Philip Marshall Brown, "The Legal Effects of Recognition," 44 AJIL 617, 621 (1950).

8. UN Doc. A/C.3/SR.644 (1955) p. 101, ¶ 15. Quoted at Duursma, *Micro-States*, 31.

9. Andrew Burghardt, "Marxism and Self-Determination: The Case of Burgenland, 1919" in *Nationalism, Self-Determination and Political Geography*. R.J. Johnston, David B. Knight & Eleonore Kofman eds. (London: Croom Helm, 1988), 57, 58.

10. On the eastern German transfers, see Nathaniel Berman, " 'But the Alternative is Despair': European Nationalism and the Modernist Renewal of International Law," 106 *Harvard Law Review* (Harv. L. Rev.) 1792, 1859–98 (1993).

11. Report of the Committee of Rapporteurs (Beyens, Calonder, & Elkens) April 16, 1921. League of Nations Council Document B7/21/68/106 [VII], 22–23. Also quoted in James R. Crawford, *The Creation of States in International Law* (Oxford: Clarendon Press, 1979), 86.

12. *See, e.g.*, Quincy Wright, "Recognition and Self-Determination," 1954 *American Society of International Law Proceedings* (ASIL Proc.) 23 (noting that, from late 1954, the United Nations began giving "great emphasis" to self-determination as an element of the requirement that, to be recognized, a polity have a stable government).

13. See, e.g., W. Ofuatey-Kodjoe, *The Principle of Self-Determination in International Law* (New York: Nellen Publishing Company, Inc., 1977); Cobban, *National Self-Determination*; Harold Johnson, *Self-Determination within the Community of Nations* (Leyden: A.W. Sijthoff, 1967); U.O. Umozurike, *Self-Determination in International Law* (Hamden, CT: Archon Books, 1972); Michla Pomerance, "The United States and Self-Determination: Perspectives on the Wilsonian Conception," 70 AJIL 20 (1976); and Lee Buchheit, *Secession: The Legitimacy of Self-Determination* (New

Haven: Yale University Press, 1978). A number of these works are also relevant to the constitutionality of independence, an issue of particular interest to American commentators. For more recent analyses of self-determination, see Nathaniel Berman, "Sovereignty in Abeyance: Self-Determination and International Law," 7 *Wisconsin International Law Journal* (Wisc. Int'l L.J.) 51 (1988); and Patrick Thornberry, *International Law and the Rights of Minorities* (Oxford: Clarendon Press, 1991); Robert McCorquodale, "Self-Determination: A Human Rights Approach," 43 *International & Comparative Law Quarterly* (ICLQ) 857 (1994); Martti Koskenniemi, "National Self-Determination Today: Problems of Legal Theory and Practice," 43 ICLQ 241 (1994).

14. Article 21, *Universal Declaration of Human Rights*, General Assembly Resolution. 217A, UN Document A/810, at 71, 75 (1948).

15. *Declaration on the Granting of Independence to Colonial Countries and Peoples*, General Assembly Resolution 1514, 15 UN GAOR Supp. (No.16) at 66, UN Document A/4684 (1961).

16. Declaration on Principles of International Law Concerning Friendly Relations and Cooperation Among States in Accordance with the Charter of the United Nations, General Assembly Resolution 2625, 25 UN GAOR Supp. (No. 28) at 121, UN Document A/80229 (1971).

17. Legal Consequences for States of the Continued Presence of South Africa in Namibia (South West Africa) notwithstanding Security Council Resol. 276 (1970). Advisory Opinion, ICJ Reports, 1971, pp. 6, 31.

18. *Western Sahara Case* (*Morocco* v. *Spain*). Advisory Opinion, ICJ Reports, 1975, p. 12, ¶¶ 31–33.

19. *Case Concerning East Timor* (*Portugal* v. *Australia*). ICJ Reports, 1995. Analyses of Namibia, Western Sahara, and East Timor appear in John Dugard, "*Namibia (South West Africa):* The Court's Opinion, South Africa's Response, and Prospects for the Future," 11 *Columbia Journal of Transnational Law* (Colum. J. Transnat'l L.) 14 (1972); Antony J.M. Zuijdwijk, "The International Court and South West Africa: Latest Phase," 3 *Georgia Journal of International & Comparative Law* (Ga. J. Int'l & Comp. L.) 323 (1973); John F. Murphy, "Whither Now Namibia?" 6 *Cornell International Law Journal* (Cornell Int'l L. J.) 1 (1972); Laurence S. Hanauer, "The Irrelevance of Self-Determination Law to Ethno-national Conflict: A New Look at the Western Sahara Case," 9 *Emory International Law Review* (Emory Int'l L. Rev.) 133, 134 (1995); Brian F. Fitzgerald, "*Portugal* v. *Australia*: Deploying the Missiles of Sovereign Autonomy and Sovereign Community," 37 Harvard International Law Journal (HILJ) 260 (1996). *See also* James Crawford, "The General Assembly, the International Court and Self-determination," in *Fifty Years of the International Court of Justice: Essays in honour of Sir Robert Jennings*. Vaughan Lowe & Malgosia Fitzmaurice eds. (Cambridge: Cambridge University Press, 1996), 585 (discussing East Timor); Antonio Cassese, *Self-Determination of Peoples: A Legal Reappraisal* (Cambridge: Cambridge University Press, 1995), 223–30, 214–18 (discussing East Timor and Western Sahara).

20. Crawford, *Creation of States*, 88–89.

21. Ibid., 81 & n. 16.

22. Ibid., 84.

23. Ibid., 99–101.

24. Crawford however documents that many writers as late as the early 1970s re-

jected self-determination as part of customary international law. Among the sceptics were Sir Gerald Fitzmaurice, 55 *Institut de Droit International, Livre du Centenaire* (1973), 196, 233; Jan Hendrik Willem Verzijl, *International Law in Historical Perspective*. vol. I (Leiden: A.W. Sijthoff, 1968), 324 (proposing self-determination "has always been the sport of national or international politics and has never been recognized as a genuine positive right of 'peoples' of universal and impartial application, and it never will, nor can be so recognized in the future."); Yehuda Z. Blum, "Reflections on the Changing Concept of Self-Determination," 10 *Israel Law Review* (Israel L.R.) 509, 514 (1975) (calling self-determination a concept "manipulated [insincerely] by the international community to suit changing political needs. . . . the exercise [of which] . . . by any given people depends not on the existence of this right in abstracto but rather on the ability of such people to implement its right to self-determination."); Rupert Emerson, "Self-Determination," 65 AJIL 459, 475 (1971) ("The realistic issue is still not whether a people is qualified for and deserves the right to determine its own destiny but whether it has the political strength, which may well mean the military force, to validate its claim."); Dermott J. Devine, "The Status of Rhodesia in International Law," 1974 *Acta Juridica* (Capetown) 109, 183 (noting post-World War II support among publicists for self-determination but doubting that state practice sustains the principle); C. Wilfred Jenks, *Law in the World Community* (London: Longman, Green and Co. Ltd., 1967), 134–49, 141 ("Though the United Nations Covenants on Human Rights provide that all peoples have the right of self-determination, it is difficult . . . to give any measurable content to such a right. . . . [T]he claim to political equality remains a political matter."). Crawford, *Creation of States*, 95–96 n. 72. Quotations not in Crawford cites.

25. On Duursma's treatment of self-determination, *see* Thomas D. Grant, "Review Article: Between Diversity and Disorder (Jorri C. Duursma, *Fragmentation and the International Relations of Micro-States: Self-Determination and Statehood* (Cambridge: Cambridge University Press, 1996))," 12 *American University Journal of International Law & Policy* (Am. U. J. Int'l L. & Pol'y) 629, 632–50 (1997).

26. This mirrors Wilson, as quoted at the beginning of this chapter.

27. Duursma, *Micro-States*, 78.

28. Ibid., 78–79.

29. *See, e.g.*, Matthew C.R. Craven, "What's in a Name? The Former Yugoslav Republic of Macedonia and Issues of Statehood," 16 *Australian Yearbook of International Law* (Austral. YIL) 199, 220–21 (1995); Malcolm N. Shaw, *International Law*. 3rd ed. (Cambridge: Grotius Publications Ltd., 1991), 302–05.

30. Duursma, *Micro-States*, 81.

31. Biafra in the late 1960s and Bosnia in the early 1990s provide cases in point. On the former, see David A. Ijalaye, "Was 'Biafra' at any Time a State in International Law?" 65 AJIL 551 (1971); John J. Stremlau, *The International Politics of the Nigerian Civil War, 1967–1970* (Princeton: Princeton University Press, 1977). On Bosnia, see Laura Silber, "Bosnia Asks Recognition from EC: Four Republics Seek Independence," *Washington Post* (Wash. Post), December 21, 1991, A15; Hans W. Maull, "Germany in the Yugoslav Crisis: From Assertiveness to Impotence" (unpublished paper under auspices of Deutsche Forschungsgemeinschaft) (on file with author); Alexander Mühlen, "Die deutsche Rolle bei der Anerkennung der jugoslawischen Sezessionsstaaten," 2 *Liberal* 9 (1992); A.V. Lowe & Colin Warbrick, "Recognition of States," 41 ICLQ 473, 474–80 (1992).

32. Duursma, *Micro-States*, 80.

33. Duursma cites the unifications of Germany and Yemen in 1990. Duursma, *Micro-States*, 81–82.

34. A number of colonies were declared by European colonial powers to constitute integral parts of the metropolitan State. Prominent examples included French Algeria and Portuguese Angola. With this fiction rejected, divorce of the colonies from the colonial power no longer posed a threat to the territorial integrity of the colonial power.

35. Duursma, *Micro-States*, 82–83. Duursma mentions the problem of heterogeneous colonies and concludes that self-determination units need not be homogeneous. I wonder however whether the problem of the ethnically multifarious territory deserves more attention. Secessionists in Biafra, Katanga, or Kashmir would probably have contested the proposition that self-determination is not effected by the presence of multiple peoples in one territorial unit. *See* Ijalaye, "Biafra," 65 AJIL 551; Stremlau, *Nigerian Civil War*; Alexis Heraclides, "Katanga," in *The Self-Determination of Minorities in International Politics* (London: Frank Cass, 1991), 71–75; John Dugard, *Recognition and the United Nations* (Cambridge: Grotius Publications Limited, 1987), 86–90; Hari Om Agarwal, *Kashmir Problem: Its legal aspects* (Allahabad: Kitab Mahal, 1979).

36. Duursma, *Micro-States*, 80–88.

37. Ibid., 89.

38. Ibid., 90–91.

39. *See Reparations for Injuries Suffered in the Service of the United Nations*. ICJ Reports, 1949, pp. 171, 185.

40. Duursma, *Micro-States*, 92.

41. Duursma acknowledges this and agrees that "[w]hether an entity is a State is a matter of fact, not of recognition." Duursma, *Micro-States*, 111. She cites to the ambundant scholarship tending to support a declaratory conception of recognition. Duursma, *Micro-States*, 111 n. 10.

42. *See* Duncan B. Hollis, "Accountability in Chechnya–Addressing Internal Matters with Legal and Political International Norms," 36 *Boston College Law Review* (Bos. Col. L. Rev.) 793 (1995) (proposing non-recognition of Chechnya evidences the constitutive doctrine in operation). *See also* Trent N. Tappe, "Chechnya and the State of Self-Determination in a Breakaway Region of the Former Soviet Union: Evaluating the Legitimacy of Secessionist Claims," 34 Colum. J. Transnat'l L. 255 (1995).

43. *See* Harry R. Strack, *Sanctions: The Case of Rhodesia* (Syracuse: Syracuse University Press, 1978), 2–3; Myres S. McDougal & W. Michael Reisman, "Rhodesia and the United Nations: The Lawfulness of International Concern," 62 AJIL 1, 3 (1968); J.E.S. Fawcett, "Security Council Resolutions on Rhodesia," 41 *British Yearbook of International Law* (BYIL) 103, 112 (1965–66).

44. *See* Louis Cavaré, "La Reconnaissance de l'État et le Mandchoukouo," XLII *Revue Générale de Droit International Public* (RGDIP) 5, 8–10 (1935); H.J. Timperley, "Japan in Manchukuo," 1934 *Foreign Affairs* (For. Aff.) 295. It is not clear how many States recognized Manchukuo. Philip C. Jessup reported that only four countries recognized Manchukuo: El Salvador, Germany, Italy, and Hungary. *See* Philip C. Jessup, *The Birth of Nations* (New York: Columbia University Press, 1974), 334. Another writer however also lists Poland, the Vatican, and the Dominican Republic.

*See* Mo Shen, *Japan in Manchuria: An Analytical Study of Treaties and Documents*, (Manila: Grace Trading Co., Inc., 1960), 299–300.

45. Duursma, *Micro-States*, 92–96. Racially discriminatory rule, Duursma proposes, might be an exception.

46. Yugoslavia is Duursma's better example here. She also mentions the USSR. Duursma, *Micro-States*, 96–97.

47. Duursma, *Micro-States*, 98–99. For the view that Chechnya possessed the attributes of a State, see Hollis. "Chechnya," 36 Bos. Col. L. Rev. 793 (1995). Hollis proposes that recognition must be constitutive of statehood, for Chechnya had the internal attributes of a State, yet did not enjoy protection under international law as a State. Chechnya was not widely recognized. Hollis reports that Kuwait and Saudi Arabia alone took steps toward recognizing Chechnya. Elsewhere, however, it has been indicated that Lithuania, Estonia, Azerbaijan, Turkey, and Iran extended recognition. *See* Bogdan Szajkowski, *Encyclopaedia of Conflict, Disputes, and Flashpoints in Eastern Europe, Russia, and the Successor States* (Harlow, UK: Longman Group, 1993), 63.

48. Duursma, Micro-States, 101. Duursma cites as evidence Eritrea, the Krajina (in Croatia), Nagorno Karabakh, the Republika Srpska (in Bosnia-Herzegovina), and Chechnya.

49. Duursma, *Micro-States*, 101. This accords with Hollis on Chechnya. He identifies human rights law as the most important contact point between the Chechen conflict and international law. The hesitancy of the international community to address a matter internal to Russia prevented the United Nations from seising itself of the issue. UN action was limited to statements and a fund-raising appeal by the UN High Commission on Refugees and a February 27, 1995, statement by the Chairman of the UN Commission on Human Rights. *See* 49 *Yearbook of the United Nations* 925, 819–20 (1995). OSCE statements concerning the conduct of warfare in Chechnya addressed humanitarian concerns, not the issue of the self-determination of the Chechens. *See* OSCE Press Communication 32/95, April 1, 1995, quoted in Antonio Tanca, "La Politique Etrangère et de Sécurité Commune de l'Union européenne en 1995," 7 *European Journal of International Law* (EJIL) 447, 454 (1996). Note, however, that James Crawford has pointed out another contact between the events in Chechnya and international law—the conventional force reduction treaties. As well as to humanitarian law, international concern over Russian conduct in Chechnya has referred to Russia's obligations under those treaties to limit the number of certain weapons in European Russia. Pursuant to its anti-secessionist campaign in Chechnya, Russia deployed military resources in excess of those permitted under the treaties. *See Treaty on Conventional Armed Forces in Europe*, Paris, November 19, 1990, Art. V. Reprinted at 30 ILM 1 (1991); James R. Crawford, Report: *State Practice and International Law in Relation to Unilateral Secession*, February 19, 1997, pp. 34–36, ¶¶ 57–58. Posted at `http://canada.justice.gc.ca/News/Communiques/1997/factum/craw_en.html` (visited February 20, 1998).

50. Duursma, *Micro-States*, 102. This last proposition is consistent with Duursma's constitutivist leaning. One of the problems commonly associated with constitutivism is that the doctrine posits entities outside the protection of international law. If rights of statehood depend on recognition, the unrecognized entity lacks those rights. The declaratory view seems more consistent with the contemporary emphasis on rights: even absent recognition, an entity or at least the people inhabiting it still enjoy the

protections of international law. Duursma apparently steps away from this view. Territorial integrity of the secessionist entity, the author writes, is guaranteed only after recognition. For the declaratist view, see James L. Brierly, *The Law of Nations: An Introduction to the International Law of Peace.* Sir Humphrey Waldock ed., 6th ed. (Oxford: Clarendon Press, 1963), 139.

51. Duursma, *Micro-States*, 103.

52. Dugard, *Recognition*, 127–131.

53. Dugard suggested that the Transkei was approaching something akin to real independence, at least to the point that it might have become a thorn in the side of its apartheid creators. John Dugard, *Human Rights and the South African Legal Order* (Princeton: Princeton University Press, 1978), 96. *See also* Dugard, *Recognition*, 100 & n. 98.

54. Fawcett, "Rhodesia," 41 BYIL at 112 (1965–66); Fawcett, "Note in reply to D. J. Devine's 'The requirements of Statehood Re-Examined' " (Devine article at 34 *Modern Law Review* (Mod. L. Rev.) 410), 34 Mod. L. Rev. 417 (1971). Devine doubted the proposition that a right to self-determination has entered the law of recognition; Fawcett took a more optimistic view.

55. Crawford, *Creation of States, passim.*

56. Fawcett, "Rhodesia," 41 BYIL at 112.

57. Crawford, *Creation of States*, 105–06.

58. McDougal & Reisman, "Rhodesia," 62 AJIL at 3. The sanctions regime against Rhodesia ultimately proved as complete as any in history. Even South Africa, the tacit patron of the Smith government, finally cut the rogue state's one link to the world. On South Africa's eventual curtailment of support for Rhodesia, see Christopher Ashley Ford, *Defensor Fidei: Explaining South African Foreign Policy Behavior: The Case of Ian Smith's Rhodesia* (Unpublished Harvard undergraduate Prize Thesis. Harvard University Library, HU89.184.756).

59. *See Status of the Transkei Act* (South Africa), July 9, 1976. Reprinted at 15 *International Legal Materials* (ILM) 1. The nominally self-governing homelands were Bophuthatswana, Venda, the Ciskei, and the Transkei. Six additional "non-independent" homelands were also created: Gazankulu, KaNgwane, KwaNdebele, KwaZulu, Lebow, and QwaQwa.

60. Note in particular the archipelago-like dispersal of Bophuthatswana. The territory of that 'Homeland' comprised a string of noncontiguous areas abutting or ensonced within three South African provinces (the Cape, Orange Free State, and Transvaal). *See The Times Atlas of the World.* comp. ed. (London: John Bartholomew & Son Limited, 1981), plates 94 & 95.

61. For discussion of the international legal status of the South African homelands, *see* John Dugard, "South Africa's 'Independent' Homelands: An Exercise in Denationalization," 10 *Journal of International Legal Policy* (J. Int'l L. Pol'y) 11 (1980), addressing in particular the effects of nonrecognition on the inhabitants of the Bantustans. Bantustan inhabitants effectively possessed no citizenship: the establishment of the homelands stripped them of South African citizenship and bestowed upon them citizenship of unrecognized states. Such citizenship was of dubious value. New, Bantustan-issued passports, for example, were of no use outside South Africa. *See also* Johan D. van der Vyver, "Statehood in International Law," 5 Emory Int'l L. Rev. 9, 13–20 (1991).

62. *See Policies of Apartheid of the Government of South Africa*, G.A. Res. 3411,

UN GAOR, 30th Sess., Supp. No. 34, at 37, UN Document A/10034 (1975).

63. *See* G.A. Res. 31/6 A, UN GAOR, 31st Sess., Supp. No. 39, at 10, UN Document A/31/39 (1976).

64. Marian Nash Leich, *Cumulative Digest of US Practice in International Law, 1981–1988* (Washington, DC: United States Government Printing Office/Department of State Publications, 1993), 272–76. Quoting from 77th plenary meeting of the 36th session of the UN General Assembly.

65. At the same time, the principle of self-determination faces constraints, especially in the form of the requirements of international order. *See, e.g.*, A. Rigo Sureda, *The Evolution of the Right of Self-Determination: A Study of United Nations Practice* (Leiden: A.W. Sijthoff, 1973), 288–293. Sureda observed that in Cyprus in the 1960s the international community moderated the principle of self-determination in order to preserve regional stability. According to another writer, "It is true that the concept of self-determination is subject to considerable doubt as regards its scope and subject." Obed Y. Asamoah, *The Legal Significance of the Declarations of the General Assembly of the United Nations* (The Hague: Nijhoff, 1966). Cited in Ofuatey-Kodjoe, *Self-Determination*, 149–151. For yet another skeptical view of self-determination, see Hanauer, "Western Sahara," 9 Emory Int'l L. Rev. 133 (proposing that self-determination remains "still no more than a political and moral ideal" and not a legal norm).

66. *East Timor.* Separate Opinion, Judge Oda, ICJ Reports, 1995 at p. 102, ¶ 29.

67. *See* Milan R. Ivanovitch, "The Servian Massacre," 84 *Contemporary Review* (July 1903) 62–78; Johnston Charles, "The Servian Tragedy," 177 *North American Review* (July 1903) 12–21; Cedomilj Mijatoic, *A Royal Tragedy: Being the Story of the Assassination of King Alexander and Queen Draga of Serbia* (New York: Dodd, Mead, 1907). It may well be that the popular press constitutes one of the important forces in a recognition crisis. Public opinion, shaped substantially by the media, indeed appears to have driven diplomatic response during the Yugoslav recognition crisis of 1991–1992, as it appears also to have done in the Serbian crisis nearly a century earlier.

68. Peterson, "Recognition," 77 AJIL at 37.

69. Ibid., 37.

70. On the importance of nonrecognition as a legal doctrine and as a tool in international affairs, see Dugard, *Recognition*, chapters 5 & 6.

71. Crawford, *Creation of States*, 260–261.

72. Mikhail Gorbachev resigned on December 26, 1991, and the Soviet Union came to an end. After the failed putsch of August 1991, dissolution of the Union had accelerated. As early as March of 1991, Lithuania had declared its intent to leave the USSR. Georgia had declared independence on April 9, 1991. Most of the remaining republics declared independence in the immediate aftermath of the attempted coup: Estonia on August 20, Ukraine on August 24, Belarus on the 25th, Moldova on the 27th, Azerbaijan on the 30th, Uzbekistan and Kyrgyzstan on the 31st, Lithuania and Latvia on September 6, Tajikistan on September 9, and Armenia on September 23. Russia itself declared independence from the USSR on August 24, 1991. Turkmenistan took its independence on October 27, and Kazakhstan waited until December 16. Central Intelligence Agency, *The World Factbook 1993–1994* (Washington: Brassey's, 1993), 124, 104–05, 352, 32–33, 229–30, 24, 362, 190, 202–03, 192–93, 332–33, 16–17, 287, 347–48, 180.

73. M. Kelly Malone, "Comment: The Rights of Newly Emerging Democratic States Prior to International Recognition and the Serbo-Croatian Conflict," 6 *Temple International and Comparative Law Journal* (Temple Int'l & Comp. L.J.) 81, 83 (1992).

74. Emphasis supplied. The Guidelines are reproduced in a number of texts. *See, e.g.*, Danilo Türk, "Recognition of States: A Comment," 4 EJIL 66, 72 (Annex 1) (1993); A.V. Lowe & Colin Warbrick, "Recognition of States," 41 ICLQ 473, 477 (1992); Roland Rich, "Recognition of States: The Collapse of Yugoslavia and the Soviet Union," 4 EJIL 36, 42–3 (1993) (in Türk and Lowe & Warbrick, in full; in Rich, paraphrased and excerpted). Original supplied to author by Sir William Nicoll, former officer, UK Foreign and Commonwealth Office.

75. Minorities were a notorious source of tension in Central and Eastern Europe long before the post-Cold War era. *See* David Turnock, *Eastern Europe: An Historical Geography 1815–1945* (New York: Routledge, Chapman and Hall, 1989), 326 & *passim*. Recent writers have noted that the old dangers of minority politics have returned to the region. *See, e.g.*, Patrick Cockburn, "Dateline USSR: Ethnic Tremors," 74 *Foreign Policy* (For. Pol'y) 168 (1989); Daniel N. Nelson, "Europe's Unstable East," 82 For. Pol'y 137 (1991); Jirí Dienstbier, "Central Europe's Security," 83 For. Pol'y 119 (foreign minister of the Czech and Slovak Federal Republic, shortly before its dissolution, discusses minority problems and the common security interests of his country, Poland, and Hungary).

76. PCIJ Reports, 1930, ser. B, no. 17.

77. Emphasis supplied. *Greco-Bulgarian Communities Case*. PCIJ Reports, 1930, ser. B, no. 17 at 19.

78. Barbara Mikotajczyk, "Universal Protection of Minorities: Selected Problems," 20 *Polish Yearbook of International Law* (Pol. YBIL) 137, 140 n. 14 (1993).

79. *Treaty of Oliva of 1660* (protecting Catholics in Livonia); *Treaty of Ryswick of 1697* (protecting Catholics in territory France ceded to Holland); *Treaty of Paris of 1763* (protecting Catholics in Canada).

80. *Treaty of Westphalia of 1648* (Protestants among the German principalities).

81. *International Convention of Constantinople of 1881* (protecting Muslims in Greece).

82. *General Act of the Congress of Berlin of 1878*.

83. Representatively, see *Treaty Concerning the Protection of Minorities in Armenia*, August 10, 1920, 12 *Nouveau Recueil Général de Traités* (NRGT) 3rd ser. 795 (1924) (between the Allied Powers and Armenia).

84. *See, e.g., Treaty of Paris*, December 9, 1919, 13 NRGT 3rd ser. 529 (1924) (between Romania and the other Allied Powers). Romania, receiving Transylvania (from Austria-Hungary) and Bukovina (from Russia), was one of the states substantially remade by the post-World War I settlement. The Treaty of Paris concerned the protection of minorities—especially Hungarians—in the aggrandized Romania. A Treaty Concerning the Recognition of the Independence of Poland and the Protection of Minorities was signed at Versailles on June 28, 1919, and had similar provisions to protect minorities in the reborn Polish state. 13 NRGT 3rd ser. 504 (1924). The minorities covered by the Polish treaty were chiefly German and Ukrainian, though also Belorussian, Lithuanian, and Jewish.

85. *Treaty of Saint-Germain-en-Laye*, September 10, 1919, 11 NRGT 3rd ser. 691 (1922). Article 57 therein provides that Czechoslovakia make treaty provisions guar-

anteeing minority rights (11 NRGT at 707); Romania was held to similar terms under Article 60 (11 NRGT at 708); and Articles 62–69 provided that Austria likewise guarantee the rights of minorities within its borders (11 NRGT 708–10).

86. *Treaty of the Trianon*, June 4, 1920, 12 NRGT 3rd ser. 423 (1922). Article 44 provided that the Kingdom of Serbs, Croats, and Slovenes (Yugoslavia) (12 NRGT at 436); and Article 47 that Romania (12 NRGT at 36) guarantee minority rights. Articles 54–60 (12 NRGT at 438–40), paralleling Articles 62–69 of the Treaty of Saint-German, provided that Hungary pledge to respect minority rights.

87. *Treaty of Neuilly-sur-Seine*, November 27, 1919, 12 NRGT 3rd ser. 323, 333–36 (1923).

88. *Treaty of Sèvres*, August 10, 1920, 12 NRGT 3rd ser. 664 (1923). Article 36 (12 NRGT at 671) pertains to minorities at Constantinople; Article 62 (12 NRGT at 677) to Kurdistan (the "Assyro-Chaldéen" people); and Article 72 (12 NRGT at 680) to Greek administration of Smyrna. Smyrna, on the Turkish Aegean coast, had a Greek majority, and the Allied Powers assigned the city and its hinterland to the Hellenic Kingdom, but with the proviso, built into Article 72, that Greece set up a 'local parliament,' giving proportional representation to all minorities. Articles 140, et seq., provided for the protection of minorities in Turkey-proper (12 NRGT at 693, et seq.).

89. Mikotajczyk, "Minorities," 20 Pol. YBIL at 141–42.

90. Consider the minority cases before the Permanent Court, *e.g.*, *Access to German Minority Schools in Polish Upper Silesia Case*, PCIJ Reports, ser. A/B, no. 40 (1931); *Treatment of Polish Nationals and Other Persons of Polish Origin or Speech in Danzig Case*, PCIJ Reports, ser. A/B, no. 44 (1932). Both cited in Mikotajczyk, "Minorities," 20 Pol. YBIL at 142.

91. GA Res. 217A (III), UN Doc. A/810 at 71 (December 10, 1948) Articles 6 & 7.

92. GA Res. 260A (III), 78 UNTS 277 (December 9, 1948).

93. GA Res. 2200 A (XXI). 999 UNTS 171 (December 16, 1966).

94. *See, e.g.*, *Lovelace* v. *Canada*, Communication No. 24/19772, HRLJ 158 (1981); *Ominayak* v. *Canada* (case concerning the Lubicon Lake Band), Communication No. 167/1984. Cited in Mikotajczyk, "Minorities," 20 Pol. YBIL at 149. For the most thorough treatment of the Committee and its work, see Dominic McGoldrick, *The Human Rights Committee: Its Role in the Development of the International Covenant on Civil and Political Rights* (Oxford: Clarendon Press, 1991).

95. The Russian minorities constitute 30.3% of the population of Estonia; 33.8% of Latvia; and 8.6% of Lithuania. Central Intelligence Agency, *Factbook*, 105, 193, 202.

96. Estonia declared independence on August 20, 1991; Latvia on September 6, 1991; and Lithuania on March 11, 1990. Central Intelligence Agency, *Factbook*, 104–05, 192–93, 202–03. After the defeat of the August 21, 1991 coup, the Russian Federation recognized the three states as independent. The EC, through the Dutch Presidency, recognized them on August 27. *See* Europe No. 5555 (N.S.) August 29, 1991 at 5. Cited in Lowe & Warbrick, "Recognition," 41 ICLQ at 474 n. 6.

97. *See* Andrea J. Haneman, "Independence and Group Rights in the Baltics: A Double Minority Problem," 35 *Virginia Journal of International Law* (Virg. J. Int'l L.) 485 (1995).

98. European Parliament, Session Documents: Report (English Edition) of the

Committee on Foreign Affairs and Security on Relations between the European Community and the Republics of the Former Yugoslavia (Rapporteur: Arie Oostlander), 7 (on file with author).

99. "Recognition of Slovenia and Croatia," European Parliament, Sess. Doc.: Relations between the European Community and the Republics of the Former Yugoslavia, 14.

100. Declaration of 'Guidelines on the Recognition of New States in Eastern Europe and in the Soviet Union.'

101. Articles 5 through 25 of the Croatian Constitutional Law of Human Rights and Freedoms and the Rights of National And Ethnic Communities or Minorities in the Republic of Croatia addresses the rights of minorities. These Articles, among other provisions, guarantee "full observance of the principles of nondiscrimination"; "the right to identity, culture, religion, public and private use of a language and alphabet and education"; in areas where a majority of inhabitants speak a different tongue or use a different alphabet, official adoption of that tongue and alphabet; use of ethnic symbols and songs; freedom of association for ethnic purposes; education in minority tongues; a minimum representation in the national parliament; and self-government in areas where a minority people in the republic possess a local majority.

102. *Texas* v. *White*, 74 U.S. (7 Wall.) 227, 240 (1868) (Chase, C.J.).

103. 74 U.S. at 243.

104. 74 U.S at 237.

105. *See, e.g.*, Holly A. Osterland, "National Self-Determination and Secession: The Slovak Model," 25 *Case Western Reserve Journal of International Law* (Case W'n Res. J. Int'l L.) 655, 697 n. 310 (1993); Keith S. Rosen, "Federalism in the Americas in Comparative Perspective," 26 *University of Miami Inter-American Law Review* (U. Miami Inter-Am. L. Rev.) 1, 6 (1994); Deborah Jones Merritt, "The Guarantee Clause and State Autonomy: Federalism for a Third Century," 80 *Columbia Law Review* (Colum. L. Rev.) 1, 9, n. 50 (1988); David P. Currie, "The Constitution in the Supreme Court: Civil War and Reconstruction, 1865–1873," 51 *University of Chicago Law Review* (U. Chi. L. Rev.) 131, 133 (1984). *But see also* Sanford Levinson, "Freedom: Politics: They Whisper: Reflections on Flags, Monuments, and State Holidays, and the Construction of Social Meaning in a Multicultural Society," 70 *Chicago-Kent Law Review* (Chi.-Kent. L. Rev.) 1079, 1117 (1995) (doubting the constitutional bar to secession).

106. Regarding the special place of the Constitution, *see* Edward S. Corwin, "The Constitution as Instrument and as Symbol," 30 *American Political Science Review* 1071 (1936); Corwin, "The Worship of the Constitution," 4 *Constitutional Review* (Const. Rev.) 3 (1920) (arguing that Lincoln's quest to subordinate the Constitution to a sense of nationhood was unusual among American political leaders). Both of these articles are reprinted in *Corwin on the Constitution*. vol. 1. Richard Loss ed. (Ithaca: Cornell University Press, 1981).

107. The view that the Constitution is the chief artifact of and reference point for American nationalism is hardly new. To my knowledge however, writers have not as yet widely noted how that view influences American approaches to international law, and in particular to self-determination and the legality of secession.

108. Brown, "Legal Effects of Recognition," 44 AJIL at 62. Quoting the Tobar Doctrine. *See also* F. Larnaude, "Les Gouvernements de fait," 28 RGDIP 498 (1921). Quoting Article 1 of the supplementary convention to *General Treaty of the Central*

*American Peace Conference (Treaty of Washington)*, December 20, 1907. Text of supplementary convention reprinted at 3 NRGT 3rd ser. 102 (1910); 2 AJIL supp. 229 (1908).

109. L.H. Woolsey, "The Non-Recognition of the Chamorro Government in Nicaragua," 20 AJIL 543, 545 (1926).

110. L.H. Woolsey, "The Recognition of El Salvador," 28 AJIL 325, 327 (1934).

111. Philip Marshall Brown, "The Recognition of New States and Governments," 30 AJIL 689 (1936).

112. For the text of the Estrada Doctrine, see 25 AJIL supp. 203 (1930), reprinting Declaration of September 27, 1930, originally printed in *Buletín Oficial de la Secretaría de Relaciones Exteriores*, Estados Unidos Mexicanos, vol. LV, no. 9, p. 9.

113. Cass R. Sunstein, "Constitutionalism and Secession," 58 U. Chi. L. Rev. 633 (*Symposium: Approaching Democracy: A New Legal Order for Eastern Europe*) (1991).

114. Akhil Reed Amar, "Some New World Lessons for the Old World," 58 U. Chi. L. R. 483, 501–502 (*Symposium: Approaching Democracy: A New Legal Order for Eastern Europe*) (1991).

115. Some have suggested it is not entirely legal. Nonrecognition of a government actually in control of the governmental machinery is, according to Borchard, a *casus belli*. Attaching conditions of 'legitimacy' to recognition Borchard went on to define as intervention. Edwin M. Borchard, "The Unrecognized Government in American Courts," 26 AJIL 261 (1932). Chen also denied a place for constitutional inquiry in international law: "With the decay of the doctrine of dynastic legitimacy in constitutional law, constitutional legality is no longer made the test of the international title to govern. . . . Hence the constitutional law test of legality should have no significance whatever in the consideration of international recognition." Ti-Chiang Chen, *The International Law of Recognition, with special reference to Practice in Great Britain and the United States* (London: Stevens & Sons Limited, 1951), 271.

116. Hersch Lauterpacht, "International Law and the Law of the State in International Law," in *Collected Papers of Hersch Lauterpacht*. vol. I-General Works. Elihu Lauterpacht ed. (Cambridge: Cambridge University Press, 1970), 151–177.

117. Hans Kelsen, *Principles of International Law*. Robert W. Tucker ed., 2nd ed. (New York: Holt, Rinehart and Winston, Inc., 1966), 290–301, 533–588.

118. *See* Article 38, Statute of the International Court of Justice.

119. This proposal echoes an editorial comment by Kunz: "[I am] . . . in complete accord with the statement that the origin of a new state or government which may be violative of pre-existing constitutional law is irrelevant from the point of view of international law. It is exactly the positive norm of effectivity of international law which validates the new state or government. Unsuccessful secession or civil war is treason; successful secession or civil war creates new law." Josef L. Kunz, "Critical Remarks on Lauterpacht's 'Recognition in International Law,'" 44 AJIL 713, 715 (1950).

120. Cobban, *National Self-Determination*, 161.

121. An uprising on Easter Sunday 1916 is identified by some historians as the beginning of the train of events which led to the independence of Ireland. Britain at the time was embroiled in World War I, and British statesmen probably viewed instability within the realm as exacerbating the threat posed by the Central Powers, the most serious threat to British security since the Napoleonic wars. Britain vio-

lently suppressed the Irish independence movement. Ireland nonetheless obtained statehood within the British Commonwealth in 1923. A new constitution, adopted in 1937, changed the name of the country from the Irish Free State to Eire (Celtic for 'Ireland'). The Governor-General was replaced by an elected president. A plebiscite the same year declared Ireland "a sovereign, independent, democratic state." British military and naval bases were evacuated, by agreement, in April 1938, and the final links to the Commonwealth were severed by the Republic of Ireland Act of 1948. Britain recognized the Republic in 1949. *See* Theodore W. Moody, Francis Xavier Martin & Francis J. Byrne eds. *A New History of Ireland.* vol. VIII (Oxford: Clarendon Press, 1982).

122. Cobban, *National Self-Determination*, 163. The first Soviet Constitution—the Constitution of the Russian Socialist Federated Soviet Republic—was adopted July 10, 1918. This most uncompromisingly 'proletarian' document was replaced in January 1924. The new constitution, one scholar of Soviet law has written, struggled to balance 'proletarian unity' and 'self-determination.' *See* Aryeh L. Unger, *Constitutional Development in the USSR: A Guide to the Soviet Constitutions* (London: Methuen & Co. Ltd., 1981), 46. Article 4 of the 1924 Constitution provided for secession: "Every union republic shall retain the right of free secession from the Union." Text at Unger, *Soviet Constitutions*, 62. The third Soviet Constitution, ratified in 1936, contained this principle as well, at Article 17: "Every union republic shall retain the right of free secession from the USSR." Unger, *Soviet Constitutions*, 143. Neither constitution, however, provided the machinery by which to advance and evaluate a request for secession. The right to secession, though explicit in the Soviet constitutions, remained "merely declaratory and bereft of any institutional backing." Unger, Soviet Constitutions, 48. Steps toward autonomy in fact met with the full force of the communist police state.

123. "Yugoslav Constitution," *Constitutions of the Countries of the World.* Albert P. Blaustein & Gilbert H. Flanz eds., Marko Pavicic trans. (Dobbs Ferry, NY: Oceana Publications, Inc., 1986), 7.

124. Cobban, *National Self-Determination*, 146.

125. Ibid., 136–139.

126. Cobban's argument may have more to do with self-determination than with constitutionality. It is noteworthy that the runaway secession argument arose very early in the debate over self-determination. When Sweden supported a plebiscite to determine the sovereignty of the Åland Islands, Finland objected on the grounds that self-determination could not practically apply to a territory with only 22,000 inhabitants. This was in 1918, at about the same time Woodrow Wilson was promoting self-determination as a principle to guide the post-World War I settlement. On the Åland crisis, see John H. Wuorinen, *A History of Finland* (New York: Columbia University Press, 1965), 297.

127. Alan James, "System or Society?" 19 *Review of International Studies* (Rev. Int'l Stud.) 269 (1993).

128. Hersch Lauterpacht, *Recognition in International Law* (Cambridge: The University Press, 1948), 31 (under §13, "Irrelevant Tests of Recognition of Statehood"). This seems to echo Lorimer, quoted at the beginning of this chapter.

129. *See* Philip Marshall Brown, "The Recognition of Israel," 42 AJIL 620, 623 (1948). Quoting Resolution Number XXII.

130. Compare Stimson's remarks to the Council on Foreign Relations on February

6, 1931, in which he declares that the Hoover Administration would not follow the Wilsonian policy of denying recognition to governments originating without popular consent. *See* Henry L. Stimson, "The United States and the Other American Republics," (address before the Council on Foreign Relations), 9 For. Aff., no. 3, special supplement (April 1931). The Stimson Doctrine arguably was resuscitated in connection with Rhodesia and the South African 'Homelands.'

131. *See* Brown, "Recognition of Israel," 42 AJIL at 622.

# 5

# AN UNSOLVED PROBLEM: THE PROCESS OF RECOGNITION

Since the Montevideo Convention of 1933, a baseline of prerequisites for statehood has been accepted widely though not unanimously.[1] Writers undeterred by deficiencies in the Convention take the view that to be regarded as a state, an entity must possess a permanent population; cover a defined territory; be presided over by an effective government; and demonstrate capacity to engage in international relations. As discussed in Chapter 4, some would include further criteria. To varying degrees, self-determination, democracy, minority rights, and constitutionality have indeed influenced the legal rule. However, the status of these criteria is ambiguous. I have meant to suggest from the ambiguity that declaratory doctrine is problematic. Declaratory doctrine may appeal to aspirations for an international society under law, because it makes recognition automatic upon attainment of the criteria for statehood and thus seemingly removes discretion from recognition. However, the possible accretion of new criteria to the definition of the state casts doubt on what "automatic" means. The new criteria—addenda to Montevideo—are themselves at least in measure politically inspired. If declaratory doctrine expels politics from recognition *per se*, it invites politics into the concept of statehood. Existing states wishing to appear to adhere to a declaratory conception can forestall recognition by taking an expansive view of what requirements an entity need fulfill to become a state. The political component shifts from recognition to statehood.

If states were to reach consensus on the criteria for statehood, the declaratory model nonetheless would leave unsettled a central question: by what process do states determine whether a putative state has fulfilled the criteria? Reducing the definition of statehood to a list of seemingly objective characteristics does not assure that the process of decision will be a legal one. Characterizing facts is not always a straightforward exercise; seemingly uncontroversial observations can be manipulated to support contradictory conclusions. In recognition law, the putative new criteria of statehood make fact-finding potentially quite complicated. The proposed addition of constitutionality further clouds the situation. If, as a matter of fact, it is virtually impossible to declare when the fulfillment of criteria necessary for statehood has occurred, then the value of the declaratory model in pinning down recognition to a set of objective criteria has been lost. When the statuses at issue are as slippery as constitutionality or even democracy, *Realpolitik* can all too readily enter the process of adjudging their attainment. The invitation to discretionary conduct inherent in deciding whether a community has met even the older, less ambiguous criteria for statehood would seem to present challenges to the declaratory model. The addenda would eviscerate it.

Declaratory doctrine was held superior because it allegedly supported legal principle, whereas constitutivism was essentially positivist. Legal idealists have indeed generally preferred the declaratory to the constitutive view.[2] The former has the attraction of seeming to remove recognition from the caprice of unprincipled foreign ministries. However, so long as the *process* of recognition remains unexamined, the positivist element to recognition endures. Under the constitutive model, the lack of legal principle is overt, the discretionary character of recognition being a hallmark of constitutivism. Decision freely made by competent authorities in the recognizing state, not the situation in the target of recognition, triggers the act. Under declaratory doctrine, such discretion in theory diminishes—recognition takes place when the criteria of statehood are in evidence. However, even if states were to agree what makes a state, the process of ascertaining whether what makes a state obtains in a given situation will still be contentious. The fact-finding process remains open to the discretionary application of individual states. If the problem is to find a model that reduces the *Realpolitik* aspect of recognition for which constitutivism was criticized, declaratory doctrine is no solution. Writers concerned about lack of legal principle therefore began to focus on the *process* of recognition.

## TOWARD A COLLECTIVE PROCESS OF RECOGNITION?

A number of writers after the Second World War approached recognition in a new way. Finding the discretionary or political element manifest in both theories of recognition and holding this undesirable, they emphasized the process of recognition, as much as the *content* of the definition of statehood. Lauterpacht, though sceptical of the constitutive model, retained the view that statehood legally commences only upon the extension of recognition by existing states. However, in a departure, Lauterpacht argued for a process restrained by principle and law. While Lauterpacht broadly assumed a constitutivist's view of recognition, his was therefore an eccentric constitutivism. The special character of Lauterpacht's theory of recognition has been widely acknowledged. Shaw treats the "Lauterpacht doctrine" as a conception distinct from both constitutivism and the declaratory view.[3] A similar classification is found in Akehurst.[4] The most conspicuous aspect of Lauterpacht's new course—indeed, the aspect emphasized by those who have classified his theory a free-standing doctrine—was its rejection of unilateral state discretion.

Lauterpacht's effort to describe and shape the law of recognition was applauded for strengthening law and reducing *Realpolitik*. Lauterpacht built a model for state recognition that remained within the general outlines of constitutive theory but rejected the positivist strand of constitutivism. Dugard described Lauterpacht's 1947 *Recognition in International Law* as "a book of immense scholarship and wisdom, which sought to bring the law of recognition into a framework of legal principle and to free it from the prison of power politics to which it had been condemned by both lawyers and politicians."[5] The aim of Lauterpacht's project was to inject a degree of legal idealism into an arena of international practice that had long been dominated by political calculation. In place of uncoordinated unilateral action of states, Lauterpacht envisioned a collectivized process of recognition. Such a process would serve to discipline otherwise unfettered and willful state conduct, and differing unilateral interpretations of the rules governing recognition would give way to global deliberation and common legal voice. In proposing to revise recognition law, Lauterpacht set the stage for change in the debate over recognition. The central controversy was whether recognition was declaratory or constitutive of statehood, but Lauterpacht's thesis foreshadowed eclipse of this doctrinal debate. Writers today still discuss recognition in terms of declaratory and constitutive effect. The terms of the old debate are vital enough that it is even said that declaratory doctrine is the better view. Looking at recognition through the lens of the old debate, I question whether a declaratory preference is justified. However, the old debate and the doctrinal questions that were its preoccupation may now be beside the point. It may well be that the central questions today are whether recognition is subject to law or political whim; and whether recognition is a collective process by the community of states or a unilateral act by a single state.

I turn first briefly to the antecedents of Lauterpacht's reconceptualization of recognition.

### Grotian International Law as Impetus for the Lauterpachtian Reconceptualization of Recognition

The Lauterpachtian reconceptualization of recognition has its origins in the foundations of modern international law. Lauterpacht joined many writers in placing the starting point of modern international law with Grotius,[6] whose treatise *De jure belli ac pacis* has been identified as the first systematic treatment of the discipline.[7] Lauterpacht proposed that eleven tenets formed the cornerstone of the Grotian thesis:

1. The subjection of the totality of international relations to the rule of law;
2. The acceptance of the law of nature as an independent source of international law;
3. Affirmation of the social character of humanity as the basis of the law of nature;
4. An essential identity between states and individuals;
5. Rejection of Machiavellian "Reason of State" as a rationale for state action;
6. Distinctions between just and unjust wars;
7. The Doctrine of Qualified Neutrality;
8. The binding force of promises between states;
9. Fundamental character of the rights and freedoms of the individual person;
10. The inherent value of peace; and
11. A tradition of idealism and progress.[8]

Lauterpacht would build from these his own revision of the positivist conception of state recognition.

First, Lauterpacht associated with Grotius a rejection of the belief that state action should be free from legal norms. The foremost Grotian innovation, in Lauterpacht's words, was to conceive "of the totality of the relations between states as governed by law." Expanding upon this, Lauterpacht argued that state conduct should know certain bounds and never be exempt from legal justification: "There are no lacunae in that subjection of states to the rule of law. Modern international law recognized for a long time the existence of gaps which obliterated altogether the border-line between law and lawlessness in international relations. Of these gaps the admissibility of war as an absolute right of states, requiring no other legal justification, is the outstanding example. In laying down the distinction between just and unjust war Grotius rejected the claim to any such right."[9] In Lauterpacht's view of Grotius, there is a normative order superior to the state.

Second, in a direct attack on the positivist view,[10] Lauterpacht shared the Grotian suspicion of *jus gentium voluntarium*—the traditional law between independent states—and embraced the Grotian advocacy of 'natural law': "[Grotius] secularized the law of nature. He gave it added authority and dignity by making it an integral part of the exposition of a system of law which became essential to civilized life. By doing this he laid, more truly than any writer before him, the foundation of international law."[11] Whereas pre-Grotian jurists defined the law of states as that law common among all branches of humanity (*jus gentium*), Lauterpacht perceived Grotius as redefining international law as derivative of natural reason. To Grotius, natural reason was a human faculty which would exclude from state practice many forms of universal but undesirable conduct (*e.g.*, warfare and slavery).[12] Consistency of a practice did not necessarily dress the practice with legality.

Two further Grotian attributes, reciprocal to one another, contributed to Lauterpacht's effort to force an evolution in the law of recognition. In Lauterpacht's reading of Grotius, the human being—not the state—is the base unit of international law. Logically flowing from this proposition, *raison d'état* cannot justify state action. On the centrality of individual persons to international law in Grotius, Lauterpacht wrote:

> The analogy—nay, the essential identity—of rules governing the conduct of states and of individuals is not asserted for the reason that states *are like* individuals; it is due to the fact that states *are composed of* individual human beings; it results from the fact that behind the mystical, impersonal, and therefore necessarily irresponsible personality of the metaphysical state there are the actual subjects of rights and duties, namely, individual human beings. This is the true meaning of the Grotian analogy of states and individuals. The individual is the ultimate unit of all law, international and municipal, in the double sense that the obligations of international law are ultimately addressed to him and that the development, the well-being, and the dignity of the individual human being are a matter of direct concern to international law.[13]

Lauterpacht's conception of international law, rooted in such an understanding of the relationship between states and real persons, could little admit Machiavellian reason of state to justify international conduct.[14]

The legal idealism he perceived in Grotius undergird Lauterpacht's effort to revise the constitutive model of recognition. Yet, perhaps ironically, it was Lauterpacht's advocacy of lawful process which rendered the constitutive theory attractive to him. Under the declaratory model, an entity becomes a state self-generatively, as it were, and thus without reference to an all-encompassing legal structure. Once the entity takes on a set of characteristics, it is a state, and other states are merely left to declare the fact. Furthermore, as I have already discussed, the declaratory model invites politics into recognition in the form of flexible criteria for statehood. By contrast, the requirement of the constitutive model that existing states formally certify the membership of newcomers to the community holds open the possibility that the attainment of statehood might be ensconced within a legal process. To Lauterpacht, it was an advantage of constitutivism that it involved other states in the legal creation of statehood. This attraction of the constitutive model was, however, diminished by its admission of unfettered state discretion. In its discretionary aspect was where Lauterpacht would have to revise the constitutive model.

### The Lauterpachtian Reconceptualization—a Constitutive Model under Law

Having rejected the positivist strands of the two prevailing theories of recognition, Lauterpacht and like-minded writers[15] had yet to address the following problem: even if there can be formulated a definition of statehood—a series of requirements clear in theory and in text—the fact-finding mission which surrounds each instance of the emergence of a new state remains susceptible to *Realpolitik*. A set of criteria defining statehood, though in form objective, will not alone cure recognition practice of the subjective, willful action of individual deciding states. How the community goes about recognizing new states thus constitutes at least as important an issue as the criteria which define statehood. Process is paramount. If deciding whether one or more of the criteria are fulfilled remains within the unilateral, discretionary province of the individual state, then the seemingly concrete legal definition of statehood, whether framed in the Montevideo Convention or elsewhere, becomes in fact an empty formality.

Lauterpacht sought a process of recognition that would prevent this result. He explained that neither the declaratory nor the constitutive view prevented the "decisive infusion of the element of national interest" into decisions on recognition.[16]

"The solution . . . of that difficulty," he wrote, "would seem to lie in transferring that function to an international organ not impeded by a conflict between interest and duty." Institutionalizing the process of recognition was Lauterpacht's answer to the problem of unfettered state discretion. It is within the formal structures of an international executive organ,[17] international courts (principally the International Court of Justice),[18] and municipal or national courts[19] that Lauterpacht envisioned the collective recognition process taking place.

Lauterpacht catalogued numerous cases that suggested a drift toward collective recognition: recognition of Greece by the Treaty of London of 1830, of Belgium by the Treaty of London of 1831, of Bulgaria, Serbia, Montenegro, and Romania by the Berlin Treaty of 1878, of the Congo State by the Berlin Treaty of 1885, of Albania by the Conference of London of 1913, of Poland, Lithuania, Latvia, and Estonia by the Allies after World War I, and of the states of Latin America by the joint action urged by Great Britain at the Congress of Verona in 1823.[20] Lauterpacht's claims for these cases were modest; he did not claim state practice and *opinio juris* to point unambiguously toward the end which he advocated. Indeed, the cases fell well short of proving that recognition was on its way to collectivization. The permanent institutional framework to which Lauterpacht argued recognition should be committed was even less in evidence than signs that there had begun a less structured collectivization of process. States hesitant to coordinate their recognition practice informally were hardly ready to hand over discretion to an international organ. Because evidence in practice was deficient, and also because the Lauterpachtian reconceptualization departed sharply from traditional positivist views of recognition, Lauterpacht's proposed revision of this area of international public order was bound to draw criticism.

The Lauterpachtian reconceptualization of the law of recognition—the revision of recognition into a matter governed by legal principle and taking place through a collective process—did in fact engender significant controversy. One writer's objections reflected the prevailing scepticism.

Josef L. Kunz rejected the thesis of Lauterpacht's *Recognition in International Law*. Dugard later would go so far as to characterize Kunz's critique as "savage."[21] The constitutive basis of Lauterpacht's discussion, Kunz argued, was faulty: "It is from [the] idea of recognition as a legal act of ascertaining the fulfillment of requirements laid down by international law that Lauterpacht's book is written, coupled with the idea of a right to, and a duty of recognition. This principal thesis the author tries to prove as positive international law from the practice of states. *In this endeavor, it must be said in the interest of scientific truth, he has failed completely* [emphasis supplied]."[22] Kunz observed that Lauterpacht's theory had met a wall of disapproval.[23] Recognition, in the view of Kunz and others, remained an instrument in the hands of individual states, to be exercised unilaterally and at the complete discretion of each state. The Lauterpachtian reconceptualization denied this, Kunz argued, in the face of reality. In the words of Kelsen, "existing states are only empowered, not obliged to recognize."[24] States, according to Philip C. Jessup, "are free to accord or to withhold the recognition of new governments," and, presumably in Kunz's view, of new states, too.[25]

The most serious objection was that Lauterpacht had been "led into what must be called a falsification of the positive law."[26] According to Kunz, Lauterpacht erred by imposing his idealist's vision of how states *should* behave onto a reality that hardly yet matched that vision. Kunz concentrated on this portrayed mistake:

> In teaching these doctrines, in contradiction to positive international law, Lauterpacht forgot that the science of international law cannot by its fiat correct the structural defects of the primitive international legal order. He forgot what his predecessor,[27] . . . what he himself recently emphasized [citation omitted]: the scholar of international law is not in the rôle of a legislator, but of a judge; of a judge, and not in the rôle of counsel for plaintiff or defendant. It is the duty of the scholar to state what the law is, whether he likes it or not. It is fundamental to distinguish between *lex lata* and *lex ferenda*. Lauterpacht's dialectic efforts to make the practice of states tell what it does not contain, however talented and powerful, are of no help; neither is the attitude of joining the now fashionable accusations against positivism.[28]

Kunz may have taken an over-narrow view of the role of scholars, whom after all the Statute of the ICJ enumerated as a source of international law.[29] Nonetheless, he made it plain that he viewed Lauterpacht's position as wishful thinking. Going beyond the observation that collective recognition lacked contemporary support, Kunz also speculated upon the future of Lauterpacht's theory.

Kunz denied that any trace of collective recognition existed—or, for that matter, could ever come into being. "Lauterpacht's proposal of collectivization of recognition," he predicted, "has little chance, as actually it has been the usual practice of the United States to refrain from participating in such joint action."[30] Kunz cited a contemporary example of American refusal to engage in collective recognition—the recognition of Israel.[31] Further to cast doubt on Lauterpacht's thesis, Kunz described the recognition of Vietnam: the United States and Great Britain recognized the Bao Dai régime; the Soviet Union recognized the rebel government, and India withheld recognition altogether.[32]

Kunz showed that not only collective *process* eluded the community of states; a single recognition incident ended in wildly disparate *results*.

The status in practice of Lauterpacht's proposed revision mirrored academic scepticism surrounding it. States, in the 1940s and 1950s at any rate, acted as if recognition was a matter for the individual state alone to decide, and there was in consequence scant indication that a collective process was taking hold. It may be that Kunz's characterization of recognition as a unilateral measure, more or less free of law, continues to be the more accurate one. However, state practice has grown significantly since Lauterpacht's *Recognition of States*. The Lauterpachtian reconceptualization merits fresh assessment.

## TRACES OF COLLECTIVE PROCESS IN RECOGNITION

A review of state practice may answer whether collectivization has become an established feature of the recognition process; whether it is an emergent norm; or whether collectivization has as yet had negligible impact on international law. Lauterpacht, in advancing a theory of collective recognition, conducted a preliminary review of state practice, leaving his critics to offer a countervailing—and hardly unpersuasive—interpretation of the evidence. A further review of cases, with an eye to traces of collective state conduct, will provide a groundwork for evaluating the current shape of the law of recognition. This section concludes with a discussion of the *Case Concerning East Timor (Portugal* v. *Australia)*. Then I will turn to the most illuminating test yet of collective recognition, the European response to the break-up of Yugoslavia.

### Past Tests of Collective Process

On occasion, states have made collective recognition decisions through the intermediation of international bodies and also through less expressly coordinate action. Independent, unilateral decision has nonetheless been sufficiently common that writers must approach with caution the proposition that collectivization is an established norm. I now turn to a number of cases where changes in international reality forced states to decide how to adapt policy and where collective process arguably had a role in recognition.

*The Ålands*

The Tsarist empire annexed Finland in 1809, in a phase of expansion facilitated by a short-lived alliance between Alexander I and Napoleon Bonaparte.[33] Since the twelfth century, Finland had been ruled by Sweden, but after the Treaty of Tilsit (June 25, 1807), Napoleon urged his new ally to "remove the Swedes farther from your capital."[34] As a grand duchy in the Russian Empire, Finland would be granted limited self-government under Alexander II (of greater fame for liberating the serfs),[35] but when the Russian political and military collapse of 1917–18 presented the Finns the opportunity to assert full autonomy, they took it. Independence was declared on December 6, 1917. Like the contemporaneous severance of the Ukraine, Belorussia, Congress Poland,[36] and the Caucasian states, the independence of Finland advanced the interests of the Central Powers. The German Kaiser, perceiving military and perhaps dynastic advantage[37] to Finnish independence, landed a contingent of German naval infantry in and around Helsingfors (Helsinki) during the first week of April 1918. Finnish secession and independence were thereby complicated from the start by foreign intervention. German troops were ordered evacuated by the terms of the November 11, 1918, Armistice, but numerous units remained. At the same time, Bolshevik forces from Russia intensified their own activities in this territory, which the new Soviet government had obvious reasons for wishing to retain.[38] Confusing the situation further, the White Russian army also took part in the ensuing fray over Finland, and indigenous communist revolutionaries fought against both these and the Germans. Multilateral warfare made it unclear who exercised *de facto* control in Finland, and a pall was cast over the legal status of the new Baltic state.

Hostilities eventually came to a close, with the Red Army defeated and the indigenous communists facing violent reprisals from the nationalist victors.[39] Lenin had recognized Finland on December 31, 1917, and by the end of January 1918, so too had Germany, France, Sweden, Norway, and Denmark.[40] Though civil war had ended and widespread recognition of the Finnish state achieved, uncertainties persisted over the geographic extent of Finnish sovereignty. These were particularly pronounced at the fringes, east and west, of the new republic. In particular, a dispute erupted over the Åland Islands.[41] At the mouth of the Gulf of Bothnia between Sweden and Finland, the Åland Islands had been inhabited by ethnic Swedes since medieval times. The archipelago was however known to Finns as *Ahvenanmaa* and ceded by Sweden to Russia in 1809 as part of Finland. The powers victorious over Russia in the Crimean War of 1856–57, at Swedish suggestion, forced Russia to neutralize the Ålands, meaning that no forces could be stationed there or fortifications built. After Finland declared independence in 1917, Sweden demanded a plebiscite be held to determine under which state the Ålanders would prefer to be governed, but Finland declared that it would not be bound by the results of any such vote. Swedish troops were landed in the archipelago in February 1918; Stockholm offered to internationalize the Ålands question that month; but Helsinki refused. In early 1919, the Paris Peace Conference took up the brewing crisis between Sweden and Finland but came to no decision. Finally, the Council of the League of Nations, at British behest, in the autumn of 1919 submitted the dispute to a panel of three international jurists, one each French, Dutch, and Swiss. Recognition lay at the heart of the dispute: did Finland possess title over the islands? And, if so, was Sweden obliged to recognize this? The decision of the jurists' panel was affirmative.[42] The panel made the initial findings that (1) the Åland question was not a matter solely within Finnish jurisdiction; and (2) the 1850s demilitarization remained valid. The panel Report to the League of Nations, submitted June 20, 1921, advised that the Ålands lay under Finnish title; that the Swedish-proposed plebiscite was invalid; but that the Åland Question was not exclusively domestic. A final settlement came later and contained six terms: (1) The islands were Finnish territory; (2) they were to become a self-governing province with its own Provincial Assembly; (3) the islanders' consent would be required for use of the Finnish language in schools or government; (4) ethnic Finns from outside the islands would not be permitted to buy land there, nor to vote before satisfying a five year residency requirement; (5) the president of Finland would appoint an Ålands governor, on the recommendation of the Provincial Assembly; and (6) the Ålands would remain demilitarized.[43] Arguably more important than the substantive result was the process behind the decision: institutionalized in a body of internationally-appointed authorities, a collective decision had been reached, and this the member states of the League of Nations followed as their own.[44]

*Manchukuo*

The 1930s brought a considerably more volatile recognition controversy, and this too was addressed by the League. Japan had begun an expansionist program in Asia when its army and navy defeated China (in 1894) and Russia (in 1905). Tokyo obtained concessions over mainland territories from Peiping and stationed soldiers along railways which it controlled as part of its concessionary interest in Manchuria. Officers of the Kwantung Army, as these troops were known, pressed Tokyo to escalate a drive for control in northeast China. The overt takeover of Manchuria began in September 1931. Using as bases the concessionary areas and its *de facto* colony in Korea, Japan completed the seizure of Manchuria by the end of 1931.[45] To lend an appearance of native consent, Tokyo installed as 'head of state' a former Chinese emperor, and from its capital at Hsinking, the government of

'Manchukuo,' as Japan referred to the territory, sought international recognition. The League of Nations, acknowledging the reality of the situation, denied any such dignity to Tokyo's new satellite state.[46] In this collective disapproval, the League found ample scholarly support. Louis Cavaré, for instance, explained that for a number of reasons Manchuria did not merit recognition: (1) the region lacked a distinct ethnic identity; (2) its history was inseparable from that of China as a whole; (3) there was no basis in law for a challenge against Chinese sovereignty there; (4) independence took place without regard for the wishes of the inhabitants; (5) the position of the Kwantung army there was inconsistent with Japanese treaty obligations; and (6) the Manchukuon state was entirely "the work of Japan."[47]

A few states did recognize Manchukuo, contrary to the League position. Most of those to recognize did so some years after the initial 1933 League decision. The first to recognize were the Vatican and El Salvador, with Poland and Hungary joining some years later. The chief powers to recognize Manchukuo were Spain; Italy (November 29, 1936); and Germany (February 20, 1938).[48] What limited recognition Manchukuo did receive was an exception which proved the rule: by the time they recognized the Japanese satellite, the most important of these states had quit the League.[49] Apart from Nazi Germany and some of its fascist allies, most of the world community adhered to the League position.

*Rhodesia*

The United Nations, recalling the League response to Manchukuo, first served as an organ for collective nonrecognition in the 1960s. Security Council Resolution 217 (November 20, 1965) declared the situation in Rhodesia following the Unilateral Declaration of Independence (UDI) invalid. General Assembly Resolution 2379 (XXIII) (October 25, 1968) called expressly for nonrecognition. Rhodesia was effectively quarantined by United Nations censure, and, accepting the verdict of the organization, no state extended recognition. By the 1970s, only two states (Portugal and South Africa) so much as maintained accredited diplomatic representatives at Salisbury, though neither claimed formally to recognize the pariah state.[50] Recognition appears to have been declined through a collective decision, at least in part institutionalized through the political organs of the United Nations.

*Namibia*

A German colony before World War I, the territory then called South West Africa was seized by South Africa in 1915. Under the mandate system established under Article 22 of the League of Nations Covenant, South West Africa was placed under South African administration. Many mandatory territories of the League system after 1945 were placed under the Trusteeship System of the UN, pursuant to Article 77 of the UN Charter. South Africa, however, declined to place South West Africa under trusteeship, and in 1949 ceased to report on the territory to the UN. Advisory opinions and judgments of the ICJ in 1950, 1955, and 1956 held that the mandatory status of the territory had not lapsed and that South Africa therefore remained responsible internationally for South West Africa. Claims against South Africa brought before the ICJ by Liberia and Ethiopia were rejected for lack of standing. General Assembly Resolution 2145 (XXI) (October 27, 1966) declared that the South African mandate, for breaches of obligations thereunder by the mandatory power, was terminated. The Security Council called upon South Africa to end its illegal administration of the territory.[51] The Council followed this up in Resolution 276 (January 30, 1970) with notification that "all acts taken by the Government of South Africa on behalf of or concerning Namibia after the termination of the Mandate are illegal and invalid." This was expressed as a policy of nonrecognition in Resolution 283 (July 29, 1970). In *Legal Consequences for States of the Continued Presence of South Africa in Namibia (South West Africa) Notwithstanding Security Council Resolution 276 (1970)*, the ICJ issued an Advisory Opinion in which South Africa was held obliged to withdraw from Namibia. Moreover, the Court held that UN member states must "recognize the illegality of South Africa's presence in Namibia and the invalidity of its acts on behalf of or concerning Namibia, and to refrain from any acts and in particular any dealings with the Government of South Africa implying recognition of the legality of, or lending support or assistance to, such presence and administration."[52] The holding went one step further still, and asked states not members of the UN to assist in the policy of nonrecognition. An international judicial organ served as collective locus of a policy of nonrecognition toward an illegal territorial situation.

*Turkish Republic of Northern Cyprus*

Cyprus, from 1878 a British protectorate, became a British colony in 1914. Under a complex system of internal governance and external guarantee, Cyprus became an independent state in 1960. The chief object of the legal instruments surrounding Cypriot independence was to balance the interests of the two principal ethno-religious communities on the island, the Greek Orthodox community and the Turkish Muslim community. The 1960 constitutional system fell apart, however, in 1963. From then onward, the Turkish community administered the northern part of the island as a zone independent of the rest of the republic. This system was cemented after unrest and Turkish invasion in July 1974. Supported by Turkish armed forces, the Turkish Cypriots declared a Turkish Federated State of Cyprus on February 13, 1975. This was refashioned the Turkish Republic of Northern Cyprus (TRNC) on November 15, 1983. Despite numerous intercommunal negotating sessions, Cyprus remained divided between the Republic of Cyprus—Greek-ruled and widely recognized—and the TRNC—Turkish-ruled and recognized only by Turkey. UN Security Council Resolution 541 (November 18, 1983) called upon "all States not to recognize any Cypriot State other than the Republic of Cyprus," and Resolution 550 (May 11, 1984) reiterated nonrecognition of the TRNC. Collective response to a claim to statehood here was expressed through the executive organ of the United Nations.[53]

### Countervailing Examples: Unilateralism Preserved

Cases such as Rhodesia, Namibia, and Turkish Cyprus notwithstanding, the litany of failed efforts at collective response raises doubts whether collectivization and institutionalization are more than embryonic features of recognition. Critics challenged the Lauterpachtian reconceptualization, and it may well have to be qualified. Two cases reinforce the point.

*American Nonrecognition of Syria*

Syria had belonged to the Ottoman Empire. With the occupation of the Levant by British forces under General Allenby in 1917–18, Ottoman power came to an end. By terms to which the Allies agreed in 1916 (the Sykes-Picot Agreement), France would control Beirut (Lebanon) and Syria. Though France perfected its claim to Beirut forthwith, it left Syria sufficiently to indigenous devices that an Arab military government under one Faysal took power in Damascus. Faysal, however, saw his claims to Syria effectively extinguished at the Inter-Allied Conference at San Remo in 1920. The Conference declared a French mandate over Syria, and France went on to govern Syria into World War II. After Nazi conquest of Western Europe (June 1940), the colonial administration in Syria recognized the Franco-German armistice and became an agent of the Vichy régime. The danger of an enemy outpost in the Levant concerned the Allies after Axis forces used Syrian airfields to support a coup attempt in Baghdad. The Allies invaded Syria in July 1941, and the Free French shortly declared the territory independent.[54] Great Britain encouraged this development and quickly extended recognition. The United States, however, would not join in recognizing the putative Syrian state.[55] A political scientist summarizes the historical background of Syrian independence, the details of which perhaps explained the American refusal to grant recognition: "At its birth, Syria had no satisfactory, indigenous state-idea, having been created by the French after World War I. As a colonial artifact, it originated through no felt need by those who lived in it and its hastily drawn boundaries ignored fundamental cultural, historical, economic, and geographic relationships within the Levant."[56]

Recognition by the predominant member of the emerging western alliance was thus denied. Even at a time when the rising tide of war had led America into the closest relations with the United Kingdom—witness material assistance under Lend-Lease and the moral support expressed by the American President[57]—collective policy on Syrian recognition proved elusive. Under circumstances less exigent than World War II, it is unremarkable that states would fail to coordinate their policies on recognition.[58]

*Independence of Israel*

An independent state of Israel was proclaimed on May 14, 1948. Widely disparate responses issued from the United Nations and several of the chief powers. Israel received a United Nations seat (May 11, 1949),[59] but Warren Austin, the United States Ambassador to the UN, quickly stated that recognition of governments and states was a power retained by member states—a power not given over to the United Nations. The American policy had been to recognize the "*de facto* authority of the new State of Israel" but not the state, *per se*. The USSR, by contrast, quickly extended *de jure* recognition, both to government and state. A letter from Molotov to Shertok, the Israeli Foreign Minister, read "the Government of the USSR has decided to recognize officially the State of Israel and its Provisional Government." Great Britain recognized neither, announcing that Israel had as yet failed to fulfill the "basic criteria" of statehood.[60] Denunciations from the Syrian representative to the Security Council added further uncertainty.[61] The atmosphere surrounding independence of Israel was quarrelsome and political rather than collective and legal.

### Case Concerning East Timor (*Portugal* v. *Australia*) (1995)

*Portugal* v. *Australia* (*Case Concerning East Timor*) called on the International Court of Justice to address the legal effect of certain United Nations resolutions. These were purported by Portugal to oblige nonrecognition of Indonesia's annexation of East Timor and acknowledgment of Portugal as administering Power for that territory.[62] *East Timor* was therefore (potentially at any rate) a test case for the competence of the UN as an organ of collective recognition.

East Timor was a vestigial appendage of a Portuguese empire which, built upon trade routes of the late fifteenth and sixteenth centuries, had once spanned the globe. Even after the loss of Brazil in 1822, Portugal had retained extensive but moribund colonies in Africa (Angola, Mozambique, and Guinea-Bissau), enclaves on the coasts of the Indian subcontinent (Diu, Daman, Goa, and Cocanada), and the East Asian possessions of Macau and East Timor. While Macau reverts to Chinese control in 1999, Portugal lost all of its other possessions by the mid-1970s. Political upheaval gripped Portugal in the early 1970s, and, among other repercussions, this accelerated retreat from colonial dominion.[63] Guinea-Bissau gained independence in September 1974, with Angola and Mozambique following the next year.[64] However, Timorese independence was not to be perfected. Indonesia, a resource-rich state occupying an immense archipelago, had inherited control of the western half of the island of Timor from the Netherlands.[65] Despite the minimal economic value of East Timor, Indonesia overran the territory in winter 1975–76 and quickly set about to eradicate indigenous opposition. In face of the invasion and a Timorese uprising at least partly orchestrated by Indonesia, Portuguese authorities evacuated the territory capital, Dili, and fled to the small nearby island of Atauro. They left Atauro shortly thereafter, thus ending all trace of Portuguese effective governmental power in that part of the world.

East Timor immediately became a subject of United Nations concern. Security Council Resolution 384 (1975) and the first of eight General Assembly Resolutions called for Indonesian withdrawal from the territory.[66] The Resolutions also called for "all states to respect the territorial integrity of East Timor as well as the inalienable right of its people to self-determination." General Assembly Resolution 3485 (xxx) of December 12, 1975 referred to Portugal as the "administering Power" for East Timor. The Security Council followed up its first resolution with a second, on December 22, 1975, condemning unanimously the Indonesian invasion. Further resolutions, in the ensuing years, rejected the incorporation of East Timor into Indonesia and continued to express that the organization would not recognize a political situation in East Timor achieved by force of arms. General Assembly Resolution 37/30 (1982) was the last. Nonetheless, the question of East Timor remained alive before the UN in a number of forms. The General Assembly agenda still included it. The list of non-self-governing territories within the meaning of Chapter XI of the United Nations Charter still included it.[67] The Special Committee on the Situation with Regard to the Implementation of the Declaration of the Granting of Independence to Colonial Countries and Peoples was still seised of the East Timor question. And the Secretary-General continued to consult with concerned parties on the matter.[68] Portugal itself would maintain a degree of pressure against Indonesia for its allegedly unlawful annexation of East Timor, but, though the international community widely accepted the Portuguese contention that Indonesia holds East Timor illegally,[69] few concrete measures were taken to sanction the delinquency. Australia did, arguably, quite the opposite. Canberra concluded a maritime delimitation treaty with Indonesia on December 11, 1989. Previous Australia-Indonesia continental shelf agreements, concluded in 1971 and 1972, had delimited the waters to the east and west of East Timor, but no agreement had been reached between Australia and Portugal or Australia and Indonesia to define rights over the waters and shelf between East Timor and Australia. The sea and its underlying strata between the opposing Australian and East Timorese coasts, an area that had become known as the Timor Gap, thus was not subject to any delimitation. The 1989 treaty however delimited it. Portugal viewed the 1989 treaty as a form of recognition of Indonesia's claim to East Timor. As such, Portugal further viewed the treaty as a delict by Australia against Portugal. Portugal filed application on February 22, 1991 to institute proceedings against Australia before the ICJ.[70]

The majority opinion (the Court held fourteen to two in favor of Australia) focused on whether, in reaching the merits of the dispute, the ICJ would have to rule on rights and obligations of a third state not party to the proceedings. Australia argued from the basic principle set forth in *Monetary Gold Removal from Rome in 1943*: third party consent is required for the ICJ to exercise jurisdiction over a matter which will decide the rights and obligations of the third party.[71] Indonesian conduct was the true target of Portugal's suit, according to Australia. It followed, then, that any holding on the merits would determine rights and obligations of Indonesia. The Court indicated that the central question for review was the locus of the power to conclude a continental shelf treaty concerning the Timor Gap: did that power lie with Portugal or with Indonesia?[72] Judgment, then, could not avoid deciding the rights and obligations of the non-consenting third party.

Portugal attempted to rebut this argument, which Australia had presented initially and which the Court, in basic form, adopted. The Court, Portugal argued, did not need to approach the issue of Indonesian rights *de novo*: these had already been settled by the General Assembly and the Security Council "acting within their proper spheres of competence."[73] The ten UN resolutions (two Security Council, eight General Assembly) were legal articles of which judicial notice could be taken, Portugal maintained. The Court differed: "[T]he argument of Portugal . . . rests on the premise that the United Nations resolutions, and in particular those of the Security Council, can be read as imposing an obligation on States not to recognize any authority on the part of Indonesia over the Territory and, where the latter is concerned, to deal only with Portugal. The Court is not persuaded, however, that the relevant resolution went so far."[74] The Majority Opinion went on to note the purport of the UN resolutions in question and acknowledged the status of East Timor as a non-self-governing territory. The Court concluded that the resolutions were not self-proving documents and thus on their own did not establish a rule of nonrecognition of Indonesian and recognition of Portuguese rights in East Timor: "The Court finds that it cannot be inferred from the sole fact that the above-mentioned resolutions of the General Assembly and the Security Council refer to Portugal as the administering Power of East Timor that they intended to establish an obligation on third States to treat exclusively with Portugal as regards the continental shelf of East Timor." The Court noted as evidence that several states had concluded treaties with Indonesia since the annexation of East Timor, and these contained no reservations regarding the disputed territory.[75] The Court held that it lacked jurisdiction over the matter.

The dispute required the Court to reach Indonesian interests (those interests not having been conclusively decided by the UN resolutions), and this the Court could not do absent Indonesian consent to ICJ jurisdiction.[76] There was, according to the Court, no international rule of recognition or nonrecognition regarding the status of East Timor, and, if the *ratio* were given general application, United Nations resolutions (at least resolutions not more explicit on the subject of recognition than those regarding East Timor) could not give rise to such a rule over any territory.

Three Separate Opinions concurred with the judgment of the Court, and two judges dissented. I turn briefly now to the Separate Opinions of Judges Oda, Shahabuddeen, and Vereshchetin, and then analyze the dissents.

Judge Shahabuddeen, as far as concerns the status of collective recognition, came closest to the view expressed in the majority opinion. The UN resolutions, Shahabuddeen agreed with the majority, do not by themselves have the meaning Portugal attributed to them. To treat them as binding rules of nonrecognition, the Court would have to interpret them as such.[77]

Judge Vereshchetin, however, emphasized a different flaw in the Portuguese case—failure to take into account the rights of the East Timorese. To Vereshchetin, the fatal flaw jurisdictionally was to omit the party most effected by the root question on review—the people of East Timor.[78] Vereshchetin's position neither necessarily confirms nor rejects Portugal's proposition that UN resolutions generated a general rule of nonrecognition.

Judge Oda, in the most interesting of the three Separate Opinions, seems to accept that a general rule of nonrecognition was established by United Nations practice. East Timor, Judge Oda wrote, was taken in an illegal use of force, and the United Nations acted within its competences when it condemned this. In joining the Court in its holding of lack of jurisdiction, Judge Oda did *not*, then, concur with the proposition that a rule of nonrecognition could be given effect only after a judicial decision as to the rights and obligations of non-party Indonesia. Judge Oda rejected jurisdiction because he rejected Portuguese standing. To Judge Oda, the important factor was that the UN resolutions were negative of Indonesian claims of right over East Timor, not affirmative of Portuguese claims: "Indonesia's claim that East Timor should be integrated into its territory was rejected *solely* in order to uphold the rights of the people of East Timor but *not* to protect the rights and duties of the State of Portugal in relation to East Timor or the status of Portugal as the administering Power."[79] One senses in Judge Oda's Separate Opinion an apprehension of perverse consequences, were Portugal granted standing. Portugal had marked itself for over a decade as one of Europe's most unreconstructed colonial powers. It administered overseas territories in defiance of United Nations resolutions. It administered them badly. And, on the eve of Timorese independence, it evacuated the territory in a 'cut-and-run' fashion almost befitting comic opera. To have construed from UN practice any right in Portugal in East Timor would have run against UN purposes, as expressed in over forty years of practice regarding non-self-governing territories.

The Dissenting Opinions, filed by Judges Weeramantry and Skubiszewski, both propose that recognition of the territorial changes effectuated since 1975 by Indonesia on the island of Timor is a delict. But the two jurists differ in their reasoning. Weeramantry posits that a general international rule regarding recognition and nonrecognition of Portuguese and Indonesian claims over East Timor could have been deduced from United Nations practice since 1975. In this, Weeramantry concludes that the law has moved toward requiring that collective process govern recognition. Skubiszewski, by contrast, takes the view that the duty of nonrecognition flowed, not from a collective decision as to the status of East Timor, but from a general international rule of nonrecognition of changes effectuated by threat or use of force.

Weeramantry wrote that the ICJ proposed incorrectly to take on work properly performed already by the United Nations—that is, the work of deciding a collective international response to the purported incorporation of East Timor into Indonesia. "The Court cannot be reduced to inaction," Judge Weeramantry wrote, ". . . by throwing upon it a burden duly discharged by the appropriate United Nations organs, acting within their proper authority."[80] No interpretative judicial lens was necessary, as the UN resolutions were already international law: "[The] resolutions of the General Assembly which expressly reject the claim that East Timor has been integrated into Indonesia, declare that the people of East Timor must be enabled to determine their own future within the framework of the United Nations, and expressly recognize Portugal as the administering Power are resolutions which are productive of legal effects."[81] The resolutions, in Weeramantry's view, are a form of collective recognition, and the ICJ could have taken notice of this without further analysis. Australia, the dissenting opinion continued, extended *de jure* recognition to the annexation of East Timor, in possible violation of East Timorese sovereignty and East Timorese self-determination.[82] Weeramantry proposes the United Nations as an organ of collective recognition.

Judge Skubiszewski was perhaps more concerned over East Timorese rights, yet in the course of his Dissenting Opinion, left less certain than Weeramantry the role of the United Nations as an organ of collective recognition. Skubiszewski noted as progenitors of a modern rule of nonrecognition Hersch Lauterpacht and, with the eponymous doctrine on Manchukuo, Henry Stimson. The rule, he declared, "now constitutes part of general international law" and is even on its way to becoming *jus cogens*.[83] Territorial change enacted by force is not to be recognized, and this, Skubiszewski posits, is a "self-executory" rule: "[T]he rule of non-recognition operates in a self-executory way. To be operative it does not need to be repeated by the United Nations or other international organizations. Consequently, the absence of such direction on the part of the international organization in a particular instance does not relieve any State from the duty of non-recognition. Nor does the absence of 'collective sanctions' have that effect."[84] Skubiszewski's Dissenting Opinion does not support an institutionalized or collective approach to the law of recognition. In placing emphasis on the prohibition against the threat or use of force and on the rule of nonrecognition that he posits flows from that prohibition, Skubiszewski takes emphasis away from collective process. The rule is free-standing, and requires no collective evaluation of factual circumstances. Skubiszewski does posit that United Nations resolutions calling for nonrecognition *amplify* the responsibility of states to withhold recognition of the annexation of East Timor;[85] but he expressly declares that these are not necessary for that responsibility to attach (*see* quotation above). Indeed, Skubiszewski reaffirms the discretionary nature of recognition, terming recognition "still a 'free act.'" To be sure, he goes on to propose that "the discretionary nature of the act has been changed by the rule on the prohibition of the threat or use of force."[86] But, apparently, in Skubiszewski's view it remains with the individual state to determine whether an illegal use of force has occurred. UN resolutions may make this determination and have binding international effect, but Skubiszewski's Dissenting Opinion does not emphasize this. In fairness, Skubiszewski leaves some room for collective recognition: the requirement of nonrecognition may be overridden by "a collective decision of the international community"—a result not obtainable by "individual acts of recognition."[87] However, in the final analysis, Skubiszewski's dissent falls further from the collective or 'Lauterpachtian' model of recognition than Weeramantry's. In his Dissenting Opinion, Weeramantry comes closest on the present Court to stating a rule for collective recognition process.

The separate writings in *East Timor* may be distinguished by how much institutional process they argue is necessary to make nonrecognition mandatory. The Majority Opinion requires not only an initiative from the political organs of the United Nations, but also ICJ interpretation. (Because of the third party problem, no judicial interpretation was possible one way or the other in the case at bar.) Judge Weeramantry views UN resolutions as sufficient. According to Judge Skubiszewski, general international law on its own indicates when nonrecognition is mandatory, and he would require accordingly no formal or collective announcement of nonrecognition whatsoever.

Notably, the Court rejected an Australian argument that there was no justiciable issue presented for review. Australia had argued that Australia was being sued as a proxy for Indonesia, for Indonesian actions. Thus, the parties at bar were not parties in altercation. The Court, however, stated that a dispute did lie. The questions presented were (1) whether Australia had failed to recognize Portugal as the administering Power for East Timor, East Timor as a non-self-governing territory, and the right of the East Timorese to self-determination; and (2), in so doing, whether Australia had committed a delict.[88] In dismissing Australia's argument that Portugal had presented no dispute, the ICJ left open the possibility that states could in the future bring actions for delictual recognition. If the Court had ruled that no dispute was presented in Portugal's pleadings, then the only action open to a party alleging injury from illegal changes in territorial status would be an action against the malfeasant which executed the changes. This would remove any chance of sanction against a third state, such as Australia, contemplating recognition, express or implied, of the illegal but *de facto* situation. Under the majority opinion in *East Timor*, the ICJ could in principle entertain a suit against a third state accused of breaking a collective rule of nonrecognition. The problem in *East Timor* was that there was no such rule. According to the ICJ, nonrecognition opposable against third states in judicial proceedings cannot emanate from the UN political organs alone. The Court only acknowledged UN resolutions on East Timor as *evidence* of a rule of nonrecognition. To treat those resolutions themselves as a general rule of nonrecognition, the Court apprehended that it would have had to consider the resolutions, if not on their merits *de novo*, then at least with an eye to determining their international legal status. The Court did not consider the resolutions final as regarded Indonesian rights. Considering the resolutions, then, was the stumbling block. In the Court's view, to do so would have decided Indonesian rights. Without Indonesian consent to ICJ jurisdiction, no matter requiring decision as to Indonesian rights could be entertained. It was the absence of a pre-existing rule of nonrecognition—not the lack of a justiciable dispute—that barred the Court from holding on the merits. If, however, a rule of nonrecognition had already existed, then the case could have gone to the merits. The reservation implicit in the majority reasoning is that third states *could* be taken to task for acts of recognition done in the face of collective nonrecognition.

This is an important reservation. Recognition can best become a subject of law if its extension in violation of the law opens the donor to negative sanction. In the case at bar, collective nonrecognition simply was not a settled issue, nor could it have been settled, as the Court saw it, without deciding nonparty rights. If however the view espoused by Judge Weeramantry had been adopted by the Court, then Indonesia's legal rights would have already been decided—by the political organs of the UN. Then Portugal's claim against Australia could have been heard on the merits, and the ICJ would have had to tell whether Australia had committed an act of recognition in violation of collective process. In any event, even under the more demanding requirements set down by the Court, an action could someday be adjudicated against a third state for alleged violation of collective nonrecognition. In at least this narrow respect, *East Timor* furthers the Lauterpachtian collective approach.

## NOTES

1. *See* Thomas D. Grant, "Defining Statehood: The Montevideo Convention and its Discontents," 37 *Columbia Journal of Transnational Law* 403 (1999) (discussing problems with the definition provided by the Convention and noting opinion critical of the Convention).

2. John Dugard, *Recognition and the United Nations* (Cambridge: Grotius Publications Limited, 1987), 7–8.

3. Malcolm N. Shaw, *International Law*. 3rd ed. (Cambridge: Grotius Publications Ltd., 1991), 247.

4. Michael Akehurst, *A Modern Introduction to International Law*. 6th ed. (London: Routledge, 1987), 63.

5. Dugard, *Recognition*, 1.

6. Brierly was one of the notable writers contesting this proposition. *See* James L. Brierly, *The Law of Nations: An Introduction to the International Law of Peace*. Sir Humphrey Waldock ed., 6th ed. (Oxford: Clarendon Press, 1963), 28: "Few books have won so great a reputation as the *De jure belli ac pacis*, but to regard its author as the 'founder' of international law is to exaggerate its originality and to do less than justice to the writers who preceded him; neither Grotius, nor any other single writer, can properly be said to have 'founded' the system."

7. Hersch Lauterpacht, "The Grotian Tradition in International Law," 23 *British Yearbook of International Law* (BYIL) 1, 17 (1946). By permission of the Royal Institute of International Affairs, London.

8. Enumerated and discussed in Lauterpacht, "Grotian Tradition," 23 BYIL 1.

9. Lauterpacht, "Grotian Tradition," 23 BYIL at 19.

10. Lauterpacht cited as a work typifying the positivist view William E. Hall, *A Treatise on International Law*. A. Pearce Higgins ed., 8th ed. (Oxford: Clarendon Press, 1924) (orig. 1890). Lauterpacht, "Grotian Tradition," 23 BYIL at 21.

11. Lauterpacht, "Grotian Tradition," 23 BYIL at 24.

12. *Compare* "*Ius naturale*" and "*Ius gentium*", in David M. Walker, *The Oxford Companion to Law* (Oxford: Clarendon Press, 1980), 657.

13. Lauterpacht, "Grotian Tradition," 23 BYIL at 27.

14. Ibid., 30.

15. Chen, writing at about the same time as Lauterpacht, like Lauterpacht reacted against the positivism of traditional recognition theory. Chen, however, unlike Lauterpacht, adhered to the declaratory view of recognition. *See* Ti-Chiang Chen, *The International Law of Recognition, with special reference to Practice in Great Britain and the United States* (London: Stevens & Sons Limited, 1951), 17–29.

16. Hersch Lauterpacht, *Recognition in International Law* (Cambridge: The University Press, 1948), 67 (chapter VI, §28, "The Procedure of Recognition").

17. Ibid., 68.

18. Ibid., pp. 69–70, §29.

19. Ibid., pp. 70–73, §30.

20. Ibid., 68–69, 362.

21. Dugard, *Recognition*, 8.

22. Josef L. Kunz, "Critical Remarks on Lauterpacht's 'Recognition in International Law,'" 44 *American Journal of International Law* (AJIL) at 714 (1950).

23. Kunz cited as criticism a book review by E.J. Cohn in 64 Law Quarterly Review 404, 404–08 (1948); and Herbert W. Briggs, "Recognition of States, Some Reflections on Doctrine and Practice," 43 AJIL 113 (1949).

24. Hans Kelsen, "Recognition in International Law—Theoretical Observations," 35 AJIL 605 (1941).

25. Philip C. Jessup, *A Modern Law of Nations: An Introduction* (New York: MacMillan, 1948), 55. *See also, generally*, Philip C. Jessup, *The Birth of Nations* (New York: Columbia University Press, 1974).

26. Kunz, "Critical Remarks," 44 AJIL at 715.

27. Kunz was referring to Oppenheim, in particular Oppenheim's, "The Science of International Law: Its Tasks and Method," 2 AJIL 313 (1908).

28. Kunz, "Critical Remarks," 44 AJIL at 716.

29. Article 38 of the Statute of the Court provides, "The Court, whose function it is to decide in accordance with international law such disputes as are submitted to it, shall apply: . . . (d) . . . judicial decisions and the teachings of the most highly qualified publicists of the various nations, as a subsidiary means for the determination of rules of law."

30. Kunz, "Critical Remarks," 44 AJIL at 718.

31. Kunz, "Critical Remarks," 44 AJIL at note 29, citing Philip Marshall Brown, "The Recognition of Israel," 42 AJIL 620 (1948).

32. Kunz, "Critical Remarks," 44 AJIL at 719. The rebel government became the government of North Vietnam after Kunz wrote.

33. Georgia and the rest of the Caucasus were other early nineteenth century additions to the Empire. On Russian territorial expansion in the region generally, *see* Thomas D. Grant, "A Panel of Experts for Chechnya: Purposes and Prospects in Light of International Law," article forthcoming in *Finnish Yearbook of International Law* (1999).

34. *See* Alan Palmer, *Alexander I, Tsar of War and Peace* (London: Weidenfeld and Nicolson, 1974), 134–143, 152–53. Alexander, for Russia, and Napoleon, for France, performed the Treaty signing ceremony on a barge in the middle of the River Niemen at Tilsit. This colorful episode holds a place in literature as well as in diplomatic history. *See* Lev Nikolaevich Tolstoi, *War and Peace*. Louise Maude & Aylmer Maude trans. (Oxford: Oxford University Press, 1991), Book Two, Part II, §§19–21, pp. 431–441.

35. Terms of annexation had guaranteed that the annexing power, Russia, respect a late eighteenth century constitution of Sweden. The Swedish text had provided for a Finnish Diet. Russia declined to allow the legislature convene, however, until 1863. Annexation was in 1809.

36. The Polish state, a commanding presence in fifteenth- and sixteenth-century Europe, dwindled in several stages. Polish territory was divided beginning in the eighteenth century, among Prussia (Poznan or Posen), Austria (Cracow), and Russia (Warsaw and Lodz). The acquisition by Russia of the largest fraction of Poland was confirmed at the Congress of Vienna in 1815. The Russian share of Poland became known by its connection to the Congress; thus "Congress Poland." This status was official from 1815 until 1864 but remained in colloquial usage into the early twentieth century. For maps illustrating the partitions, see Norman Davies, *God's Playground: A History of Poland*, vol. II (Oxford: Clarendon Press, 1982), 83, 113, 140.

37. The parliament of Finland voted in August 1918 to elect a king. On the advice of Wilhelm II, the Finnish legislators chose one of the Kaiser's brothers-in-law, Prince Frederick Karl of Hesse. Acknowledging a changed political reality after the German surrender in November 1918, however, the prospective monarch of Finland renounced the crown. John H. Wuorinen, *A History of Finland* (New York: Columbia University Press, 1965), 232–33.

38. If historical tenure gave Russia basis for a claim to Finland by prescription, geography gave Russia strategic reasons to prevent Finnish independence, or at least a hostile régime taking power there: Finland, as then constituted, had its southeast-

ern frontier less than 100 kilometers from Petrograd, one-time capital and Russia's second largest city; and the principal Russian naval base in the Baltic, at the island of Kronstadt, communicated with the rest of the sea through narrow lanes formed on their northern side by the Finnish littoral. *See The Times Atlas of the World*. comp. ed. (London: John Bartholomew & Son Limited, 1981), plate 51.

39. Many of the surviving communists fled to Russia; others, interestingly, formed a substantial emigration to the United States. On the Finnish Civil War, see Wuorinen, *Finland*, 216–224.

40. Wuorinen, *Finland*, 216. The United States, United Kingdom, and Japan held off recognizing Finland until May 1919. This delay possibly reflected concern that the Finnish state relied too heavily on German military assistance. Armed forces from Germany, in the form of irregular *Freikorps* units, remained in Finland after the November 11, 1918 Armistice. Wuorinen, *Finland*, 234.

41. Also, on the eastern frontier, a contest arose over Finnish sovereignty in Karelia. *See Eastern Carelia Case*. PCIJ Reports, 1923, ser. B, no. 5. *See also* Manley O. Hudson, "The Eastern Carelia Question," 18 AJIL 7 (1924).

42. *See* "The Controversy Between Finland and Sweden over the Status of the Aaland Islands" in *Survey of International Affairs: 1920–1923*. Arnold J. Toynbee ed. (Oxford University Press: 1925), 234–238.

43. Wuorinen, *Finland*, 297–298.

44. *See League of Nations Official Journal* (Leag. Nat. O.J.), Special Supplement 4, 8–9 (1920).

45. On the origins of Japanese aggression in China, *see* James B. Crowley, *Japan's Quest for Autonomy: National Security and Foreign Policy, 1930–1938* (Princeton: Princeton University Press, 1966).

46. 112 Leag. Nat. O.J. 56 (1933).

47. Louis Cavaré, "La Reconnaissance de l'État et le Mandchoukouo," XLII *Revue Générale de Droit International Public* (RGDIP) 5, 8–10 (1935).

48. For perhaps the most comprehensive survey of diplomatic ties to Manchukuo, *see* Mo Shen, *Japan in Manchuria: An Analytical Study of Treaties and Documents* (Manila: Grace Trading Co. Inc., 1960), 299–300.

49. On Japan's own withdrawal from the League of Nations, *see* Sadako N. Ogata, *Defiance in Manchuria: The Making of Japanese Foreign Policy, 1931–1932* (Berkeley: University of California Press, 1964); Ian H. Nish, *Japan's Struggle with Internationalism: Japan, China and the League of Nations, 1931–3* (London: Kegan Paul International, 1992).

50. Harry R. Strack, *Sanctions: The Case of Rhodesia* (Syracuse: Syracuse University Press, 1978), 5–6, 52. For contemporaneous analysis by distinguished publicists, *see* Myres S. McDougal & W. Michael Reisman, "Rhodesia and the United Nations: The Lawfulness of International Concern," 62 AJIL 1, 3 (1968). A survey after the demise of white-ruled Rhodesia is provided in Jericho Nkala, *The United Nations, International Law, and the Rhodesian Independence Crisis* (Oxford: Clarendon Press, 1985), 53–76. *See also* Michael Charlton, *The Last Colony in Africa: Diplomacy and the Independence of Rhodesia* (Oxford: Basil Blackwell, 1990); Vera Gowlland-Debbas, *Collective Responses to Illegal Acts in International Law: United Nations Action in the Question of Southern Rhodesia* (Dordrecht: Martinus Nijhoff Publishers, 1990), 273–361.

51. SC Resolutions 264 and 269 (1969).

52. *Legal Consequences for States of the Continued Presence of South Africa in Namibia (South West Africa) Notwithstanding Security Council Resolution 276 (1970)*, Advisory Opinion. ICJ Reports, 1971, p. 46.

53. Collective nonrecognition of the TRNC may also have been determined by other multilateral organizations. The British Commonwealth, the Council of Europe, and the EC/EU expressly recognize only the Republic of Cyprus. Thomas Oppermann, "Cyprus," *Encyclopedia of Public International Law*, vol. one, Peter Macalister-Smith ed. (New York: North-Holland, 1992), 923, 926.

54. *See* "Proclamation of Syrian Independence by General Catroux," September 27, 1941. *Quoted in Répertoire de la Pratique Française en Matiére de Droit International Public* (Pratique Française ). vol. V (Paris: Centre National de la Recherche Scientifique, 1965), 152–53.

55. *See* "Telegram from Secretary of State to the Diplomatic Agent and Consul General at Beirut," 1943 *Foreign Relations of the United States*, vol. iv, 966. Crawford attributed nonrecognition to the American assessment that the purported grant of colonial independence lacked substance in reality. James R. Crawford, *The Creation of States in International Law* (Oxford: Clarendon Press, 1979), 66–67. Britain's acceptance of the Free French statement as a valid grant of independence arguably reflected Britain's aim of maintaining influence over its own colonies. If it was unavoidable that international law was to require independence for colonies, perhaps the definition of independence could be shaped in a way tolerant of residual rights in the former colonial power. The United States, having few overseas dependencies, did not perceive its interests threatened by a definition requiring removal of metropolitan influence. Rejecting the Syrian independence grant cost the United States little. Britain, by contrast, may have apprehended that a strict definition of independence (i.e., one allowing little post-independence influence on the part of the former colonial power) would cost Britain a great deal, when Britain set about acceding to demands by international society to grant independence to its colonies. Britain and the United States are seen in the Syrian case trying to develop state practice toward independence in different ways, either power conditioned in its law-making efforts by its perceived political interests.

56. Alasdair Drysdale, "National Integration Problems in the Arab World: The Case of Syria," in *Nationalism, Self-Determination and Political Geography*. R.J. Johnston, David B. Knight & Eleonore Kofman eds. (London: Croom Helm, 1988), 90.

57. The Lend-Lease Act was signed in March 1941. Franklin D. Roosevelt delivered his "Arsenal of Democracy" speech on December 29, 1940, in which he said, "We must be the great arsenal of democracy. For us this is an emergency as serious as war itself. We must apply ourselves to our task with the same resolution, the same sense of urgency, the same spirit of patriotism and sacrifice as we would show were we at war." Franklin D. Roosevelt, "Fireside Chat on National Security from the White House," *The Public Papers and Addresses of Franklin D. Roosevelt.* Speech 14, December 29, 1940, 1940 vol. (London: MacMillan and Co., Limited, 1941), 643. The Alliance would be formalized in August 1941 with the Atlantic Charter.

58. Iceland, for example, recognized Lithuania in February 1991, a measure at variance with the cautious approach taken by the principal state actors. *See* Debra Rowland & Martin Zabell, "Lithuanians Mark Independence Day," *Chicago Tribune* (Chi. Trib.) Monday February 18, 1991, p. 7 and, for a characterization of the

conservative stance of the United States, see "U.S. on Secession: Maybe," *New York Times*, June 28, 1991. Online at 1991 *Westlaw* 2085744, 6/28/91, *New York Times Abstracts* 8.

59. On the admission of Israel to the United Nations, *see* Dugard, *Recognition*, 60–63.

60. *See* Brown, "Recognition of Israel," 42 AJIL at 620.

61. Ibid., 621.

62. The objects of recognition may be divided into four categories:

1. new states;
2. extraconstitutional changes of government;
3. changes of territorial possession; and
4. claims of belligerent status by insurgent movements within a recognized state.

Edwin L. Fountain, "Out from the Precarious Orbit of Politics: Reconsidering Recognition and the Standing of Foreign Governments to Sue in U.S. Courts," 29 *Virginia Journal of International Law* (Virg. J. Int'l L.) 473, 510 (1989). *East Timor* concerned the third of these categories. Recognition, to be sure, means different things for different categories of object. Whatever the object of recognition however, recognition involves acknowledging a new situation containing an international dimension, and it makes some aspect of the situation opposable against the recognizing state. Whether acknowledging the new situation should be performed by individual states or in a collective framework is a potent issue for all objects of recognition.

63. General Salazar, long-time military dictator of Portugal, suffered a debilitating stroke in September 1968. The prime minister, Caetano, formed a government and, upon Salazar's death in July 1970, became head of state. Caetano was ousted in a socialist coup, known as the 'Carnation Revolution,' in April 1974. Portugal enacted the *Law of 27 July 1974* acknowledging that all non-self-governing territories under Portuguese administration had a right to self-determination, including a right to independence. A summary of this history appears in *Case Concerning East Timor (Portugal* v. *Australia)*. Separate Opinion, Judge Oda, ICJ Reports, 1995, p. 110, ¶¶ 12, *et seq*.

64. Guinea-Bissauan independence, September 10, 1974; Mozambican independence, June 25, 1975; Angolan independence, November 11, 1975. Central Intelligence Agency, *The World Factbook 1993–1994* (Washington: Brassey's, 1993), 142–43, 236–37, 9–10.

65. Indonesia gained independence in 1949, after thwarting two desultory police actions by the Netherlands. *See* Wilfred T. Neill, *Twentieth Century Indonesia* (New York: Columbia University Press, 1973), 323–32.

66. The first General Assembly Resolution was 3485(XXX). It was followed by resolutions 31/35, 32/34, 33/39, 34/40, 35/27, 36/50, and 37/30. For discussion of relevant UN practice, see Roger S. Clark, "The 'decolonisation' of East Timor and the United Nations norms on self-determination and aggression," chapter 4 in *International Law and the Question of East Timor* (London & Leiden: Catholic Institute for International Relations & International Platform of Jurists for East Timor, 1995), 65–102.

67. East Timor had been declared a non-self-governing territory by General Assembly Resolution 1542(v) of December 15, 1960.

68. *East Timor*. Opinion of the Court, 1995, ICJ Reports at 97.

69. Reporting international consensus that the presence of Indonesia in East Timor

is illegal, *see* "In East Timor, A Quiet Rite," *International Herald Tribune*, July 18, 1996, p. 4. Further suggesting continued international interest in the issue, a number of states reportedly recognized East Timor as an independent state in 1975 and have given no indication that they 'retract' their recognition. The recognizing states were Angola, Cape Verde, Guinea-Bissau, Mozambique, Sao Tome and Principe, Albania, Benin, Cambodia, the People's Republic of China, Congo (Brazzaville), Guinea (Conakry), North Korea, Laos, Vietnam, and Tanzania. Clark, " 'Decolonisation' of East Timor," 70–71 n. 29.

70. For initial motions in the case, see *East Timor*. ICJ Reports, 1991 at 9; ICJ Reports, 1992 at 228; and ICJ Reports, 1993 at 32.

71. *Monetary Gold Removal from Rome in 1943*. ICJ Reports, 1954, p. 32.

72. *East Timor*. Majority Opinion, ICJ Reports, 1995 at pp. 101–02, ¶ 27.

73. *East Timor*, Majority Opinion, p. 103, ¶ 30.

74. *East Timor*, Majority Opinion, p. 103, ¶ 31.

75. *East Timor*, Majority Opinion, p. 104, ¶ 32.

76. *East Timor*, Majority Opinion, p. 105, ¶ 35. Considering that the core of operative fact in East Timor was an alleged delict by Indonesia, it is curious that Portugal did not bring suit against Indonesia. Portugal may well have decided that Indonesia was very unlikely to consent to jurisdiction. By contrast, Australia was probably assumed to be amenable. There however may have been an advantage in targeting Australia besides its greater willingness to participate in an ICJ action. Portugal moved on the proposition that there is an international norm, obliging collective nonrecognition of statuses achieved by illegal use of force, and, perhaps, that, even if the Court declined to accept the existence of such a norm, Australia and its opinion-forming polity would be sensitive to the charge of a violation. Public disapprobation is a more powerful force in the effective power processes of a liberal democratic state than of an authoritarian one. Accordingly, challenging Australia before the ICJ might have triggered political reactions beneficial to Portugal's cause. Though a favorable internal dynamic might not have been entirely lacking in Indonesia, the role of civil society in shaping international legal policy there is probably less pronounced than in Australia. An ICJ action against Indonesia, even in the unlikely event Indonesia had consented, would have eventuated little internal pressure to change policy toward East Timor. An ICJ action against Australia, even in the event of dismissal before a hearing on the merits, probably furthered Portugal's cause in the political processes of the respondent. For some thoughts on whether an impleaded but non-appearing state can be a 'party' to ICJ proceedings, see Hugh W.A. Thirlway, *Non-Appearance Before the International Court of Justice* (Cambridge: Cambridge University Press, 1985), 46–63.

77. *East Timor*, Separate Opinion, Judge Shahabuddeen, 123.

78. *East Timor*, Separate Opinion, Judge Vereshchetin, 135.

79. *East Timor*, Separate Opinion, Judge Oda, p. 116, ¶ 15. Judge Oda, like Judge Shahabuddeen, expressed concern over the indigenous people.

80. *East Timor*, Dissenting Opinion, Judge Weeramantry, 155.

81. *East Timor*, Dissenting Opinion, Judge Weeramantry, 186. Citations omitted.

82. *East Timor*, Dissenting Opinion, Judge Weeramantry, 204.

83. *East Timor*, Dissenting Opinion, Judge Skubiszewski, p. 262, ¶ 125.

84. *East Timor*, Dissenting Opinion, Judge Skubiszewski, p. 263, ¶ 130.

85. *East Timor*, Dissenting Opinion, Judge Skubiszewski, p. 263, ¶ 129 (noting,

in addition to a general rule requiring nonrecognition of changes achieved by force, UN resolutions on the status of East Timor).

86. *East Timor*, Dissenting Opinion, Judge Skubiszewski, p. 263, ¶ 129.

87. *East Timor*, Dissenting Opinion, Judge Skubiszewski, p. 265, ¶ 132.

88. *East Timor*, Majority Opinion, 100.

# 6

# THE YUGOSLAV RECOGNITION CRISIS

The close of the Cold War brought unexpected changes to the map of Europe. The breakup of the USSR fortunately was negotiated with minimal friction, but the advent of new states in the space of the Socialist Federal Republic of Yugoslavia was not so peaceful. Serbia and Montenegro, the political core of the federation, resisted the secession of the other constituent republics. For the first time since the 1940s, Europe was confronted by the spectre of warfare on the Continent, and it was not at all clear how to react to the emergence of several putative new states in the center of the conflict. In connection with this problem, the early 1990s brought a test of the law of recognition.

The critical question surrounding recognition of the Yugoslav secessionists—Slovenia, Croatia, and later Bosnia and Macedonia—was whether a collective process could be maintained in the face of differing national priorities and the lingering conviction that to recognize a new state is an act of sovereign discretion. Collectivization of recognition was indeed espoused in European practice toward the new states. The extent to which recognition in reality took place in collective fashion is less clear. Still less clear is whether practice recast the law of recognition or simply reflected political expediency.

## HISTORICAL OVERVIEW

To analyze the Yugoslav crisis as a crisis in the law and politics of recognition, it is useful first to summarize the historical context in which the crisis arose.

The Yugoslav civil wars of the 1990s stemmed from a combination of contemporary problems and remote antecedents. Writers in the social and political sciences debate how the earlier history of the region interacted with its modern social, political, and economic problems.[1] A review of the origins of the Yugoslav civil wars is beyond the scope of the present treatment, but a number of features of the Balkan past are salient to an analysis of European response to the secessions of 1991–92.

The space of the former Yugoslavia straddled two ancient ethno-religious dividing lines, that separating Catholic from Orthodox Europe and that separating Christian from Islamic civilization. The legacy of those divides is plainly in evidence. The Croatian and Serbian peoples, though linguistically and ethnically very similar, adhere respectively to the Catholic and Orthodox faiths. Their political cultures arguably reflect the divide, with Croats perhaps taking after Central Europe in their civic organization, the Serbs after the European East. The Croats use Latin script; the Serbs Cyrillic. The Croats were unsure from its inception in 1918 whether they wanted part in a Yugoslav state; the Serbs were the driving force behind that state.[2] Croatia gravitated geopolitically toward Germany; Serbia, variably, toward France and Russia. Accommodating both groups in a single state was one of the challenges in which Yugoslavia failed.

A further challenge had been the Islamic heritage. Especially in Bosnia, but in Kosovo as well, substantial Muslim minorities added to the patchwork appearance of the ethno-religious map. The Bosnian Muslims (or 'Bosniacs') were Slavic converts, brought into the Islamic fold during Ottoman Turkish rule. Though playing a comparatively minor role in crises earlier this century, the Bosnian Muslims found themselves at the center of the most damaging strife in the 1990s Yugoslav breakdown.

For purposes of the recognition of new states in the space of the former Yugoslavia, perhaps the most complicating factor was past involvement of outside powers in the region. Turkey had once ruled much of the Balkans, and a sense of obligation to Bosnia's Muslims posed some risk of embroiling Turkey in the 1990s strife.[3] Russia long had taken the view that, as a Slavic Orthodox country, it ought to defend Serbia. However, most important in the crisis over recognition was past involvement in the region by Germany and Austria.

The Austro-Hungarian Empire until 1918 ruled Slovenia, Croatia, Bosnia, and part of Serbia. The influence of its reign may well still be detected in culture and politics.[4] German involvement replaced Austrian after World War I. In the 1920s and 1930s, to be sure, German involvement was indirect—investment and attempts (initially unsuccessful) at diplomatic penetration. Nazi conquest of Yugoslavia in 1941 radically intensified the German role in the area. Siding with the Germans, Croat nationalists set up a state including Croatia and Bosnia, less annexations to Germany's allies Italy and Hungary. Though a satellite of the Third Reich under occupation by German and Italian armies, World War II Croatia perpetrated atrocities against Serbs, Gypsies, Jews, and Muslims. The vigor with which the Ustashi (the fascist Croat movement favored by Hitler) prosecuted religious and ethnic slaughter may well have exceeded that of any Nazi ally.[5] This tragedy of the Yugoslav past has continued to shape perceptions about Germany and Croatia. Combined with the problem of Germany's World War II conduct generally, this factor made German policy during the 1990s dissolution of Yugoslavia a keenly sensitive matter. Debate over how to respond to the dissolution of the Balkan federation frequently made reference to the liabilities of the German past.

The immediate predicate to civil war was the degradation of two systems—of a federal state structure divided only approximately along ethnic lines; and of a communist political monopoly.[6] One contemporary problem was economic disparity between comparatively wealthy republics (Slovenia and Croatia) and poorer members of the Socialist Federal Republic of Yugoslavia (Serbia, Montenegro, Macedonia, and Bosnia-Herzegovina). The more prosperous republics may well have contributed disproportionately to federal budgets, and central government expenditures may well have been targeted disproportionately to Serb-speaking areas. Foreign exchange proceeds, it was complained, were not allocated fairly by the central bank, and this exacerbated the active policy of transfer payments to poorer republics. Internal fiscal and organizational problems were a source of discontent in Yugoslavia.

At the same time, external affairs arguably began in the late 1980s to disfavor the polyglot federation. Western pressure to maintain debt service schedules has been identified as a factor aggravating the Yugoslav situation.[7] Arguably more important was the waning of the Soviet threat. The peoples of Yugoslavia, some writers argue, tolerated integration under a federal state because they apprehended that disunity would invite a Russian move on the region and possibly end in reduction of the peoples to satellite status within the Soviet sphere. Soviet retreat after 1989 ended this fear, making safe in theory a breakup of the SFRY. The death in 1980 of Marshall Tito, leader of wartime anti-Nazi resistance, removed a personal force that apparently had played by turns a mediating and enforcing role. A renaissance of nationalism, starting in Croatia in the 1970s, provided an impetus for breakdown, once the various unifying influences declined. When states of the soon-to-be-dissolved Warsaw Pact accelerated their transitions to free market economies, the example made free-market-leaning republics all the more impatient for change in Yugoslavia. Slovene deputies at an extraordinary party congress quit the League of Communists of Yugoslavia in January 1990, and the unravelling of the SFRY came into open view. The process of dissolution continued through spring 1991. Slovenia and Croatia declared themselves independent states on June 25, 1991. The federal government, increasingly an organ of the two Serb-majority republics, Serbia and Montenegro, resisted secession. Federal armed forces fought Slovene secessionists briefly, giving up the small homogeneous republic by early July. In Croatia, however, in which nearly a third of the territory was inhabited by ethnic Serbs, federal forces prosecuted a vigorous and destructive campaign to prevent secession. Violence escalated in Eastern Slavonia, and by August the first of two civil wars in the space of Yugoslavia was underway.

## EUROPEAN RESPONSE

Western Europe had apprehended violence in Yugoslavia some months before the breakdown of summer 1991. The EC assembled a troika of foreign ministers—Jacques Poos (Luxembourg), Gianni De Michelis (Italy), and Hans van den Broek (the Netherlands)—and the troika was sent numerous times to Yugoslavia in efforts to mediate.[8] The foreign ministers had visited Yugoslavia in April 1991 to try to fend off the disintegration of Yugoslavia which some were then beginning to believe possible.[9] On British motion at a May 13 EC meeting, the steadily-brewing crisis formally entered the EC agenda. Consensus was reached at that meeting that Jacques Santer, as prime minister of Luxembourg and chairman of the European Council, and Jacques Delors, as EC Commission president, also visit the federation. The EC intensified its efforts after the June 25 secessions and, moreover, after war broke out in Croatia. On June 28, the foreign ministers troika returned to Belgrade. The EC and the CSCE (Council for Security and Cooperation in Europe) discussed various options for peace negotiations under joint auspices, and the United Nations Security Council was also proposed as a framework for a Yugoslavia conference. The EC however emerged the chief institution in international response to the crisis. Lord Peter Carrington headed the European Conference on Yugoslavia at the Hague starting on September 7, 1991.[10]

In addition to putting in motion an active shuttle diplomacy, the EC issued a number of statements. A Declaration on the Situation in Yugoslavia issued at Brussels on July 2, 1991 demanded that parties to hostilities "immediately abstain from all acts of violence." A Joint Statement on the Situation in Yugoslavia was issued at Washington, DC, on July 3 by Hans van den Broek (in his capacity as representative of EC presidency incumbent, the Netherlands), Frans Andriessen, the Vice-President of the European Commission, and James Baker, the United States Secretary of State. The Joint Statement noted that the Yugoslav military had "rejected civilian control;" condemned this and the use of force; and called for "an immediate halt to the violence." The Joint Statement also indicated support for an international observer mission to monitor the cease-fire which the Joint Statement had urged. A Statement on Yugoslavia (issued July 19) welcomed the withdrawal of the Yugoslav Peoples' Army (JNA) from Slovenia and invited those parties still engaged in hostilities to negotiate under EC auspices. After breaches in the first EC cease-fire, an Extraordinary Ministerial Meeting of the EC issued a Declaration on Yugoslavia expressing "grave concern at the infringements of the ceasefire," and "appeal[ing] to the parties concerned to do everything within their power to ensure that the negotiating process will not be marred by further violence." This Declaration reiterated that the EC and its member States would "continue to keep the situation in Yugoslavia under close review."[11]

Closely tied to the European Conference was an EC Arbitration Commission (variously termed a "committee" and a "commission"), set up in August under the same EC Declaration as the Conference. The Arbitration Commission would be chaired by the president of the French Constitutional Council, Robert Badinter. The Badinter Commission, as this five-member body became known, was part of a broader European effort to mediate the crisis which had erupted in the space of the former Yugoslav federation.

Though the United States, the Soviet Union, and various West European states and organizations stated their disapproval of Croat and Slovene unilateral declarations of independence, Germany quickly began to suggest that it would extend recognition to the putative states. As early as August 7, 1991, the German government expressed support for the secessionists. Far in advance of any other power, Germany, on November 27, 1991, pledged recognition to the republics, assuring, moreover, that recognition would come "before Christmas." Despite a December 16 decision by EU foreign ministers to delay recognition until January 15, 1992, and to condition it upon various political and legal assurances,[12] Germany recognized Croatia and Slovenia on December 23, 1991. The response of the United States, the EU, and of individual EU member states (especially the United Kingdom) was highly adverse. Nonetheless, the EU extended recognition on January 15, 1992, while the United States would refuse to recognize until April 7. After German and EU recognition, the organs of public opinion formation, including many government ministries, leveled a barrage of criticism against the German diplomatic act. Some would accuse Germany of dragging an unwilling Europe into an ill-advised extension of recognition and, later, of precipitating the civil war in Bosnia-Herzegovina. This was the immediate European background of the Yugoslav recognition crisis.

## THE BADINTER COMMISSION: RECOGNITION BY ARBITRATION?

The International Court of Justice, as will be recalled from Chapter 5, in its *East Timor* decision proposed that the United Nations does not contain an apparatus for collective recognition. One result of the holding is, arguably, that, though the UN is competent to decide questions of recognition for its own purposes, its decisions on the matter are not universally binding.[13] *East Timor* did not however preclude some UN role in recognition, nor did it rule out the possibility that some other multilateral organ could address recognition. Faced at the end of the Cold War with a sudden efflorescence of state formation, Western Europe attempted to establish an *ad hoc* mechanism for recognition. Civil war precipitated the Peace Conference on Yugoslavia, and with the Conference was convened a Commission of Arbitration. Known by the name of its chairman, Robert Badinter,[14] the Badinter Commission was set up under a European Community Declaration on Yugoslavia of August 27, 1991. The Commission delivered its first opinion on November 29.

### Sources of the Badinter Commission Mandate

The establishment of the Conference on Yugoslavia and the Arbitration Commission was announced by the EC on August 27 in a *Declaration on Yugoslavia*.[15] Robert Badinter presided over the arbitral body, the other four members of which were the Presidents of the Constitutional Courts of Germany and Italy (Roman Herzog and Aldo Corrasaniti), of the Court of Arbitration of Belgium (Irène Petry), and of the Constitutional Tribunal of Spain (Francisco Tomas y Valiente).[16] The Badinter Commission was created by the European Community and its member States. This implied that the authority of the Commission—however the scope of that authority was to be defined—derived from two related but distinct sources: from the European Community as a legal entity unto itself and from the constituents of the Community. Such dual authorization is common to many bodies set up by the Community.

The source of the Commission's authority and its composition may have been clear, but other matters were not. The scope of the Commission's mandate was nowhere explicitly set out. Even in the estimation of Alain Pellet, a champion of the body,[17] "[t]he mandate given the Committee was somewhat vague."[18] The August 27 EC *Declaration on Yugoslavia* establishing the Arbitration Commission read in pertinent part:

> The Community and its member States cannot stand idly by as the bloodshed in Croatia increases day by day. An agreement on the monitoring of the cease-fire and its maintenance[19] should allow the Community and its member States to convene a peace conference and establish an arbitration procedure. This peace conference will bring together:
>
> – on the part of Yugoslavia, the Federal Presidency,[20]
>
> – the President of the Council,[21] representatives of the member States and the Commission.[22]
>
> The arbitration procedure in the framework of this peace conference will be established as follows. The relevant authorities will submit their differences to an Arbitration Commission of five members chosen from the Presidents of Constitutional Courts existing in the Community countries. The composition of the Arbitration Commission will be:
>
> – two members appointed unanimously by the Federal Presidency;
>
> – three members appointed by the Community and its member States.

> In the absence of agreement of the members to be appointed by the Federal Presidency [of Yugoslavia], they will be designated by the three members appointed by the Community.
>
> This Arbitration Commission will give its decision within two months.[23]

The phrasing of the *Declaration* was very broad. No specific instructions were offered as to procedure,[24] and other aspects essential to constituting a judicial organ were omitted. The *Declaration* did not define what parties enjoyed standing before the organ, referring only to "relevant authorities." Reference to "bloodshed in Croatia" suggests momentarily a focus limited to that republic; it was the escalating violence there that in summer 1991 most aroused public concern. (The civil war in Bosnia had yet to erupt). However, the *Declaration* elsewhere embraces all the constituents of the Yugoslav federation, so a more expansive jurisdiction was apparently intended. Other paragraphs of the August 27 *Declaration* hint at the subject matter which the EC intended the Arbitration Commission to reach. Matters mentioned in the *Declaration* included changes of frontiers by force, other illegal uses of force, and human rights ("protection of the rights of all"). Beyond this, however, the *Declaration* was sketchy. No procedures for Commission deliberations were set, no mechanisms for compliance described. Such a loosely-textured mandate could be concretized only by reference to previous EC statements and perhaps by future elaborations of the Commission's scope and procedures.

EC declarations from the several months leading up to the August 27 *Declaration* gave some indication as to the scope intended for the Arbitration Commission. An EC Declaration of July 2 concentrated on Slovenia. A Joint Statement on the Situation in Yugoslavia of July 3 (issued by the EC and the United States at Washington) encompassed the situation in Yugoslavia generally and the deployment of federal armed forces specifically. A July 19 EC Statement on Yugoslavia addressed itself to the Yugoslav collective presidency, and a August 20 Extraordinary Ministerial Meeting produced a Declaration on Yugoslavia emphasizing "the rights of peoples and minorities in all the Republics." If read in view of its predecessors, the August 27 *Declaration* would seem to contemplate for the Arbitration Commission a mandate covering the whole of Yugoslavia and diverse substantive issues. The August 27 *Declaration* can be identified as the "legal basis" for the Commission[25] only in a relative sense.

Declarations after August 27 supported a broad scope for the Commission. An October 5 Declaration, resulting from an informal meeting of EC foreign ministers at Haarzuilens, criticized Serbia and Montenegro for their takeover of the Yugoslav collective federal presidency, in derogation of the constitutional role of the federal parliament. The same ministerial meeting produced a Declaration on October 6, in which the ministers expressed the opinion that persons responsible for loss of life in Yugoslavia "should be held accountable under international law." A September Declaration had welcomed the fact that "*all Yugoslav parties* have accepted the goals and instruments for a solution to the crisis as contained in the EC Declaration of 27 August 1991" [emphasis supplied]. The *Declaration* of August 27 itself emphasized only the situation in Croatia; and that was the situation precipitating public agitation for diplomatic or other intervention.[26] However, the EC considered itself seised of all facets of the crisis in Yugoslavia. It is this broad understanding of the EC role that framed the *Declaration* of August 27 and set the agenda of the Badinter Commission.[27]

The Arbitration Commission was intended to have a geographic scope co-terminous with that of the EC Peace Conference—that is, the whole of Yugoslavia. It was less evident what precise issues within that geographic scope were subject to the Commission's jurisdiction. Again, however, the overall context made it reasonably apparent that the Commission should reach a broad variety of issues. Minority rights, use of force, border changes,[28] the rule of law, state succession, and recognition all eventually fell within the Commission's brief.

A moment of tension arose when the Federal Republic of Yugoslavia (FRY) challenged the competence of the Commission to pass on the matter of the recognition of the FRY.[29] The FRY, through the presidents of its two constituent republics, argued that the Commission derived its competence from the Brioni Agreement alone, which on July 7, 1991, had provided for a cease-fire in Slovenia.[30] According to the FRY, the scope of the Commission mandate was narrow, and the arbitrators had no *compétence de la compétence.* To take up questions of recognition, succession, or state dissolution was in the Yugoslav view an *excès de pouvoir* on the part of the arbitrators. The Commission, in an unnumbered Interlocutory Decision preceding Opinions 8, 9, and 10, rejected FRY jurisdiction arguments. The Commission held that it was not the Brioni Agreement but the August 27 Extraordinary Meeting of Ministers in the context of European Political Cooperation (EPC)[31] that gave the Commission its mandate. Moreover, the Commission cited decisions concerning the power of international tribunals to decide their own competence. The ICJ, in *Nottebohm*, had stated that "in the absence of any agreements to the contrary, the international tribunal has the right to decide as to its own jurisdiction and has the power to interpret for this purpose the instruments which govern that jurisdiction."[32] The ICJ had added in *Nottebohm* that the principle of *compétence de la compétence* operated with special vigor, where an arbitral tribunal, rather than springing from a special agreement among the parties, "is an instrument which has been preestablished by an international instrument defining its jurisdiction." The Badinter Commission determined itself to be that type of tribunal, and, moreover, a tribunal contemplated by its mandating document (the August 27 *Declaration*) to possess a very broad scope. The status of the rump Yugoslavia was held to fall within the jurisdiction of the Commission.[33]

The next most critical instrument in defining the role of the Badinter

Commission was the December 16 *Declaration on the "Guidelines on the Recognition of New States in Eastern Europe and the Soviet Union."* The December 16 *Guidelines* were accompanied by a separate *Declaration* detailing a procedure for applying for recognition. These documents resulted from an Extraordinary EPC Ministerial Meeting, held at Brussels on December 16, 1991. The *Guidelines* and the *Declaration* they accompanied purported to establish a collective mechanism for the recognition of new states. This mechanism consisted of several steps. First, a set of threshold requirements was enumerated in the separate *Declaration*. On or before December 23, 1991, any republic of Yugoslavia wishing to be recognized by the EC and its member States would formally announce its wish to be recognized. Along with indicating its wish to be recognized, the putative state had to affirm

1. acceptance of provisions laid down in a Draft Convention on Yugoslavia,[34] including provisions on human rights and on the rights of national and ethnic groups;

2. continued support for

(a) the peace efforts of the Secretary-General and the Security Council of the United Nations and

(b) the continuation of the Conference on Yugoslavia; and

3. acceptance of the commitments contained in the *Guidelines on the Recognition of New States*.

The separate *Declaration* set an application procedure that the claimant to recognition was required to follow, if its claim was to be evaluated on the merits. Whether the threshold criteria were satisfied was to be determined by the Conference. A complete application (that is, one satisfying items 1 through 3 above) the Conference chair was to submit to the Arbitration Commission on behalf of the claimant. In no case did it appear that the Conference declared an application for recognition to fail to satisfy these threshold criteria. (The fate of an application by the ethnic Albanian "shadow government" of Kosovo is unclear.) Indeed, there is no indication that the Conference subjected applications to more than facial inspection.

In the second step of the procedure, the Commission evaluated the application in view of the *Guidelines*. The December 16 *Declaration* provided that any republic submitting its application by the December 23 deadline would receive a response from the arbitrators before January 15, 1992. The arbitrators would study the application and conditions then obtaining in the applicant republic to adjudge conformity with the *Guidelines*. The *Guidelines* stated:

The Community and its member States confirm their attachment to the principles of the Helsinki Final Act and the Charter of Paris,[35] in particular the principle of self-determination. They affirm their readiness to recognise, subject to the normal standards of international practice and the political realities in each case, those new

States which, following the historic changes in the region, have constituted themselves on a democratic basis, have accepted the appropriate international obligations and have committed themselves in good faith to a peaceful process and to negotiations.

Therefore, they adopt a common position on the process of recognition of these new states, which requires:

–respect for the provisions of the Charter of the United Nations and the commitments subscribed to in the Final Act of Helsinki and in the Charter of Paris, especially with regard to the rule of law, democracy and human rights;

–guarantees for the rights of ethnic and national groups and minorities in accordance with the commitments subscribed to in the framework of the CSCE;[36]

–respect for the inviolability of all frontiers which can only be changed by peaceful means and by common agreements;

–acceptance of all relevant commitments with regard to disarmament and nuclear non-proliferation as well as to security and regional stability; [and]

–commitment to settle by agreement, including where appropriate by recourse to arbitration, all questions concerning State succession and regional disputes.

The Community and its member States will not recognise entities which are the result of aggression. They would take account of the effects of recognition on neighbouring States.

The commitment to these principles opens the way to recognition by the Community and its member States and to the establishment of diplomatic relations. It could be laid down in agreements.

One additional criterion for recognition was included in the December 16 Declaration:

The Community and its member States also require a Yugoslav republic to commit itself, prior to recognition, to adopt constitutional and political guarantees ensuring that it has no territorial claims towards a neighboring Community State and that it will conduct no hostile propaganda activities versus a neighboring Community State, including the use of a denomination which implies territorial claims.

In an otherwise loosely textured document this last requirement stands out for its precision. Greek politicians were under pressure from their constituents to check any territorial ambitions which Macedonia might harbor over Greece's northern province. Many Greeks believed that that province, bearing the same name as the republic, was a target of Macedonian expansionists. The specific clause appears to have been the price of Greek cooperation in setting up an EC collective recognition mechanism and illustrates the political hurdles to establishing such a mechanism.

The third and final step in the procedure outlined on December 16 was "implementation." If the Arbitration Commission opined that an applicant republic satisfied all the relevant criteria, then on the date prescribed in the *Declaration*—January 15, 1992—the Community and each member State would recognize that republic.

The December 16 EC meeting thus produced a procedure and a set of substantive criteria for the Badinter Commission to employ in its previously inchoate role of collective recognition organ.

### The Badinter Commission Opinions

The Commission issued fifteen opinions from November 29, 1991 to August 13, 1993. Four of these addressed applications for recognition;[37] others addressed questions raised by Yugoslavia[38] and by the Chair or Co-Chair of the European Conference.[39] Additionally, after the FRY challenged its competence, the Commission published an unnumbered opinion (May 26, 1993); and the Commission also published *Observations on Croatian Constitutional Law of 4 December 1991 as Amended on 8 May 1992* (July 4, 1992). The Commission findings most pertinent to recognition are contained in Opinions 1 through 10, summarized here *seriatim*.

*Opinion 1* (November 19, 1991). Lord Carrington inquired of the Arbitration Commission, on November 20, 1990, if the Yugoslav federation survived secessions of several of its constituent republics, or if the secessions resulted in disintegration of that state. The question had implications for state succession. If the old SFRY had disintegrated, then all the resultant pieces, including the federation of Serbia and Montenegro, were new states and legally equal successors. If it simply had lost certain of its former constituents, then these former constituents were not automatic successors to Yugoslav rights—only Serbia and Montenegro would enjoy that status.[40] Noting that Croatia, Slovenia, Macedonia, and Bosnia had declared independence (or had moved decisively toward independence); that the federal organs of Yugoslavia had ceased to function; that elements of the Federation were in armed conflict with one another; and that federal authorities were powerless to guarantee enforcement of cease-fires, the Badinter Commission concluded "that the Socialist Federal Republic of Yugoslavia is in the process of dissolution."[41]

*Opinion 2* (January 11, 1992). Serbia put the following question to the Commission, through Lord Carrington: "Does the Serbian population in Croatia and Bosnia-Herzegovina, as one of the constituent peoples of Yugoslavia, have the right to self-determination?"[42]

The Commission had to balance two principles in its answer: (1) *uti possidetis juris* (maintenance of frontiers existing at the time of independence); and (2) the rights of minorities (rights the Commission characterized as part of a "now peremptory" norm of international law). The Commission declined to attribute to the Serb minorities a right to independent statehood and thus assured the existing republican borders. In the same breath, however, the Commission indicated that the Serb minorities "have the right to recognition of their *identity* under international law" (emphasis supplied). Opinion 2 further indicated that the minorities must be given the right to choose their nationality. The aim of the Commission seems to have been to urge fair treatment of the minorities, while also restraining them from assertions of independent statehood.

*Opinion 3* (January 11, 1992). For a second time, Serbia placed a question before the Arbitration Commission: "Can the internal boundaries of Croatia and Serbia and between Bosnia-Herzegovina and Serbia be regarded as frontiers in terms of public international law?"

The arbitrators used this question firmly to reiterate that boundaries may not be changed by force. In its first substantive citation to the ICJ, the Commission referred to the case between *Burkina Faso and Mali (Frontier Dispute)*.[43] The ICJ had examined frontiers established by France, the former colonial power in West Africa, and affirmed that *uti possidetis* is a "general principle" of international law. Opinion 3 observes that the constitution of the SFRY itself provided that inter-republic borders could not be altered without the republics' consent. Again, the arbitrators had to balance two considerations. First, they wished to avoid declaring the secessionist republics independent states; and, second, they wished to avoid sanctioning any change of borders within Yugoslavia for fear that such change would result in violence. The two considerations were in tension, Serbia arguing that the borders, if not international, were not subjects of international law, and thus open to revision. This meant in other words that Serbia reserved the right to redraw the inter-republic borders—a project the arbitrators aimed to avoid. Yet Serbia could be blocked from making such changes only if the borders were borders of *states*—and the statehood of the secessionist republics the arbitrators were not at that time ready to concede. The Commission acknowledged that "the process in the SFRY" would eventually lead to "the creation of one or more independent States," but declined to declare that this had already happened. That said, the Commission listed authorities for the principle of *uti possidetis*.[44] Difficulty was posed by the conflicting aims of avoiding recognition of new states and sanctifying internal administrative boundaries.[45]

*Opinion 4—On International Recognition of the Socialist Republic of Bosnia-Herzegovina by the European Community and its Member States* (January 11, 1992).[46] The arbitrators specifically noted that the executive authorities of Bosnia had undertaken to fulfill the requirements of the December 16 *Declaration* and the *Guidelines on the Recognition of New States*. However, the Bosnian application for recognition would be denied. The Commission reasoned that two flaws made recognition impossible. First, the Serb minority of Bosnia did not participate in the declarations and undertakings of Bosnia, though these had been made in the name of the Presidency and the Government of Bosnia; and, second, the Constitution of Bosnia required popular sovereignty to be exercised either through a representative assembly or through a referendum, and there had been neither. In reaching its decision, the Commission acknowledged that Bosnia was a multi-ethnic state, consisting of Muslims, Croats, and Serbs. It also acknowledged that the Serb element of Bosnia had, since November 10, taken steps to sever itself from Bosnia, in the event of Bosnian secession from Yugoslavia. In conclusion, Opinion 4 suggested that a referendum of all Bosnians, carried out under international supervision, was necessary to determine whether Bosnia was an appropriate subject for international recognition.

*Opinion 5—On the Recognition of the Republic of Croatia by the European Community and its Member States* (January 11, 1992).[47]

Croatia applied for recognition on December 19, 1991. The Commission held that Croatia satisfactorily affirmed its commitment to the December 16 *Guidelines* principles and to other principles required of recognition applicants. However, the arbitrators found that the Constitutional Act of December 4, 1991,[48] promulgated by Croatia in an attempt to demonstrate acceptance of the provisions of the Draft Convention on Yugoslavia of November 4, was unsatisfactory. Chapter II, Article 2(c) of the Draft Convention was the particular focus of the Commission's concern. The article addressed minority rights, under the heading 'special status.' The constitution of Croatia as amended did not in the arbitrators' assessment assure acceptance of Chapter II, Article 2(c) of the Draft Convention. But for this flaw, though, Croatia "[met] the necessary conditions for its recognition." The Commission implicitly invited Croatia to correct the December 4 Constitutional Act as a condition for recognition.[49]

*Opinion 6—On the Recognition of the Republic of Macedonia by the European Community and its Member States* (January 11, 1992).[50] Macedonia, through its minister of foreign affairs, requested recognition on December 20, 1991. The Commission noted that Macedonia had undertaken to "base[ ] its international position and its relations with other States and international organizations on the generally acknowledged principles of international law." The Constitution of Macedonia satisfied the minority rights criteria through its provision for a Council for Interethnic Relations and its Articles 48 (separate cultural identity and institutions), 19 (right to private ethnic and religious schools), 7 (official use of local language), and 9 (prohibition against discrimination). Other criteria (accession to arms control treaties, agreement to settle disputes through arbitration, renunciation of territorial ambitions) were also satisfied through letters and faxes from Macedonia to the Arbitration Commission. The Republic expressly assured that it would abide by the provisions of Chapter II of the Draft Convention of November 4. In contrast to Bosnia, Macedonia had held a referendum (on September 8) in which a majority chose independence, and the Assembly of the Republic had passed a Declaration on September 17 favoring independence. Opinion 6 noted these measures with approval. Of unique concern in the Macedonian case was the clause contained in the December 16 *Declaration* pertaining to hostile propaganda toward a neighboring EC member State. A letter from the minister of foreign affairs of Macedonia on January 11 assured that "the Republic would refrain from any hostile propaganda against a neighboring country which was a Member State of the European Community." Moreover, the arbitrators held that "the use of the name 'Macedonia' cannot . . . imply any territorial claim against another State." This holding was intended to assuage Greek concerns that the nomenclature of the republic was in itself a claim against Greek territory.

*Opinion 7—On the Recognition of the Republic of Slovenia by the European Community and its Member States* (January 11, 1992).[51] Slovenia applied for recognition on December 19, 1991. Referring to events in June 1991, the Arbitration Commission noted an Assembly vote adopting a Declaration of Independence and a plebiscite showing 88.5 per cent support for independent statehood. Slovenia pledged to adhere to all relevant international texts, as required in the EC *Guidelines*. Democratic institutions and human rights law were, according to Opinion 7, enshrined within the Slovenian constitution, legal system, and electoral mechanisms. The constitution of the republic contained general ethnic rights provisions, as well as specific guarantees to the Italian and Hungarian minorities. The arbitrators enumerated a list of specific constitutional provisions guaranteeing various rights. The Commission concluded, in summary, that Slovenia satisfied all the particulars of the EC recognition criteria.

*Opinion 8* (July 4, 1992). Lord Carrington, as the Peace Conference chairman, made a three-part inquiry on May 18, 1992. He asked (1) whether the FRY was a new State requiring recognition under the December 16 *Guidelines*; (2) whether the (SFRY) could now be regarded as completely dissolved; and (3) if the SFRY indeed no longer existed, how state succession should be handled. The arbitrators addressed the second inquiry first, on the reasoning that the first and third hinged on it.

The Badinter Commission concluded that "the SFRY no longer exists."[52] It noted international references to "the former SFRY"[53] and "the former Yugoslavia."[54] It noted a referendum choosing independence in Bosnia on February 29 and March 1; the formation by Serbia and Montenegro of a new state called the Federal Republic of Yugoslavia and the adoption by the FRY of a new constitution on April 27; mutual recognition among the former SFRY republics;[55] disappearance of all SFRY federal bodies; international recognition of Bosnia, Croatia, and Slovenia; UN resolution 757 noting international rejection of continuity between the SFRY and the FRY; and the fact of effective control of the former territory and population of the SFRY by new states. Teaching generally about federal states, the Badinter Commission added, "[T]he existence of a federal State, which is made up of a number of separate entities, is seriously compromised when a majority of these entities, embracing a greater part of the territory and population, constitute themselves as sovereign States with the result that federal authority may no longer be effectively exercised."[56] Opinion 8 ratifies effectiveness as a defining feature of statehood and furnishes some clues as to determining in federal context when effectiveness has lapsed.

*Opinion 9* (July 4, 1992).[57] The Commission addressed the troublesome issue of state succession in Opinion 9. The FRY was held not to constitute the sole successor to the SFRY. The Commission indicated that membership of the SFRY in international organizations should be terminated and that no single successor state to the SFRY should be allowed to claim membership rights exclusively. The arbitrators did not propose a specific mechanism for state succession issues, but they acknowledged inherent complexity in a process that would apportion SFRY debts and assets, including properties in third countries. Opinion 9 urged pacific resolution of succession disputes within the framework of international conventions and general principles of international law.

*Opinion 10* (July 4, 1992).[58] Lord Carrington asked the arbitrators on May 18, 1992, whether the FRY is a new State, the recognition of which had to be determined under the December 16 *Guidelines*. Having decided in Opinion 8 that the SFRY no longer existed, the Commission concluded that the FRY was indeed a new state and not a simple continuation of the old Yugoslavia. Opinion 10 reiterated the view, expressed earlier by the arbitrators, that recognition is "purely declaratory in its impact." But Opinion 10 added that recognition is discretionary on the part of the recognizing states. The arbitrators concluded that the FRY "meets the criteria of international public law for a State" but was an as yet unrecognized one. Recognition, the arbitrators concluded, would have to take place under the December 16 *Guidelines*: "It is . . . for other States, where appropriate, to recognize the new State."[59]

*Opinions 11–15.*[60] Opinions eleven through fifteen addressed various aspects of state succession and fall out of the scope of the present discussion.[61]

### Evaluation

Perhaps for the first time, a segment of the community of states had set up an ad hoc body with the purpose of evaluating claims for recognition.[62] The record of the Badinter Commission could provide a reference point for future attempts at governing recognition through international institutions.

Robert Badinter, chairman of the Commission, equated the Commission process to conciliation and arbitration and observed that such a process will not always work: "Once . . . the situation has degenerated into violent confrontation . . . the time for conciliation and arbitration is passed, and does not return until the end of hostilities."[63] Any assessment of the Arbitration Commission must take into account the contemporary situation in Yugoslavia. External political concerns as well, including apprehension over stability in southeastern Europe and, more ominously, the Soviet Union, influenced decision-making in 1991–92. A balanced analysis starts by observing that the operative decision-makers faced an uncertain and potentially dangerous trajectory of events.

The work of the Badinter Commission may be evaluated in a number of dimensions. I will address four, through the following questions:

1. Were the Opinions of the Commission followed by the EC and its member States?

2. Was the Commission supported by actors in the world community besides those which instated it?

3. Did an expectation arise that the Opinions of the Commission should be treated as binding? and

4. Did the Commission push recognition away from political and toward legal categories?

It has been widely remarked that compliance with the findings of the Badinter Commission was incomplete. One commentator declared that there was "no uniformity in the responses or the results" after issuance of the Opinions,[64] and another wrote, "[T]he Opinions of the Arbitration Commission were not entirely determinative of State practice."[65] Weller reserved particularly critical words for the output of the body: "[T]he generally very brief opinions of the Commission are likely to attract considerable and probably hostile scholarly interest. They are underpinned by the shallowest of legal reasoning and do not appear destined to assist the international community greatly when addressing the potentially dangerous problem of secession in the future."[66] Arguably the most disappointing aspect of the record of the Commission was that its findings were indeed followed with little consistency by the states which had constituted it. Slovenia the Commission recommended be recognized, and it was. Though Opinion 5 found that Croatia had fallen short in its guarantees of "special status" to minorities, a pledge of correction from President Tudjman satisfied the EC and the member States sufficiently that Croatia won recognition on January 15, the date that the EC had identified as the earliest possible.[67] Macedonia, by contrast, receiving a clean bill from the arbitrators, would not receive recognition for some time.[68] Thus, in two applications for recognition, the Opinions of the Arbitration Commission were not strictly followed.

The case of Bosnia was somewhat more complicated. Several writers have suggested that recognition of that republic was premature and the Commission's handling of the case incorrect. Echoing Judge Pound's remark about the "man in the street" and recognition of Russia—but to opposite effect—Roland Rich wrote in 1993, "[E]very newspaper reader in the world knew . . . not only could Bosnia and Herzegovina not be accurately described as independent, but it could hardly be described as a state."[69] However, the record of the Commission on Bosnia may not be as clearly unsatisfactory as Rich suggests. Opinion 4 recommended *not* to recognize and, indeed, the

EC and the member States withheld recognition of that republic until Bosnia conducted the referendum the lack of which Opinion 4 had indicated was Bosnia's one shortcoming. UN General Assembly admission (a process that Dugard argues is at least cognate to recognition) was also held off until spring. Because the UN admitted Croatia, Slovenia, and Bosnia essentially at once, it is difficult however to draw conclusions as to the extent of UN deference to the Badinter Commission holdings.[70]

In regard to Bosnia, it may be that the Commission erred in focusing on a referendum, when other substantive deficiencies arguably ought also to have stayed recognition. But at least two considerations favor the Commission. First, the situation in Bosnia might not have been as unambiguously against recognition as Rich and other writers have suggested. Second, the Commission acted judiciously within the constraints facing it. The arbitrators may well have discerned any number of defects in the Bosnian application. However, their mandate, vague and unclear in its origins, stemmed from the consent of its subjects as much as from the will of its framers.[71] Accordingly, the arbitrators could little declare the rude fact that Bosnia was in crucial senses not a state. The arbitrators' position was a delicate one, and they had to find polite expressions for an unfortunate reality. That the EC withheld recognition from Bosnia on January 15, 1992, makes Opinion 4, in terms of the first question posed above, at least a temporary 'success.'[72]

Opinion 1 and its follow-ups, Opinions 8 and 10, were also arguably adhered to. Serbia and Montenegro were not recognized as the successors to Yugoslavia, nor did they receive recognition as a state. Withholding recognition was recommended by the arbitrators.[73] It is noteworthy in this connection that the FRY itself viewed the Opinions of the Badinter Commission as having produced results. This conclusion came forth in a letter of complaint to the Peace Conference from the foreign minister of the FRY on July 2, 1993. The FRY, the letter indicated, rejected that the Badinter Commission enjoyed competence to decide succession issues, and complained that the Commission's opinions "were taken as judgments and served as a basis for making concrete decisions on the relevant issues concerning the Yugoslav crisis."[74] In rejecting use of a judicial mechanism to resolve the succession problem, the FRY obliquely ratified the Badinter Commission as a collective recognition organ.

This leads to the second evaluative inquiry: did the Commission enjoy outside support? On balance, the record reflects support for the Arbitration Commission. Apart from the EC and the governments of its member States, a number of actors endorsed the collective recognition mechanism embodied in the Commission. The print media was generally sympathetic.[75] At the very least, the press increased the profile of the Commission, making it a focus of public awareness.[76] Publicity arguably amplified the force of Commission opinions. The United Nations Security Council also lent support to the procedures set up under the August 27 *Declaration*. Security Council Resolution 713 (September 25, 1991) imposed an arms embargo on Yugoslavia. Resolution 713 also "commended" the EC, especially for "the convening of a Conference on Yugoslavia, including the mechanisms set forth within it." The Resolution further indicated Security Council support for "the smooth functioning of the process instituted within the framework of the Conference on Yugoslavia." The North Atlantic Treaty Organization also endorsed the process. A NATO press communique of November 8 expressed support for the EC peace efforts, and, more specifically, in discussing recognition of the republics of Yugoslavia, the communique affirmed several of the principles soon to appear in the EC *Guidelines*, including respect for international norms and obligations, "especially those embodied in the Helsinki Final Act, the Charter of Paris, and other CSCE documents." NATO also welcomed the framework of the Peace Conference headed by Lord Carrington.[77] The Badinter Commission attracted support from a number of quarters.

Whether an expectation arose that the Opinions of the Commission would be treated as binding provides another test. Existence of such an expectation is perhaps best determined by examining international reaction when a country failed to follow the Opinions.

The most notorious deviation from the Badinter Commission's recommendations came on December 23 when Germany recognized Croatia and Slovenia.[78] This measure took place outside the framework of the EC procedure set up on December 16, and thus could be seen as a test of the Commission's mandate. The international reaction to German recognition provides an index of views toward Germany; it also provides an index of perceptions of the Badinter Commission. In fact, the view was widespread that Germany had committed a delict in recognizing early. Even before recognition was formally extended, at least one German editorialist apprehended that, if strife and instability in Yugoslavia were to persist, "ill-wishers might get the idea of pillorying Germany's haste as the reason."[79] The accusation appeared in the press many times after December 23 that Germany had gone off track,[80] and commentators from the academic and diplomatic arenas would reach the conclusion as well that recognition before the January 15 deadline was inappropriate.[81] Some even proposed that German recognition was to blame for disasters which followed.[82] That recognition outside the Badinter Commission process earned rebuke tends to suggest that there had arisen an expectation that states (at least within the EC/EU) would adhere to the process.

## Nature of the Badinter Commission: Legal Organ or Political Forum?

"[T]he work of the Arbitration Commission attached to the EC peace conference on Yugoslavia," one writer complained, "has had only a limited influence on the attempts to manage and end the Yugoslav crisis. While this is largely due to political factors, the EC's Arbitration Commission has failed to clarify many of the controversial legal issues raised by cases of secession or the dissolution of states."[83] A multilateral organ with competence to decide questions of recognition must involve one of the chief tensions in the field: that between politics and law. Efforts to institutionalize recognition were not entirely new in 1991. Organs addressing recognition in the past and the Badinter Commission alike however found it difficult to set a proper balance between politics and law in their institutional processes.

At the San Francisco Conference of 1945 (where the United Nations Charter was adopted), Norway proposed amendments to the Dumbarton Oaks Proposals. The amendments would have given the General Assembly "the right to present recommendations to Member states with regard to the recognition of new Governments or new States."[84] Though the proposal was rejected, the United Nations returned to the matter of recognition in 1950. At that time, the UN considered criteria for credentialing a government, in cases where two or more competing authorities claimed to control a country. These were presented as a Draft Resolution by the British and Cuban delegations. They bear a certain resemblance to the criteria of the December 16 *Guidelines on the Recognition of New States* and accompanying *Declaration*:

¶ 1 (a) [W]henever more than one authority claims to be the government entitled to represent a Member State in the United Nations, and this question becomes the subject of controversy in the United Nations, it should be considered in the light of the purposes and principles of the Charter and the circumstances of each case; [and]

(b) [t]he following should be among the factors to be taken into consideration in determining any such question:

i. the extent to which the new authority exercises effective control over the territory of the Member State concerned and is generally accepted by the population;

ii. the willingness of that authority to accept responsibility for the carrying out by the Member State of its obligations under the Charter; [and]

iii. the extent to which that authority has been established through internal processes in the Member State.[85]

Points ii and iii roughly parallel the requirements of the December 16 criteria: acceptance of international obligations and evidence that authority (in the case of the 1991 criteria, independence) was by indigenous choice.

The Draft Resolution on recognition criteria however settled neither the criteria nor the related question of where to vest authority to tell whether a putative state satisfied the criteria. Debate simmered over the proper locus of a UN recognition procedure,[86] and, moreover, representatives disagreed over the balance between law and politics in recognition. Some UN organs seemed better suited to legal determinations, others to political process. Those representatives who argued for a legal approach to recognition favored the International Court, the Sixth Committee, or the International Law Commission. Those who viewed recognition as essentially political preferred the UN Secretariat, the *Ad Hoc* Political Committee, or the General Assembly.[87] The organ in which authority to recognize is vested may reflect whether the operative decision-makers embrace a legal or a political view of recognition.

Vesting an arbitration panel with authority to study and advise on recognition is not the same as vesting such an organ with authority to recognize. However, that the Badinter Commission was set up with terms of reference appropriate to an international judicial organ suggests movement toward a view of recognition as a form of legal decision. The Commission itself did not decide the questions of recognition facing Europe in 1991–92, but to some extent its Opinions influenced state practice. Where its Opinions were ignored (*i.e.*, German recognition of Croatia), popular and diplomatic criticism followed. In vesting competence over recognition in an arbitral panel (however uncertain a competence), the leaders of Western Europe at least announced an intention that recognition be a matter regulated by law.

The extent to which the Badinter Commission introduced a new legality into recognition is controversial. Whether recognition is a subject of law or of politics is indeed one of the centers of debate over recognition today.

Danilo Türk notes "difficulties involved in the political implementation of a legal opinion," and these he identifies as having prevented the political organs of the EC from following the Badinter Commission Opinions.[88] Joe Verhoeven takes the view that, in fact, the Badinter Commission promoted a legal approach to recognition—though, he argued, recognition had only recently become to any great extent politicized.[89] Colin Warbrick, by contrast, argues that the Yugoslav crisis brought about a new politicization of recognition,[90] not reinforcement of its legal character. The Commission will likely be viewed as a body with judicial form, but one which served more a consultative than judicial function. For its accomplishments, the Commission has received reserved applause:

> [T]he Opinions of the Arbitration Commission, taken as a body, represent a unique and important examination of the legal issues that attach to the dismemberment of a State. It has rarely been the case that an independent body of legal experts has been asked to consider the whole range of issues relating to Statehood, recognition, self-determination, territorial integrity, and succession, in relation to the break-up of a single State, and to map their development as events unfold. It is equally rare for a judicial body to play such an active part in the process of dismemberment itself. As has been noted, even if the opinions of the Arbitration Commission were delivered in a consultative capacity (a point which was not entirely clear in the early stages) and for that reason did not form part of the *res judicata*, they nevertheless played an influential part in creating the necessary framework within which subsequent State practice developed.[91]

## COORDINATED DIPLOMACY: A NON-INSTITUTIONAL COLLECTIVE APPROACH

As seen so far, collective recognition can take place through formal institutions, either permanent or *ad hoc*. The International Court of Justice has addressed recognition in the context of particular inter-state disputes. *East Timor* involved recognition of a territorial situation. Proceedings under the *Convention on the Prevention and Punishment of the Crime of Genocide* (*i.e.*, *Bosnia and Herzegovina* v. *Yugoslavia*) have also elicited ICJ commentary on the effects of recognition and the nature of statehood.[92] The potential of the United Nations as a forum for collective recognition has been studied by Dugard.[93] Temporary international organs, too, have played roles in recognition. The League of Nations convened a Commission of Jurists to assess the territorial status of the Åland Islands. Lord Lytton's fact-finding mission to Manchuria (likewise under League auspices) arguably served the community of states as a helpmate in reaching a collective nonrecognition policy. And, most notably, the Badinter Commission set up in August 1991 by the European Peace Conference on Yugoslavia was expressly charged with producing legal analyses of recognition.

Collective action however need not be—and in practice perhaps seldom is—formalized within international institutions. States shun commitment of critical areas of 'sovereign' competence to the international sphere. Formalizing such commitment in structured bodies draws all the more attention to it and makes it seem less open to reservation or retraction. To adopt the view that the international community has a role in certain areas of legislation may challenge the interests of important groups of authoritative decision makers in the national community, and if the decision-making bureaucracies in the municipal arena apprehend that a competing international bureaucratic structure is absorbing what formally were their competences, they are afforded a clear target on which to focus political efforts to impede the process of internationalization. A more diffuse mode of internationalization may facilitate the process, first, by drawing less attention to itself; second, by denying domestic opponents of the process the clear target afforded by international organizations; and third, by assuaging domestic concern that the process may be difficult to reverse and prone to uncontrolled continuation. Conducting collective policy informally rather than within structures such as the UN or *ad hoc* commissions may avert the harsher reactions 'at home' which sometimes result from express assignments of state functions to the international sphere—and in particular to international bodies. To be complete, an analysis of the collective development of recognition requires an analysis of informal coordination among recognizing states. The Yugoslav crisis of 1991–92 presented a signal test of collective recognition in a non-institutional context.

### Western Europe Promotes a Collective Approach

In the years leading up to the Treaty on European Union signed at Maastricht in December 1991, twelve European states had assigned a wide array of competences to institutions of the EC. Often described as 'pillars,' the different areas of EC activity are usually divided into three or four categories. First, the 'classic Community' includes the European Commission which possesses legislative initiative and responsibility for monitoring member state compliance; the Parliament which has a consultative role as well as a 'limited right to reject' proposed legislation; the Council which represents the member states; and the Court of Justice which interprets provisions of the European treaties. Monetary union is usually described as the second pillar. This too has formal institutional structures. Two further pillars however consist only of inter-governmental cooperation and have little standing institutional or bureaucratic strcuture of their own. One of these is cooperation among law enforcement agencies. The other is the so-called CFSP—'Common Foreign and Security Policy.'[94]

CFSP is arguably the weakest pillar of the EU. Its one institutional manifestation, the Western European Union (WEU), is a bare skeleton of an international military organization, and the relationship between the WEU and the dominant collective security apparatus, NATO, remains uncertain and in flux.[95] Unlike policy-making in such areas as agriculture, fisheries, external tariffs, and transportation, foreign and security policy-making does not take place within EC/EU structures.[96]

Member states indeed have resisted assigning the EU responsibility over foreign and security policy. According to one writer commenting on Greek policy toward Macedonia, "The member states retain sole authority over national foreign policies, although some level of coordination is attempted."[97] Recognition of new states fell under the umbrella of CFSP and, like most CFSP matters, was not decided within formal institutions.[98] Moreover, the debate over recognizing the secessionist republics, because it involved states not members of the EC/EU, could not wholly have been addressed within a standing CFSP bureaucracy, even if one adequate to deal with the debate had existed. Austria and Hungary in particular as states proximate to the crisis played active roles in recognition but did not belong to the EC/EU. Rather than through EC/EU organs, Western European efforts to coordinate recognition of the new states in the space of the former Yugoslavia took place, though under the nominal aegis of the EC/EU, in the traditional forum of inter-state relations.

Various sources suggest that an expectation was arising in Western Europe that a collective approach had to be adopted toward recognizing new states. Official statements by Western European governments suggested a shared conviction that the region needed a single diplomacy. Government ministers began voicing this conviction quite pointedly in late 1991. The foreign minister of Belgium said on November 29, 1991, that the EC states could resolve whether and when to recognize Croatia and Slovenia only "at the community level."[99] Apart from such direct statements, still other evidence suggested collectivization of the Western European position. Press and media treatment, for example, reflected an emergent expectation of collective conduct. Both the press and governments were keen to criticize particular instances of state conduct when these arguably deviated from collective process. Indeed, accusations of 'breaking rank' or 'unilateral action' became characteristic of the debate over the Yugoslav republics. That unilateralism earned rebuke offered one indication that collective process was emerging as part of recognition law.

The governments of individual Western and Northern European states announced straight-forwardly that they would support collective discipline in the recognition process. State leaders and media sources also *implied* the operation of a collective component in the norm governing recognition. High-ranking government officials were quick to defend against accusations of their own noncompliance, and press and governments alike criticized non-compliance by others. A review of policy statements and reportage surrounding the Yugoslav recognition crisis illustrates the pattern which was taking shape.

*Germany*

German views relating to the Yugoslav recognition crisis can be divided among three categories: affirmative support for collective process; implication, by denial of unilateral conduct, that collective process was required; and public criticism of the German government for ignoring a supposed European consensus.

A number of expressions of support for a collective approach to recognition took the form of affirmations of such an approach. The recognition crisis in Yugoslavia occurred amid sweeping change in post-Communist Europe. Likewise, German policy toward that crisis took form not in isolation but as part of a broader effort to define the country's direction after the fall of the Soviet empire. Avowals of collective process were made in relation to the Yugoslav crisis and also to the general European situation of the day. The government of Germany portrayed its diplomacy as collective in regard to many issues.

German officialdom, from the highest levels, stressed the need for a collective approach to the economic rehabilitation and political stabilization of the states of the former Warsaw Pact. At his annual New Year's reception for the diplomatic corps in Bonn, German President Richard von Weizsäcker called for a pan-European, and even a pan-Western, policy toward Eastern Europe. The aim of the collective effort, he urged, should be to support the nascent democratization of the East and to tender economic assistance. He further called for "cooperative pluralism" within Europe on matters of politics, economics, and culture. Such collective policy and attitude, Weizäcker argued, would put a "pan-European peace structure" within reach. The stumbling block which might prevent the realization of the promises of this new collective view of state relations, Weizäcker warned, was the "unholy temptation" to lapse back into nationalist excess. That temptation Weizäcker blamed for the bloodshed in Yugoslavia. A message implicit in the presidential New Year's address was that a solution to the Yugoslav crisis depended on collective world, or at least collective Western European, policy.[100]

Other German officials expressed hope and predicted that the European Union would act as a single body in recognizing Croatia and Slovenia. The German government evidently perceived it important to establish a collective approach to the recognition of the Yugoslav successor states. Foreign diplomats and German foreign ministry spokesmen expressed confidence, according to the December 1 *Süddeutsche Zeitung*, that the Yugoslav crisis would "not split the EC but that an agreement [would] be reached on the basis of the German position."[101] Collective policy on recognition was a central theme in a contemporaneous article by Hans-Dietrich Genscher. Genscher stressed the common European approach to recognition:

> [W]e have worked in the European Community for the following goals:
>
> —for the recognition of the republics that so wish it.
>
> —for equal protection of all minorities in the republics.
>
> —against a change of existing borders by force.
>
> —against the use of force.
>
> We have continued these efforts in the interests of a common attitude of the European Community and in doing so, went to the limit of what can be reasonably expected. We can say today that we first won the support of all EC states and then that of all CSCE states. Under our chairmanship, we achieved the Western European Union decision to dispatch peace-keeping forces under the umbrella of the United Nations and caused the UN Security Council, of which we are not a member, to deal with the situation in Yugoslavia.

Genscher framed the recognition question in collective terms: the EC, the CSCE, the Security Council, and the UN. Further, in mentioning a June 25 communication with Yugoslav Foreign Minister Budimir Locar, Genscher underscored that Germany took this diplomatic measure not alone, but in tandem with Italian Foreign Minister Gianni de Michelis. Genscher went on to point out that the Vatican, too, expressed solidarity with the European Union (*i.e.*, the German) position on recognizing the new republics.[102] Germany was eager to demonstrate that its Balkan diplomacy took place in concert with other states and with multilateral organizations.

Indicative of the breadth of expectation for collective action, the German foreign ministry espoused a collective approach toward situations other than the Yugoslav crisis. For example, Genscher in the wake of the dissolution of the Soviet Union urged a joint European response to the establishment of the Commonwealth of Independent States.[103]

Further exemplifying the German show of commitment to collective European diplomacy, Genscher advocated that the CSCE states take steps to stanch the flow of advanced weapons from the former East Bloc. Speaking too of the need for an extra-European collectivization of weapons control, Genscher said, "[T]he community of peoples has to do everything to clamp down on the irresponsible continuation of wasting resources through the export of weapons and armaments."[104] Genscher and Weizsäcker, representative of German leaders, expressed intent to follow a collective path to the recognition decision, and their avowal of collective policy extended to matters beyond the Balkan crisis. Peace and stability, in their words, would be fostered by collective response.

A number of statements, while not expressly supporting collective recognition, implied that international law required it. These statements denied that Germany was 'breaking rank' with European consensus. In assessing adverse reactions abroad to German assertiveness in foreign policy, one German commentator stressed the need to act in coordination with Europe. "The sovereignty of German foreign policy," wrote Jochen Siemens on January 22, 1992, in the *Frankfurter Rundschau*, "is not shown by lonely advances . . . but by moderately coordinating one's own conviction with that of one's neighbors and allies."[105] This proposition represented a general class of assertions from German sources during the Yugoslav recognition crisis. When confronted with an accusation that Germany had acted unilaterally, German spokespersons, both in government and media, stepped in to defend state policy. That accusations of unilateral behavior elicited defenses may illustrate that decision-makers in Germany had begun to apprehend a collective requirement in the law governing recognition.

President Tudjman of Croatia and Chancellor Kohl met during the first week of December 1991, and one radio report of their talks reinforced the impression that the German government was sensitive to avoid appearances of breaking rank with Western European collective strategy. Kohl assured Tudjman, and earlier (December 3) Slovene President Milan Kucan, that Germany would soon extend recognition. But the chancellor emphasized that his government was "proceed[ing] from the assumption that more than five or six other countries may take this step as well."[106] German recognition may have been looming earlier than some wished, but, Kohl said, this did not mean Bonn was breaking rank. By German reckoning, early recognition did not violate the emerging rule against unilateral conduct, so long as a number of states joined the act.

Even with the Maastricht Summit of December 10–11 finished and thus no longer the chief concern in the foreign ministries of Europe, Germany qualified its insistence on recognizing Croatia and Slovenia. Germany would not proceed with recognition, Bonn assured its European partners, without taking into consideration the general Western European view. Dieter Vogel, speaking for the chancellor, and Hans Schumacher for the foreign ministry, informed the press on December 13 that recognition would not be granted before the December 16 conference of EC foreign ministers.[107] Such portrayal of German thinking was repeated elsewhere.

The view that collective diplomacy was becoming an imperative was reflected by German defenses against accusations of hasty recognition. Media scrutiny of German recognition policy reached a notable mark when the *New York Times* criticized Germany for "dragging" an unwilling Europe toward early recognition. The newspaper cited Chancellor Kohl declaring the EC resolution to recognize Croatia and Slovenia a "great victory for German foreign policy." Vogel, the cabinet spokesman, denied that the Chancellor had chosen such an aggressive phrase. Kohl had allegedly issued the celebratory characterization of the recognition plan at a Christian Democratic Union party congress in Dresden, but, according to Vogel, the minutes of the congress recorded a much less inflammatory statement. Vogel indicated that Kohl had said that the EC measures constituted "a great *success* for German and European policy," not a unilateral German "victory."[108] The federal government believed it incumbent to rebut charges that Germany viewed diplomacy as a matter of contest between itself and the rest of Europe. To do this, German officials assured the world that their recognition policy belonged to a collective plan.

Criticism of unilateral action lent further support to collective process. Though advocated by many Germans, early recognition was questioned by some. Indicative of a rising expectation for collective conduct, critics of German recognition policy identified the alleged unilateral character of German diplomacy as a delict. Dieter Schröder, writing in the December 21 *Süddeutsche Zeitung*, expressed dismay at "Bonn's unilateral proceeding." Such a nationalist and non-collective diplomacy would, in Schröder's estimation, harm the fabric of international order. "[I]n open disregard of the EC formula," German policy, in his opinion, was a throwback to "19th-century European power politics."[109]

Sympathy for the secessionists notwithstanding, inroads of collectivization into the recognition process proved sufficiently deep that a government policy violative of the collective spirit earned public rebuke. The press broadly supported—indeed insisted upon—the substance of German measures; early recognition was promoted to support the Yugoslav separatists. The government came under fire however when it appeared to deviate from collective process. The press, as well as authoritative decision-makers in government, expressed the belief that collective action in recognizing the new states was mandatory. This was not confined to Germany.[110]

*France*

France stood in the forefront of the collective approach to recognition. Moreover, when calling for collective diplomacy toward Yugoslavia, French President François Mitterand also suggested that recognition not be accorded as early as some states had been urging. The president left these states unnamed. Deliberateness, Mitterand counselled, was particularly demanded by the fact of still-unsettled borders and anxious minorities. He asked whether those states which were insisting on immediate recognition planned to dispatch troops to support the fact of Croat and Slovene statehood. This rhetorical query was a fairly transparent barb against Germany and Italy for their independent and allegedly precipitous move toward recognition.[111] Not only did Mitterand criticize the leaders in the drive for recognition for their departure from European process; he expressed concern over their hastiness, too.

In contrast with the president, who, albeit thinly, veiled his criticisms, the French foreign minister was unambiguous in his disapproval of German action. Roland Dumas on December 5 warned all European Community states against unilateral recognition of the secessionist republics. "We are striving to make our partners understand, starting with Germany," Dumas said, "that it would be prejudicial for Europe as a whole and that this attitude of unilateral recognition could be damaging for the Community." In the same radio interview, the foreign minister said it was in Europe's interests to pursue within the EC a "reasonable and collective approach."[112]

As criticism of German diplomacy increased, France assumed the difficult task simultaneously of censuring German conduct and preserving the appearance of collective EC action. This indeed had become a preoccupation of much of the foreign policy community in Western Europe. It was feared that Germany was moving too fast on recognition, but leaving the Federal Republic on its own threatened to damage the project of European unity. President Mitterrand stepped in to assure that the EC member states continued to share core principles. "I have always said that I could not be against self-determination," the French leader indicated in response to queries whether Germany was encouraging recognition imprudently.[113] At the same time, Mitterrand emphasized that "[the] choice of sovereignty and independence must take place under acceptable conditions, for example, with respect for minorities." The determination of whether such respect had been guaranteed could not be left to individual states; only through collective process could Europe decide whether and when to recognize.[114] French leaders confronted a tension between their concerns over precipitate action on the Yugoslav question and the risk of fracturing the EU. They wished, in short, to discourage an acceleration of the Balkan breakdown yet apprehended the cost of deviating from CFSP.

French commitment to collective process on recognition was amplified in statements President Mitterrand made to French television on December 15, 1991: "Recognition can be automatic [if certain conditions are fulfilled]. It carries risks, especially that of not changing what is actually happening on the ground. But if [it] is to become the reality, then it must take its place in the organization of the whole of Europe and not be a risky undertaking between two peoples who are fighting and are ready to start again."[115]

Mitterrand announced that collective process must embrace, not only the recognition decision, but, indeed, the entire effort to obtain a peaceful resolution to the crisis in the space of the former Yugoslavia.

*Belgium*

Adhering to the EC collective policy, Belgium announced its recognition of Croatia and Slovenia on January 15. In support of the Belgian measure, Foreign Minister Mark Eyskens cited the resolve of the EC to stand together on the issue. Eyskens drew attention to guarantees which Croat President Franjo Tudjman had issued in regard to minorities and democracy. These in particular, Eyskens said, supported the Belgian declaration.[116] Belgium carefully framed its decision to recognize as an incident of collective EC diplomacy. Also underlined were the substantive merits of the Croat case. Eyskens numbered among these assurances on ethnic rights and governance. Like French policy at the time, Belgian policy reflected two possible emerging evolutions in the recognition norm: incorporation of guarantees concerning internal order into the criteria for recognition; and, more concretely, the requirement that recognition be subject to collective discipline.

*Great Britain*

The United Kingdom Foreign and Commonwealth Office announced on January 15 that the UK supported the collective EC decision to recognize Croatia and Slovenia. "We are glad the European Community has reached a common position on this very complex question," an FCO spokesman said. The United Kingdom simultaneously stated that it would follow the EC decision to withhold recognition for the time being from Macedonia and Bosnia-Herzegovina. Deficiencies in those republics' laws on minorities, Whitehall stated, made recognition as yet inappropriate.[117] From the British standpoint, then, recognition and nonrecognition both flowed from the European process, not from national decision alone. As in the Belgian and French statements, the details of domestic governance in the new states entered the evaluation of whether and when to recognize. The dual evolution was thus again in evidence—new substantive criteria and collective process.

*Denmark*

Slightly prior to the EC announcement to recognize the former Yugoslav republics, Denmark issued its own statement of recognition.[118] Nonetheless, it was on the same day and amid the collective EC decision that the Copenhagen government extended recognition to Croatia and Slovenia. Individual state conduct was fashioned to conform to the collective movement.

*Italy*

Italy announced on December 16 that it would recognize Croatia and Slovenia only in coordination with other EC member states. Foreign Minister Gianni De Michelis announced that "reaching a common position of as many European countries as possible" was the goal of Italian policy. Because Italian policy would "remain pegged to the European position," Italy would not join Germany if Germany in recognizing Croatia and Slovenia parted ways with the other member states.[119] This position, however, ran against Italy's initial lead in supporting Croat and Slovene independence. Indeed, the president of Italy, Francesco Cossiga, had early tendered moral support to the new republics and, in addition to issuing sympathetic statements, had made the first visit by a head of state to the republics' capitals. (Cossiga had gone to Ljubljana and Zagreb earlier in the year.) The Italian foreign minister, in joint statements with his German counterpart in early autumn 1991, had further identified Italy as a promoter of rapid recognition. Even though Italy's policy in practice may have displayed independent characteristics similar to Germany's, the pressure to adhere to a collective plan sufficed to induce Italy, like other EC member states, to emphasize the multilateral nature of its decision to recognize.

*Portugal*

Portugal was an important player at the time of recognition, as it then occupied the rotating presidency of the EC. Like the other EC member states, Portugal expressed that its recognition of Croatia and Slovenia occurred within the EC collective framework. A Portuguese government communique issued on January 16, the day following EC and Portuguese recognition, emphasized that recognition was taking place within "the framework of the EC declaration on Yugoslavia."[120] Lisbon, during its term in the EC presidency, promoted CFSP and by extension evolution of a multilateral recognition process.

*Sweden*

Sweden, though not an EC member at the time, announced that it would take careful note of the EC foreign ministers' meetings on Yugoslavia. Maragaretha af Ugglas, the foreign minister of Sweden, stated to the press: "We have close contacts with various European capitals in this matter. We shall try to fulfill our policy to handle this matter *in accord with the rest of the European nations*" [emphasis supplied]. Asked by a reporter what would happen if Germany alone among EC member states were to insist upon recognition, Foreign Minister Ugglas indicated that Sweden would have to formulate a response on the basis of Sweden's unilateral judgement. She said further that some observers believed that "recognition would . . . intensify the fighting." She cited Cyrus Vance as representative of this view.[121] Stockholm aimed to mold its action in conformity with the EC and identified Germany as a linchpin to collective recognition diplomacy. Significantly, the Swedish foreign minister held open the possibility that her country would revert to unilateral, discretionary conduct in the event collective discipline dissolved. Though promoting a multilateral approach to recognition, Sweden carefully reserved a space for traditional state practice, should the need for that arise.

*Finland*

In principle strongly favoring recognition, Finland qualified its stance. According to the Finns, recognition could not occur without reference to the policies of the United Nations and of the community of states. Finnish diplomats observed that Estonia, Latvia, Lithuania, and Ukraine had extended recognition but that this was not enough. Finland came to the conclusion that a few governments alone did not constitute a wide enough compass by which to gauge whether a collective decision on recognizing the new states had yet been reached.[122] Collective process, implied in the Finnish view to be mandatory, involved broad participation. According to the government in Helsinki, consensus among a narrow collection of governments in isolation failed to meet the emergent expectation for collective action. The Finnish commitment to collective recognition led that country to disregard even multiple signs of approval from its near community (the Baltic states); a broad community enunciation alone would satisfy Finland's leaders that the requisite consensus obtained. For such consensus, Finnish policy makers looked to the EC and the broader world stage, rather than just to the Baltic and Finland's neighbors. In view of the conduct of other states, however, how broad a basis satisfied the evolving expectation of collective action would remain unclear.

*The Vatican*

The Vatican announced its recognition of Croatia and Slovenia on January 13, 1992. As early as the end of November, the Vatican had proposed "agreed and conditioned" international recognition of Croatia and Slovenia. In a late November letter to the CSCE, the Holy See had urged, in effect, an approach at once collective ("agreed") and based upon legal principles ("conditioned"). What exactly Vatican diplomats meant by the term 'conditioned' is not clear. If they intended to express that recognition would be accorded only when the communities claiming statehood had satisfied certain legal prerequisites, then the Holy See viewed recognition as governed by international law. It is arguable, however, that by 'conditioned,' the Vatican meant that recognition would be granted only in partial form, with full recognition coming upon complete attainment of the characteristics of a state, as the prevailing norm defined these. Under this interpretation, recognition would be conditional upon satisfaction of certain internationally mandated guarantees. The second interpretation seems less likely, given the plain meaning of the Vatican's words. Assuming the former interpretation, the Vatican more closely than most states approximated the ideal of collective and principled action proposed by Hersch Lauterpacht. The Holy See stated that it would recognize only when the community of states, acting as a body, had ascertained that the claimants had fulfilled the legal requirements for recognition. The Vatican approach provides an interesting model for possible evolution in recognition law.

At the same time as they declared recognition of the secessionist republics, Vatican spokesmen assured that the Holy See continued to recognize the Federal Republic of Yugoslavia, Msgr. Piero Pennacchini noting that "[Yugoslavia's] death certificate has so far not been signed." The Vatican closely tracked the policy of the EC on recognition, echoing the collective EC position that the new republics, in order to win recognition, would have to illustrate respect for the principles enumerated in the Helsinki Final Act and the Paris Charter.[123] The Vatican particularly emphasized that Croatia and Slovenia must make provision for human rights and fundamental liberties, implement safeguards for minorities, and promote democratization.[124] Assurances toward Belgrade and Serb minorities kept Church diplomacy closely in line with the European collective process, as such assurances stayed recognition.

The pains which the Vatican took to assure Serbs and to adhere to collective process may in part have been conditioned by the history of the Catholic Church in Yugoslavia. Important Roman Catholic clerics such as Archbishop Stepinac had collaborated, according to many Serbs wholeheartedly, with the NDH (the Croat state set up under Nazi aegis in 1941). Atrocities perpetrated under the NDH indelibly marked Yugoslav politics, and doubtless many Serbs in 1991–92 continued to harbor suspicion toward the Vatican. Church diplomacy in the 1990s showed great sensitivity to the burdens of Balkan history.[125]

*Austria*

Austrian political opinion took cognizance of the collective trend in the European approach to recognition. Though Austria did not yet belong to the EC, politicians and statesmen in Vienna kept close watch on Community policy. On December 5, the Social Democratic Party of Austria, the Austrian People's Party, the Freedom Party of Austria, and the Greens unanimously motioned to urge the government of Austria to recognize Croatia and Slovenia. In addressing recognition, however, this bloc urged that the "respective schedule of other European states" and the decisions of the United Nations Security Council be taken into account.[126] Austrian politicians professed the need to keep their nation in line with the emerging collective expectation.[127] A principle of multilateral conduct had permeated discussion of the secession crisis, and this reached beyond the borders of the EC.

Shortly after the parliamentary motion, the Austrian government announced through its foreign minister, Alois Mock, that the cabinet would agree as soon as possible on recognition, perhaps before the EC held a scheduled December 18 meeting to debate the issue. In announcing this, Austria emphasized that Germany, Italy, the Benelux states, Denmark, Iceland, and Australia also contemplated early recognition. The Austrians cast the decision to recognize as one which had to parallel the conduct of other states. Extending recognition in a vacuum was not an option. Austria had apparently identified a state interest in abiding by collective decision—or, short of that, in taking major foreign policy initiatives only in conjunction with at least several other states. Austria's policy of avoiding unilateral action was further evidenced in an address to the Diplomatic Press Association by Chancellor Franz Vranitzky. Recognition, Vranitzky said, "can only be effective if several countries adopt the same approach."[128] Though the chancellor seems to have broadly outlined a principle of collective recognition, his remarks left unanswered a critical question of the mechanics of the emergent process. How many states had to participate in the multilateral process of recognition—or in any multilateral process—before the process could accurately be described 'collective'? The ambit of collective decision-making is a crucial element in the norm governing recognition, but Austrian practice left it indeterminate. I will turn to the scope of collective action below.

On January 15 (the recognition deadline set in the December 16 EC declaration), journalists asked Foreign Minister Alois Mock whether West Europe and Austria should press Serbia to surrender territory gained in battle against the Croats in Slavonia and elsewhere. Mock responded, "[T]he EC has stated at least 10 times in official communiques that border changes must not be brought about through the use of force."[129] The foreign minister underlined the importance of collective resolve on the question of territorial changes, and by implication, on the effort generally to bring peace to the Balkans. The linking of recognition to an overall peace process was suggested by the French president as well. Insofar as the overall peace process was concerned, Austria seemed to define collective diplomacy to embrace the whole of Europe. Whether Vienna deemed such broad consensus necessary for recognition is less clear. Austria closely followed German recognition diplomacy, and, though the Vienna government, also like Bonn, asserted the importance of collective process, Austrian recognition was pledged early and came early.

The expressed intention of most European states was to coordinate recognition under the aegis of the EC at the inter-governmental level (rather than within EC institutions). However, Austrian and German conduct would evidence that recognition was not in fact extended in strict compliance with the proposed collective process.

### Lapses in Collective Discipline

A number of challenges to collective discipline confronted Western Europe during the Yugoslav recognition crisis. On the one hand, that energetic efforts were made to answer these challenges and that a substantial degree of common policy survived the differences among various states' conduct, further demonstrated the inroads of collective expectation into the norm governing recognition. On the other hand, that differences in recognition diplomacy persisted began to suggest the limits of collectivization.

*Mending the German Tear*

By November 1991, it had become clear that Germany and similarly disposed states (Austria, Hungary, and Italy in particular) were committing themselves to recognition, at a date significantly forward of that preferred by Western Europe as a whole. A problem for European comity in general, the emerging disjunction between Germany and the other eleven EC member states posed problems for EC cohesion specifically. All the more so because the Maastrict Summit was soon to address the vital but yet undecided question of monetary union, mending the German tear in EC diplomacy became imperative.

The EC foreign ministers meeting at Brussels on December 16, 1991, fashioned a compromise between Germany and member states less anxious to proceed with recognition. Reportedly, Italian Foreign Minister Gianni de Michelis acted as a broker between the Germans and less enthusiastic Europeans, especially the Dutch. Dutch cooperation was viewed as particularly important, because the Netherlands at the time held the revolving EC presidency. Characterized by his German counterpart, Hans-Dietrich Genscher, as "[going] out of his way with Venetian enthusiasm," Michelis brokered a compromise, wherein recognition would be carried out in practice on January 15—later than initially desired by Germany but earlier than desired by other powers, especially the Netherlands, the United Kingdom, and, outside the EC, the United States. Some foreign ministers stated that the prospect of isolated German recognition threatened to fissure the nascent European Union and that agreement to the Italian compromise date was as much an effort to prevent disunity as an expression of readiness to acknowledge Croat and Slovene legal personality. Accepting the Michelis date resulted in a general European position on the new republics. To be sure, the compromise reached in Brussels did not satisfy all parties. The United States, already having expressed concern to Austria over what the State Department judged to be that country's overly forward policy on recognition, was dissatisfied with the European position. But within Germany the Social Democratic Party (SPD) was dissatisfied, too—with the *lateness* of recognition. Calling the compromise a "diplomatic failure," SPD foreign policy expert Norbert Gansel stated that "if the EC keeps to its schedule, it will possibly only recognize dead bodies and ruins [on January 15]." At the same time, even the German government's ambassador in Belgrade criticized the compromise.[130] It was against the current of domestic sentiment that Germany agreed to the later recognition deadline (January 15, 1992). Whether Germany would adhere to its bargain in spirit and in letter, as of the middle of December when the compromise date was chosen, remained to be seen.

*Reproaching Austria and Germany for Sanctions*

Germany imposed stiff sanctions against the rump Yugoslav state starting on December 10, 1991. Serbian and Montenegran ships, aircraft, and trucks would no longer enjoy access to German territory, and German carriers would cease to call at Yugoslav destinations. In these penalties, Austria, Italy, and Hungary quickly followed suit. Four states acting in concert, however, did not constitute sufficient consensus to satisfy the growing demand for collective action. Chancellor Vranitzky and Foreign Minister Mock both reiterated Austrian commitment to collective action, but this would fail to assuage the concerns of cautious powers such as the United Kingdom, France, and the United States. Vranitzky stated to Austrian radio that recognition would take place "as soon as we are sure that others will follow our example," and his interviewer interpreted the government position as follows: "[A] basic yes to recognition, but within an internationally coordinated schedule." Vranitzky left open the possibility for unilateral recognition, but only if the European Community collectively deemed unilateral action acceptable: "[T]he question has to be clarified whether the EC agrees on individual countries deciding for or against recognition of Croatia and Slovenia. This is how the doctrine must be understood, in which the attempt is made to find a common EC line on this topic."[131] The chancellor took pains to place his policy in collective terms—even were Austria to 'go it alone,' it would do so only after receiving a collective green light on unilateral recognition. Vranitzky evidently hoped that waiting for a multilateral cue to engage in unilateral diplomacy would satisfy the European requirement of collective conduct. Vranitzky's effort to ensconce unilateral action in an additional layer of collective procedure however did not succeed. Raising any possibility that Vienna might recognize ahead of the jointly-decided deadline caused worry abroad.

On December 11, Mock described the content of Austrian sanctions against Serbia and Montenegro—the freezing of assets and a transportation ban similar to that adopted by Germany. Mock pointedly emphasized that Austria did not behave unilaterally in these sanctions, but, rather, enjoyed the company of Germany, Hungary, Italy, and, perhaps, the EC. His characterization of the sanctions would not please the more cautious powers. Mock said, "There will be transport sanctions corresponding to the model that was adopted by Germany and that is currently being discussed in Hungary and Italy. In this respect, the EC principle will serve as a basis, according to which a distinction is made between the Yugoslav republics that are ready to cooperate with the peace conference in The Hague and those that do not recognize the EC peace plan."[132] EC *principle* would guide Austria, but Vienna would work out the details alone. This posture, on examination, left little to collective diplomacy. States in Europe mostly agreed on the broadest formulations of foreign policy. Assurances on minority rights and other internal constitutive provisions, as well as the basic criteria for statehood—these were not bones of contention in a theoretical sense. Assessing whether the requirements for recognition had been met in a particular case, however, lay open to debate. Expressions of adherence to EC principle meant little, absent consent to collective decision-making.

A pattern emerged in the effort to characterize Austrian diplomatic action as non-unilateral. Vranitzky and Mock tried to paint Austria's policies as imitations of the conduct of its neighbors, rather than unilateral invention. The sanctions, Mock stated, paralleled the measures Germany had taken and, reassuringly, which Hungary and Italy too planned to take. Implicit was a notion that any state assuming the diplomatic vanguard had acted improperly. Austria sought to immunize itself against charges of unilateralism and invention by casting its conduct as derivative of other states' policies or, better yet, derivative of collective processes. Despite the effort, Mock and Vranitzky do not seem thoroughly to have convinced the sharper critics of Austrian policy.

The governments of the United States and Great Britain formally reproached Austria for sanctioning rump Yugoslavia. A written note from London emphasized in particular that precipitate conduct, in the form either of recognition or sanctions, could compromise peace-keeping efforts. The American State Department, in an oral opinion to Vienna, criticized the Austrian decisions roundly. These communiques signalled that lone action on Austria's part might carry high diplomatic costs. Accordingly, the Vranitzky government sought a compromise with the forces in parliament which had urged early, and if necessary unilateral, recognition and sanctions. Compromise however would prove elusive.

By withholding recognition from Croatia and Slovenia, the Vranitzky government may have assuaged its critics in London and Washington, but it began to run into the obstacles of democratic process in its own country. Austrian opinion, as expressed by a unanimous resolution of the parliament, strongly favored recognition and sanctions. Domestic constraints thus began to demarcate the ground which the cabinet could concede in order to appease foreign governments. Vienna's Balkan diplomacy had to confront the barriers presented by the sensibilities of the Austrian public. With one party secretary declaring that the government by declining immediately to recognize Croatia and Slovenia had acted in "gross disregard of parliament," the Vranitzky cabinet now faced a minor crisis of its own.[133] The experience of Austria illustrated that domestic political forces can constrict the possibilities for conforming to a collective norm on international conduct.

*Disjunction over Croatia*

With the approach of January 15, the EC and its member states reiterated their support for recognition, but they did so with various qualifications. In common among the qualifications were demands that, in order to receive recognition, Slovenia, and moreover Croatia, provide for fair treatment of their minority communities. (The EC had already announced the substance of these demands at Brussels on December 16.) The decision on recognizing the new states would hinge, for some EC member states, upon a final report assessing the secessionist republics' adherence to the Brussels criteria. A chief purpose of the Badinter Commission was to state, in the judgment of the jurists who composed it, whether the republics seeking recognition had fulfilled the substantive criteria set out on December 16, especially those criteria concerning minority rights. The opinions of the Commission were professed by most member states to inform their deliberations on recognition of the new republics. Germany, however, assured that it would recognize Croatia and Slovenia, notwithstanding the Commission findings.[134] This marked a signal German independence from collective European diplomacy. Though bearing on the Balkan crisis generally, Bonn's decision to move ahead whatever the outcome of the Badinter Commission assessment was relevant for Croatia in particular.

As the January 15 deadline drew closer, it became apparent that, in weighing recognition, the Western European states harbored greater doubts toward Croatia than toward Slovenia. Slovenia is substantially homogeneous, and the practical administrative separation of Slovenia from Yugoslavia had been comparatively clean. Croatia by contrast contains a Serb minority comprising some 11.5 per cent of the republic's population, and Croat secession had triggered warfare which raged through the recognition debate. Lord Carrington, chairman of the EC Yugoslav peace conference, and Douglas Hurd, foreign minister of the United Kingdom, expressed concern on January 10 that Croatia might fail to meet EC requirements on minority rights. At the same time, however, the German government reiterated its forward stance on recognition, regardless of minority rights assurances.[135] From the Spanish foreign ministry, too, came expressions of concern over Croatia. Spanish Foreign Minister Francisco Fernandez Ordonez stated on January 12 that recognition of Slovenia posed no problem, but that other Yugoslav republics such as Bosnia-Herzegovina and Macedonia would unlikely qualify for recognition so soon. Croatia, too, raised "serious dilemmas" in the Spanish foreign minister's estimation.[136] Germany, notwithstanding collective doubt over Croatia's satisfaction of critical recognition prerequisites, would continue to lobby the EC to recognize on January 15. Though the EC recognized both republics on January 15, individual member states, reflecting continued doubt over Croatia, appended to their recognition statements qualifications and "conditions."

### *Macedonia and Greek Particularism*

As much as any other aspect of the crisis surrounding Yugoslavia, recognition of Macedonia exposed the complications of the Common Foreign and Security Policy toward which EC member states professed to aspire. According to one publicist, "The ease by which [Macedonia] achieved independence stands in stark contrast to the unduly protracted process by which the Republic gained international recognition."[137]

Macedonia, in the south of the former SFRY, is bounded on the north by Serbia, the west by Albania, the south by Greece, and the east by Bulgaria. An ethnic mosaic, its population consists of Macedonian Slavs (66.5%), Albanians (22.9%), Turks (4.0%), Serbs (2.0%), Gypsies (2.3%), and

Vlachs (0.4%). Its territory has been claimed by all of its neighbors at different times this century and, in modern times, had never been an independent state. Macedonia made a declaration of sovereignty from the SFRY on January 25, 1991. The overwhelming majority of voters elected on September 8, 1991, to declare independence, and the republic declared independence on September 17. By April 15, 1992, JNA forces had withdrawn from Macedonia. The transition to free statehood was accomplished without bloodshed.[138] On January 11, 1992, Opinion No. 6 of the Badinter Commission recommended that Macedonia be recognized.

Though Bulgaria proceeded to recognize the new republic on January 16, widespread recognition would be delayed for some fifteen months.[139] Hindering recognition was the relationship between Macedonia and the northern region of Greece by the same name. It was widely agreed that Macedonian statehood had no fundamental defects. The FYROM had not violated international law in the process of gaining independence; its continued existence did not rely on any violation of international law; and, as determined by the Badinter Commission, it fulfilled the basic criteria of statehood.[140] Greece however objected to certain national symbols and to the adoption by the republic of the name "Macedonia" itself.[141] The EC Presidency seems to have encouraged the unusual Greek objections in a statement of May 4, 1992, calling for a "name that can be recognised by all parties concerned."[142] Greece therefore continued to block normalization of ties between the Community and FYROM.

The Greek position complicated European efforts to sanction Serbia and Montenegro for misconduct in Bosnia and Croatia. Macedonia proved porous to a European embargo and unready to assist so long as its own status was kept in doubt by the controversy over national symbols and nomenclature.[143] A more serious breach in Europe's collective external policy opened on February 16, 1994. As of that date, Greece implemented a trade embargo against the FYROM, despite an EU decision within the framework of common commercial policy to open economic ties with the new state.

The embargo prompted the European Commission to move against Greece. The resultant case before the Court of Justice of the European Communities, *Commission of the European Communities* v. *Hellenic Republic*,[144] was decided on June 29, 1994. Greece argued that it had made proper use of Articles 223 and 234 of the EC Treaty of 1957, which permit unilateral measures by a member state confronted with domestic disorder, threat of war, or international tension. Greece specifically argued that the FYROM 'situation' caused "serious international tension constituting a threat of war." The Commission applied to the ECJ for interim measures to suspend the Greek blockade. Though the Court found that the blockade was contrary to Community rules regarding free movement of goods and common commercial policy, it rejected the Commission argument that the breach did the "serious harm" which was necessary to permit the Court to order interim measures. In reaching its decision, the ECJ took notice that Macedonia had amended its constitution in order to comply with the December 16, 1991, Brussels Declaration provisions against "hostile propaganda activities versus a neighboring Community state." (Greece had portrayed maps, calenders, car stickers, school texts, and clauses of the Macedonian constitution as part of a campaign of hostile propaganda against Greece).[145] The Court further noted that Greece had rejected a proposal advanced at a European Council Meeting in Edinburgh on December 11–12, 1992, whereby Macedonia would have done four things in return for recognition by all member states: (1) adopt the name "Republic of Macedonia (Skopje)"; (2) pledge by treaty the inviolability of the border with Greece; (3) amend Article 49 of its constitution to remove all reference to the "status" and "rights of citizens of neighboring countries who are of Macedonian origins"; and (4) enter into a treaty of good relations and exchange letters on important issues with Greece.[146] Six EU member states recognized the FYROM in December 1993, but Greece persisted in nonrecognition.

The EC encountered difficulties in maintaining collective discipline over the recognition of the former Yugoslav republics. Nevertheless, the evidence suggests that a collective impetus had entered the norm on recognition. That the leaders of many states expressed concern over deterioration of collective discipline and that they took affirmative steps to repair breaks in consensus reflect the importance which had attached to multilateral process.

## DETERMINANTS AND LIMITS OF THE COLLECTIVE RESPONSE

Through ad hoc diplomacy and permanent intergovernmental bodies alike, Western European states attempted to approach the Yugoslav crisis in collective fashion. The process of recognizing Croatia and Slovenia did reflect a trend toward collectivization, but this only reached so far. A number of limits became evident in the capacity of Western Europe to maintain a joint recognition policy. Albeit against a backdrop of an emerging expectation for collective conduct, there lingered acceptance of recognition as unilateral and discretionary. Two reservations of state discretion in particular limited the collectivization of the recognition process.[147] First, though a degree of collectivization had entered the norm on recognition, the exact scope of this development remained ill-defined and its terms highly malleable. To engage in a collective process, participants must know the extent of the community involved in the process. Is the relevant community a small one, numbering perhaps a few neighboring states? Or is it larger, embracing an entire region? To assess whether a decision is collective in any meaningful sense, the authoritative decision makers must first decide what entities comprise the relevant community. How the decision to define the scope of the relevant community is reached may be as important as the process of policy-making which follows.

A review of state practice during the Yugoslav crisis suggests that, at least to an extent, it still rests in the hands of the individual state to decide the scope of the relevant community. Put differently, the individual state retains the discretion to define the compass of its collective reference. States, then, enjoy the discretion to define what might be termed the *collective referential community*—that group of states to which the authoritative decision-makers look when assessing whether consensus has arisen behind a given policy. It is as if parliamentary procedure permitted an individual delegate to choose how many delegates constitute a quorum and, moreover, which delegates are eligible to be counted toward the quorum. The power to choose its own quorum, as it were, leaves a substantial discretion in the hands of the individual state. A decision to recognize a claimant community may have been reached in the ministries or cabinet, outside any multilateral framework and before interstate deliberation has begun in earnest. Where a state has arrived *ex ante* at the decision to recognize, a given assemblage of states might reject that decision; another however might ratify it. If collective action is mandatory, then the power to redefine a state's point of reference—to redefine its collective referential community—is potent. International practice indeed appears to permit the state unilaterally to define what assemblage of states it will join in collective deliberation. Though unilateral recognition may be against current usage (and perhaps even law), a state is free to choose that collective referential community likely most nearly to affirm the state's own views.

The second reservation of state discretion is closely related to the first. As a state can define the compass of its own collective reference, so too can it join pre-existing groups of states likely to reach multilateral decisions consonant with its own. Such groups may be loose and informal, bound only by common heritage or geopolitical outlook; or they may form international institutions with discrete legal personality and solid bureaucratic foundations. Either way, the state and the group possess common interests predating the recognition crisis and independent of it. Italian foreign minister Gianni De Michelis, for example, noted the role of such groups even before the Yugoslav recognition crisis of 1991–92.[148] The practice of states during the crisis further testified to the influence of preexisting state groups. The groups may indeed demarcate where collective process is likely to take place. The collectivization of recognition appears to go little further than the limits of *a priori* common interest. Organizations of states such as NATO and the EC (or before 1989, the Warsaw Pact) possess common bonds, overarching any single recognition incident. Groups of states bound by common interest, in the economic, political, cultural,[149] or historic[150] spheres, are more likely to form consensus than states lacking extant ties. Where the bonds of economics, politics, culture, or history have been formalized in institutions and treaties, then the likelihood of consensus is greater still. The states of the EC endeavored to maintain a collective front on the Yugoslav recognition crisis; these states shared intimate ties, of all types, and many of the ties were strengthened by the EC and its institutions. It may well be that if any group of states were able to maintain collective recognition diplomacy, it would be a group like the EC. That diplomatic consensus frayed even within a set of such closely related states as the EC suggests the limits on collective recognition process. Though collectivization may well be sustainable outside groups of states which have preexisting reasons for collective action, practice surrounding Yugoslavia did not clearly point that way.

### A Reservation of State Discretion—Defining the Compass of Collective Reference

Zvonimir Separovic, foreign minister of Croatia, visited Finland on December 13, 1991, in part of a campaign of shuttle diplomacy to broaden the European consensus for recognition. Finnish radio reported at the time of Separovic's visit that UN Secretary General Javier Perez de Cuellar had just reiterated an appeal to delay recognition of the separatist republics. Recognition, the Secretary General argued, would exacerbate the crisis in Yugoslavia. Finnish radio simultaneously noted that Finland's new neighbors, the Baltic states of Estonia, Latvia, and Lithuania, as well as Ukraine, had already recognized the Yugoslav secessionists, but that no other states had yet followed suit. Finland's neighbors were acting in concert toward the republics, but such a small collective referential community did not satisfy policy makers in Helsinki. Though noteworthy, nearly simultaneous recognition by a handful of states lacked sufficient compass to persuade Finland too to recognize. Helsinki delayed its own recognition and awaited the advent of a broader consensus.[151]

The discretion to define collective referential community was exercised by some states conservatively. Others however employed this discretion to promote rapid recognition. Austria and Germany in particular defined the compass of collective reference in a manner likely to ratify their own preference for early action.

#### *The Austrian Case*

Austria at once acknowledged that an expectation had emerged for collective recognition and reserved for itself the freedom to define what group of states constituted the collective referential community. Chancellor Vranitsky commented upon the meeting of EC foreign ministers which had taken place in Brussels on December 16: "The conclusion that we are drawing from the EC deliberations is that we will stick to Austria's line. In reality, the EC foreign ministers decided to do what we had decided two-and-a-half months ago on principle, namely to recognize Slovenia and Croatia if another group of states decides to do so." The collective decision-making underway at Brussels had become the indispensable reference point. Leaders within and without the EC framed their own policy in EC terms. Vranitzky was no exception. However, the Austrian government rather boldy stated that critical to its decision to join EC diplomacy on Yugoslavia was the congruence between EC views and Austria's own.

Chancellor Vranitzky explained that Austria would identify a group of states which conformed to the Austrian view. As things appeared on December 17, the EC fit the bill. However, if an alternate set of decision-makers more closely approximated Austria's views, Vienna would redefine the compass of collective policy. Chancellor Vranitzky explained that Austria was currently watching to see "whether *another group of states* indeed decides to [extend recognition]" [emphasis supplied]. He added that Austria was not bound to follow the particular collective decision reached by the EC: "For us the dates set down by the EC are not as relevant as they are for EC members, because our basic position proceeds from the premise of declaring recognition as soon as a group of other states follow suit. As soon as we can be certain that there is such a group, we will take the necessary steps."[152] Defining that group Austria reserved to itself. Vranitzky's remarks reflected that the collective process emerging at the end of 1991 was malleable. Austria, the chancellor said, would recognize only amidst a group of states. Collective recognition was expected. Austria remained free however to define which and how many states would constitute a suitable group. Echoing Vranitzky's position, Foreign Minister Mock expressed respect for the collective decision of the EC member states, but simultaneously underlined that that decision appeared to conform to the Austrian view on recognition: "I consider the decision made in Brussels to be an important, positive step in the right direction, because the 12 EC states clearly said that they agree on recognizing the republics which so desire."[153] The foreign minister reiterated that the EC was a critical reference point but noted too that the EC agreed with Austria's position. The EC, by Mock's description, endorsed recognizing any republics requesting recognition. Mock referred approvingly to EC collective process, but it was no mere coincidence that EC process had yielded a result Mock characterized as consonant with Austrian aims. Both the head of Austria's government and her senior diplomat thus affirmed the collective influence on recognition, but they also reserved discretion to their own national decision-making mechanisms. The Austrian leaders left open whether the EC would form the collective referential community for purposes of assessing whether and when to recognize the new states in Yugoslavia.

Some hours later on the same day as the Mock-Vranitzky interviews, Mock announced to parliament that the Austrian government had decided to recognize Croatia and Slovenia on January 15, 1992.[154] In a live interview later in the evening, Mock and his Croat counterpart, Zvonimir Separovic, discussed the Austrian measure. Mock reiterated the collective component of the recognition process: "[W]e will follow the course of other countries, that is to say to recognize in principle, but implement recognition on 15 January."[155] Though Mock took pains to associate Austrian policy with the EC, the position announced on December 17 stood notably forward of other European states. Mock explained later in the same interview that the January 15 Brussels deadline did not mark full recognition by all EC states; hesitant states viewed January 15 as a date for "recognition in principle" only. Austria by contrast was recognizing "in principle" on the very day Mock was speaking—December 17. The fifteenth of January would, in Mock's words, bring full implementation of recognition by Austria. The EC constituted a collective reference point only insofar as its decision comported with Austria's.

While Austrian statesmen took care to emphasize the collective component of the recognition process, they nonetheless exercised a degree of unilateral discretion. At the heart of this discretion lay the freedom to define a collective referential community suitable to state interests.

The actions of European leaders were demarcating the collective character of the recognition process. While diplomatic conduct during the crisis of Yugoslav recognition suggested that purely unilateral and discretionary action was inappropriate, the scope of collectivization remained malleable. The states most concerned with Croatia and Slovenia espoused collectivization of the recognition process, but the compass of that process was largely self-determined. In assessing whether a consensus has been reached, one must first gauge the scope of the referential community. By constricting or enlarging the scope of the referential community, one can alter one's assessment of whether consensus exists. Austria, Germany, and other states committed themselves in principle to the proposition that recognition must no longer be a process restricted to individual chanceries and foreign ministries but, rather, that recognition must be a collective process embracing a number of states. However, what number of states amounts to the quorum necessary to make recognition "collective" remained unclear. In defining a reference for collective process, the individual state retained a type of *Kompetenz-Kompetenz*. The state defined its own referential community; the state defined its own quorum. It was left to the individual state to identify the community to which to look in assessing whether a consensus had developed. Whether collective process survives such unilateral discretion is uncertain. Freedom to define the collective referential community was however a prominent feature of state practice in 1991–92.

A disagreement between Germany and the United Nations further illustrated this limit on collective process.

*The German Case*

The chief rationale for slowing the process of recognition was to enable international bodies and the negotiations under their auspices to achieve a cease-fire in the Serbo-Croat war. The loci of effort to stop the fighting—and to slow recognition—were the United Nations, the Vance-Owen Mission, and Lord Carrington's Conference on Yugoslavia. The United Nations Security Council recommended that countries and groups of countries refrain from "actions that would prevent the implementation of a cease-fire, and would prevent or delay a peacefully negotiated solution to the conflict." Many observers assumed that Germany, though not targeted specifically by the Council, prompted the most concern. German Foreign Minister Hans-Dietrich Genscher discussed his country's position toward the Yugoslav successor states and toward the world community and UN. Genscher raised two matters in particular. Firstly, the collective nature of recognition: "The FRG's position is very clear. It is fully in line with what the European Community has decided. The EC set a deadline of one or two months for the political process on 10 October. This deadline expired on 10 December. Therefore, it is necessary for the EC to deal with the recognition of those republics in Yugoslavia that wish to be recognized. The EC will meet on this problem tomorrow."[156] Genscher declared that a collective process should prevail over the recognition decision—but a process with certain limits. The fact of a deadline implied that collective political action deserved a chance, but, failing a collective solution, recognition would take place regardless of EC views. Secondly, Genscher declared that recognition decisions would have to follow from a list of substantive criteria. The list itself, Genscher took pains to emphasize, resulted from *joint* Franco-German action. This meant that the substantive criteria for recognizing a new state derived from multilateral (or at least bilateral) process. "The Community," Genscher said, "should not decide on a case-by-case basis, but should have a catalogue of principles that would make it easier for the EC to decide on a given case." He went on to cite a "catalogue of principles" set forth in cooperation between France and Germany.[157] Asked whether France would concur with Germany's estimation that Croatia and Slovenia had met the criteria for recognition, Genscher indicated that the key step in the conference scheduled for the next day (December 16) was adopting the catalogue of principles. This left unclear whether that catalogue was the product of bilateral talks between Paris and Bonn or of the multilateral process scheduled to go on at Brussels. Nor did Genscher answer whether France would join the German position advocating recognition. The foreign minister acknowledged the need for broad-based action but left uncertain whether broad-based action was a requirement under the law of recognition or an expedient of German foreign policy. Speaking to an interviewer, Genscher added, "This very complicated process . . . shows that this is a problem that cannot be solved easily. It is important to win as many countries as possible over to our position because only broad recognition has the desired effect for the peoples concerned."[158] Genscher's objective appears to have been to amass enough support for recognition to obscure the unilateral character of German foreign policy. Such an objective differs from that of making policy through collective process. Creating an appearance of joint decision may well have taken precedence over reality. German statecraft nonetheless further evidenced the development in recognition noted already in the Austrian case. A state is restrained from acting alone on recognition, but the state remains at liberty to define the community which will serve as a reference for collective process. If Genscher's citing of talks with France was any indication, then Germany believed itself free even to constrict the collective referential community to a single bilateral relationship.

Genscher also remarked upon the difficulty involved in trying "to achieve . . . coordinated action" as requested by the United Nations Secretary General. Thus, the leading German foreign policy decision-maker expressed concern over the role of the UN in the recognition process. "We wished," Genscher said, "that . . . a global settlement had come about. However, the European Community was also in agreement that those who prevent a global settlement must not prevent a political solution. Or, in other words, this means that those who refuse to accept peace and those who refuse to accept independence are not granted the right of veto." The parties to which Genscher here alluded were the Yugoslav federal government and its armed forces. At the same time, Genscher appeared to criticize the UN for obstructing independence as well. Confronted with an international organization that did not share the German view on recognition, the foreign minister tried to shift the locus of authority elsewhere. The Kohl government failed to find ratification of its views in the world's most broadly constituted assembly, so it turned to an organization of narrower scope. The EC, Genscher seemed to anticipate, would be more likely to concur with German recognition policy than the UN. Under this precedent, a policy-maker dissatisfied by the collective decisions of a given multilateral body may direct public focus away from that body and toward an alternative reference point. This redirection is executed in the hope that the alternative reference point will provide a collective decision more agreeable to state policy.

The liberty to define the collective referential community provides a powerful tool with which to forge affirmance of national policy. The impact of this goes beyond domestic decision-making and individual incidents. Indeed it shapes public international law. The reservation of a right to select which states constitute the relevant community for purposes of deliberation imposes a limit on the evolution of a collective process of recognition.

### Extant Common Interest—Collectivization Delimited?

The collectivization of recognition during the Yugoslav crisis was most pronounced amidst a group of states possessing mutual affinities independent of their assessment of the crisis. Ties among Western European states superseded the events of 1991–92. Historical, cultural, economic, and political similarities and interests brought the region into an unprecedented degree of cooperation after World War II, and this operated on the recognition process at least as markedly as did any shift in the legal norm governing recognition. Amid the EC member states, similarities and relationships exerted particular influence, and the institutionalization of ties amplified their effect. While the norm governing recognition has moved discernibly toward collective process, it is no mere coincidence that collective process showed up in clearest relief among states already sharing reasons and precedents for coordinate action.

Pressing short-term concerns (or long-term developments anticipated soon to come to a head) can add impetus to collective conduct among states already tied by other factors. Where a community project of overarching importance intervenes, the collective process of recognition is reinforced. Whether collective recognition is possible without such a project to impose discipline is as yet unclear. The incident of the recognition of Croatia and Slovenia suggests that a superseding crisis among states infuses them with incentive to behave collectively. The states apprehend that failure to reach a multilateral decision on recognition may endanger some other consensus deemed vital to the community.

Maintenance of consensus was indeed central to EC discipline on Croatia and Slovenia for reasons independent of recognition. European monetary and political union had reached a critical juncture in late 1991, and the delicacy of that situation concentrated the cooperative energies of the EC member states. Confronted by crisis in the Balkans, the member states took care lest foreign policy disagreements jeopardize the union project. This resulted in forging a collective position on recognition, not only because the collective process might have been becoming mandatory, but because to guarantee the success of the Maastricht Treaty unity had to be maintained across the board. Arguably the most powerful force sustaining the drive for collective recognition was independent of the Yugoslav crisis or broader currents of public international law.

Long-term interests and affinities and the exigencies of union-building at the time of the Balkan crisis alike contributed to the collective conduct of the EC in 1991–92. The question arises whether collective recognition derives at all from imperatives of public international law, or whether it is simply a product of political factors. Further, the experience of 1991–92 leaves unanswered how far collective process might spread in the future.

Arguably, the most pressing concern that faced the member states of the EC at the time of the crisis of recognition was the European economic and monetary treaty. A brief history of the EC assists in understanding the relation between the treaty and Western European development.

The European Communities comprised three separate institutions. The first of these, the European Coal and Steel Community (the ECSC), was set up under the Treaty of Paris of 1951. The Treaties of Rome of 1957 created the Atomic Energy Community (Euratom) and the European Economic Community (the EEC). The ECSC and Euratom regulated the activities suggested by their titles, with all other sectors of the economy left to the EEC. The Single European Act of 1986 removed all trade barriers among the then-twelve member states.

In addition to the three Communities, a number of political and judicial institutions were established to foster European integration. The European Parliament, sitting in Strasbourg, has been elected by direct universal suffrage since 1979. A European Council, established in 1974, meets twice yearly and consists of the Heads of State or Government of the member states. A representative from the European Commission also sits on the Council. The European Commission consists of representatives of the member states and sits for five year terms. Membership requires the approval of the European Parliament. The Commission, based in Brussels and Luxembourg, is supported by fifteen thousand officials divided among roughly thirty directorates-general. The Commission initiates enforcement actions against breaches of European rules, especially in the area of competition law, and it promulgates regulations under various treaty articles. The laws which guide the Commission are passed through any one of a complex of legislative procedures.[159] A Court of Justice was established in 1952, and this sits in Luxembourg. In 1989, a Court of First Instance was established to hear actions brought by private persons and businesses. Other institutions include a Court of Auditors (monitoring expenditures), an Economic and Social Committee (representing three groups: employers, workers, and other interests), a Committee of the Regions (addressing local and regional concerns), the European Investment Bank (set up under the Treaty of Rome to promote balanced development within the EC), and a European Monetary Institute (set up in 1994 and based in Frankfurt, with the mission to prepare for a single European currency).

The original members of the communities were France, West Germany, Italy, the Netherlands, Belgium, and Luxembourg. In 1973, Ireland, the United Kingdom, and Denmark joined, and Greece in 1981. Spain and Portugal brought membership to twelve in 1986. In 1990, the space of the former German Democratic Republic was integrated into West Germany and the EC. The most recent expansion came in 1995 with the accession to the Treaty on European Union of Sweden, Finland, and Austria.

It was this step toward integration—the Treaty on European Union—which most concerned the member states at the time of the Yugoslav crisis.

The Treaty on European Union was signed at Maastricht on February 7, 1992 and entered into force on November 9, 1993. The Treaty declared that the twelve member states of the three European communities (the ECSC, Euratom, and the EEC) formed a European Union. The European Union (EU) was envisioned as an overall structure tying together three parts of European integration: (1) The three communities; (2) common foreign and security policy; and (3) common judicial and home affairs policies. The second and third parts involved the judicial, legislative, and executive activities of the several European institutions described above. The Treaty on European Union broadened the competences of the Council of the European Union and governs the organization and membership of the Council. Though some member states take the view that the EU lacks international legal personality, the Union does provide the constitutional structure for integrated European institutions. The Maastricht Treaty, as the Treaty on European Union is commonly called, was the essential step toward this structure and any further economic, monetary, or political integration to arise within it.[160]

The urgency of completing the Maastricht Treaty was a principal theme in Western Europe at the time of the Yugoslav recognition debate. "One does not have to be a prophet to say that if we do not create political and economic unity now, then it will take more than a generation before we get this opportunity again," declared Helmut Kohl in late November 1991.[161] In the same set of remarks, Kohl emphasized the need to reach compromise on the Maastricht Treaty: "[A]nyone," he said, "who thinks: My concept is the only conceivable one—they need not even bother to go to Maastricht."[162] The Maastricht summit of EC members, on December 9 and 10, would have to resolve vexing questions about the economic and institutional structure of the nascent Union. Failure to iron out differences in December would have threatened delay—and possibly derailment—of the Treaty on European Union. Exemplifying the difficult issues facing the summit, the member states had yet to decide whether to vest monetary policy power in the future EU central bank alone (the structure preferred by German leaders, desiring to achieve as much economic unity as possible) or to leave such policy to the discretion of a legislative chamber with deliberative capacities (an approach favored by the economically less powerful states, fearful of the overshadowing influence of a European central bank). In this connection, German Secretary of State for Finance Horst Koehler repeated Chancellor Kohl's advice that consensus and compromise were imperative.[163] That critical issues remained on the table added more urgency to maintaining European agreement. Important compromises had yet to be worked out, and an overall atmosphere of comity promised to facilitate these.[164]

Germany took the lead in insisting that Europe maintain comity during the run-up to the Maastrict summit. It is unsurprising, then, that Germany's breaking rank on recognition aroused criticism and puzzlement. Chancellor Kohl addressed the Bundestag on November 27, 1991, and indicated that Germany would implement recognition of Croatia and Slovenia before Christmas, even if the other states of the EC did not concur. "There is no obligation for unanimity," Kohl was reported to have said.[165] When Belgian officials stated the need for collective Western European response to the Yugoslav crisis, they emphasized the connection between recognition and the impending Maastricht talks. Belgian Foreign Minister Eyskens addressed the precarious position of the nascent union. On the evening of November 28 he stated that European unity would be jeopardized if individual member states broke from the common Community foreign policy and recognized Croatia and Slovenia unilaterally. Eyskens emphasized that the summit scheduled for December 9 and 10 was much more likely to go smoothly if the member states arrived at Maastricht amid a spirit of joint action on Yugoslavia.[166]

The Maastricht summit overtly influenced the Greek position on recognition, too. Domestic sympathy in Greece was with the Serbs, so the drift of Western Europe toward recognition of Croatia and Slovenia and toward isolation of Belgrade was resisted. Nonetheless, policy-makers in Athens, as elsewhere in Europe, worked to avoid jeopardizing the comity which they believed would speed accession to the Union Treaty. At Brussels in the first week of December, the EC foreign ministers had reiterated their resolve to sanction Serbia and Montenegro for complicity in the civil war. Greece, represented at Brussels by its foreign minister Andonios Samaras, declared that it opposed selective sanctions against Serbia and Montenegro. However, Samaras was quick to reassure that Greece wished to avoid disrupting the Maastricht talks. Rather than fray the emerging EC collective policy by voting against sanctions, Athens abstained. Even when pressed by pro-Serb domestic opinion, the Greek government stood by its commitment to make Maastricht work.[167]

European leaders continued to emphasize the importance of the Union Treaty. After the Maastricht summit, Helmut Kohl addressed the Bundestag:

> [T]he path toward European union has become irreversible. Now and in the future the EC member nations are linked in such a way that is its impossible for them to break out or to relapse into the past way of thinking of nation-states with all its terrible consequences. With this we have implemented in practice a central goal of Germany's European policy. Maastricht is proof of the fact that the united Germany actively accepts its responsibility in and for Europe and lives up to what we have always said, that German unification and European unity are two sides of the same coin.[168]

The Maastricht Treaty was consistently portrayed as cornerstone for European integration; and maintenance of comity over Yugoslavia as imperative for the Maastricht Treaty.

The delicacy of the Maastricht consensus was much noted in the press at the time of the debate over recognition. An editorial analyzing progress toward the Union Treaty appeared in the *Düsseldorf Handelsblatt* on January 15, the date by which the EC had agreed to recognize the secessionist republics. The commentator, Eberhard Wisdorf, noted several factors which might disturb the Maastricht project. First, the financial system in place since February 1988 was set to expire shortly, and the design and implementation of its successor promised to be difficult. Second, political, economic, and monetary union remained tenuous. That the poorer member states (*e.g.*, Greece, Portugal, Spain, and Ireland) joined many EC initiatives only when financial promises induced their cooperation demonstrated how loose were the underpinnings of integration. Third, foreign policy and foreign aid commitments placed a heavy burden on the richer EC states (Germany in particular), and such disproportionate cost-sharing strained relations within the EC.[169] Facing problems already, the nascent union could little afford a foreign policy confrontation over the Balkans.

The delicacy of the European monetary arrangement became all the more evident when the Danish electorate declined to ratify the Maastricht Treaty. Though this failure in the union process would be corrected by a second referendum, the precariousness of the EU project was evident. An editorialist in Denmark was acutely aware that EC disagreements unrelated to monetary union could unravel the progress achieved at the Maastricht Summit: "The closer EC cooperation becomes, the more important it is to straighten out situations that are subject to criticism." Matters not directly related to the Union Treaty threatened to absorb the energies of the member states and even to rent the fragile European structure. Though the Copenhagen commentator did not specify particular "situations," he intended a caveat to avoid tension wherever possible.[170] If domestic commentators were awake to the destructive potential of breaking rank with EC consensus, it should come as little surprise that leading policy-makers of the EC were as well.

Two limits on the collectivization of the recognition process came to light during the Yugoslav crisis: first, the reserve of substantial discretion in the individual state to define the collective referential community; and, second, the tendency of collective recognition to operate within groups of states already tied together by common aims. As in the first, in this second limitation the individual state retains substantial discretion. Joining international bodies and formulating national policy objectives are municipal, not international, decision processes.

This is not to say that the process of collectivization is hollow. The Yugoslav recognition incident illustrated that states and the public had come to expect some collective aspect in recognition. Leaders were loathe to describe their policy toward Croatia and Slovenia without reference to the community of states. Pains were taken to give individual policy the appearance of originating in consensus. Each foreign ministry carefully regarded the others, and none in the EC were so bold to declare recognition absent some acknowledgment of multilateral deliberation. The day was long past when an ambassador might declare that recognition was a matter of 'sovereign' decision that "no nation on earth can question."

A degree of collective process by 1991–92 had entered the norm governing recognition. The extent of collectivization was uncertain, but its impact was strongly felt. Domestic sentiment favored early recognition, especially in Germany and Austria, and government officials could little ignore the chorus of public sympathy for the secessionist republics. At the same time, an obligation was emerging under international law to approach recognition collectively. The decision-makers of Bonn and Vienna in 1991–92 confronted tension between national political will and new expectations of international order. Managing policy in the midst of such tension indeed proved a test for the emergent collectivization of recognition.

## NOTES

1. Woodward, for example, takes the view that the civil wars are to be blamed more on modern policy failures than on ancient ethnic or religious antagonism. Susan L. Woodward, *Balkan Tragedy: Chaos and Dissolution after the Cold War* (Washington, DC: Brookings Institution, 1995), 1–5, 7–8.

2. On establishment of Yugoslavia, see Alex N. Dragnich, *The First Yugoslavia: Search for a Viable Political System* (Stanford: Hoover Institution Press, 1983), 70 *ff.*

3. This risk has presented itself again in Muslim-Albanian-majority Kosovo. For background, see Julie A. Mertus, "Nationalism and Nation-Building: Milosevic Turns to Montenegro and Kosovo," 26 *New York University Journal of International Law & Politics* (N.Y.U. J. Int'l L. & Pol.) 511 (1994). On the risk of escalation, see Thomas D. Grant, "The New Tinder Box: The Kosovo Crisis," *Seattle Times*, March 22, 1998, p B5.

4. *See* Robert A. Kann, *A History of the Habsburg Empire, 1526–1918* (Berkeley: University of California Press, 1974).

5. On the pro-Nazi régime in Croatia, see John A. Armstrong, "Collaborationism in World War II: The Integral Nationalist Variant in Eastern Europe," 40 *Journal of Modern History* 396, 401–03, 405, 407, 408–09 (1968); Edmond Paris, *Genocide in Satellite Croatia, 1941–1945: A Record of Racial and Religious Persecutions and Massacres*, Lois Perkins trans. (Chicago: American Institute for Balkan Affairs, 1961), *passim*; Elizabeth Wiskemann, "Partitioned Yugoslavia," in *Hitler's Europe*, Arnold Joseph Toynbee & Veronica M. Toynbee eds. (London: Oxford University Press, 1954), 684.

6. Details on the breakup of Yugoslavia are furnished by a number of sources. *See, e.g.*, *Report of the Foreign Affairs Committee of the House of Commons: Soviet Union/Developments in Central Europe*, HC 1991–1992, 2-I, November 6, 1991, 46–49; Marc Weller, "The International Response to the Dissolution of the Socialist Federal Republic of Yugoslavia," 86 *American Journal of Internatinonal Law* (AJIL) 569 (1992); Carnegie Endowment for Peace, *Breakdown in the Balkans: A Chronicle of Events, January 1989 to May 1993*, Samantha Power ed. (Washington, DC: Carnegie Endowment Special Publications, 1994).

7. *See* Woodward, *Balkan Tragedy*, 15–16.

8. *Keesing's Record of World Events* (Keesing's), vol. 37:6, June 1991, p. 38275.

9. Among those closely observing Yugoslav affairs, signs of breakdown had been reported a year or two before the fact. *See, e.g.*, Alex N. Dragnich, "The Rise and Fall of Yugoslavia: The Omen of the Upsurge of Serbian Nationalism," 23 *East European Quarterly* 183, 187, 189 (1989).

10. Peter Lord Carrington served as Foreign Secretary of the United Kingdom from 1979 to 1982, resigning over the Argentine invasion of the Falklands. He earned international respect for coordinating the Lancaster House talks (leading to the transition from white-led Rhodesia to majority-led Zimbabwe), and he served as Secretary-General of NATO from 1984 to 1988. The Peace Conference he headed would meet on a continuing basis at the Peace Palace in the Hague. Lord Carrington resigned a year after the establishment of the Conference. Barbara Crossette, "Europe's Envoy

in Yugoslav crisis Quits," *New York Times* (N.Y. Times), August 26, 1992; John M. Goshko, "Carrington Quits as Mediator: Surprise Announcement Made as Conference on Yugoslavia Opens," *Washington Post* (Wash. Post), August 26, 1992, A20.

11. August 20, 1991 Declaration, The Hague (on file with author).

12. These assurances were

1. that the republics would accept the UN Charter and the CSCE Helsinki Accords;
2. that the republics would guarantee the rights of ethnic minorities;
3. that the republics would respect internationally recognized borders;
4. that the republics would uphold arms control and disarmament treaties; and
5. that the republics would support the political resolution of disputes.

*Breakdown in the Balkans: A Chronicle of Events, January 1989 to May 1992*, Samantha Power ed. (Washington, DC: Carnegie Endowment for International Peace, 1993), 28.

13. The most thorough analysis of the subject is Dugard's *Recognition and the United Nations*. Dugard may be over-optimistic about the mandate of the UN to decide recognition questions for its member states. *See* M.J. Peterson, 82 AJIL 391 (1988) (reviewing *Recognition and the United Nations* and doubting whether UN is independent of its member states).

14. Robert Badinter, "L'Europe du Droit," 3 *European Journal of International Law* (EJIL) 15 (1993).

15. *Declaration of European Community Foreign Ministers on Yugoslavia*, from an Extraordinary Meeting of Foreign Ministers, Brussels, August 27, 1991 (on file with author). The press, scholars, and official publications have variously referred to the Conference on Yugoslavia as the 'Conference,' the 'Peace Conference,' the 'European Peace Conference,' and the 'Carrington Peace Conference.' Its official long-form name appears to have been 'International Conference for Peace in Yugoslavia,' later changing to 'International Conference for Peace in the Former Yugoslavia.'

16. Alain Pellet, "The Opinions of the Badinter Arbitration Committee: A Second Breath for the Self-Determination of Peoples," 3 EJIL 178 (1992).

17. Pellet, professor at University of Paris X and at the IEP (Paris) and Member of the International Law Commission, served as legal advisor to the Badinter Commission. He wrote of the Commission in 1992, "Through its balanced and impartial decisions, the Arbitration Committee of the Peace Conference on Yugoslavia has furnished proof that such an organ can provide a great service. This example must be recognized and used as a building block in the search for mechanisms to resolve ethno-territorial conflicts." 3 EJIL at 181. Professor Pellet substantially contributed to the drafting of the Opinions of the Commission.

18. 3 EJIL at 178.

19. The large number of cease-fires brokered and then broken during the summer and autumn of 1991 makes keeping track of them difficult. The ministerial troika secured a first, brief cease-fire on June 28. It failed in hours, to be replaced by another on June 30. Keesing's, 38275. An agreement reached on July 7 at the Adriatic island of Brioni established an ambitious cease-fire, including a three-month "suspension of implementation" of the Croatian and Slovenian independence declarations. This was followed by an intensification of fighting between Serbs and Croats. Keesing's, 38374, 37:8, August 1991. The Peace Conference established on August 27 would broker numerous further cease-fires. Keesing's, 38420, 37:9, September 1991. On the Brioni cease-fire and its failure, see Henry Wynaendts, *L'engrenage: Chroniques*

*Yougoslaves, juillet 1991-août 1992* (Paris: Editions Denoël, 1993), 13–14.

20. The Yugoslav federation cannot be argued to have remained intact past December 20, 1991, when Ante Markovic quit as SFRY prime minister. On Markovic's resignation, precipitated by his opposition to excessive appropriations for the federal armed forces, see Laura Silber, "Bosnia Asks Recognition from EC: Four Republics Seek Independence," *Washington Post*, December 21, 1991, A15. In fact, the declarations of independence of June 25 had sounded the death-knell for Yugoslavia. On July 30, President Tudjman of Croatia boycotted a meeting of the collective presidency, signalling the withdrawal of Croatia from federal organs. On August 4, remaining formal ties between Croatia and Serbia were severed. Keesing's, 38375, 37:8, August 1991.

21. The presidency of the Council of the European Communities rotates among the member States, each in turn holding the office for a six-month term. Order is alphabetical by the name of the member States, as spelled in their own tongues. The EC presidency during the relevant period was held by Luxembourg (January to June 1991); the Netherlands (July to December 1991); Portugal (January to June 1992); and the United Kingdom (July to December 1992). On the Council generally, see Sir William Nicoll & Trevor C. Salmon, *Understanding the New European Community* (London: Prentice Hall, 1994), 67–74.

22. The Commission is the executive organ of the EC (after February 1992, of the EU).

23. *Declaration on Yugoslavia*, August 27, 1991 (on file with author).

24. Additional guidance on procedure would be provided in a Declaration of September 3, stating, "The rules of procedure for the arbitration will be established by the Arbitrators, after taking into account existing organizations in the field." The Arbitration Commission adopted an unpublished rules of procedure on December 22. *See Opinion 4*, 92 *International Law Reports* (ILR) 175, Elihu Lauterpacht & Christopher J. Greenwood eds. (Cambridge: Grotius Publications Limited, 1993). Pellet summarizes the procedure in fact employed by the Arbitration Commission. Alain Pellet, "Note Sur la Commission d'Arbitrage de la Conférence Européene Pour la Paix en Yugoslavie," 37 *Annuaire Français de Droit International* (AFDI) 329, 332 (1991).

25. *See* Matthew C.R. Craven, "The European Community Arbitration Commission on Yugoslavia," 66 *British Yearbook of International Law* (BYIL) 333, 337–38 (1995) (calling August 27 Declaration legal basis for Badinter Commission and discussing constitution of the Commission generally).

26. It was not in the press alone where Croatia prevailed as the chief topic. The exchanges among diplomats in late summer 1991 also focused on the war between Croat separatists and Serb irregulars and their JNA ally. A report by Dutch ambassador Henry Wynaendts on his fourth mission to Yugoslavia (August 27 to 1 September) illustrates the centrality of the Croatian war at that moment. (on file with author (CPE/PRES/HAG 734: 01-09-1991)).

27. The Republics of Serbia and Montenegro, it must be noted, at several points argued for a narrower mandate for the EC Conference. According to Yugoslavia (then representing only Serbia and Montenegro), it was from the Brioni Agreement of July 7, 1991, alone that the EC mandate flowed, and the Arbitration Commission was committing an *excès de pouvoir* in seizing itself of questions of state succession and the dissolution of Yugoslavia. *Opinions* 8, 9, & 10, 92 ILR 194–95.

28. Borders quickly became a particular source of controversy. Ambassador Wijnaendts, in his September 1, 1991 report, noted that the President of Croatia attempted to reserve the issue of borders and avoid putting it before the Commission. Serb irregulars and the JNA had occupied roughly one third of Croatia's territory by the autumn of 1991. Croatia wanted to exclude any international legal validation of the fact that it had lost effective control over much of the territory it claimed. The Croatian reservation of the border issue is noted in A.V. Lowe & Colin Warbrick, "Recognition of States," 41 *International and Comparative Law Quarterly* (ICLQ) 478–79 (1992).

29. The FRY challenge was in response to the questions that the arbitrators would later answer in Opinions 8 through 10.

30. *See* 92 ILR 195 n. 3.

31. "EPC" stands for "European Political Cooperation" and refers to the objective of the EC member States to coordinate external policy through multilateral conferences. EPC, after the February 1992 Maastricht Treaty, came to be known as CFSP—Common Foreign and Security Policy. Nicoll & Salmon, 185–212.

32. *Interlocutory Decision of the Arbitration Commission*, 92 ILR 197 (quoting *Nottebohm (Preliminary Objection), ICJ Rpts.*, 1953 at 199). This, the first of a pair of challenges to the Commission's jurisdiction, is discussed at some length in Craven, 66 BYIL at 342–49.

33. In reaching this conclusion, the arbitrators also noted a form of estoppel. Serbia had itself submitted three questions to the Commission in November 1991, and, at that time, had not "made the least mention of any incompetence on the Commission's part . . . thereby recognizing its competence." 92 ILR 198. The November 1991 Serbian questions were addressed in Opinions 2 and 3. *See* 92 ILR 167–172. The arbitrators further noted that all six republics had accepted the arbitration arrangements, upon the September 7 opening of the Conference for Peace. 92 ILR 197.

34. The Draft Convention on Yugoslavia had been drawn up by the European Conference on Yugoslavia and issued November 4, 1991. As of December 16, the Draft Convention was under review by the Conference.

35. The Final Act of the Conference on Security and Co-operation in Europe was signed by thirty-five states on August 1, 1975, at Helsinki. The Conference had convened on July 3, 1973, and met intermittently at Helsinki and Geneva. The Helsinki Final Act, though without binding legal effect, contained a number of statements on human rights and the security of Europe. The security aspect included confirmation of the post-1945 borders of Europe, and critics charged that the Final Act merely validated Soviet hegemony over Eastern Europe. The human rights provisions of the Helsinki Final Act later were seen to take on a force independent of their original context. "Remarks of Richard A. Falk," 1993 *American Society of International Law Proceedings* (ASIL Proc.) 198, 199. *See also* Oscar Schachter, "The Twilight Existence of Nonbinding International Agreements," 71 AJIL 296, 304 n. 29 (1977) (acknowledging that the "Third Basket" of the Helsinki Final Act concerning human rights may exert influence on national policy). Among the sections of the Final Act of particular concern to the framers of the December 16, 1991 EC *Declaration* were Chapter III (concerning inviolability of frontiers) and Chapter VII (concerning "Respect for human rights and fundamental freedoms, including the freedom of thought, conscience, religion or belief"). For the text of the Helsinki Final Act see 14

ILM 1492 (1975). Chapters III & VII appear at 14 ILM 1294 & 1295.

The Charter of Paris (*Charter of Paris for a New Europe: A New Era of Democracy, Peace and Unity*) was signed by the thirty-four members of the CSCE at Paris on November 21, 1990. The Charter signing was the second occasion of a summit-level meeting of the CSCE (the first was the August 1, 1975, Helsinki signing of the Final Act). The Charter of Paris adopted new CSCE institutional mechanisms, and it addressed human rights, military security, and environmental and scientific co-operation. *See* 30 ILM 190 (1991) (giving background to the Charter); 30 ILM 193 (reproducing text of the Charter). The Charter included an extensive list of human rights. 30 ILM at 194–95.

36. The Conference for Security and Co-operation in Europe was a product of the Helsinki Final Act of 1975. In the final provisions of the Final Act, the signatories called for "follow-up to the Conference" in the form of multilateral meetings. The CSCE was the institutional manifestation of this. The CSCE was re-invigorated by the Charter of Paris of 1990. The Charter section entitled *New Structures and Institutions of the CSCE Process* called in general terms for an extension of CSCE activities and of the structures to support these. A *Supplementary Document* to the Charter (*see* 30 ILM 209–219 (1991)) gave the details of a new CSCE, including emergency meeting provisions to address crises such as that which erupted in Yugoslavia less than a year after the signing of the Charter. Members of the CSCE in 1990 were France, Germany, Italy, the USSR, the United Kingdom, the United States, Canada, Belgium, the Netherlands, Poland, Spain, Sweden, Austria, the Czech and Slovak Federation, Denmark, Finland, Hungary, Norway, Switzerland, Greece, Romania, Turkey, Yugoslavia, Bulgaria, Ireland, Luxembourg, Portugal, Cyprus, the Holy See, Iceland, Liechtenstein, Malta, Monaco, and San Marino. 30 ILM 219–20.

37. Opinions 4 through 7.

38. Serbia, for the Federal Republic of Yugoslavia, posed questions answered in Opinions 2 and 3.

39. Opinions 1 & 8–15.

40. On state succession and Yugoslavia, see Paul R. Williams, "State Succession and the International Financial Institutions: Political Criteria v. Protection of Outstanding Financial Obligations," 43 ICLQ 776 (1994); Rein Mullerson, "The Continuity and Succession of States, by reference to the former USSR and Yugoslavia," 42 ICLQ 473 (1993).

41. 92 ILR 162–163.

42. 92 ILR 167–169.

43. ICJ Reports, 1986, p. 554.

44. Among these were the United Nations Charter; the Declaration on Principles of International Law (General Assembly Resolution 2625 (XX)); the Helsinki Final Act; Article 11 of the Vienna Convention of August 23, 1978 on the Succession of States in Respect of Treaties; *Burkina Faso and Mali (Frontier Dispute)*; Article 5 of the SFRY Constitution; the Hague Conference of September 7, 1991; and the Draft Convention of November 4, 1991, of the Conference on Yugoslavia.

45. On *uti possidetis*, see Craven, 66 BYIL at 385–90.

46. 92 ILR 173–178.

47. 92 ILR 179–181.

48. On file with author.

49. The Badinter Commission issued Observations on Croatian Constitutional

Law (Comments on the Republic of Croatia's Constitutional Law of 4 December 1991, as Last Amended on 8 May 1992) on July 4, 1992. The Observations stated that the amended constitution generally satisfied the essential principles of the EC Draft Convention. 92 ILR 209–211.

50. 92 ILR 182–187.

51. 92 ILR 188–194.

52. 92 ILR 202.

53. UN Security Council Resolutions 752 (May 15, 1992) & 757 (May 30, 1992). In resolution 777 (September 19, 1992), the Council, affirming the Badinter Commission observation, stated that "the state formerly known as the Socialist Federal Republic of Yugoslavia has ceased to exist."

54. Lisbon European Council Declaration of June 27, 1992.

55. *See* Saskia Hille, "Mutual Recognition of Croatia and Serbia (+Montenegro)," 6 EJIL 598 (1995).

56. 92 ILR 201.

57. 92 ILR 203–205.

58. 92 ILR 206–208.

59. 92 ILR 208.

60. 96 ILR 719–737 (1994).

61. Opinion 11 (July 16, 1993) addressed the dates of state succession of the various successors to the SFRY; Opinion 12 (July 16), the legal principles for determining state succession; Opinion 13 (July 16), financial responsibility for war damages; Opinion 14 (August 13, 1993), division of SFRY assets and liabilities; and Opinion 15 (August 13), authority of the National Bank of Yugoslavia and of the central banks of the successor states to decide rights, interests, and obligations concerning property and debts. Craven addresses the succession issues in 66 BYIL at 354–55; 401–08.

62. The League of Nations in connection with Manchuria in the early 1930s engaged an arguably similar body. After Japan had invaded and declared the northeastern province of China an independent state, the League dispatched a commission, under Lord Lytton, to investigate. Part of the task of the Lytton Commission was to evaluate the recognition claim. *See* Ian Nish, *Japan's Struggle with Internationalism: Japan, China and the League of Nations, 1931–3* (London: Kegan Paul International, 1993), 107–86; H.J. Timperley, "Japan in Manchuria," 1933 *Foreign Affairs* 294; Mo Shen, *Japan in Manchuria: An Analytical Study of Treaties and Documents* (Manila: Grace Trading Company, 1960) (Appendix G and Appendix H—*Proclamation on the Establishment of Manchukuo, March 1, 1932*), 401–406.

63. Badinter, 3 EJIL at 23 (1993).

64. Roland Rich, "Recognition of States: The Collapse of Yugoslavia and the Soviet Union," 4 EJIL 36, 44 (1993).

65. Craven, 66 BYIL at 335.

66. Marc Weller, "International Law and Chaos," 52 *Cambridge Law Journal* (Camb. L.J.) 6, 9 (1993).

67. Rich, 4 EJIL at 48–89.

68. Rich, 4 EJIL at 52–53; Badinter Commission Opinion 6. The EC, meeting at Lisbon on June 26–27, 1992, indicated that the republic could not be recognized under the name 'Macedonia,' despite the Arbitration Commission holding that, given the republic's renunciation of territorial ambitions, the nomenclature was innocu-

ous. Earlier, on May 2, the EC foreign ministers had declared their willingness to recognize "under a name that can be accepted by all parties concerned." *See* Weller, 86 AJIL 569. The US recognized Macedonia on February 9, 1994. *See* White House Office of Communications, "U.S. Recognition of the Former Yugoslav Republic of Macedonia," 1994 *Westlaw* (WL) 35346. The republic was admitted to the UN on April 8, 1993. A/RES/47/225 (April 8, 1993), "Admission of the State whose application is contained in document A/47/876-S/25137 to membership in the United Nations." Note the verbal formula avoiding reference to the disputed name 'Macedonia.'

69. Rich, 4 EJIL at 49.

70. Croatia was admitted to the UN by General Assembly resolution 46/238 (May 22, 1992) on the recommendation of the Security Council in resolution 753 (May 18, 1992); Slovenia by General Assembly resolution 46/236 (May 22, 1992) on the recommendation of the Security Council in resolution 754 (May 18, 1992); and Bosnia-Herzegovina by General Assembly resolution 46/237 (May 22, 1992) on the recommendation of the Security Council in resolution 755 (May 20, 1992).

71. On September 7, 1991, at the start of the Peace Conference, each of the six Yugoslav republics agreed to participate in the Arbitration Commission proceedings.

72. *The Guidelines for the Recognition of New States* were applied by the EC by itself, directly, as well as through the recommendations of the Badinter Commission. After January 15, the mandate to evaluate recognition claims appears to have reverted to the EC and its member States. Recognition extended after January 15, 1992 is therefore arguably not part of the Arbitration Commission's record.

73. *See* Hille, 6 EJIL 598.

74. Reactions of the Members of the Arbitration Commission of the International Conference on the Former Yugoslavia to the Statement Made by the Federal Republic of Yugoslavia Government on its Competence (May 26, 1993), 96 ILR 713–718 (1994).

75. *See, e.g.*, Sarah Lambert, Adrian Bridge, & Marcus Tanner, "Yugoslavia: Serbia says EC erased Yugoslavia from map; Serbs reject plan to recognize states," *The Independent* (London), December 18, 1991, p. 8 (citing Badinter Commission opinions as useful to the peace process); Tom Walker, *London Times*, January 11, 1992 (noting that even Germany at times emphasized the role of the 'Badinter Report'); Graham Brown, "EC Splits on Recognition of Croatia," Agence France Press, January 14, 1992 (noting that most states considered the Badinter Commission 'reports' a key source in evaluating recognition).

76. *See, e.g.*, Paul L. Montgomery, "Europe Plans Yugoslav Peace Talks," N.Y. Times, September 4, 1991 (detailing the composition and initial guidelines of the Arbitration Commission); BBC Summary of World Broadcasts Spec. Supp., EE/1243/c1/1, November 30, 1991, (reporting that the foreign minister of Yugoslavia, Vladislav Jovanovic, on November 28 protested to Lord Carrington and Robert Badinter over remarks Badinter made to the press about the work of the Commission); "Political Cooperation: Peace Conference on Yugoslavia Kicks Off," *European Report*, September 11, 1991, p. 2 (reporting the establishment of the Arbitration Committee).

77. *The Situation in Yugoslavia: Statement Issued by the Heads of State and Government Participating in the Meeting of the North Atlantic Council in Rome on 7th-8th November 1991*, NATO Press Communique S-1 (91) 88, November 8, 1991 (on

file with author).

78. "Slovenia, Croatia to Be Recognized after 16 December," Hamburg DPA in German 1117 GMT 13 Dec 91, *Foreign Broadcast Information Service* (FBIS) WEU-91–240.

79. Dieter Buhl, "The Reward of Speed," *Die Zeit* in German 20 Dec 91 p. 1 (FBIS-WEU-91–246). Buhl is the Op-Ed Page editor at *Die Zeit*. Letter to author, March 8, 1996.

80. *See, e.g.*, William Drozdiak, "Germany Vows Balkan Recognition; EC's Criteria for Ties not Binding, Genscher tells Foreign Ministers," Wash. Post, January 11, 1992, A14 (questioning Genscher's statement that the Badinter 'Report' is *not* a condition for recognition); "EC and Yugoslavia: Countdown to Recognition," *The Economist*, January 3, 1992, p. 57 (noting that the Badinter Commission opinions appeared important to all states but Germany). Even some German press sources criticized early recognition. *See, e.g.*, Dieter Schröder, "Germany's Lone Hand," *Süddeutsche Zeitung* in German 21 Dec 91 p 4 (FBIS-WEU-92–006) (commenting after a December 19 'recognition in principle' which made clear that formal recognition would be extended by Bonn to Croatia and Slovenia on December 23); Eberhard Wisdorff, "Dubious Triumph," *Düsseldorf Handelsblatt*, January 16, 1992, p. 2 (FBIS-WEU-92–012); Jochen Siemens, "The Uneasiness About the Germans," *Frankfurter Rundschau* in German, January 22, 1992, p. 3 (FBIS-WEU-92–015).

81. *See, e.g.*, "France to Recognize Croatia Conditionally," Reuters, January 15, 1992 (reporting French protest over German recognition prior to Badinter Commission opinion); K. Iordanidis, "Hasty Move on the Yugoslav Issue," *I Kathimerini* in Greek, December 22, 1991, p. 4 (FBIS-WEU-92–011) (reporting Greek government disapproval over German recognition decision); Werner Stanzl, "Genscher: U.S. Criticism of Recognition Unfounded," *Der Standard* (Vienna) in German, January 9, 1992, p. 4 (FBIS-WEU-92–006) (noting American government disapproval and German rebuttal). For a summary of adverse reaction to the German recognition act, see Marie-Hanine Calic, "Jugoslawienpolitik am Wendepunkt," B37/93 *Außen Politik und Zeitgeschichte* (1993) 11.

82. Hans W. Maull suggests that premature recognition may have in part contributed to the civil war in Bosnia. "Germany in the Yugoslavia Crisis: From Assertiveness to Impotence" (unpublished research paper on file with author). *See also* Alexander Mühlen, "Die deutsche Rolle bei der Anerkennung der jugoslawischen Sezessionsstaaten," 2 *Liberal* 9 (1992). The former American ambassador to Yugoslavia (and last to the SFRY) Warren Zimmermann sharply criticized recognition, though it is not clear whether he meant to censure Germany for deviating from the December 16 process or all states for recognizing sooner rather than later. Warren Zimmermann, "The Last Ambassador: A Memoir of the Collapse of Yugoslavia," 74(2) *Foreign Affairs* 13, 16–17 (1995). *See also* Heinz-Jürgen Axt, "Hat Genscher Jugoslawien entzweit? Mythen und Fakten zur Außenpolitik des vereinten Deutschlands," 48 *Europa Archiv* 351 (1993).

83. Weller, 52 Camb. L.J. at 6.

84. Yuen-Li Liang, "Notes on Legal Questions Concerning the United Nations," 45 AJIL 689 (1951) (quoting UNCIO (vol. III) Doc. 2, G/7(n)(1) May 4, 1945, 366–367).

85. Draft Resolution presented to the *Ad Hoc* Political Committee (UN Doc. A/AC.38/L.45, 21 Nov. 1950) (quoted in Yuen Li Liang, 45 AJIL at 689).

86. Candidates included the ICJ, the Sixth Committee (the Legal Committee of the UN), the International Law Commission, the UN Secretariat, the Ad Hoc Political Committee, and the General Assembly. 45 AJIL at 701. Other international organs had previously been nominated, at least by writers, as possible loci of recognition competence. The Permanent Mandates Commission of the League of Nations, it was suggested, had functions akin to recognition. Quincy Wright, "Proposed Termination of the Iraqi Mandate," 25 AJIL 436 (1931). Quincy Wright later noted that the UN Trusteeship Council determined which territories are capable of self-government—again, a recognition-like competence. Quincy Wright, "Recognition and Self-Determination," 1954 ASIL Proc. 23.

87. Yuen-Li Liang cites the General Assembly debate over recognition organs and the nature of recognition. 45 AJIL at 700 n. 48 (citing GA, 5th Sess., Official Recs., Gen. Com., 70th meeting (September 22, 1950) 10).

88. Danilo Türk, *Recognition of States: A Comment*, 4 EJIL 66 (1993) 70.

89. Joe Verhoeven, "La Reconnaissance Internationale: Déclin ou Renouveau?" 39 AFDI 7, 28 (1993). Verhoeven proposes that, in the Yugoslav crisis, political process failed, and, facing this failure, political authorities deferred to judicial mechanisms. These, too, however, in Verhoeven's view, did not entirely succeed: "Le droit y a perdu ce que la politique n'a pas gagné."

90. Warbrick, "Recognition of States," 41 ICLQ 473, 482 (1992).

91. Craven, 66 BYIL at 409–10.

92. *See* Thomas D. Grant, "Territorial Status, Recognition, and Statehood: Some Aspects of the Genocide Case (*Bosnia and Herzegovina* v. *Yugoslavia*)," 33 *Stanford Journal of International Law* (Stan. J. Int'l L.) 305 (1997).

93. John Dugard, *Recognition and the United Nations* (Cambridge: Grotius Publications Limited, 1987).

94. Nicoll & Salmon, 286–87.

95. Nicoll & Salmon, 207–11.

96. On how EU institutions make law, see Alan Dashwood, "Community Legislative Procedures in the Era of the Treaty on European Union," 19 *European Law Review* (Eur'n L. Rev.) 343 (1994).

97. Anne Peters, 89 AJIL 376, 378 (1995).

98. Strictly speaking, CFSP was initiated under the terms of the Maastricht Treaty only in November 1993. However, the principle on which it was built—European Political Cooperation (EPC)—was associated since the Single European Act of 1986 with a 'European foreign policy.' Geoffrey Edwards, "Common Foreign and Security Policy: Incrementalism in Action?" in *International Law Aspects of the European Union*, Martti Koskenniemi ed. (The Hague: Kluwer Law International, 1998), 3.

99. "Foreign Minister on Recognizing Slovenia, Croatia," Belgrade, *Tanjug* in English 0055 GMT, November 29, 1991 (FBIS-WEU-91–231). Mark Eyskens was foreign minister at the time.

100. "Weizsäcker Urges More Help for Eastern Europe," Hamburg DPA in German 0709 GMT January 9, 1992 (FBIS-WEU-006).

101. "Recognition by the EC Possible," *Süddeutsche Zeitung* in German November 30-December 1, 1991, p. 1 (FBIS-WEU-91–231) (remarks attributed to German government spokesman Dieter Vogel and Foreign Ministry spokesman Hans Schumacher).

102. "The EC Should Offer Croatia and Slovenia an Associate Status," *Welt am Sonntag* (Hamburg) in German, December 1, 1991, p. 9 (FBIS-WEU-91-231).
103. "Genscher Wants European Response to Commonwealth," Hamburg DPA in German 1158 GMT, January 2, 1992 (FBIS-WEU-92-001).
104. "Genscher Supports Reductions in Weapons Exports," Hamburg DPA in German 0000 GMT, January 1, 1992, citing *Hamburger Abendblatt* article (FBIS-WEU-001).
105. Jochen Siemens, "The Uneasiness About the Germans," *Frankfurter Rundschau* in German, January 22, 1992, p. 3 (FBIS-WEU-92-015).
106. "Tudjman Briefs Kohl on SFRY Situation," Hamburg DPA in German 1403 GMT, December 5, 1991 (FBIS-WEU-91-234).
107. "Slovenia, Croatia to Be Recognized after 16 December," Hamburg DPA in German 1117 GMT, December 13, 1991 (FBIS-WEU-91-240).
108. "Kohl Speaks of 'Great Victory' in Foreign Policy," Berlin ADN in German 1720 GMT, January 7, 1992 (FBIS-WEU-92-005) [emphasis supplied]. Attributing the words 'Great Victory' [*Große Sieg*] to Helmut Kohl might have been politically damaging to the Chancellor because these words had connotations of Nazi hubris. Allusions to the Nazi past constituted a recurring theme in debate over German diplomacy toward Yugoslavia in 1991–1992. That such a subtle cue as the word 'victory' could trigger the worst associations indicates the sensitivity of the matter.
109. Dieter Schröder, "Germany's Lone hand," *Süddeutsche Zeitung* in German, December 12, 1991, p. 4 (FBIS-WEU-92-006).
110. Nor were such assertions confined to the immediate period of crisis. German foreign ministry spokesperson Michael Gerdts would assert, a year and a half after Germany recognized the republics, "The decision to recognize Croatia and Slovenia was a joint decision." "Christopher Blames Germany for Bosnia's Woes," Agence France-Presse, June 17, 1993, 1993 WL 10735406.
111. "EC Recognition for Croatia, Slovenia Supported," Paris AFP in English 1932 GMT 5 Dec 91 (FBIS-WEU-91-325).
112. "EC Recognition Warned Against," Paris AFP in English 1031 GMT 6 Dec 91 (FBIS-WEU-91-235).
113. A wry observer might ask whether the French President weaved a double entendre here: perhaps his response meant that France respected *Germany's* right to self-determination, as regarded recognition diplomacy—rather than Croatia and Slovenia's right to self-determination, as regarded independence.
114. Paul Taylor, "Recognition of Croatia, Slovenia Conditional, Mitterrand Says," Paris, Reuters December 15, 1991, 17:26 (on file with author).
115. France Statements, The French Embassy and Information Service, Excerpts from an interview with Francois Mitterrand, President of the Republic, Broadcast on French Television, December 15, 1991 (on file with author).
116. "EC Meets: Belgium Recognizes Croatia, Slovenia," Paris AFP in English 1211 GMT 15 Jan 92 (FBIS-WEU-92-011).
117. Chris Moncrieff, "Government Recognizes Croatia, Slovenia," London Press Association in English 1320 GMT, January 15, 1992 (FBIS-WEU-92-012).
118. "Recognition of Croatia, Slovenia Announced," Stockholm Radio Sweden in English 1930 GMT, January 15, 1992 (FBIS-WEU-92-011).
119. "Government Cites Position on Slovenia, Croatia," *Tanjug* in English 1419 GMT, December 16, 1991, (FBIS-WEU-91-242).

120. "Communique Issued Recognizing Croatia, Slovenia," Lisbon RDP Commercial Radio Network in Portuguese 2200 GMT January 16, 1992 (FBIS-WEU-92-012).
121. "Foreign Minister Remarks on Croatian Recognition," Stockholm Sveriges Radio Network in Swedish 1700 GMT, December 12, 1991 (FBIS-WEU-91-240).
122. "Croatian Foreign Minister Seeks Recognition, Aid," Helsinki Suomen Yletsradio Network in Finnish 1600 GMT, December 13, 1991 (FBIS-WEU-91-241).
123. This document was signed on November 21, 1990 to declare the end of the Cold War.
124. "Vatican Officially Recognizes Slovenia, Croatia," Rome ANSA in English 0803 MT, January 14, 1992 (FBIS-WEU-92-009).
125. On the history of the relationship between the Catholic Church, the Croats, and Yugoslav politics, see Jill A. Irvine, *The Croat Question: Partisan Politics in the Formation of the Yugoslav Socialist State* (Boulder, CO: Westview Press, 1993), 236-241.
126. "Slovenia, Croatia Resolution Adopted Unanimously," Vienna ORF Teletext in German 1911 GMT, December 5, 1991 (FBIS-WEU-91-235).
127. Whether Austrian diplomats succeeded, however, in balancing domestic pressures and foreign policy concerns is open to question.
128. "Our Neutrality Would Not Be an Obstacle to a Common Defense," *Le Figaro* in French, December 4, 1991, p. 4 (FBIS-WEU-91-235).
129. "Mock Discusses Situation," Vienna ORF Television Network in German 2100 GMT, January 15, 1992 (FBIS-WEU-92-011).
130. "Kohl: Brussels Decision is Success for German Policy," *Süddeutsche Zeitung* in German, December 18, 1991, p. 1 (FBIS-WEU-91-243).
131. "Vranitzky on Recognizing SFRY, Soviet Entities," Ernest Hauer report on press conference by Chancellor Franc Vranitzky after the Cabinet meeting in Vienna, Vienna Österreich Eins Radio Network in German 1100 GMT, December 10, 1991 (FBIS-WEU-91-238).
132. Rupert Haberson, "Mock: Boycott Against Serbia to be Increased," *Wiener Kurier* in German, December 11, 1991, p. 5 (FBIS-WEU-91-239).
133. "Vienna's Lone Action: London, Washington Objections," *Die Presse* in German, December 12, 1991, p. 2 (FBIS-WEU-91-239).
134. "EC 'Poised' for Recognition," Paris AFP in English 1620 GMT, January 10, 1992 (FBIS-WEU-92-008).
135. "UK Warns of 'Difficulties,'" London Press Association in English 1938 GMT, January 10, 1992 (FBIS-WEU-92-008).
136. "Spain's Fernandez Comments," Belgrade *Tanjug* in English 2149 GMT, January 12, 1992 (FBIS-WEU-92-008).
137. Matthew C.R. Craven, "What's in a Name? The Former Yugoslav Republic of Macedonia and Issues of Statehood," 16 *Australian Yearbook of International Law* (Austral. YIL) 199, 204 (1995).
138. Craven, 16 Austral. YIL at 202-05.
139. The UN would admit Macedonia on April 8, 1993, and then only after a Security Council resolution (resol. 817 (1993)) recommending admission under the name "Former Yugoslav Republic of Macedonia." The United States recognized the so-called FYROM on February 9, 1994; Albania on April 9, 1993; China on October 12, 1993; and Russia on February 3, 1994. 16 Austral. YIL at 206 n. 58.

140. 16 Austral. YIL at 210*ff*.
141. Among the symbols to which Greece objected were the Star of Vergina, evidently associated with the Greek past; and waves, argued by Greece to evince Macedonian designs on Greek coastal territory. Anne Peters, "*Commission of the European Communities* v. *Hellenic Republic*," 89 AJIL 376, 377 (1995). Craven argues that forcing Macedonia to change its name and flag was unlawful. He notes in support that the *Declaration on Principles of International Law Concerning Friendly Relations and Cooperation among States in Accordance with the Charter of the UN*, GA resol. 2625 (XXV)(1970) provides that each state "has the right freely to choose and develop its political, social, economic and cultural system." 16 Austral. YIL at 234. I would propose, too, that the 1966 *International Covenant on Economic, Social, and Cultural Rights* may invalidate the Greek demands for changes in symbolism and nomenclature.
142. Presidency Statement, Europe, No. 5722 (N.S.), May 4, 1992. Quoted in Colin Warbrick & A.V. Lowe, "Recognition of States, Part 2," 42 ICLQ 433, 437 (1993).
143. House of Commons Hansard, vol. 215, cols. 120–23, November 30, 1992; quoted in Warbrick & Lowe, 42 ICLQ at 438.
144. *Commission of the European Communities* v. *Hellenic Republic* [1994] ECR I-3037; 100 ILR 222.
145. ECJ Opinion at 227.
146. ECJ Opinion at 229.
147. *See, e.g.*, the statement of the Czech Republic, pertaining to its view of the Yugoslav recognition crisis. The decision to recognize, according to Czech diplomats, "is the prerogative of a sovereign state." Thus, Germany's decision to recognize the secessionist Yugoslav republics was "something which solely concerned Germany, Croatia and Slovenia." Letter from Rudolf Hykl, Press Secretary of the Embassy of the Czech Republic, Washington, DC (March 2, 1994) (on file with author).
148. Gianni De Michelis, "Reaching Out to the East," 79 *Foreign Policy* 44, 50–51 (1990) (discussing quadripartite collaboration among Austria, Hungary, Italy, and Yugoslavia).
149. The Latin American states may exemplify a group tied by cultural affinity. Though not bound by a formal union or treaty-enshrined institutions, the states of Latin America have sometimes followed parallel diplomacy in certain matters. Consider for example the Tobar Doctrine, under which Latin American states withheld recognition from any government among them that came to power by unconstitutional means. The doctrine was stated in the General Treaty of Peace and Amity of 1907. Green Haywood Hackworth, *Digest of International Law*. vol. I (Washington, DC: United States Government Printing Office, 1940), 186; 2 AJIL Supp. 229 (1908).
150. Historic bonds might be strongest where negative. Groups of states sharing common animosities or anxieties perhaps tend to form the basis for collective diplomacy more often than groups sharing affinities. The common antagonism in Serbia and Greece toward the Macedonian Republic and Turkey comes to mind as an example of a negative impetus to collective action. The fear in Central European states of German revanchism suggests another such grouping.
151. "Croatian Foreign Minister Seeks Recognition, Aid," Helsinki Suomen Yleisradio Network in Finnish 1600 GMT, December 13, 1991 (FBIS-WEU-91-241).
152. "Vranitzky, Mock Comment on SFRY Recognition," Vienna Österreich Eins

Radio Network in German 1100 GMT, December 17, 1991 (reporting on press conference by Chancellor Franz Vranitzky and Foreign Minister Alois Mock) (FBIS-WEU-91-243).

153. Vranitzky-Mock press conference (FBIS-WEU-91-243).

154. "Recognition on 15 January," Vienna ORF Television Network in German 1830 GMT, December 17, 1991 (FBIS-WEU-91-243).

155. "Mock, Croatia's Separovic Discuss Recognition" (Interview with Croatian Foreign Minister Zvonimir Separovic and Austrian Foreign Minister Alois Mock by Robert Hochner; Separovic is in the studio in Zagreb, and Mock is in the parliament in Vienna live) Vienna ORF Television Network in German 2107 GMT, December 17, 1991 (FBIS-WEU-92-243).

156. "Genscher on SFRY Republics, USSR Weapons" (Interview by Hans-Jörg Krieger) Cologne Deutschlandfunk Network in German 1000 GMT, December 15, 1991 (FBIS-WEU-91-241).

157. Ibid. The criteria in this catalogue Genscher enumerated as follows: "the peoples' right of self-determination, human rights, minority rights, and the inviolability of borders."

158. Ibid.

159. *See* Dashwood, 19 ELR 343 (enumerating five principal routes to legislation and some twenty variations upon these). The complexity of the law making process has been noted as a flaw of European institutions.

160. On the history and structure of the EC and EU, see Directorate-General for Information, Communication, Culture, and Audiovisual Media, *The Institutions of the European Union* (Brussels: European Commission, May 1995).

161. "Kohl Urges Europe not to Miss Chance for Unity," Hamburg DPA in German 1305 GMT, November 27, 1991, (FBIS-WEU-91-229).

162. Elsewhere at approximately the same time, Kohl declared the willingness of Germany to compromise at the Maastricht Summit and urged all other Member States to assume a similar stance. "Kohl Willing to Compromise at EC Summit," Hamburg DPA in German 1516 GMT, November 29, 1991 (FBIS-WEU-91-231).

163. *See* "Official Sees Good Chances for Economic Union," *Düsseldorf Handelsblatt* in German, November 27, 1991, p. 1 (FBIS-WEU-91-229).

164. *See* Rolf H. Fricke, "Agreement Required: Potential Differences with France at Maastricht," Düsseldorf Handelsblatt in German, November 26, 1991, p. 2 (FBIS-WEU-91-229).

165. "Government to Recognize Croatia, Slovenia," Hamburg DPA in German 1230 GMT, November 27, 1991 (FBIS-WEU-91-229).

166. "Foreign Minister on Recognizing Slovenia, Croatia," Belgrade, *Tanjug* in English 0055 GMT, November 29, 1991 (FBIS-WEU-91-231). Eyskens made the statement in reaction to a plan announced by German Chancellor Helmut Kohl and Italian Prime Minister Giulio Andreotti in Bonn on November 29 to grant diplomatic recognition before Christmas to the Yugoslav successor states. "We are close to the position of Germany and Italy but we are also anxious about another goal, the maintenance of unity among the Twelve," said Eyskens.

167. "Government States Position on Yugoslav Crisis," *Athens News* in English, December 4, 1991, p. 3 (FBIS-WEU-91-234). Recognition was perceived in Athens to implicate the sensitive Macedonian question. To abstain on the vote represented a substantial Greek concession to EC comity.

168. "Kohl Speech," Hamburg ARD Television Network in German 0800 FMT, December 13, 1991.
169. Eberhard Wisdorff, "Maastricht Summit Decision and New Foreign Policy Will Become Expensive," *Düsseldorf Handelsblatt* in German, January 15, 1992, p. 2 (FBIS-WEU-92–011).
170. "EC Proponents on the Offensive," *Berlingske Tidende* (Copenhagen) in Danish, December 17, 1992, p. 10 (FBIS-WEU–92–011).

# CONCLUSION

The preceding chapters have reviewed an old debate and traced the outlines of a new one. The old debate—the once "Great Debate"—concerned the legal nature of recognition. One theory as to that nature, the constitutive, held that recognition created states. The other theory, the declaratory, took recognition only to mark—at most, to ratify—facts that had already created a state. The constitutive doctrine raised logical problems and was associated with a "positivist" school of thought that seemed to accept unilateral state competence over recognition and exclude any significant role for international society in the matter. Those features, intellectually and professionally unattractive for the international lawyer, arguably account for why writers began to call the declaratory doctrine the better view of recognition. At the same time, declaratory doctrine exerted a positive attraction of its own. Declaratory doctrine accommodated more readily than constitutivism the contemporary trend toward attributing competence to international society over matters previously assumed to be strictly municipal.

Statehood has come to be defined as more than effectiveness. New criteria of statehood such as compliance with *jus cogens* norms, guarantee of minority rights, and democracy, reflect new claims to international competence over internal governance. If recognition is permissible when some of these new criteria are missing, then the aspiration of international law to regulate matters traditionally reserved to sovereign states is frustrated. Declaratory doctrine held that existing states extended recognition when all criteria of statehood in a community aspiring to recognition were in place. Declaratory doctrine gave the criteria of statehood, whatever they may be, an important position in the process of recognition and thus, if the new criteria are accepted, enlisted recognition practice as a support for the new criteria. The declaratory theory of recognition allowed the international legal system to regulate internal order through the definition of statehood.

Insofar as the declaratory preference stemmed from an aspiration to strengthen claims of international law to regulate certain aspects of internal organization, it is a preference conditioned on old assumptions about the process of recognition. Recognition was traditionally assumed to be a preserve of the individual state, a quintessentially "sovereign" matter. Whether or not to recognize was decided unilaterally and formed a discretion that "[no] country on earth can question."[1] If decisions concerning recognition are made solely by organs at the municipal level and involve no international consultation, perhaps the only way for international law to harness recognition as a tool for regulating internal order in new states would be to establish criteria for statehood comporting with the international legal vision of how those states should be organized. Then, even if the recognizing state continued to admit no international aspect in the *process* of recognition, the *substantive* rules governing recognition would reflect international values. Recognition would in turn project international values into new states. An existing, recognizing state would have to decline recognition where the new criteria of statehood did not obtain, and, consequently, the international aspiration to regulate certain aspects of domestic order, notwithstanding the lack of an internationalized process of recognition, would be felt in entities aspiring to statehood. The new entities would have to conform with the new criteria in order to receive recognition. The threat of the withholding of recognition would induce constitutional regimes to include compliance with *jus cogens* norms, guarantee of minority rights, and democracy.

However, it may well be the case that the process of recognition has not remained an exclusively municipal one. State practice concerning recognition of new states in the space of the former Socialist Federal Republic of Yugoslavia evidences a shift of competence to international levels. Even in states such as Germany and Austria, where authoritative decision-makers for diverse reasons aimed to conduct recognition diplomacy independently, an expectation was acknowledged that recognition occur collectively. The extent to which recognition of Croatia, Slovenia, Bosnia, and Macedonia was international and collective may have been conditioned by factors not obviously related to recognition or the Yugoslav crisis. The Treaty on European Union, imminent at the time of the Yugoslav recognition crisis, was chief among these. Expressions of the expectation that recognition occur through a collective process have nonetheless been persistent in the 1990s.

A collective recognition process changes the relationship between doctrines of recognition and the aspiration to regulate internal order through international law. Declaratory doctrine was arguably more consistent with the aspiration, so long as recognition was a unilateral process little coordinated across borders. If recognition does involve coordination among states—if the process of recognition has become in some measure *collec-*

*tive*—then international society has a direct role every time a decision is required about recognition. If the individual state had exclusive competence over the mechanics of recognition, then international society could involve itself in recognition only by prescribing substantive guidelines for recognition—by telling states what criteria made an entity a state. Formulating recognition case-by-case at the international level was not an option. A substantive international law of recognition substituted for international recognition process. International society now however has some purchase on the mechanism of recognition. Having acquired a claim to participate every time recognition is in issue, international society can influence one recognition incident other than by prescribing substantive rules over all recognition incidents.

A collective recognition process changes how substantive rules of recognition affect international society. To writers who sought a greater role for international society, substantive rules were useful when the object was *to contain* discretion over the mechanics of recognition. Now, arguably, the object may well be *to expand* discretion. Whilst international society had little or no competence over particular recognition incidents, international society increased its role relative to states by making substantive rules stricter. With at least some competence acquired, however, international society increases its role by liberalizing the substantive rules. Constitutivism has generally been understood to accent the discretionary aspect of recognition, conditioning recognition more on decisions in the recognizing authority than on changes in the community receiving recognition. Though not all writers who characterized themselves as constitutivists in the old debate favored discretion,[2] the association seems to have stuck. Declaratory doctrine may have been "the better view" for an international society aspiring to regulate certain aspects of internal order at a time when the state monopolized recognition process, but constitutivism begins to look more attractive once international society has successfully asserted a claim to participate in that process. Insofar as the terms of the old debate continue to appear in contemporary writing, a new receptiveness is indeed discernible toward the constitutive view of recognition.

Once international society holds a share of the competence over recognizing new states, international society increases its own power by increasing the discretionary aspect of recognition. This may explain the observation, at first paradoxical, that recognition in recent practice has demonstrated a continued deficit in substantive rules and a strengthening in its collective aspect. Recent practice witnesses groups of states coordinating recognition policy but extending recognition to entities such as Bosnia and Monaco which, albeit in widely different ways, have been deficient in view of the standard criteria for statehood. Recognition appears to have become more collective but also more discretionary. If so, then critical issues today are the process of recognition and the content of substantive norms. Correspondingly, the old doctrinal debate becomes less and less illuminating, if ever it illuminated recognition much at all. The fading of the debate is an intellectual development more significant than any recent shift from one doctrine to the other.

Changes in how we think about recognition may mirror trends of thought in other parts of the law and even academic culture at large. A more than somewhat amorphous concept,[3] "postmodernism" in at least one of its dimensions[4] seems to involve a reaction against a preoccupation with "the ways in which legal language represents, depicts, and captures the world."[5] Erosion of debate over how to describe recognition may well be a "postmodernist" development. The "Great Debate" was very much, after all, a debate over how to describe recognition. How recognition works today in practice has become a more important focus than its legal nature. And how recognition works may itself interest self-described postmodernists.[6] Making decisions about recognition was once assumed to be a competence of the individual state. The process of recognition was unilateral, discretionary, and, moreover, in most states, believed to be vested constitutionally in certain executive officers. If, however, an international element is admitted into the process of recognition, former certainties as to the locus of authority to recognize a new state are cast in doubt. "Postmodernists" have identified as a development central to their school of thought the erosion of "monopolies of interpretation" and the replacement of such monopolies by multiple "interpretive communities."[7] At a time when doctrinal debate was more prevalent in writing on the subject, municipal processes of authority organized rather tightly around national organs, particularly executive organs, were believed to govern recognition with little challenge from alternative sources of authority. Writers little doubted where recognition decisions took place, so there was little to discuss about process. The strengthening of claims by groups of states to control recognition changes this. A shift in state practice toward collective recognition means that more than one "interpretive community" may have a say in recognition. Not just the individual state acting in its "sovereign" discretion, but also groups of states pursuing coordinated diplomacy arguably serve as loci of decision-making. The fading of doctrinal debate over the legal meaning of recognition; growth of academic interest in the process or mechanism by which recognition is actually granted; and, lastly, evidence that international society now challenges the individual state as a source of interpretation, thus pressing the process of recognition toward polycentricity, may well fit a "postmodern" paradigm.[8]

Contemporary residues of the "Great Debate" as well may be of interest from the standpoint of jurisprudence. I have noted in the preceding chapters that declaratory doctrine was recently widely assumed to be the "better view" as to the nature of recognition. However, I have argued that some of the cases often noted as pointing toward a declaratory conception of recognition are not unequivocal in this regard; and the declaratory view was not unanimously accepted. The debate, while dimming, has shifted perceptibly toward the constitutive theory. This, too, may signal a growing polycentricity in decision process. Declaratory doctrine, more readily than constitutivism, implied an automaticity in recognition: once an entity attained all the marks of statehood, recognition was appropriate, possibly required. If one put aside the problem of identifying the criteria of statehood and the associated problem of how to determine in a given incident whether those criteria had been attained, the declaratory theory eroded state discretion. Once a state, an entity was to be recognized. Of course, variance in decision results were inevitable under a declaratory conception, for in practice there was never perfect accord as to the criteria for statehood, and states have seldom coordinated fact-finding in international incidents. In theory, though, a declaratory approach should have yielded similar results in similar cases. Constitutivism, by contrast, would appear to have contained an in-built tendency toward polycentric decision-making. Recognition was not a response to statehood already achieved, compelled by facts in international society exerting themselves upon all existing states; it was instead an act of state-building in which each existing state had discretion to indulge. Accordingly, recognition as seen through the constitutive lens would continue to result from many decisions reached in many different centers of authority. It is not coincidental that most writers who adopted a constitutive viewpoint in the heyday of the "Great Debate" also took the view that recognition was decided by each state at its independent discretion and that recognition, insofar as it formed a coherent institution, was one more of politics and statecraft than of law. Even if the process of recognition has shifted from municipal to interstate arenas, a theory of recognition that emphasizes its political nature leaves greater room for variable decision-making results than one that contains recognition with substantive rules. That the European Union followed some recommendations of the Badinter Commission but not others illustrates this flexibility.

However much the "Great Debate" was about doctrine, it may well have contained an undercurrent concerning where to locate competence. Though the correspondence was not exact, constitutivists tended to emphasize state discretion; declaratists at least the possibilities for internationalization. Insofar as the location of authoritative decision-making concerned earlier writers, then contemporary debate may be a continuation of the "Great Debate"—only without the encumbrance of the doctrinal categories that were at the center of the "Great Debate." As noted, the doctrinal categories do continue to attract some interest, but they no longer prevail in informed discourse on the subject. A much more important issue today is the locus of authority to recognize—Is recognition entirely a municipal discretion? Or is international society an authority in the matter as well? This issue was arguably one that underlay the old doctrinal debate from the start, with the collective view manifested more among declaratists and the unilateral view among constitutivists. Today, if one can speak of a collectivist/unilateralist debate, that debate has had its links to the old debate essentially severed. Little if any correspondence remains between declaratory doctrine and collective recognition or between constitutivism and the unilateral approach.[9] The intellectual history of recognition arguably displays continuity in one dimension, closure in another.

There may even be emerging debate as to whether there exists a coherent international *legal* institution of recognition. The continuing vitality of recognition in the *political* dimension is in little doubt: witness the European crisis over recognition of the Yugoslav secessionists. But, considering how municipal legislation at least in certain dimensions purposefully erodes the legal consequences of nonrecognition,[10] writers must ask what legal content recognition retains.

Why, then, has discussion about recognition evolved? As I alluded earlier, contemporary suspicion of doctrine, preference for polycentric decision process, and focus generally on mechanisms of decision rather than theories about the subject of decision are broad intellectual currents consistent with the change in how recognition is discussed. On balance, however, general trends in academic thought do not satisfactorily explain the evolution in how we think about recognition. States, through their practice, are legislators of international law. They may make law suddenly, as happened in certain areas involving radical advances in technology (space law, telecommunications), or they may reshape law over time. A shift in practice concerning recognition of states appears to have started in the early 1990s. An expectation began to be expressed that decisions about recognition take place among states, rather than at the municipal level alone. Municipal processes of authority have never been entirely insulated from events outside the state territory, but a threshold has nevertheless been crossed when authoritative decision-makers in a state overtly acknowledge at the international level competences that those decision-makers hitherto claimed exclusively for themselves.

Debate over the recognition of states has evolved from one of doctrine to one of mechanics; from "what is the legal nature of recognition" to "what are the processes through which recognition is conferred." The new debate implicates one of the key points of tension facing international law today: the competence of states versus the competence of international institutions. Is recognition a decision process over which competences have drifted to the international level? Or is it one that remains essentially municipal? International society increasingly puts claims to matters once held to fall exclusively under national jurisdiction. Some of these claims have hardly crystallized into binding norms. The catalogue of "soft law" assertions of international competence over matters traditionally accepted as "sovereign" is lengthy.[11] However, some such matters, in some situations, have indeed lost their once exclusively internal character.[12] Evolution from a debate over the nature of recognition to a debate over the decision-making process and its locus parallels change in what states do and in which questions most concern international law.

## NOTES

1. Warren Austin, quoted in Philip Marshall Brown, "The Recognition of Israel," 42 *American Journal of International Law* (AJIL) 620, 621 (1948).

2. Lauterpacht notably adopted the constitutive view but called for recognition to be governed by law rather than discretion.

3. Some have called it "notoriously ambiguous." *See* Costas Douzinas, Ronnie Warrington, & Shaun McVeigh, *Postmodern Jurisprudence: The Law of Text in the Texts of Law* (London: Routledge, 1991), 14.

4. On the multiplicity of forms "postmodernism" has taken, see Jennifer Wicke, "Postmodern Identity and the Legal Subject," 62 *University of Colorado Law Review* (U. Col. L. Rev.) 455, 456 (1991).

5. Dennis Patterson, *Law and Truth* (Oxford: Oxford University Press, 1996), 169.

6. Postmodernist legal writers include Balkan, Douzinas, Warrington, McVeigh, and Schlag. *See* J.M. Balkin, "Understanding Legal Understanding: The Legal Subject and the Problem of Legal Coherence," 103 *Yale Law Journal* (Yale. L.J.) 105 (1993); Douzinas, Warrington, & McVeigh, *Postmodern Jurisprudence*; Pierre Schlag, "Normativity and the Politics of Form: L.A. Law's Empire," 139 *University of Pennsylvania Law Review* (U. Penn. L. Rev.) 801 (1991).

7. B. de Sousa Santos, "The Postmodern Transition: Law and Politics," in *The Fate of Law*. Austin Sarat & Thomas R. Kearns eds. (Ann Arbor; University of Michigan Press, 1991), 79, 108. *See also* Jacques Chevallier, "Vers un droit postmoderne? Les transformations de la régulation juridique," 1998(3) *Revue du Droit Public et de la Science Politique en France et à l'Étranger* 659, 672–75 (contrasting monist conception characteristic of modern law with pluralist conception characteristic of post-modernism).

8. Trends in thought about recognition may also sound in *pragmatism*. Richard Rorty describes pragmatism as a viewpoint rejecting the proposition that

> "There is something out there in addition to the world called 'the truth about the world' " (what James sarcastically called "this tertium quid intermediate between the facts *per se*, on the one hand, and all knowledge of them, actual or potential, on the other").

Richard Rorty, *Consequences of Pragmatism: Essays, 1972–1980* (Minneapolis: University of Minnesota Press, xxvi). Pragmatism in turn has been linked to postmodernism. *See* M.D.A. Freeman, *Lloyd's Introduction to Jurisprudence*. 6th ed. (London: Sweet & Maxwell Ltd., 1994), 1152.

9. The severance of doctrines was prefigured by Lauterpacht and Chen. It is instructive that those writers both advocated lodging competence over recognition in international society, yet took opposite sides in the constitutivist-declaratist debate. *See* Hersch Lauterpacht, *Recognition in International Law* (Cambridge: The University Press, 1948), 38; Ti-Chiang Chen, *The International Law of Recognition, with special reference to Practice in Great Britain and the United States* (London: Stevens & Sons Limited, 1951), 14.

10. Recall Foreign Corporations Act 1991 (UK); Foreign Corporations (Application of Laws) Act 1989 (Australia); Taiwan Relations Act of 1979, 22 U.S.C. §§3301 *et seq*. These are discussed in Chapter 4, Section 3, "The Public/Private Distinction in Municipal Legislation."

11. Consider the Rio Convention, the International Covenant of Civil and Political rights, the International Covenant of Economic, Social, and Cultural Rights, the Convention on the Rights of the Child. On environmental law, see Pierre-Marie Dupuy, "Soft Law and the International Law of the Environment," 12 *Michigan Journal of International Law* 420, 422–35 (1991).

12. International intervention in northern Iraq to protect a minority Kurdish population, in the traditional view, would have been inappropriate, as the state was held to have unlimited discretion to suppress rebellion within its borders. Intervention in Haiti, to restore a democratically elected government, would have been viewed as dubious under an international legal regime suspicious of second-guessing constitutive changes in municipal systems, however shocking to the conscience those changes might have been. The International Monetary Fund and its chief contributors, conditioning emergency programs for Mexico and several Pacific Rim states on implementation of free market reforms, have also taken advantage of contemporary tolerance for international regulation of municipal order.

# SELECTED BIBLIOGRAPHY


Agarwal, Hari Om. *Kashmır Problem: Its Legal Aspects.* Allahabad: Kitab Mahal, 1979.

Akehurst, Michael. *A Modern Introduction to International Law.* 6th ed. London: Routledge, 1987.

Alexandrowicz, C.H. "The Theory of Recognition *In Fieri*," 34 BYIL 176 (1958).

Amar, Akhil Reed. "Some New World Lessons for the Old World," 58 U. Chi. L. R. 483 (1991).

American Law Institute, *The Restatement (Third) of the Foreign Relations Law of the United States.* vol. I. St. Paul: American Law Institute Publishers, 1986.

Anzilotti, Dionisio. *Cours de droit international.* Gilbert Gidel trans., 3rd ed. Paris: Recueil Sirey, 1929. Orig. *Corso di diritto internazionale.* 3rd ed. Rome: Athenaeum, 1928.

Attix, Cheri. "Between the Devil and the Deep Blue Sea: Are Taiwan's Trading Partners Implying Recognition of Taiwanese Statehood?" 25 *California Western International Law Journal* 357 (1995).

Axt, Heinz-Jürgen. "Hat Genscher Jugoslawien entzweit? Mythen und Fakten zur Außenpolitik des vereinten Deutschlands," 48 *Europa Archiv* 351 (1993).

Badinter, Robert. "L'Europe du Droit," 3 EJIL 15 (1993).

Blum, Yehuda Z. "Reflections on the Changing Concept of Self-Determination," 10 Israel L.R. 509 (1975).

Borchard, Edwin M. "The Unrecognized Government in American Courts," 26 AJIL 261 (1932).

Brierly, James L. *The Law of Nations: An Introduction to the International Law of Peace.* Sir Humphrey Waldock ed., 6th ed. Oxford: Clarendon Press, 1963.

Brierly, James L. *The Outlook for International Law.* Oxford: Oxford University Press, 1944.

Briggs, Herbert W. "Recognition of States, Some Reflections on Doctrine and Practice," 43 AJIL 113 (1949).

Brown, Philip Marshall. "The Recognition of Israel," 42 AJIL 620 (1948).

Brown, Philip Marshall. "The Recognition of New States and Governments," 30 AJIL 689 (1936).

Brownlie, Ian. "Recognition in Theory and Practice" in *The Structure and Process of International Law: Essays in Legal Philosophy, Doctrine, and Theory*. R.S.J. MacDonald & Douglas M. Johnston eds. The Hague: Nijhoff, 1983.

Brownlie, Ian. *International Law and the Use of Force by States*. Oxford: Clarendon Press, 1963.

Brownlie, Ian. *Principles of Public International Law*. 3rd ed. Oxford: Clarendon Press, 1979.

Burghardt, Andrew. "Marxism and Self-Determination: The Case of Burgenland, 1919" in *Nationalism, Self-Determination and Political Geography*. R.J. Johnston, David B. Knight & Eleonore Kofman eds. London: Croom Helm, 1988.

Burley, Anne-Marie. "Law Among Liberal States: Liberal Internationalism and the Act of State Doctrine," 92 Colum. L. Rev. 1907 (1992).

Calic, Marie-Hanine. "Jugoslawienpolitik am Wendepunkt," B37/93 *Außen Politik und Zeitgeschichte* (1993).

Casey, James A "Sovereignty by Sufferance: The Illusion of Indian Tribal Sovereignty," 79 Corn. L. Rev. 404 (1994).

Cass, Deborah Z. "Rethinking Self-Determination: A Critical Analysis of Current International Law Theories," 18 Syracuse J. Int'l L. & Com. 21 (1992).

Cavaré, Louis. "La Reconnaissance de l'État et le Mandchoukouo," XLII RGDIP 5 (1935).

Charlton, Michael. *The Last Colony in Africa: Diplomacy and the Independence of Rhodesia*. Oxford: Basil Blackwell, 1990.

Chen, Ti-Chiang. *The International Law of Recognition, with special reference to Practice in Great Britain and the United States*. London: Stevens & Sons Limited, 1951).

Cheyne, Ilona. "The Foreign Corporations Act," 40 ICLQ 983 (1991).

Chiang, Huang-Chih. *The International Legal Status of Taiwan*. Thesis Presented for the Degree of Doctor of Philosophy to the Faculty of Laws in the University of London. Queen Mary and Westfield College: 1996.

Clark, Roger S. "The 'decolonisation' of East Timor and the United Nations norms on self-determination and aggression," chapter 4 in *International Law and the Question of East Timor*. London & Leiden: Catholic Institute for International Relations & International Platform of Jurists for East Timor, 1995.

Cockburn, Patrick. "Dateline USSR: Ethnic Tremors," 74 For. Pol'y 168 (1989).

Connick, Louis. "The Effect of Soviet Decrees in American Courts," 34 Yale L.J. 499 (1925).

Corten, Olivier. "La résolution 940 du Conseil de sécurité autorisant une intervention militaire en Haïti: l'émergence d'un principe de légitimité démocratique en droit international?" 6 EJIL 116 (1995).

Corwin, Edward S. "The Constitution as Instrument and as Symbol," 30 *American Political Science Review* 1071 (1936).

Corwin, Edward S. "The Worship of the Constitution," 4 Const. Rev. 3 (1920).

Corwin, Edward S. *The President: Office and Powers 1787–1957. History and Analysis of Practice and Opinion*. 4th rev. ed. New York: New York University Press, 1957.

Craven, Matthew C.R. "The European Community Arbitration Commission on Yugoslavia," 66 BYIL 333 (1995).
Crawford, James R. "The Criteria for Statehood in International Law," 48 BYIL 93 (1976–77).
Crawford, James R. *The Creation of States in International Law*. Oxford: Clarendon Press, 1979.
Crowley, James B. *Japan's Quest for Autonomy: National Security and Foreign Policy, 1930–1938*. Princeton: Princeton University Press, 1966.
Currie, David P. "The Constitution in the Supreme Court: Civil War and Reconstruction, 1865–1873," 51 U. Chi. L. Rev. 131 (1984).
Delbrück, Jost; and Wolfrum, Rüdiger. *Völkerrecht*. Berlin: Walter de Gruyter, 1989.
DeMarchi, Virginia K. "United States-Taiwan Relations: *New York Chinese TV Programs, Inc.* v. *U.E. Enterprises, Inc.*, No. 91–7694, slip op. (2d Cir. January 24, 1992)," 33 HILJ 631 (1992).
De Michelis, Gianni. "Reaching Out to the East," 79 For. Pol'y 44 (1990).
Devine, Dermott J. "Requirements of Statehood Re-examined," 34 Mod. L. Rev. 410.
Devine, Dermott J. "The Status of Rhodesia in International Law," 1974 *Acta Juridica* (Capetown) 109.
Dickinson, Edwin D. "The Unrecognized Government or State in English and American Law," 22 Mich. L.R. 29 (1923–24).
Dienstbier, Jirí. "Central Europe's Security," 83 For. Pol'y 119 (1992).
Doswald-Beck, Louise. "The Legal Validity of Military Intervention by Invitation of the Government," 56 BYIL 189 (1985).
Dragnich, Alex N. *The First Yugoslavia: Search for a Viable Political System*. Stanford: Hoover Institution Press, 1983.
Dragnich, Alex N. "The Rise and Fall of Yugoslavia: The Omen of the Upsurge of Serbian Nationalism," 23 *East European Quarterly* 183, 187, 189 (1989).
Drysdale, Alasdair. "National Integration Problems in the Arab World: The Case of Syria," in *Nationalism, Self-Determination and Political Geography*. R.J. Johnston, David B. Knight & Eleonore Kofman eds. London: Croom Helm, 1988.
Dugard, John. *Human Rights and the South African Legal Order*. Princeton: Princeton University Press, 1978.
Dugard, John. "*Namibia (South West Africa)*: The Court's Opinion, South Africa's Response, and Prospects for the Future," 11 Colum. J. Transnat'l L. 14 (1972).
Dugard, John. *Recognition and the United Nations*. Cambridge: Grotius Publications Limited, 1987.
Dugard, John. "South Africa's 'Independent' Homelands: An Exercise in Denationalization," 10 J. Int'l L. Pol'y 11 (1980).
Duursma, Jorri C. *Fragmentation and the International Relations of Micro-States: Self-Determination and Statehood*. Cambridge: Cambridge University Press, 1996.
Edwards, Geoffrey. "Common Foreign and Security Policy: Incrementalism in Action?" in *International Law Aspects of the European Union*, Martti Koskenniemi ed. The Hague: Kluwer Law International, 1998.
Emerson, Rupert. "Self-Determination," 65 AJIL 459 (1971).
Emiliou, Nicholas. "Cypriot import certificates: some hot potatoes," 20 ELR 202 (1995).

Engle, Karen. "Views from the Margins: A Response to David Kennedy," 1994 Utah L. Rev. 105.

Farer, Tom J. "The United Nations and Human Rights: More Than a Whimper Less than a Roar," 9 Hum. R. Q'ly 550 (1987).

Fawcett, J.E.S. "Security Council Resolutions on Rhodesia," 41 BYIL 103 (1965–66).

Fawcett, J.E.S. *The Law of Nations*. London: The Penguin Press, 1968.

Field, Michael E. "Liberia v. Bickford. The Continuing Problem of Recognition of Governments and Civil Litigation in the United States," 18 *Maryland Journal of International Law and Trade* 113 (1994).

Ford, Christopher Ashley. Defensor Fidei: *Explaining South African Foreign Policy Behavior: The Case of Ian Smith's Rhodesia*. Unpublished Harvard undergraduate Prize Thesis. Harvard University Library, HU89.184.756.

Förster, Stig; Mommsen, Wolfgang J.; and Robinson, Ronald eds. *Bismarck, Europe and Africa: The Berlin African Conference 1884–1885 and the Onset of Partition*. Oxford: Oxford University Press, 1988.

Fountain, Edwin L. "Out from the Precarious Orbit of Politics: Reconsidering Recognition and the Standing of Foreign Governments to Sue in U.S. Courts," 29 Virg. J. Int'l L. 473 (1989).

Franck, Thomas M.; and Sughrue, Dennis M. "Symposium: The International Role of Equity-as-Fairness," 81 Georgetown L.J. 563 (1993).

Friedmann, Wolfgang. Legal Theory. 5th ed. London: Stevens & Sons, 1944. Garris, Christian J. "Bosnia and the Limitations of International Law," 34 *Santa Clara Law Review* 1039 (1994).

Gasser, Hans-Peter. "Internationalized Non-international Armed Conflicts: Case Studies of Afghanistan, Kampuchea, and Lebanon," 33 Am. U. L. Rev. 145 (1983).

Gowlland-Debbas, Vera. *Collective Responses to Illegal Acts in International Law: United Nations Action in the Question of Southern Rhodesia*. Dordrecht: Martinus Nijhoff Publishers, 1990.

Grant, Thomas D. "Defining Statehood: The Montevideo Convention and its Discontents," 37 *Columbia Journal of Transnational Law* 403 (1999).

Grant, Thomas D. "A Panel of Experts for Chechnya: Purposes and Prospects in Light of International Law," article forthcoming in *Finnish Yearbook of International Law* (1999).

Grant, Thomas D. "Territorial Status, Recognition, and Statehood: Some Aspects of the Genocide Case (*Bosnia and Herzegovina* v. *Yugoslavia*)," 33 Stan. J. Int'l L. 305 (1997).

Grant, Thomas D. "The New Tinder Box: The Kosovo Crisis," *Seattle Times*, March 22, 1998, p B5.

Greenwood, Christopher J. "Gibt es ein Recht auf humanitäre Intervention?" 4 Eur. Arch. 93 (1993).

Greenwood, Christopher; and Lowe, A. Vaughan. "Unrecognised States and the European Court," 54 Camb. L. J. 4 (1995).

Guggenheim, Paul. "La Validité et la Nullité des Actes Juridiques Internationaux," 74 Hag. Rec. 191 (1949).

Hackworth, Green Haywood. *Digest of International Law*. vol. I. Washington, DC: United States Government Printing Office, 1940.

Hall, William E. *A Treatise on International Law*. A. Pearce Higgins ed., 8th ed. Oxford: Clarendon Press, 1924. Orig. 1890.

Hanauer, Laurence S. "The Irrelevance of Self-Determination Law to Ethno-national Conflict: A New Look at the Western Sahara Case," 9 Emory Int'l L. Rev. 133 (1995).

Haneman, Andrea J. "Independence and Group Rights in the Baltics: A Double Minority Problem," 35 Virg. J. Int'l L. 485 (1995).

Harris, D.J. *Cases and Materials in International Law*. 4th ed. London: Sweet & Maxwell, 1991.

Hart, H.L.A. *The Concept of Law*. Oxford: Clarendon Press, 1961.

Harty, Mark J. "United States-Taiwan Relations. Taiwan Relations Act," 20 HILJ 731 (1979).

Heraclides, Alexis. "Katanga," in *The Self-Determination of Minorities in International Politics*. London: Frank Cass, 1991.

Heraclides, Alexis. "Secessionist Minorities and External Involvement," 44 Int'l Org. 341 (1990).

Higgins, Rosalyn. "Derogations Under Human Rights Treaties," 48 BYIL 281 (1976–77).

Higgins, Rosalyn. *Problems and Process: International Law and How We Use It*. Oxford: Clarendon Press, 1994.

Hille, Saskia. "Mutual Recognition of Croatia and Serbia (+Montenegro)," 6 EJIL 598 (1995).

Hollis, Duncan B. "Accountability in Chechnya–Addressing Internal Matters with Legal and Political International Norms," 36 Bos. Col. L. Rev. 793 (1995).

Hyde, C.C. "Acquisition of Sovereignty Over Polar Areas," 19 Iowa L. Rev. 286 (1934).

Ijalaye, David A. "Was 'Biafra' at any Time a State in International Law?" 65 AJIL 551 (1971).

Ipsen, Knut. *Völkerrecht*. Munich: C.H. Beck'sche Verlagsbuchhandlung, 1990.

James, Alan. "System or Society?" 19 Rev. Int'l Stud. 269 (1993).

James, Alan. *Sovereign Statehood: The Basis of International Society*. London: Allen & Unwin, 1986.

Jenks, C. Wilfred. *Law in the World Community*. London: Longman, Green and Co. Ltd., 1967.

Jennings, Sir Robert. *The Acquisition of Territory in International Law*. Manchester: Manchester University Press, 1963.

Jessup, Philip C. *A Modern Law of Nations: An Introduction*. New York: MacMillan, 1948.

Jessup, Philip C. *The Birth of Nations*. New York: Columbia University Press, 1974.

Jones, J. Mervyn. "The Retroactive Effect of the Recognition of States and Governments," 16 BYIL 42 (1935).

Kelsen, Hans. "Recognition in International Law, Theoretical Observations," 35 AJIL 605 (1941).

Kelsen, Hans. "Théorie Générale du Droit International Public: Problèmes Choisis; Chapter III: La Détermination par le droit international du Domaine de Validité des différents Ordres Juridiques Étatiques," XLII(iv) Hag. Rec. 268 (1932).

Kelsen, Hans. *Principles of International Law*. Robert W. Tucker ed., 2nd ed. New York: Holt, Rinehart and Winston, Inc., 1966.

Kirgis, Frederic L. Jr. "Admission of 'Palestine' as a Member of a Specialized Agency and Withholding the Payment of Assessments in Response," 84 AJIL 218 (1990).

Kocs, Stephen A. "Explaining the Strategic Behavior of States: International Law as System Structure," 38 Int'l Stud. Q'ly 535 (1994).

Koh, Harold Hongju. *The National Security Constitution: Sharing Power after the Iran-Contra Affair*. New Haven, Yale University Press, 1990.

Kunz, Josef L. "Critical Remarks on Lauterpacht's 'Recognition in International Law,'" 44 AJIL at 714 (1950).

Larnaude, F. "Les Gouvernements de fait," 28 RGDIP 498 (1921).

Lauterpacht, Hersch. *An International Bill of the Rights of Man*. New York: Columbia University Press, 1945.

Lauterpacht, Hersch. "International Law and the Law of the State in International Law," in *Collected Papers of Hersch Lauterpacht*. vol. I-General Works. Elihu Lauterpacht ed. Cambridge: Cambridge University Press, 1970.

Lauterpacht, Hersch. "The Grotian Tradition in International Law," 23 BYIL 1 (1946).

Lauterpacht, Hersch. *Recognition in International Law*. Cambridge: The University Press, 1948.

Lawrence, Thomas Joseph. *The Principles of International Law*. Sir Percy H. Winfield ed., 7th ed. Boston: Macmillan, 1923.

Le Normand, René. *La Reconnaissance Internationale et ses Diverses Applications: états, gouvernements, belligerants, principes du droit international*. Paris: Imprime Camis, 1899.

Lerner, Natan. *Group Rights and Discrimination in International Law*. London: Martinus Nijhoff Press, 1991.

Levinson, Sanford. "Freedom: Politics: They Whisper: Reflections on Flags, Monuments, and State Holidays, and the Construction of Social Meaning in a Multicultural Society," 70 Chi.-Kent. L. Rev. 1079 (1995).

Lillich, Richard B.; and Newman, Frank C. eds. *International Human Rights: problems of law and policy*. Boston: Little, Brown and Co., 1979.

Liszt, Franz von. *Le Droit International: exposé systematique*. Gilbert Gidel & Leon Alcindor trans. Publications of the Carnegie Endowment for International Peace. Paris: Pedrone, 1927.

Lorimer, James. *The Institutes of the Law of Nations*. Edinburgh: William Blackwood and Sons, 1883.

Lowe, A.Vaughan; and Warbrick, Colin. "Recognition of States," 41 ICLQ 473 (1992).

Malone, M. Kelly. "Comment: The Rights of Newly Emerging Democratic States Prior to International Recognition and the Serbo-Croatian Conflict," 6 Temple Int'l & Comp. L.J. 81 (1992).

Marston, Geoffrey. "The Incorporation of Continental Shelf Rights into United Kingdom Law," 45 ICLQ 13 (1996).

Maull, Hans W. "Germany in the Yugoslav Crisis: From Assertiveness to Impotence." Unpublished paper under auspices of Deutsche Forschungsgemeinschaft. On file with author.

McDougal, Myres S.; and Leighton, Gertrude C.K. "The Rights of Man in the World Community: Constitutional Illusions versus Rational Action," 59 Yale L.J. 60 (1949).

McDougal, Myres S.; and Reisman, W. Michael. "Rhodesia and the United Nations: The Lawfulness of International Concern," 62 AJIL 1 (1968).

McDougal, Myres S.; and Reisman, W. Michael. *International Law in Contemporary Perspective: The Public Order of the World Community*. Mineola, NY: The Foundation Press, Inc., 1981.

McDougal, Myres S.; Lasswell, Harold D.; and Chen, Lung-chu. *Human Rights and World Public Order: The Basic Policies of an International Order of Human Dignity*. New Haven: Yale University Press, 1980.

McGoldrick, Dominic. *The Human Rights Committee: Its Role in the Development of the International Covenant on Civil and Political Rights*. Oxford: Clarendon Press, 1991.

McKinney, Kathryn M. "The Legal Effects of the Israeli-PLO Declaration of Principles: Steps Toward Statehood for Palestine," 18 *Puget Sound Law Review* 93 (1994).

Menon, P.K. "Some Aspects of Recognition: Recognition of States," 67(3) RdDIdS-DeP 161 (1991).

Merritt, Deborah Jones. "The Guarantee Clause and State Autonomy: Federalism for a Third Century," 80 Colum. L. Rev. 1 (1988).

Mertus, Julie A. "Nationalism and Nation-Building: Milosevic Turns to Montenegro and Kosovo," 26 N.Y.U. J. Int'l L. & Pol. 511 (1994).

Mikotajczyk, Barbara. "Universal Protection of Minorities: Selected Problems," 20 Pol. YBIL 137 (1993).

Moore, John Bassett. *Digest of International Law*. vol. I. Washington, DC: Government Printing Office, 1906.

Morrison, Fred L. "Recognition in International Law: A Functional Reappraisal," 34 U. Chi. L. Rev. 857 (1967).

Mosler, Hermann. "Subjects of International Law," in 7 *Encyclopedia of Public International Law*. Rudolf Bernhardt ed. Amsterdam: North-Holland Publishing Company, 1984.

Mugerwa, Nkambo. "Subjects of International Law," in *Manual of Public International Law*. Max Sørensen ed. London: Macmillan, 1968.

Mühlen, Alexander. "Die deutsche Rolle bei der Anerkennung der jugoslawischen Sezessionsstaaten," 2 *Liberal* 9 (1992).

Mullerson, Rein. "The Continuity and Succession of States, by reference to the former USSR and Yugoslavia," 42 ICLQ 473 (1993).

Nardin, Terry. "International Ethics and International Law," 18 Rev. Int'l Stud. 29 (1992).

Nash Leich, Marian. *Cumulative Digest of US Practice in International Law, 1981–1988*. Washington, DC: United States Government Printing Office/Department of State Publications, 1993.

Nelson, Daniel N. "Europe's Unstable East," 82 For. Pol'y 137 (1991).

Nicoll, Sir William; and Salmon, Trevor C. *Understanding the New European Community*. London: Prentice Hall, 1994.

Niles, Margaret A. "Judicial Balancing of Foreign Policy Considerations: Comity and Errors Under the Act of State Doctrine," 35 Stan. L. Rev. 327 (1983).

Nish, Ian H. *Japan's Struggle with Internationalism: Japan, China and the League of Nations, 1931–3*. London: Kegan Paul International, 1992.

Nkala, Jericho. *The United Nations, International Law, and the Rhodesian Independence Crisis*. Oxford: Clarendon Press, 1985.

O'Connell, Daniel P. *International Law*. vol. 1, 2nd ed. London: Stevens & Sons, 1970.

Oppenheim, Lassa F.L. *International Law: A Treatise*. Sir Hersch Lauterpacht ed., 8th ed. London: Longmans, Green and Co., 1955.

Oppermann, Thomas. "Cyprus," *Encyclopedia of Public International Law*, vol. one, Peter Macalister-Smith ed. New York: North-Holland, 1992.

Orent, Beatrice; and Reinsch, Pauline. "Sovereignty over Islands in the Pacific," 35 AJIL 443 (1941).

Orlow, Daniel. "Of Nations Small: The Small State in International Law," 9 Temple Int'l & Comp. L.J. 115 (1995).

Osinbajo, Yemi. "Legality in a Collapsed State: The Somali Experience," 45 ICLQ 910 (1996).

Osterland, Holly A. "National Self-Determination and Secession: The Slovak Model," 25 Case W'n Res. J. Int'l L. 655 (1993).

Patel, Satyavrata R. *A Textbook of International Law*. London: Asia Publishing House, 1964.

Patterson, Dennis. *Law and Truth*. Oxford: Oxford University Press, 1996.

Pellet, Alain. "Note Sur la Commission d'Arbitrage de la Conférence Européene Pour la Paix en Yugoslavie," 37 AFDI 329 (1991).

Pellet, Alain. "The Opinions of the Badinter Arbitration Committee: A Second Breath for the Self-Determination of Peoples," 3 EJIL 178 (1992).

Peterson, Martha J. "Political Use of Recognition: The Influence of the International System," 34 *World Politics* 324 (1982).

Peterson, Martha J. *Recognition of Governments: Legal Doctrine and State Practice, 1815–1995*. New York: St. Martin's Press, Inc., 1997.

Power, Samantha ed. *Breakdown in the Balkans: A Chronicle of Events, January 1989 to May 1992*. Washington, DC: Carnegie Endowment for International Peace, 1993.

Ratner, Steven R. "The Cambodia Settlement Agreements," 87 AJIL 1 (1993).

Redslob, Robert. "La Reconnaissance de l'État comme Sujet de Droit International," 13 RdDI 429 (1934).

Reisman, W. Michael. "International Incidents: Introduction to a New Genre in the Study of International Law" in *International Incidents: The Law That Counts in World Politics*. W. Michael Reisman & Andrew R. Willard eds. Princeton: Princeton University Press, 1988.

Rich, Roland. "Recognition of States: The Collapse of Yugoslavia and the Soviet Union," 4 EJIL 36 (1993).

Rorty, Richard. *Consequences of Pragmatism: essays, 1972–1980*. Minneapolis: University of Minnesota Press, 1982.

Santos, B. de Sousa. "The Postmodern Transition: Law and Politics," in *The Fate of Law*. Austin Sarat & Thomas R. Kearns eds. Ann Arbor: University of Michigan Press, 1991.

Scelle, Georges. *Precis de Droit des Gens: Principes et Systematique*. Paris: Recueil Sirey, 1932.

Scharf, Michael P. "Musical Chairs: The Dissolution of States and Membership in the United Nations," 28 Corn. Int'l L.J. 29 (1995).

Schlag, Pierre. "Normativity and the Politics of Form: L.A. Law's Empire," 139 U. Penn. L. Rev. 801 (1991).

Schroeder, William A. "Nationalism, Boundaries, and the Bosnian War: Another Perspective," 19 *Southern Illinois University Law* 153 (1994).

Schwarzenberger, Georg. *Power Politics: A Study of International Society*. 2nd ed. London: Stevens & Sons Limited, 1951.

Seidl-Hohenveldern, Ignaz. *Corporations in and under International Law*. Cambridge: Grotius Publications Limited, 1987.

Shaw, Malcolm N. *International Law*. 3rd ed. Cambridge: Grotius Publications Ltd., 1991.

Shaw, Malcolm N. *Title to Territory in Africa: International Legal Issues*. Oxford: Clarendon Press, 1986.

Small, Michael C. "Enforcing International Human Rights Law in Federal Courts: The Alien Tort Statute and the Separation of Powers," 74 Georgetown L. J. 163 (1985).

Sneesby, Kevin. "National Separation: Canada in Context-A Legal Perspective," 53 Louisiana L. Rev. 1357 (1993).

Sørensen, Max. "Souveraineté Territoriale de l'État," 101 Hag. Rec., III, 141 (1960).

Sperduti, Giuseppe. "L'Individu et le Droit International," 90 Hag. Rec., II, 733 (1956).

St. John, Ronald Bruce. "The Boundary Dispute Between Peru and Ecuador," 71 AJIL 322 (1977).

Starke, J.G. "Recognition in International Law" in Starke, *Studies in International Law*. London: Butterworths, 1965.

Starke, J.G. "The Acquisition of Title to Territory by Newly Emerged States," 41 BYIL 441 (1965–66).

Starke, Joseph G. *Introduction to International Law*. 10th ed. London: Butterworths, 1989.

Stojanovic, Svetozar. "The Destruction of Yugoslavia," 19 Ford. Int'l L.J. 337 (1995).

Strack, Harry R. *Sanctions: The Case of Rhodesia*. Syracuse: Syracuse University Press, 1978.

Strang, David. "Anomaly and Commonplace in European Political Expansion: Realist and Institutional Accounts," 45 Int'l Org. 143 (1991).

Stremlau, John J. *The International Politics of the Nigerian Civil War, 1967–1970*. Princeton: Princeton University Press, 1977.

Sunstein, Cass R. "Constitutionalism and Secession," 58 U. Chi. L. Rev. 633 (1991).

Suzuki, Eisuke. "The New Haven School of International Law: An Invitation to a Policy-Oriented Jurisprudence," 1 Yale Stud. W. Pub. Ord. 1 (1974).

Symmons, Clive R. "Irish Policy and Practice on Recognition," 28 Irish Jur. 175 (1995).

Szasz, Paul C. "The Protection of Human Rights through the Dayton/Paris Peace Agreement on Bosnia," 90 AJIL 301 (1996).

Talmon, Stefan. "Recognition of Governments: An Analysis of the New British Policy and Practice," 63 BYIL 231 (1992).

Tanca, Antonio. "La Politique Etrangère et de Sécurité Commune de l'Union européene en 1995," 7 EJIL 447 (1996).

Tappe, Trent N. "Chechnya and the State of Self-Determination in a Breakaway Region of the Former Soviet Union: Evaluating the Legitimacy of Secessionist Claims," 34 Colum. J. Transnat'l L. 255 (1995).

Taylor, Hannis. *International Public Law.* London: Sweet & Maxwell, 1902.

Thirlway, Hugh W.A. *Non-Appearance before the International Court of Justice.* Cambridge: Cambridge University Press, 1985.

Timperley, H.J. "Japan in Manchukuo," 1934 For. Aff. 295.

Triepel, Heinrich. *Völkerrecht und Landesrecht.* Tübingen: Verlag von T.C.B. Mohr, 1899.

Tuck, Richard. *Natural Rights Theories: Their Origin and Development.* Cambridge: Cambridge University Press, 1979.

Türk, Danilo. "Recognition of States: A Comment," 4 EJIL 66 (1993).

Türk, Danilo. "The Dangers of Failed States and a Failed Peace in the Post Cold War Era," 27 N.Y.U. J. Int'l L. & Pol. 625 (1995).

Turnock, David. *Eastern Europe: An Historical Geography 1815–1945.* New York: Routledge, Chapman and Hall, 1989.

Unger, Aryeh L. *Constitutional Development in the USSR: A Guide to the Soviet Constitutions.* London: Methuen & Co. Ltd., 1981.

van der Vyver, Johan D. "Statehood in International Law," 5 Emory Int'l L. Rev. 9 (1991).

Van Walt van Praag, Michael C. *The Status of Tibet: History, Rights, and Prospects in International Law.* London: Wisdon, 1987.

Vause, W. Gary. "Tibet to Tienanmen: Chinese Human Rights and United States Foreign Policy," 42 Vand. L. Rev. 1575.

Vedder, Christoph; and Folz, Hans-Peter. "The International Practice of the European Communities: Current Survey," 7 EJIL 112 (1996).

Verdross, Alfred; and Simma, Bruno. *Universelles Völkerrecht.* Berlin: Duncker & Humboldt, 1984.

Verhoeven, Joe. "La Reconnaissance Internationale: Déclin ou Renouveau?" 39 AFDI 7 (1993).

Verzijl, Jan Hendrik Willem. *International Law in Historical Perspective.* vol. I. Leiden: A.W. Sijthoff, 1968.

von der Heydte, F.A.F. "Discovery, Symbolic Annexation and Virtual Effectiveness in International Law," 29 AJIL 448 (1935).

von Glahn, Gerhard. *Law among Nations: An Introduction to Public International Law.* 4th ed. New York: MacMillan Publishing Co., Inc., 1981.

Wagner, Wolfgang. "Zwischen Neuer Weltordnung und Wachsender Anarchie," 1991/92 Int. Pol. 1.

Waldock, Humphrey M. "Disputed Sovereignty on the Falkland Islands Dependencies," 25 BYIL 331 (1948).

Walker, David M. *The Oxford Companion to Law.* Oxford: Clarendon Press, 1980.

Warren, Charles. *The Supreme Court in United States History.* vol. I i. Boston: Little, Brown & Company, 1922.

Weber, Eugen. *A Modern History of Europe: Man, Cultures, and Societies from the Renaissance to the Present.* New York: W.W. Norton & Company Inc., 1971.

Weiner, Justus R. "Hard Facts Meet Soft Law: The Israel-PLO Declaration of Principles and the Prospects for Peace: A Response to Katherine W. Meighan," 35 Virg. J. Int'l L. 931 (1935).

Weller, Marc. "International Law and Chaos," 52 Camb. L.J. 6 (1993).

Weller, Marc. "The International Response to the Dissolution of the Socialist Federal Republic of Yugoslavia," 86 AJIL 569 (1992).

Weston, Burns H.; Falk, Richard A.; and D'Amato, Anthony. *International Law and World Order*. 2nd ed. St. Paul: West Publishing Co., 1990.

Wheaton, Henry. *Elements of International Law*. Richard Henry Dana, Jr. ed. (as originally published in 1866). James Brown Scott ed., 1936 ed. Oxford: Clarendon Press, 1936.

Whiteman, Marjorie M. *Digest of International Law*. Washington, DC: Government Printing Office, 1973.

Wicke, Jennifer. "Postmodern Identity and the Legal Subject," 62 *University of Colorado Law Review* 455 (1991).

Wieruszewski, Roman. "International Response to the Human Rights Violations in the Territory of the Former Yugoslavia," 19 Pol. YBIL 203 (1991–92).

Williams, Paul R. "State Succession and the International Financial Institutions: Political Criteria v. Protection of Outstanding Financial Obligations," 43 ICLQ 776 (1994).

Wiskemann, Elizabeth. "Partitioned Yugoslavia," in *Hitler's Europe*, Arnold Joseph Toynbee & Veronica M. Toynbee eds. London: Oxford University Press, 1954.

Woodward, Susan L. *Balkan Tragedy: Chaos and Dissolution after the Cold War*. Washington, DC: Brookings Institution, 1995.

Woolsey, L.H. "The Non-Recognition of the Chamorro Government in Nicaragua," 20 AJIL 543 (1926).

Woolsey, L.H. "The Recognition of El Salvador," 28 AJIL 325 (1934).

Wright, Quincy. "Recognition, Intervention and Ideologies," 7 Ind. Y. Int'l Aff. 89 (1958–59).

Wynaendts, Henry. *L'engrenage: Chroniques Yougoslaves, juillet 1991–août 1992*. Paris: Editions Denoël, 1993.

Zimmermann, Warren. "The Last Ambassador: A Memoir of the Collapse of Yugoslavia," 74(2) For. Aff. 13 (1995).

# INDEX

## ABOUT THE AUTHOR

THOMAS D. GRANT is a Fulbright Scholar at Cambridge University, where he is a junior member of Wolfson College. A member of the bars of Massachusetts, New York, and Washington, D.C., he received his JD from the Yale Law School and clerked on the U.S. Court of Appeals for the First Circuit. His articles have appeared in the *Virginia Journal of International Law* and *Columbia Journal of Transnational Law* among others.

www.ingramcontent.com/pod-product-compliance
Lightning Source LLC
LaVergne TN
LVHW011448011025
822429LV00002B/166